JUNG`S RED BOOK FOR OUR TIME

Searching for Soul under Postmodern Conditions

Murray Stein
and
Thomas Arzt
Editors

Volume 3

 CHIRON PUBLICATIONS • ASHEVILLE, NORTH CAROLINA

© 2019 by Chiron Publications. All rights reserved. No part of this publication may be reproduced, stored in a retrieval system, or transmitted, in any form by any means, electronic, mechanical, photocopying, recording, or otherwise, without the prior written permission of the publisher, Chiron Publications, P.O. Box 19690, Asheville, N.C. 28815-1690.

www.ChironPublications.com

Interior and cover design by Danijela Mijailovic
Printed primarily in the United States of America.

ISBN 978-1-63051-716-8 paperback
ISBN 978-1-63051-717-5 hardcover
ISBN 978-1-63051-718-2 electronic
ISBN 978-1-63051-719-9 limited edition paperback

Library of Congress Cataloging-in-Publication Data Pending

TABLE OF CONTENTS

Introduction

Murray Stein and Thomas Arzt

It has again been an astonishing experience to see how powerfully Jung's *Red Book* has excited the imagination of our invited authors. Each of their essays challenges readers to expand and deepen our thinking about this unique work and does so with the same qualities of individuality and brilliance that we saw in the first two volumes of the series, *Jung's Red Book for Our Time: Searching for Soul under Postmodern Conditions.*

What creating the *Red Book* did for Jung is what this work can do for present-day readers: stretch, expand, enliven, and inspire the mind to develop new modes of thinking and perception. It is not just our thoughts (mental contents) that are challenged but also our way of thinking (mental process). *The Red Book,* when taken seriously and read deeply, has an enlivening effect: It frees the mind from old habitual tracks and patterns, breaks the spirit free to adventure into new territory, and releases a flow of creativity. The result can be the creation of a new master narrative for the individual and for postmodern culture, something so desperately lacking today as French philosopher and sociologist Jean-François Lyotard has convincingly diagnosed as the state of affairs in our age of postmodernity.

In this third volume of the series, we encounter 18 new essays that pick up on one or more of the many facets of Jung's groundbreaking work and extend them into greater intelligibility. Each essay is unique, and yet all of them converge on the themes that we as editors outlined at the outset of the project in asking for thoughts about the relevance of *The Red Book* for our postmodern era. In a letter to the prospective authors, we asked them to consider the following questions:

> Can Jung's *Red Book* help us to navigate meaningfully through the rough waters we find ourselves in today

individually, professionally, politically, and culturally? Considering "the spirit of this time" today, how can "the spirit of the depths" be found in a way that is meaningful in our contemporary world? Does *The Red Book* help us possibly to formulate a new worldview and god-image that can sustain people in the present crisis the world finds itself in?

In the present volume, each of the authors addresses one or more of these pivotal questions. The result again is a set of original contributions to our ongoing reflection on the value of *The Red Book* for our times.

The volume opens with an essay by Murray Stein, who proposes that Jung's *Red Book* is a new link in the *aurea catena* ("Golden Chain") of imaginative literature extending from ancient narratives such as the Epic of Gilgamesh to modern and postmodern times. He asks the question: "What is *The Red Book* for Analytical Psychology?" and answers that it is not merely another addition to the shelf of works by C.G. Jung and to the library of thousands of works created by the successive generations of contributors to the field. It is unique in that it is "prophetic" in the sense of the biblical prophets who speak for the spirit of the Deity. This does not confer sacrality upon *The Red Book* such as believers have projected upon other sacred writings, but it does challenge the reader to catch a glimpse of the spirit that motivated the creation of the field of Analytical Psychology and continues to sustain it.

Paul Brutsche's essay, titled "The Creative Power of Soul," proposes a similar theme and one that is conspicuous in many of the essays, namely that *The Red Book* demonstrates the creativity of the imagination, which is embedded in the unconscious and directed by an agency called "Soul." This figure is pivotal in the narrative that flows so richly from Jung's imagination as he leaves "the spirit of this time" and follows "the spirit of the depths" into the interior spaces of the psyche. Soul challenges Jung's thinking and his feeling from her first appearance in *Liber Primus* to her last in "Scrutinies." She is omnipresent throughout the narrative.

Joseph Cambray's essay follows and offers an insightful reflection on Jung's genial use of images for advancing his psychological thinking. Cambray underscores the key insight that for Jung conceptualization follows imagination, not the other way around. This was based on the conviction that image is psychologically more fundamental than concept or language. *The Red Book*, as Cambray convincingly argues, is an example of how this process unfolds in the creation of Jung's later psychological theory.

Serbian psychoanalyst Velimir Popović takes up the theme of the centrality of imagination in Jung's creative work and finds that this pioneering method allowed Jung to break free from the tight constraints that modernity had imposed on theory construction in his time. The use of imagination in the construction of narrative is a key element in postmodern psychology and philosophy, as Popović shows, and this turn in postmodernity thereby renders Jung's work exceptionally suitable for our times. Popović finds that Jung uncannily anticipated this postmodern turn of thinking in his *Red Book*. In the essay that follows Popović's, his colleague in Belgrade, Serbia, Žanet Prinčevac de Villablanca, continues this line of thought by looking at the prizewinning documentary film "No One's Child" as a poignant expression of loss of soul in postmodern times and as a telling representation of the postmodern condition. She brings this into play with a reflection on similar motifs in Jung's *Red Book*.

Lebanese scholar Samir Mahmoud in turn also highlights the role of imagination in *The Red Book* and finds that this provides a way for religious Muslims to read Jung with interest and respect. His discussion of the rejection of secular depth psychology, which has no space for transcendence, by the advocates of religious psychology, which is guided by the notion of transcendence and the existence of transcendent beings, is concise and instructive. *The Red Book* offers the devout Muslim an entry into Jung's thought, he argues, because it relies on what Henry Corbin discusses as the role of imagination in the works of the great mystic of Islam, Ibn 'Arabi. Jung's similar understanding of imagination opens a space for appreciative consideration of the possibilities of transcendent interventions in postmodern human consciousness.

In the next chapter, Japanese psychoanalyst Toshio Kawai brings his refined Japanese sensibility into play as he reflects on *The Red Book* as a chapter in Jung's personal individuation process and on the possibilities of Jung's display of imagination to dismantle that barriers between consciously scripted narratives and the more open and generously endowed perspectives of the unconscious that are not limited by the restrictions of one's culture. Kawai's astonishment at Jung's achievement in navigating the influx of imagery that came to him during his journey through the depths of the inner world is described with a deep feeling of appreciation and respect.

Considering two types of imagination in the essay that follows, Mexican Jungian psychoanalyst Patricia Michan takes up the distinction made by Jung between false and true imagination and reworks this dichotomy in a thoughtful essay on the usefulness of both types in clinical practice. Having worked extensively with Mesoamerican and particularly Mexican mythologies, Michan has a finely honed sensitivity to the creative possibilities of imagery that looks at first glance to be merely pathological and worthless. She teaches us to look for the "golden seed" in the dross and offers graphic examples from her practice as a Jungian psychoanalyst.

Swedish Jungian psychoanalyst Gunilla Midboe picks up on a similar theme and develops the issue of shadow integration in *The Red Book* and in Norse mythology, using as a backdrop her own childhood experiences in Norway and Sweden. The Japanese Jungian psychoanalyst Mari Yoshikawa then looks at the image of the serpent in *The Red Book* and traces its presence throughout the entire text. The issue of integration of shadow and instinct lie at the base of both essays and constitute a common theme. One of the remarkable outcomes of these many culturally diverse reflections on Jung's *Red Book* in our series is that the themes Jung presents and takes up in that work are universal and apply to ancient traditions and to postmodern cultures to an equal degree. This is one of the most significant features of Jung's genius, namely that by following the spirit of the depths, he reaches a level of the collective unconscious that is multispecific.

Linda Carter's essay, which follows upon Yoshikawa's, views Jung's meticulous care in constructing his *Red Book* as the work of an artist-craftsman. She makes the important distinction between craft and art and reflects on how the hand of the craftsman in Jung offered his imagination the opportunity to reveal its contents and to fix them in time and space. She speaks of craftsmanship as knowing with one's hands and compares it to the work of alchemists in their laboratories. Irish scholar Mathew Mather then continues the reflection on the alchemical nature of *The Red Book* and focuses his comments on the theme of *coniunctio*, the union of the opposites, a motif that would become central in Jung's later work on the psychology of the transference. Transformation through imagination that flows through the hands is a common feature of Carter's and Mather's essays.

Japanese Jungian psychoanalyst Megumi Yama leads us then to the theme of the dead in *The Red Book* and compares Jung's confrontation with the spirits of the dead with *kami* spirits in Japanese Shintō religion. Following upon Yama's touching portrayal of Japanese religion and culture, the notion of invisible spirits inhabiting the material world and having distinct effects on the lives of humans is taken up in a creative way by Anna Milashevich in her remarkable exploration of the presence of the trickster in the postmodern business world, especially in start-up enterprises. The presence of the unconscious and its energies is not limited to religious rite and ritual but is equally manifest in the most secular of all domains, the world of business. *The Red Book* argues the same in its insistence that the spirit of the depths underlies and influences the spirit of the times whatever it might be or wherever it might go.

The famous psychiatric case of Daniel Paul Schreber catches the perspicacious eye of Chicago-based George Hogenson. Jung's appreciation of Schreber's delusions and fantasies as prophetic and as having prospective value and indeed spiritual significance for Schreber, as he claimed in court when he argued for his release from the asylum, follows from Jung's understanding of the creative nature of the unconscious and its forward-looking perspective. This induced Jung to revalue the works of the imagination and to see imagination as a primary creative agency within the psyche. Paradoxically, Schreber was a forerunner of the experimental work that Jung engaged in when undertaking his form of active imagination and creating the material that would go into his *Red Book*.

French Jungian scholar Christine Maillard and German Jungian psychoanalyst Ingrid Riedel, both university professors in Religious Studies with many years of academic experience and numerous publications in their native French and German to their credit, take a look at Jung's revisioning of the Christian doctrine of Christ and the Christian tradition. Maillard analyzes Jung's Christology and his proposals for how to integrate this religious symbol into modern and postmodern consciousness, while Riedel focuses on Jung's projection of a new god-image and his pioneering efforts to create a new psychology of religion. Both essays regard *The Red Book* as a major contribution to the future of religious life and thought in the present and future.

Concluding this volume, the well-known American Jungian scholar and international lecturer and teacher, Stephen Aizenstat, recommends reading *The Red Book* meditatively, as a dream. In his autobiographical essay, "The Quest for One's Own *Red Book* in the Digital Age," he offers a moving personal testimony to the power of imagination to open inner space as he honors the extraordinary capacity of Jung's *Red Book* to guide us through psychic worlds that are largely inaccessible to the rational mind and therefore unknown and possibly frightening. While reminding us of the dangers of being sucked up totally into the cyberspace of the Digital Age, Aizenstat ingeniously considers ways of using its technologies for enlarging and vivifying inner space, thus transforming this threat to a means for psychic enrichment. For this purpose he finds *The Red Book* to be a precious resource for facing the unsettling unique challenges of these postmodern times with courage and creativity.

In summary, the essays in this third volume of the series on Jung's *Red Book*'s relevance for our postmodern time again offer many angles of vision and point to a variety of directions for further reflection on this remarkable work that we are beginning to recognize as a new link in the *aurea catena* extending far back into ancient times and suggesting new possibilities for meaning in the present and future.

Jung's *Red Book* as a New Link in the *Aurea Catena*

Murray Stein

Although the field of Analytical Psychology as it exists today in the 21st century displays the marks of diverse bloodlines in its genetic intellectual heritage, deriving from a number of generative figures whose theoretical and cultural perspectives have varied considerably, C.G. Jung towers over everyone else as the singular ancestor of all who identify themselves with it. Even after more than 50 years since his death, Jung's published *oeuvre* continues to define the field's fundamental identity.[1] Its practicing members often go by the title of Jungian analysts. It is the family name.

While some of Jung's works are generally considered to be essential and central, however, others are seen as peripheral and even dispensable. People will always have their favorites among the many books and papers that Jung left as a heritage, and they will also have their most disliked pieces. Which of them should be viewed as canonical and which as secondary or dispensable has thus far not been officially determined. Besides, who would be in a position to make this judgment? The field is, so far, without a pope and a College of Cardinals. It is more a far flung family of independent-minded individuals who nevertheless concede that they share a common forefather.

In 2009, a remarkable and much belated addition to the *oeuvre* arrived at the field's doorstep: *The Red Book*. For more than 70 years, this medieval-like illuminated calligraphic manuscript lay first on the shelves of Jung's private library and then in a bank vault. Evidently, Jung himself was at least somewhat ambivalent about its place in his overall *oeuvre*, since he kept it to himself and a very few close associates in his lifetime, and when he passed away, he left behind no instructions concerning its publication posthumously.[2] Moreover, it is an unfinished work, a fragment. *Liber Novus* (Jung's title for this work) comes into the field somewhat like a long-concealed illegitimate child into an established and distinguished family. This mysterious member of the family may turn out to be quite exceptional and display remarkable gifts, but there is also some trepidation concerning potential embarrassment. With its public appearance, *The Red Book* must now be considered as part and parcel of the field's heritage, whether one likes it or not.

What is *The Red Book* for Analytical Psychology? Does it belong to the body of seminal works beside Jung's other major writings, or is it to be ranked as the equivalent of a writer's personal diary and sketchbook, akin to Leonardo's *Notebooks*, which shows the early workings of a brilliant mind as the creator prepares for his more serious later contributions to a scientific or cultural enterprise? Conversely, one can also wonder if all of Jung's later writings were nothing more than an attempt to explicate this monumental foundational work and make its ideas and insights, which are here expressed in colorful image and high-flown rhetorical style, digestible for modern readers and thinkers.

As a commercial publishing venture, *The Red Book* has been phenomenally successful, with sales figures soaring far beyond anyone's wildest calculations. Whether the people who purchase it read it or not (I have called it the "unread red book," although this now appears to be changing), its surprising popular reception and its ubiquity in the media show that it has an astonishing appeal to general audiences, especially in the United States but also in other countries and now in several other translations. The sudden wave of attention generated by this remarkable work has had the unintended consequence, moreover, of greatly increasing the visibility of Jung and Jungian analysts in public awareness. Some people have celebrated this, while others have found it threatening or distasteful. Putting its success on this level aside, I would here like to consider the question of *The Red Book's* place and possible role in the tradition of Analytical Psychology as it has taken form over the course of the last 100 years.

Analytical Psychology, the Tradition

The professional members of the field of Analytical Psychology belong to a tradition that is now nearly 100 years old since its founding in Zurich, Switzerland, by Jung and a group of others who were separating themselves from Freud's school of psychoanalysis in Vienna. By using the term "tradition" (from the Latin *tradere*—hand over, deliver), I mean a received culture-with-a-history that contains a more or less well defined and precise set of values, perspectives, ideas and attitudes that is delivered or handed over from one generation to the next for an indefinite period of time. There are long, venerable, and very old traditions, and there are new ones. If one looks at how traditions are transmitted, one discovers a variety of channels. A tradition may be borne along importantly by texts (Scriptures and Sacred Books); it may be handed on primarily through oral narratives and rituals, as in nonliterate cultures; it may be (as in our tradition of depth psychology and praxis) handed down by a combination of texts, oral transmissions from teachers and supervisors to students, trainees, and supervisees, and rituals of initiation (passing exams, receiving diplomas, advancing from analyst to training analyst to supervising analyst, etc.).

The Jungian psychoanalysts of today are in what can be thought of as the third, fourth, fifth and perhaps even in some cases the sixth generation of a tradition of clinicians who work in and with the perspectives offered by the progenitor, C.G. Jung. The first and founding generation was made up of Jung himself (perhaps one may also include Freud) and a few others who were close to him, such as Emma Jung and Toni Wolff; the second generation was composed of people who worked directly with Jung in analysis and supervision of cases and by attending his seminars (e.g., H.G. Baynes, Gerhard Adler, James Kirsch, Esther Harding, C.A. Meier, Erich Neumann, Marie-Louise von Franz, Barbara Hannah, and Joseph Henderson, among others); in the third generation were those who studied and analyzed with the members of the second generation (importantly, Michael Fordham, Elie Humbert, Hans Dieckmann, Mario Jacoby, Adolf Guggenbühl-Craig, James Hillman, Helmut Barz, June Singer). Each of us contemporary Jungians can determine our own specific generation by tracing the lineage directly back to Jung. In my case, I am of the fourth generation, and those who worked with me in analysis and supervision would be the fifth generation, and so on.

Many of our teachers had a more direct link to Jung himself than we do, and our students have a yet more distant one than we have had. What difference does this make? Does Jung's figure grow smaller in the distance and the influence of his ideas fade with the passing generations, or do they change in other ways and gain new features due to projections from afar?

Here I would like to consider how a tradition may maintain itself *spiritually speaking* (that is, "in the spirit of the founding figure") and how it may retain a living sense of the symbolic presence of its founder(s), also what this means and what its importance may be for the future generations of the tradition. Into this reflection I will then fold the discussion of a potential role for *The Red Book* in Analytical Psychology.

The Transmission of Spirit in Tradition

To begin, I reach back to a somewhat obscure source, to one of Jung's earliest pieces, his fifth and last *Zofingia Lecture*, given in January 1899, titled "Thoughts on the Interpretation of Christianity, with reference to the Theory of Albrecht Ritschl." In that lecture, which he delivered to his fraternity brothers at the university of Basel and composed in the year before he took up residency in psychiatry in Zurich, Jung displays his interest in theology. He boldly criticizes some of the views expressed by the important liberal Protestant theologian Albrecht Ritschl (1822-1889), who held that the spiritual influence of Christ is passed on from generation to generation more or less mechanically through a rational process of teaching and learning within the communities of believers that make up the Christian church. He holds to a strictly causal, nonmystical theory of historical transmission. The image of Christ is kept alive in the minds and hearts of believers by a process of education. The community transmits Christ from one generation to the next by rigorous teaching and learning. A text like the Bible is important as an object of study and as a sourcebook for orientation, but the understanding and personal integration of its spiritual meaning is strictly dependent upon the effectiveness of the teaching of the community in which one participates as a Christian. The Bible's inspirational power and its spiritual effects on believers do not depend on the working of the Holy Spirit or any other supernatural agents. Ritschl was intent on purging theology of its metaphysical baggage and of reliance on the influence of mystical or supernatural elements. To achieve this, he crafted his theological views to harmonize with the positivistic learning theories of the day. In his view, the spiritual reality of Christ, no matter how numinous, is transmitted through the ages strictly by the educational means available to communities of faith who pass their teachings and collective memories on from the earliest generations down to the latest ones, each generation investing these received materials anew with its own human energy. One believes what one learns and receives in the community of faith. There is nothing metaphysical or mystical about this process. It is cognitive-behavioral psychology pure and simple, to put it into today's psychological language. For the theologian Ritschl and others who followed this line of thinking, spiritual transmission has nothing to do with archetypal images and energies, or with synchronicity.

As a 24-year-old medical student with only a youthful amateur's understanding of theology, for which he apologizes profusely in the introduction, Jung objects vehemently to this theory of transmission of spiritual reality.[3] His objection hinges precisely on the point that Ritschl deletes the mystical element from his theology: "The mystery of a metaphysical world, a metaphysical order, of the kind that Christ taught and embodied in his own person, must be placed in center stage of the Christian religion," Jung argues. "No religion has survived, or ever will, without mystery, to which the devotee is most intimately bound."[4] In describing Ritschl, quite correctly, as having shorn theology of metaphysical and mystical elements, Jung puts his finger accurately on a basic problem in late-19th-century liberal Protestant theology. Jung regards numinous experience of the Divine Other (in this case, Christ) as foundational for a living spiritual tradition. Without the mystical element, religious traditions become sterile, nothing more than the habit-ridden repetitions of learned doctrines. This was, as we now know from his autobiography, his own experience of the Swiss Reformed Church. As he reports in *Memories, Dreams, Reflections*, this is what he diagnosed to be the source of the spiritual illness of his pastor father, Paul Jung.[5]

What is surprising to us today as we read this early essay is Jung's explicitly positive regard for the term "metaphysical." In all of his later psychological writings, he would eschew anything having to do with the "metaphysical," emphasizing repeatedly that he is speaking only as a psychologist about psychic images and not as a theologian about ontological realities. We can see that in his theory of archetypes and the collective unconscious he discovered a channel of communication through the generations whereby numinous figures and powers can be transmitted without requiring any sort of metaphysical or supernatural grounding. This is identical to what science has done by explaining the creation of the universe, electromagnetic force, gravity, the nature of light, and other phenomena without reference to a Divine Force or God. What was previously attributed to supernatural powers has been explained by natural ones. Jung did the same with respect to the forces of the mental world. Visions and mystical experiences are best not understood as the revelations of supernatural beings and divine energies to human consciousness; rather they are now seen as the manifestations of the activities of autonomous archetypes at the psychoid level of the psyche.[6]

Later in life, when he added the theory of synchronicity, he introduced the notion of objective meaning due to the manifestation of "creative acts ... the continuous creation of a pattern that exists from all eternity ... "[7] Synchronistic events, however, are neither the eternally predestined actions of God (John Calvin) nor the products of a subtle chain of causality in the physical world (Albert Einstein), but rather the regular discontinuities in the psycho-physical cosmos that are not predictable (except in a statistical sense) but which convey the impact of an objective source of meaning ("meaningful coincidences"). They imply objective meaning.[8]

Jung could speak, therefore, of the power of numinous archetypal images, energies, and processes emerging within the space-and-time-limited world as the consequence of synchronistic concatenations in the depths of the collective unconscious where psyche and matter are one and constitute two sides of a single whole. These occur at moments of significance in the lives of individuals and communities, and they have the effect of enlivening and energizing them with a sense of transcendent meaning. It is these acausal meaningful events that most deeply keep a spiritual tradition alive and vital, and not the rational teachings of texts and techniques that go on within the communities of the committed. They are, in religious terms, signs of the working of the Holy Spirit and the continuous presence of God within the historical process.[9] In other words, Jung concludes that it takes spirit to keep spirit alive.

Transmission of "Jung" in Analytical Psychology

What about the transmission of "Jung" in our tradition of Analytical Psychology and psychoanalytic practice? I deliberately put quotation marks around the name of the founding figure. By asking how is "Jung" transmitted in our tradition, I do not mean to ask how veneration for C.G. Jung the man is fostered through the generations but rather how the spirit that he embodied for the circle that gathered around him is kept alive, a spirit that nourished their hearts and minds and inspired them to form a tradition that continues to thrive today. Does what Jung says in that early *Zofingia Lecture* have relevance for this question? Does a transmission of symbolic and numinous images that convey transcendence and meaning take place in the tradition of Analytical Psychology?

In purely practical and mundane terms, the tradition of Analytical Psychology is today passed down, though only in part, by means of the training programs that have been created by professional Jungian institutions worldwide, all of which are housed within the International Association for Analytical Psychology. In addition to these recognized institutional channels, there are many others that pass through academic circles, study groups, Friends of Jung societies, readers of Jungian books, and nowadays denizens of the internet. In the training programs of the professional institutes, candidates are required to study the texts of the discipline and to master the methods and techniques needed to practice Jungian psychoanalysis competently, legally, and with some measure of confidence. But as the Swiss Reformed tradition did for Jung, our psychological tradition can lose its aliveness and deeper qualities of significance and meaning if there are no archetypal and synchronisitic supports. If people read Jung's works and are not moved by something deeply embedded within their own souls, in other words if symbolic resonance is absent, then the text quickly fades in significance and dies. The words become marks on a page, and such students may become teachers who are dogmatic and dry manipulators of words, concepts, and techniques. More likely, new influences when they arrive on the scene capture their interest, and the "ancestor" becomes an old-fashioned portrait of a fine gentleman hanging on the wall of an antiquated house. As time goes by, the picture fades, and newer and more exciting images beckon the later generations, who go off in other directions and build new houses of their own, occasionally lifting a toast to the old Swiss ancestor with a funny mustache who was a bit cranky and eccentric but thankfully left them some money to do their own thing. In this way, the tradition fades and passes into history. In time, it withers as a living matrix for inspiration and will become a footnote in the history of depth psychology, which is itself a footnote in the history of psychology, which is a footnote in the history in philosophy, and so forth. History moves on.

On the other hand, if the transmission of "Jung" is augmented by numinous experience, including synchronicities, by dreams and life-transforming "moments of meeting" with the spirit that Jung the man embodied and voiced in his writings, the tradition will continue to be revitalized over long and indefinite and perhaps even endless stretches of time. The fading that mundane movements suffer over time for want of transcendent grounding will not then be characteristic of this one.

Does this mean that we should look upon Jung as a sort of god, a Christ figure to be worshipped and mystically united with in ecstatic visions? Personally, I find this approach quite distasteful and in fact seriously off the mark, because it leads to obscurantism and defensive distortions of history. However, one does need to discover and experience an archetypal ground in, around, or beneath the ancestor figure, one that can emanate transcendence and constellate symbolic resonance. There must be synchronicities involved in "meeting Jung," whether in dream or text. If this numinous figure cannot be the biographical Jung himself, then what is this image in our tradition? What or who symbolizes "Jung" for us?

The Red Book

The belated publication of Jung's *Liber Novus* and "Scrutinies" (*The Red Book*) landed right in the middle of the field of Analytical Psychology with a big splash. For some among us it is an awkward embarrassment ("We have not become psychologists in order to listen to revelations and to adopt a pseudo-religious ideology of 'the self' (or each develop our own one)"[10], while for others it is an awesome and inspiring addition to the Jungian heritage ("Now, for me, this material is some of the most exquisite you will find in any religious or spiritual tradition: Beauty in the Dark. Jung grapples with human embodiment on its own terms, graphically sacrificing body and soul for the sake of Soul. This book is a literary masterpiece because it embodies Jung's deepest personal, spiritual transformation, taking the reader on that perilous journey along with him."[11]) Thus far, there has been considerable uncertainty among Jungians about how to receive this astonishing and complex gift from our common ancestor. Is it a curse or a blessing?

As with all such anomalous inheritances from founding figures in intellectual or religious traditions, there is a variety of possible interpretations of its meaning. For example, Martin Luther discounted the importance of several books of the Bible and considered the last book, The Revelation to John, to show no evidence of inspiration by the Holy Spirit. For other serious readers of the Bible, Revelation lies at the very center of what the Holy Scriptures mean to communicate. It is hard to be neutral about texts like this. It seems to me that it does matter how one comes down on the value of *The Red Book*, but whatever the judgment of individuals may be, the tradition itself must from now on include this work as a major item in its inventory of received texts. For some, it will be a book of inspiration, for others a work to be avoided except perhaps for historical and biographical interest or as a preparation diary or notebook for the scientific works to follow.

For myself, I consider *The Red Book* as a potentially powerful transmission device for the numinous images that underlie and ground our tradition and link it to even deeper and older historical traditions.[12] It can also serve as a text that offers people useful guidance for how to deal with experiences of the numinous images of the collective unconscious when they befall one. I would therefore locate it in the center, albeit somewhat uneasily as I will explain later, rather than on the periphery of our inheritance as Jungians. *The Red Book* is, as one person in the epicenter of the current Jungian world who prefers to remain anonymous said, "precious," and meant that in the genuine sense of the word and not ironically.

As a potentially active transmitter of the numinous ground underlying Analytical Psychology, *The Red Book* would play the role of a foundational text with a symbolic value beyond the literal meaning of the words inscribed in it. Such texts inspire later work and thought along certain precise lines and are returned to again and again by later generations because they transmit a foundational genius for a particular cultural domain. I use "genius" here in the Latin sense of the word: "In ancient Rome, the genius was the guiding spirit or tutelary deity of a person, family, or place *(genius loci)*. The noun is related to the Latin verb *gigno, genui, genitus,* 'to bring into being, create, produce.' Because the achievements of exceptional individuals seemed to indicate the presence of a particularly powerful *genius*, by the time of Augustus the word began to acquire its secondary meaning of 'inspiration, talent.'"[13] *The Red Book* contains such a genius in the figure of Philemon, I would argue, and makes it available for transmission to the tradition.

Philemon, Genius of *The Red Book*

What we find in *The Red Book* is the story of a very time-bound and human-all-too-human narrator/protagonist (i.e., Jung) setting out at midlife on a journey with "the spirit of the depths"[14] to rediscover his lost soul ("My soul, where are you? Do you hear me?"[15]). In the course of his wanderings, he passes through a number of gripping inner experiences that we can only view as profound initiations into archetypal mysteries. Moreover, in passing from passive witness to active participant in these interior visions and dialogues, the protagonist also becomes a vital actor in the transformation of the figures he encounters. In the course of the narrative, he plays a role in giving birth to a new god-image, Phanes, who unites the opposites in his being. Finally, the protagonist discovers that the "genius," who is "the spirit of the depths" and responsible for all the images and experiences in this realm, is "Philemon."

Who is Philemon? And what does he stand for? What is his symbolical value and meaning? It is important to become acquainted with him, since Philemon is the primary symbol for the authorial spirit that shapes *The Red Book*, and this is what will be transmitted therefore by this work to later generations of the tradition in which this work is housed.

In *The Red Book*, Philemon appears as a figure of importance primarily in the third section, "Scrutinies." However, he is introduced to the reader in the last chapter of *Liber Secundus*, titled "The Magician." Jung, the Protagonist in the story, has had to work hard to get to Philemon. A prefiguration of Philemon who appears earlier in the work, in *Liber Primus*, is Elijah. By the time he approaches Philemon, Jung has undergone major initiations and encounters with many other figures. He goes in search of Philemon because, having been given the "wand of magic," he has to find out what it means. So he sets out to find "the Magician." This is Philemon.

He finds him in retirement, working quietly in his garden tending tulips.[16] Philemon's wife, Baucis, is present but does not play a role. The old man initially ignores Jung and his persistent questioning, saying he is now retired from the world and no longer interested in teaching. Philemon's extreme reticence does not augur well, but in the end he relents and instructs Jung in the paradox of magic. Magic, he teaches, is the complement of rationality. Rationality can comprehend the part of the world that is rational but no more. It cannot understand or grasp the part that is nonrational. Much of reality is not nonrational, and this can only be comprehended by another type of thinking. This is "magic." Magic proceeds by way of imagination and denotes intuitive understanding of the nonrational. Magic can comprehend the portion of reality that rationality misses. In our language, magic is the intuitive understanding of unconscious processes that purely rational methods cannot grasp, a kind of mythopoetic approach to knowledge. The magician is an intuitive comprehender whose mind reaches into spaces that science cannot approach directly with its methods and tools. This is Philemon's first teaching. He makes no further appearances in *Liber Secundus*.

It is at first surprising that Philemon should be the figure selected to be Jung's teacher about magic. In myth, he is a simple farmer whose only claim to fame is his hospitality to the gods Hermes and Zeus as they wander the roads of the earth and look for a place to stay the night.[17] His attitude of pious receptivity to the divine strangers is the key to Philemon's good fortune and immortality as a figure in myth. This virtue is also precisely what Jung, the protagonist of *The Red Book*, must develop in himself. The task that is set before him throughout the text again and again is to get over his egoistic ambition and narcissistic pride and to transform his conscious attitude into a receptive womb for the seeds of the future. For this, Philemon would be a model. More than that, though, it is Philemon's receptivity precisely to the divine that is essential. He represents the religious attitude.

In "Scrutinies," Philemon's role is much more prominent than in *Liber Secundus*. Here he is the dominant figure and assumes the persona of sage and wisdom figure. In his most significant extended appearance in *The Red Book*, he delivers the "Seven Sermones to the Dead." It is particularly the Seventh Sermon, where Philemon teaches the dead about their eternal destiny and directs them to their trans-cendent home as symbolized by a star, that finally puts to rest the souls of the dead who are unsatisfied after returning from their trip to Jerusalem.

Throughout *The Red Book*, the protagonist is confronted with the problem of restless ghosts desperately searching for an answer that will show them the Way to they know not what. This theme of disturbance and dissatisfaction in the ghostly world culminates in a visitation that Jung describes both in *The Red Book* and in *Memories, Dreams, Reflections*. Here is the original version as told in *The Red Book*:

> But one night a dark crowd knocked at my door, and I trembled with fear. Then my soul appeared and said in haste, "They are here and will tear open your door."
>
> "So that the wicked herd can break into my garden? Should I be plundered and thrown out onto the street? You make me into an ape and a child's plaything. When, Oh my God, shall I be saved from this Hell of fools? But I want to hack to pieces your cursed webs, go to Hell, you fools. What do you want with me?"
>
> But she interrupted me and said, "What are you talking about? Let the dark ones speak."
>
> I retorted, "How can I trust you? You work for yourself not for me. What good are you, if you can't even protect me from the devil's confusion?"
>
> "Be quiet," she replied, "or else you'll disturb the work."
>
> And as she spoke these words, behold, Philemon came up to me, dressed in the white robe of a priest, and lay his hand on my shoulder. Then I said to the dark ones, "So speak, you dead." And immediately they cried in many voices, "We have come back from Jerusalem, where we did not find what we sought. We implore you to let us in. You have what we desire. Not your blood, but your light. That is it."
>
> Then Philemon lifted his voice and taught them, saying (and this is the first sermon to the dead):
>
> "Now hear: I begin with nothingness."[18]

Throughout the following several nights, Philemon delivers seven sermons in the style of a Hellenistic Gnostic teacher, whom Jung renamed "Basilides" after the historical Gnostic of the second century in the privately published version of *Septem Sermones ad Mortuos*.[19] In the seventh sermon, Philemon teaches them of their destiny and their eternal home, the star.

> This star is the God and the goal of man.
> This is his lone guiding God,
> in him man goes to his rest,
> toward him goes the long journey of the soul after death,
> in him everything that man withdraws from the greater
> world shines resplendently.[20]

This teaching finally satisfies the dead, as the text reports in one of its most beautiful poetic passages:

> But when Philemon had finished, the dead remained silent. Heaviness fell from them, and they ascended like smoke above the shepherd's fire, who watches over his flock by night.[21]

They can now move on to their resting place in eternity.

Who are these ghosts, and what do they mean? In *Memories, Dreams, Reflections*, Jung vividly recalls the experience of their visitation and says of them: "From that time on, the dead have become ever more distinct to me as the voices of the Unanswered, Unresolved, and Unredeemed."[22] They are representatives of the unhoused souls of people who have died without a sense of meaning, conflicted, faithless. Jung would have known well the New Testament's classic definition of faith: "Now faith is the assurance of things hoped for, the conviction of things not seen. For by it the men of old received divine approval. By faith we understand that the world was created by the word of God, so that what is seen was made out of things which do not appear" (*Hebrews 11:1-3*). These restless and disoriented dead are the spirits of modernity who die without mythic symbols that would contain their souls and give them guidance. Being without a guiding myth, they search for an unknown solution to an unstatable problem. They travel fruitlessly to ancient places where faith is supposed to have its home (Jerusalem, for instance), but they come away empty. This was Jung's own predicament as a "modern man."

The comforting image of the star as a symbol of transcendence would return to Jung much later in life, in a dream, and give him solace. He recounts this in a letter to Victor White, which he wrote while recovering from a serious illness in 1946:

> The aspectus mortis is a mighty lonely thing, when you are stripped of everything in the presence of God … Yesterday I had a marvelous dream: One bluish diamondlike star high in heaven, reflected in a round, quiet pool—heaven above, heaven below—. The imago Dei in the darkness of the Earth, this is myself. The dream meant a great consolation. I am no more a black and endless sea of misery and suffering but a certain amount thereof contained in a divine vessel.[23]

It was precisely this notion of a link between the human and the Divine, as symbolized by the star, which had settled the disquiet of the unsatisfied dead and given them peace. Now it provides the same settling containment for Jung in his later years. In *The Red Book*, Philemon is the mediator of this knowledge. From his own testimony, it is clear the Jung struggled to hold on to this piece of *gnosis*.

In Philemon's final appearance, which takes place in the last chapter of *The Red Book*, he welcomes Jung into his garden. Then, a figure dressed in blue, identified as Christ, enters the scene, and they converse with him. Surprisingly, Christ identifies Philemon as a reincarnation of Simon Magus. Christ wonders whose garden this is, his own or Philemon's. In this decisive moment of encounter, recognition, and questioning, Philemon informs Christ that this is his, Philemon's, garden and not Christ's. Thus, the scales are rebalanced between an image of human wholeness (Philemon as Anthropos) and a god-image, putting them into a more evenly calibrated relation, a result that Jung has been struggling mightily to achieve in earlier pages. This is the thematic culmination of the whole narrative, and it leads directly into Jung's late reflections on the reciprocal relation between the human and images of the divine in *Answer to Job* and his magisterial late work, *Mysterium Coniunctionis*.

Philemon himself is a figure who can pass between worlds—time and eternity—and who speaks from personal knowledge and experience and not from received doctrine, theory, or belief. He also links depth psychology to ancient Gnosticism because of his association with Simon Magus. He is a mediator, an image for what Jung would call "the transcendent function." But he is not final or ultimate. He is a symbol for an archetypal power and a mystery beyond himself, which can never be exhaustively described or imagined.

Jung's Philemon, it should be noted, descends to him from Goethe's *Faust* and not in the first place from Ovid's *Metamorphoses*. The *Faust* connection is important because, as it turns out in the final scene of *The Red Book*, Philemon is recognized to be a reincarnation of the unscrupulous magician Simon Magus (Simon the Sorcerer) of New Testament origins (*Acts 8: 9-24*), who by tradition is the prototype of the European Faust. Faust, who embodies overweening pride and egocentricity and who with the able assistance of Mephistopheles grasps greedily for the ring of power, destroys the humble cottage of Philemon and Baucis in order to realize a utopean plan of his own perverse creation. Now, in *The Red Book*, Philemon is identified as Simon Magus (aka Faust), so obviously a great transformation, indeed a kind of reversal, has taken place in the figure.

This transformation of ego ambition into wisdom is the result of several important sacrifices undertaken in the course of the protagonist's pilgrimage, starting with the slaying of the hero Siegfried.[24] In recognition, Jung carved a dedication to Philemon over the doorway of his tower at Bollingen: *Philemonis Sacrum—Fausti Poenitential* (Shrine of Philemon—Repentance of Faust).[25] Clearly, Jung was struggling personally with a strong will to power, and Philemon represents the transformation of the trickster (Simon Magus) and powermonger (Faust) into a teacher of wisdom and transcendence.

What does the Jungian tradition receive from *The Red Book*?

Overall, my conclusion is that *The Red Book* can come to function within the field of Analytical Psychology as a transmission instrument for the archetypal "genius" that lies beyond Jung the man and inscriber of the stories, reflections and images found in it. This genius, moreover, as symbolized in *The Red Book* by Philemon, exists beyond this work itself and has its roots in the "metaphysical" (or, as we say, in the metapsychological) world of the archetypes of the collective unconscious. It can enliven and sustain the tradition.

The danger is that we absolutize any particular symbol of this genius and turn it into a monotheistic idol or into an archetypal fundamentalism. The genius responsible for our dreams and visions, we must remember, is compensatory to our conscious world; it does not offer absolute guidance but rather balance and wholeness when brought into relation with consciousness. It can also produce states of possession (or "intoxication"—German: *Rausch*—as Jung says of his exposure to Philemon in *The Red Book*), from which consciousness must be freed. Jung does not succumb to religious mania with *The Red Book*, as well he could have had he been so inclined, but rather he comes to earth and concludes his adventure with a crucial scene in a garden owned by Philemon, not by Christ, where archetypal images and humans converse on a common level. In an important sense, Jung is struggling throughout *The Red Book* to get beyond the power of the archetypal images he meets up with, including the soul, to dictate their wishes and ambitions to a servile mortal who must obey or face doom. The effort brings them into the human world where they can be integrated and made useful for humanity's consciousness as metaphors that map the unconscious psyche. On the other hand, he knows that the psyche's deepest mystery can never be completely known but must forever be allowed to show itself in new symbols, which in turn must again be integrated and relativized. This is the message of *The Red Book*—encounter and disidentification with the archetypal images of the collective unconscious. The work functions, therefore, as a model for how the human ego can meet and interact with the numinous archetypal powers of the collective unconscious (made available by the genius of the work) and can work creatively and modestly with them.

In the final analysis, Jung's *Red Book* offers a ground plan for an enlarged anthropology and humanism, which receives and embraces the divine with its awesome powers but does not fall on its face before Deity and become enslaved to it. The human maintains its dignity before the Divine, respectfully, and helps the Divine to become conscious by letting it pass through the doorway of human consciousness and enter into relationship with the human world.

Where I will put *The Red Book* in my arrangement of Jung's literary legacy is beside *Memories, Dream, Reflections*. Neither is a scientific work, both are autobiographical, and both can inspire, fascinate, and offer a touchstone for postmodern men and women. They are "timeless documents of the soul." In the chapter in *Memories, Dreams, Reflections* titled "Confrontation with the Unconscious," which is Jung's retrospective account of his experiences as recorded in *The Red Book*, he implies a connection of this work of imagination to a "Golden Chain" of imaginative explorations of the inner world: "It is considered the path of error, of equivocation and misunderstanding. I am reminded of Goethe's words: 'Now let we dare to open wide the gate/Past which men's steps have ever flinching trod.' The second part of *Faust*, too, was more than a literary exercise. It is a link in the *aurea catena* ["Golden Chain"] which has existed from the beginning of philosophical alchemy and Gnosticism down to Nietzsche's *Zarathustra*. Unpopular, ambiguous, and dangerous, it is a voyage of discovery to the other pole of the world."[26] It should be noted that *Liber Secundus*, the second Part of *The Red Book*, is titled "The Images of the Erring." Jung is aligning himself with "the series of great wise men, beginning with Hermes Trismegistos" whose works link "earth with heaven."[27] *The Red Book* is Jung's contribution to the *aurea catena*[28] and offers those of us who are entangled in the postmodern condition of turmoil and confusion, mythlessness, and the dismaying absence of a coherent master narrative a glimpse of the underlying tradition of wisdom that has sustained many generations and can sustain us as well.

Endnotes

1 There is by now also a vast library of secondary works that must be included as central though perhaps not canonical if one speaks of Analytical Psychology as a field, some of which have achieved nearly the status of Jung's own foundational texts, e.g., books by Erich Neumann and Marie-Louise von Franz.

2 The publication of one piece of it in his lifetime, *Septem Sermones ad Mortuos*, he looked upon as "a sin of his youth and regretted it," according to Aniela Jaffé (C.G. Jung, *Memories, Dreams, Reflections*, ed. Aniela Jaffé (New York, NY: Vintage, 1963), 378.

3 In *Memories, Dreams, Reflections*, Jung says: "Ritschl's theology was much in fashion in those days. Its historicism irritated me, especially the comparison with a railway train." Aniela Jaffé adds the footnote: "Albrecht Ritschl compared Christ's coming to the shunting of a railroad train. The engine gives a push from behind, the motion passes through the entire train, and the foremost car begins to move. Thus the impulse given by Christ is transmitted down the centuries." See Jung, *Memories, Dreams, Reflections*, 97.

4 C.G. Jung, *The Zofingia Lectures* (Princeton, NJ: Princeton University Press, 1983), par. 289.

5 Jung, *Memories, Dreams, Reflections*, 91-98.

6 Jung presents this argument, for instance, in his late work, *Mysterium Coniunctionis*, in the concluding section titled "The Self and the Bounds of Knowledge." See C.G. Jung, *Mysterium Coniunctionis*, in *CW*, vol. 14 (Princeton, NJ: Princeton University Press, 1963), pars. 776-789.

7 C.G. Jung, "Synchronicity: An Acausal Connecting Principle," in *CW*, vol. 8 (Princeton, NJ: Princeton University Press, 1969), par. 967.

8 Ibid.

9 Jung, *Memories, Dreams, Reflections*, 98.

10 Wolfgang Giegerich, "*Liber Novus*, That is, the New Bible: A First Analysis of Jung's *Red Book*," *Spring: A Journal of Archetype and Culture* 83 (Spring 2010), 380.

11 Kathryn Evans (2011), International Association for Jungian Studies [Electronic mailing list message. Sent: Saturday, February 19, 2011 10:07 PM. To: The IAJS Online Discussion Forum].

[12] Jung was ever in search of links to older traditions, which he found in alchemy and gnosticism, as he writes in *Memories, Dreams, Reflections* in the chapter titled "The Work," where he makes known his need to put Analytical Psychology on a historical basis.

[13] Wikipedia entry for "genius." See http://en.wikipedia.org/wiki/Genius.

[14] C.G. Jung, *The Red Book: Liber Novus*, ed. Sonu Shamdasani, trans. John Peck, Mark Kyburz, and Sonu Shamdasani (New York, NY: W.W. Norton, 2009), 229.

[15] Ibid., 232.

[16] Ibid., 312.

[17] Ovid, *Metamorphoses*, Bk. VIII.

[18] Jung, *The Red Book*, 346.

[19] Jung, *Memories, Dreams, Reflections*, 378ff.

[20] Jung, *The Red Book*, 354.

[21] Ibid.

[22] Jung, *Memories, Dreams, Reflections*, 191.

[23] Ann Conrad Lammers and Adrian Cunningham, eds., *The Jung-White Letters* (London: Routledge, 2007), 59-60.

[24] Jung, *The Red Book*, 241ff.

[25] Jung, *Memories, Dreams, Reflections*, 235 fn5.

[26] Ibid., 188-189.

[27] Ibid., 189 fn2.

[28] The *aurea catena* ("Golden Chain"), as I am using the term, refers to the immense series of literary works of elevated imagination that reaches back in time to the ancient Sumerian *Epic of Gilgamesh* (whom Jung encounters importantly in *The Red Book* in the figure of Izdubar) and continues onward to include (among many other works) the Bible, the *Tao-te-Ching*, the Homeric epics and Virgil's *Aeneid*, the pre-Socratic philosophers, the Gnostic writers and the philosophical alchemists of antiquity and the Middle Ages, Dante's *Divine Comedy*, the poetical works of William Blake, and, as Jung writes in *Memories, Dreams, Reflections*, Goethe's *Faust* and Nietzsche's *Zarathustra*. In a letter to Max Rychner and responding to a questionaire about Goethe upon the centenary in 1932 of the German poet's death, Jung writes: "*Faust* is the most recent pillar in that bridge of the spirit which spans the morass of world history, beginning with the Gilgamesh epic, the *I Ching*, the Upanishads, the *Tao-te-Ching*, the fragments of Heraclitus, and continuing in the Gospel of St. John, the letters of St. Paul, in Meis-

ter Eckhart and in Dante." (See Gerhard Adler, *C.G. Jung Letters*, trans. by R.F.C. Hull. Vol. 1, 1906-1950 (Princeton, NJ: Princeton University Press, 1973), 80). *The Red Book* can be considered a new modern/postmodern link in the immense Golden Chain of the world's imaginative literature.

The Creative Power of Soul:
A Central Testimony of Jung's *Red Book*

Paul Brutsche

One may well ask, is it worthwhile to study *The Red Book* in detail? If so, why? After all, we know that the substance of this document has been absorbed into Jung's later theoretical works and is more easily accessible in this later form. Is *The Red Book* of importance only or mainly to bibliographically interested academics who want to follow the lines of development from this work to the later writings and try to show the hidden references to *Red Book* material in other of the author's thoughts?

In response to this I would say: The vital psychological interest of *The Red Book* lies in the fact that here we encounter the searching and creative Jung. In this work, Jung takes an attitude toward the reality of the soul that is also valuable for psychologists today and for people of the 21st century in general. It manifests a relationship with the soul that values it as a living reality *sui generis*. It shows a way of dealing with it that brings it alive, as it were, in its original primal state—as a mysterious and extremely powerful reality. *The Red Book* does not offer a theory of soul, a psychology, but something much more fundamental. It offers an experience of soul, an existential testimony of an encounter with the soul. While writings about the soul can easily turn into theoretical studies about psychological phenomena that could be studied, examined, and explained, *The Red Book* puts the reality of the soul as such at the center of attention. Jung realized in his *Red Book* how much he had fallen into a Zeitgeist-inspired surface perspective.

The Red Book is an experiential book documenting Jung's handling of the autonomous reality of his soul. It bears witness to his individual story and his personal experiences. But the attitudes taken by him are of more general validity. They emphasize the soul as an autonomous, creative force and show the conditions under which it can unfold in its own autonomy.

We can also understand *The Red Book* as an empirical representation of soul's creativity under specific conditions. Soul-creativity is different from creativity in science, technology, medicine, economics, politics, and sports. It is a creativity that plays in the medium of imagination and visual perception, is based on subjectivity and personal experience, creates symbolic signification and meaning, includes feelings and the unconscious, and aims at expression and creative design. It is akin to the creativity in art and poetry, where individuals create and shape symbolic reality on the basis of inner experience and through an exchange with the unconscious.

In the following, I wish to consider some of the conditions for experiencing the soul in its autonomous existence as they become evident in *The Red Book*.

The Zeitgeist and the "Hero" as Impediments to the Soul

At the outset, *The Red Book* draws attention to two mental attitudes that stand in the way of the soul's creativity. The one is a "spirit of this time" (Zeitgeist), which is opposed to a "spirit of the depths." Jung describes this Zeitgeist as the dominant way of thinking that determines how people think and behave in a particular epoch. The Zeitgeist of his time is characterized by a complacent "reason" that sees itself as an absolutely autonomous and sovereign guiding principle, which does not want to submit to any ideas suggested by the soul. "The spirit of this time considers itself extremely clever ..."[1]

The Zeitgeist considers dreams as "foolish and ungainly,"[2] and itself as filled "with ripe thoughts."[3] It considers itself superior due to its developed logical-discursive thinking. It faces simple visual thinking with condescending disdain. This thinking in the mode of the Zeitgeist is dominant, anticipatory, abstract, and self-confident. It is thinking in the style of scientifically methodical knowledge, or absolutized "directed thinking," as Jung says in his book *Symbols of Transformation*. It is a type of thinking that often appears in fairy tales as the archetypal *topos* of arrogant and know-it-all older siblings in contrast to the instinctive knowledge of the simpleton.

Jung's *Red Book* emphasizes that a certain mental attitude stands in the way of true soul-inspired creativity. This includes a critically depreciative and dogmatically biased state of mind. Soul-creativity requires openness to "the spirit of the depths," namely a sense for the pictorial, intuitive and childlike playful element in the psyche.

> You think that the dream is foolish and ungainly. What is beautiful? What is ungainly? What is clever? What is foolish? The spirit of this time is your measure, but the spirit of the depths surpasses it at both ends. Only the spirit of this time knows the difference between large and small. But this difference is invalid, like the spirit which recognizes it.[4]

This spirit also has a problematic relation to time. It knows only linear progress, the forward movement. It is incapable of dwelling in the here and now:

> The spirit of this time has condemned us to haste. You have no more futurity and no more past if you serve the spirit of this time. We need the life of eternity. We bear the future and the past in the depths. The future is old and the past is young.[5]

Under the cipher of the "Zeitgeist," Jung thus characterizes an uncreative attitude that is detrimental to the experience of the reality of soul. He does not mean a certain specific time period or epoch. Rather, he means the Zeitgeist of all times, an attitude that in the name of what is *à jour* and corresponds to collective consensus negates the opposite, "the spirit of the depths," which nourishes itself from the unconscious that transcends all times. The spirit characterized as Zeitgeist is a spirit that runs counter to all creativity and experience of the soul. It is a spirit that can interfere with both creative activities and therapies of contemporary people. It prevents, for example, analysands from descending from the high horse of intellectual reasoning to engage with dreams, to paint pictures, and to allow feelings of grief and helplessness. Often, a Zeitgeist dominates that misunderstands therapy as quasi-medical treatment in accordance with the collective consciousness. There is then no willingness to entrust oneself to the "spirit of the depths" and to engage in an inner process under the leadership of the unconscious.

The attitude of the *hero* is the other attitude that stands in the way of creative activity and experience of soul, according to *The Red Book*. On the one hand, this consists of pursuing high performance goals with the object of achieving something perfect and ideal. In this perfectionist quest for something higher and better, the imperfect is suppressed as if it had no right to exist. Such a one-sided strategy of perfection, which excludes the conditional opposite, contradicts the dynamics of a creative antithesis in psychic reality:

> The heroic in you is the fact that you are ruled by the thought that this or that is good, that this or that performance is indispensable, this or that cause is objectionable, this or that goal must be attained in headlong striving work, this or that pleasure should be ruthlessly repressed at all costs. Consequently you sin against incapacity. But incapacity exists. No one should deny it, find fault with it, or shout it down.[6]

The other soul-destroying component of the hero consists in the fact that this attitude leads to nonauthentic imitation. This becomes apparent in two ways: On the one hand, one follows outwardly set ideals; on the other hand, one gains role model status for others and seduces them into apish imitation. This runs counter to the fact that everyone is called to creative self-experience for themselves. *The Red Book* declares:

> Imitation was a way of life when men still needed the heroic prototype. The monkey's manner is a way of life for monkeys, and for man as long as he is like a monkey. ... but the time will come when a piece of that apishness will

fall away from men. ... Then there will no longer be a hero, and no one who can imitate him. ... The hero must fall for the sake of our redemption, since he is the model and demands imitation. ... If you are in yourself, you become aware of your incapacity. You will see how little capable you are of imitating the heroes and of being a hero yourself. So you will also no longer force others to become heroes.[7]

To what extent is a heroic attitude counterproductive to an existentially creative experience? It implies a shift from the honest effort of self-development from within to mere imitation of an ideal set from the outside. Instead of choosing one's individual reality with its possibilities and limits as the true place of self-formation, one chooses a high goal outside. Instead of completeness, one strives for perfection; instead of authenticity, one seeks for exclusivity; instead of being creative "from within oneself,"[8] one aims for the unreachable ideal. Jung recognizes in the heroic tendency, with its incapacitating and self-alienating approach, a great danger to a real inner experience. This can be seen again in the context of today's analyses. People who are bonded to a particular ideal have difficulty really getting involved in a fruitful analytical experience. These are people who, for instance, are trapped in unquestioned religious beliefs as to how to lead a godly life, or people who cling fanatically to political ideals and socio-critical convictions that rob them of openness to other positions and their own shadow aspects. In the field of creative experience also, ideal or perfectionist ideas hinder a creative process. In a creative process, an overly ambitious attitude moves from the immediate here and now and the unplanned and fortuitous to becoming a faraway goal difficult to attain. In such a case, the work cannot develop itself out of itself. It is steered in advance to a predetermined result. This reduces its creative quality, because then the creative process cannot generate freely the unexpected new, the real symbol.

Recognition of Soul's Creativity in Its Antagonism

According to the elementary basic experience documented by Jung in *The Red Book*, soul in its innermost essence is a reality determined by opposites. Insofar as opposites mean energy and are the starting point of creative endeavors, the soul characterized by opposites is a living energetic and creative reality. The image of soul drawn by Jung in *The Red Book* is very new in the history of psychology and is still unique today. He sees soul as an autonomous reality that lives from *inner opposites*. The special feature of this conception is that the opposition is not only seen as that between different psychic components, e.g., between consciousness and the unconscious, between ego and self, between the individual and the collective, between present and past (although these entities are not excluded as causes for inner conflicts), but also as an inherent, autochthonous antagonism of the soul in its very nature. This is an antagonism that does not arise from different claims from inside and outside and between different inner voices, in the sense of the usual psychic conflicts, but from the very core of the creative soul itself. It is an actual process of birth initiated by the soul itself, in which division and distinction serve transformation and creative production of a new third. Since it is an amazingly autonomous and sublime event, Jung symbolically speaks of a "divine child." With this term he describes the origin of this antagonism as a transcendent, i.e. extraordinarily effective, creative power.

> The divine child approached me out of the terrible ambiguity, the hateful-beautiful, the evil-good, the laughable-serious, the sick-healthy, the inhuman-human and the ungodly-godly.[9]

Jung represents the antithetical quality of psychic reality also with the image of the *serpent*. With this image, he describes a dialectical dynamic within opposing poles that corresponds both to life and to the essence of soul and creativity.

The way of life writhes like the serpent from right to left
and from left to right, from thinking to pleasure and from
pleasure to thinking. Thus the serpent is an adversary and
a symbol of enmity, but also a wise bridge that connects
right and left through longing, much needed by our life.[10]

This describes an antithesis that is peculiar to all creative individuals.
This is an antithesis between Dionysian sensuality and Apollonian
depth of thought, which is not only described in Hermann Hesse's
Narcissus and Goldmund or by Friedrich Nietzsche or C.G. Jung but
belongs to the reality of the creative par excellence.

However, the antithetical quality of psychic and creative reality
does not only consist in the ambiguity of opposite aspects or of
dialectics between opposing poles, as we have seen, but it also
includes the *connection between opposites.*

I saw a new God, a child, who subdued daimons in his
hand. The God holds the separate principles in his power,
he unites them. The God develops through the union of
the principles in me. He is their union.[11]

Jung recognizes a powerful, autonomously creative principle in
himself, "a new God, a child," that subdues the "daimons in his hand,"
i.e., that reconciles diverging opposite tendencies through creative
activity. "The God develops through the union of the principles in
me. He is their union." This means that the union of opposites creates
the sublime reality of a superordinate, transcendent symbolic reality,
allowing God to develop inside man.

Finally, Jung addresses the theme of opposites in connection
with the contrast between *man and woman.* Is the soul female or is it
male? The position of *The Red Book* is:

You can hardly say of your soul what sex it is. But if you
pay close attention, you will see that the most masculine
man has a feminine soul, and the most feminine woman
has a masculine soul.[12]

Jung points to the fact that the soul not only contains opposites within itself, but that it stands in contrast to the conscious person. It is thus not only ambivalent, paradoxical and transcends opposites, but it also behaves in a compensatory way to the conscious mind. In summary, it can be said that soul in the sense of *The Red Book* is essentially determined by the aspect of polarity. It is therefore seen as a living energy, as an independent counterpart to consciousness and as an autonomous capability for transformation.

Creative action and expression also must be determined by opposites if they are to be more than merely an intellectual endeavor but spring from the imaginative reality of soul itself. Through opposites the soul expresses itself in its amazing liveliness and dialectical nature. When, however, creative expression is too uniform, obvious, and rational, it becomes a matter of intentional production and intellectual manufacture, of kitsch and propaganda. Such works are boring because they are one-dimensional, too obvious and deliberate, and because they lack the liveliness of psychic polarity.

Recognition of the Soul as an Autonomous Reality

In his inner experience, Jung is led to recognize the soul as an autonomous reality. First of all, this implies a double *reversal* of the previous view anchored in his own ego. On the one hand, he learns that all life goals and relationships are about something beyond the achievement of concrete self-set goals, namely the fundamental search for one's own soul. On the other hand, he must realize that he is not directing his own projects, but that he is guided by the soul and that he is more actor than author.

> Like a tired wanderer who had sought nothing in the world apart from her, shall I come closer to my soul. I shall learn that my soul finally lies behind everything, and if I cross the world, I am ultimately doing this to find my soul. Even the dearest are themselves not the goal and end of the love that goes on seeking, they are symbols of their own souls.[13]

> I had to recognize that I am only the expression and symbol of the soul. In the sense of the spirit of the depths, I am as I am in this visible world a symbol of my soul, and I am thoroughly a serf, completely subjugated, utterly obedient. The spirit of the depths taught me to say: 'I am the servant of a child.' Through this dictum I learn above all the most extreme humility, as what I most need. ... This dictum was repugnant to me and I hated it. But I had to recognize and accept that my soul is a child and that my God in my soul is a child.[14]

To be the servant of a child means to be determined by an inner creative principle that shapes one's life in the sense of constant renewal and playful transformation. For the adult ego, which sees itself as a determining force, this subordination to an unpredictably imaginative, childlike soul-reality is a big challenge.

People with compulsive symptoms show to what an extent the recognition of this childlike divine autonomy of the soul, i.e., the recognition of its powerful transformative energy, can be frightening. They are lacking "humility" in the sense of the above text, they are not ready to submit themselves to the autonomy of the soul, to its "God-character," and to recognize its "child-quality" as the organ of change. Psychologically speaking, people plagued by obsessions struggle to assert self-control over the non-ego reality of soul and to keep themselves free of the influence of its childlike ideas and impulses for change.

The recognition of the soul as an autonomous reality is mentioned in *The Red Book* under yet another image: the experience of the *desert*:

> My soul leads me into the desert, into the desert of my own self. I did not think that my soul is a desert, a barren, hot desert, dusty and without drink.
> Why is myself a desert? Have I lived too much outside of myself in men and events? ... I should also rise up above my thoughts to my own self. My journey goes there, and

that is why it leads away from men and events into solitude.[15]

The desert experience symbolically means an experience of the total emptying of one's own consciousness. This is intended to create an absolute receptivity toward the soul and its autochthonous ideas. The passage into the inner desert corresponds to a radical loss of conscious thoughts and assured knowledge. This brings about a process of melancholic doubting of all certainties. This skeptical path through the "barren, hot and dusty desert" questions any skill and established knowledge. These are experienced as merely dry formulas and phrases. What *The Red Book* describes under the suggestive image of the desert corresponds to the typical experience of an unavoidable loss of *a priori* certainties whenever new original knowledge begins to emerge. In philosophy, we know this systematic questioning of all certainties. It extends from Descartes' *Discours de la Méthode* to Hegel's *Phenomenology of the Spirit* and Husserl's method of the Epoché, the negation of all qualities of *Dasein*. These skeptical approaches each lead to elementary new evidence. In *The Red Book*, however, the experience of the desert does not lead to a *cogito ergo sum*, but to an *esse in anima*, to the vivid experience that the human being is founded in the autonomous imaginative soul.

This phenomenon of process-immanent experiences of desert-like negativity occurs also in creative processes. These are the moments when the creative individual becomes infested with depressing un-creativity. These moments usually have a final goal: They serve to remove people from their previous skills and knowledge and to make them receptive to radically different and new discoveries, which is suggested by an inner creative counterpart. These are humbling and at the same time absolutely enriching experiences. They give evidence of the fact that ultimately creative imagination does not spring from one's own ability but from the will of a soul, in which a "child" and a "god" appear.

In the context of analysis, such an existential desert experience can also be observed in the experience of a soul-initiated loss of conscious control for the purpose of recognizing autonomous psychic reality. As we have said, disturbing symptoms can take over this function by showing a too dominant consciousness the limits of its self-determination. It is forced to admit the autonomy and presence of a different inner reality. The remarkable extinction of former values and faculties so typical of a midlife crisis can also be understood in this sense. It is a matter of inner-psychically constellated "desert situation" in which former strengths and convictions are wiped away. This allows a reversal of perspective that is needed for further life. The essential content of this new view is to realize that one has an autonomous soul and that one is guided by it.

The recognition of the autonomy of the soul, in the view of *The Red Book*, ultimately means the consciousness of a *creative depth* of the human being. Humans are able to create always new meaning out of the soul. With this symbolizing faculty, they can change the fixed structures of the world. The imaginative power of the soul enables new conceptions and new meanings. This opens up "the way of what is to come," namely a perspective of meaning that results from an intuited future and a continually surmounted past. At the same time, "life can flow again" by flowing in the streambed of the changing symbolic meanings of things. The symbolic power of the soul recreates anew the established world of created things.

> Therefore, whoever considers the event from outside always sees only that it already was, and that it is always the same. But whoever looks from inside, knows that everything is new. The events that happen are always the same. But the creative depths of man are not always the same. Events signify nothing, they signify only in us. We create the meaning of events. …
> Because of this we seek in ourselves the meaning of events, so that the way of what is to come becomes apparent and our life can flow again. …
> The meaning of events is the way of salvation that you create. The meaning of events comes from the possibility of life in this world that you create. It is the mastery of this world and the assertion of your soul in this world.[16]

If we apply *The Red Book's* conception of the autonomy of the soul as a meaning-creating faculty to analysis, we can say that analysis can also be understood as a creative reinterpretation of life and personality stimulated by the soul of the analysand. In the symbolic vessel of an understanding relationship between analysand and analyst, and with a symbolic understanding of the contents of the unconscious, an interpretive attitude to the analysand's reality takes place. The analysand's life is released from its meaningless factuality and transformed into a suggestive story. This symbolic opening of life from its trivial factuality to a meaningful gestalt has a healing effect. Life is recognized as an expression of a psychically determined event and thus experienced as something "more than" mere facts. Even if someone has little sense of dreams and symbolic understanding, the contemplative attention to actual life as such is a beneficial creative achievement. It opens "a way of salvation," i.e., blind being is transformed into revelation of meaning.

Dealing with the Archetypal Forms of the Soul

> But as I became aware of the freedom in my thought world, Salome embraced me and I thus became a prophet, since I had found pleasure in the primordial beginning, in the forest, and in the wild animals.[17]

This sentence could be understood as follows: When Jung, on his way to a more immediate experience of the soul, had gained freedom from his one-sided theoretical attitude, he could also take a new approach to the reality of his unconscious. He could enter into a personal dialogue with its contents. In this new attitude he was "embraced by Salome," i.e., supported by an inner intuition that made symbolic understanding and expression possible in the sense of the transcendent function. In this way, he "became a prophet." This is because new insights became possible through the connection with the living figures of the unconscious and their visual expression, which would not have been possible by pure reflection. *The Red Book* as a whole is an expression of this "prophetic" dimension of visual creation. As Jung commented later about his experiences, his inner images became the "stuff and material for more than only one life."[18] These images not only anticipated his later personal insights and thus proved to be prophetic in an individual context, but they also laid the groundwork for insights that are universally valid and significant for later times. This prophetic, future-opening dimension is something that characterizes all true symbolic creation. This is visible, for example, in the precursor function of art, which in all times has given rise to new forms of consciousness and new worldviews in the collective psyche of peoples. "For I had found pleasure in the primordial beginning, in the forest and in the wild animals" could mean that he became interested in the primordial archetypal conditions and in the basic factors of the soul. Likewise, he became interested in the "forest" of the unconscious: the dark background of the psyche. He also turned to the "wild animals" of the archaic driving forces, the primordial instincts and the psyche of the primitive. In symbolic language and condensed form, the entire horizon of Jung's psychological interests is thus unfolded here in a snapshot.

Jung's way of dealing with the unconscious is even more clearly described in the following passage. It describes the method that he will later call active imagination.

> I earnestly confronted my devil and behaved with him as with a real person. This I learned in the Mysterium: to take seriously every unknown wanderer who personally inhabits the inner world, since they are real because they are effectual. ... I must have it out with him, as I cannot expect that he as an independent personality would accept my standpoint without further ado.[19]

The most important thing about active imagination is the idea of taking the "unknown wanderer" seriously and dealing with it as a "real person." In this act of serious and genuine dialogue with the inner figures, Jung shows most clearly his understanding of the soul as a real entity. This is his original experience of soul, his central idea, his most important legacy. Because *The Red Book* documents this conception of soul so clearly and vividly, it is of great importance.

The idea that the inner figures are "real because they are effectual" is another basic idea in Jung's work. It reveals his understanding of psychic reality in contrast to external reality. In the outer reality, real is what is; in the psychic reality, real is what has an effect. Imagination is real because it has a psychic effect on the human being. With his emphasis on a psychic reality *sui generis*, which is defined entirely by the energetic quality of effectiveness, Jung has a conception of soul that is unique and continues to cause incomprehension in the academic world. Nevertheless, it is probably the only empirical evidence in relation to the reality of the soul, as it points directly to real manifestations and effects that can be measured.

A final thought on active imagination as described in the quotation above: It is about dealing with the inner figures, e.g., the devil, in real terms, "as I cannot expect that he as an independent personality would accept my standpoint without further ado." What comes along as an ironic remark is meant quite seriously. The point is to take the inner counterpart so seriously that, as with real people, I grant him his own point of view and allow him to understand mine. Active imagination is not mere fantasizing but a real confrontation between opposing positions and the creative production of a surprising third, a symbol.

The concrete examination of the contents of the unconscious, as we have discussed here by following *The Red Book*, is of great importance for today's analyses. Certainly, most of the analytical work with the unconscious takes place in the form of working on dreams during analytic sessions. But if analysands are ready to enter into such an active dialogue through painting or active imagination, they can have several positive experiences. They may experience that an energetic blockage that manifests itself in the form of a physical symptom—headache, tension, back pain and so forth, or a mental discomfort, grief, emptiness, anxiety and the like—dissolves into a surprising picture or inner fantasy. It is as if the soul finds expression in a symbol. And with the symbol various effects come into being that basically belong to the symbolic: the feeling of astounding meaning, even if it does not express itself in an explicit under-standing of the symbol but merely in a foreboding sense of a certain coherence; the wondering consciousness of being in contact with an imaginative unconscious that supplies ideas and participates actively in the formation of images; and finally the invigorating feeling of participating in a creative process that produces something new and unique.

The Existential Realization of Soul-inspired Creativity

The Red Book shows various ways in which soul-inspired creativity permeates and enhances an individual's life. It also shows the conditions for this to happen.

A. *Existential experience of negativity and blockage*: It is an astonishing and irritating aspect of soul-creativity that it manifests not only and not primarily as a positive, constructive force but also as a force of negation and painful dialectical experience:

> Is there anyone among you who believes he can be spared the way? Can he swindle his way past the pain of Christ? I say: 'Such a one deceives himself to his own detriment. ... No one can be spared the way of Christ, since this way leads to what is to come. You should all become Christs.'[20]

Jung does not mean an imitation of Christ or a conversion to Christianity. What he means is to become Christ in the figurative sense of the crucifying experience, to be at the mercy of insur-mountable opposites and to suffer paralyzing powerlessness. The experience of creative people is always to be blocked by adverse obstacles. These can turn out to be so massive that they take on superhuman proportions. But in this "Christ" quality, they have a redemptive effect. They lead to the "way of what is to come," that is, they open a person's consciousness beyond itself by making it experience the limitations of its own creative possibilities. This is the trajectory enforced by the creative power, not to be able to eliminate the paralyzing blocks with a voluntary effort, but to be dependent on a third one. It is about existential humility, which has to acknowledge the dependence on another, a non-ego.

B. *Experience of meaning and chaos*: Soul-creativity also feeds on the disordered, the meaningless, and the chaotic, which opposes the orderly world of consciousness. Nietzsche put it thus in his famous poetic thought: "One must still have chaos in oneself to be able to give birth to a dancing star."[21] Jung writes:

> If you take a step toward your soul, you will at first miss the meaning. You will believe that you have sunk into meaninglessness, into eternal disorder. ... Nothing will deliver you from disorder and meaninglessness, since this is the other half of the world. ... You open the gates of the soul to let the dark flood of chaos flow into your order and meaning. If you marry the ordered to the chaos you produce the divine child, the supreme meaning beyond meaning and meaninglessness.[22]

Creativity needs to unfold the experience of the disordered and chaotic, in order to create a new order and new meaning. That's why routine and an over ordered world of proven traditions and matters of course are the death of all creativity. It takes uncertainty, instability, and the experience of the strange. For creative solutions, it is well-known that in group processes the possibility of uncontrolled brainstorming is needed, where meaningless ideas have space. Also in the creative endeavor of an individual, there is a need for phases of creative aimlessness, so that ideas can be born and the creative thought can emerge from the mass of meaningless associations and tentative approaches. Also in analysis, it is important to give room to chaos. Jung writes in "General Problems of Psychotherapy": "My aim is to bring about a psychic state in which my patient begins to experiment with his own nature—a state of fluidity, change, and growth where nothing is eternally fixed and hopelessly petrified."[23]

The Supreme Meaning or Symbolic Reality

The meaning of events is the way of salvation that you create. The meaning of events comes from the possibility of life in this world that you create. It is the mastery of this world and the assertion of your soul in this world.[24]

"The meaning of events is the way of salvation that you create"—this is what Jung will later call "religio," the close attention to the meaning of events and the understanding of their symbolic dimension. This symbolic understanding is what allows the soul to live. This is its very specific need, as opposed to the needs of the body and of the cognitive function. Symbolic understanding is the way the soul can prevail and assert itself over and against the mundane world. It does so by creating meanings, by giving a symbolic dimension to things, and by doing so, it "redeems" itself from the pressures of sheer existence.

The captured Jews in the Nazi concentration camp Theresienstadt survived by staging all kinds of theatrical and musical performances and by holding lectures on literature, religion, and philosophy in the dead of night. They survived thanks to the "meanings" that were linguistically conveyed or artistically staged. The fact that the soul lives thanks to meaning-creating expression and is able to survive under restrictive conditions is also evidenced by the paintings of mentally ill people in clinics. People with a diagnosis of cancer are also often able to survive psychologically thanks to artistic expression and occasionally even overcome the cancer somatically thanks to the retroactive effect of the imaginatively revitalized soul.

Children also demonstrate that the soul relies essentially on meaning-creating expression. The child translates everything into fantasy reality, which offers an opportunity for play. In the child's view, things are not only what they were made for. They are not only their function. Rather, they present the subject for a possible staging. The child symbolically converts them into props of an inventive imagination. The purpose of their being, their function, stands in contrast with an antithesis: "To this chair, which is usually intended for sitting on, I assert an antithesis. This chair here on the floor is a horse, and from this I create another meaning: The horse takes a role in an emerging fantasy." Jung continues:

> This meaning of events[25] is the supreme meaning,[26] that is not in events,[27] and not in the soul, but is the God standing between events[28] and the soul, the mediator of life, the way, the bridge and the going across.[29]

The transcending meaning is not in the thing (or events) and not in the soul. It is easy to understand that the transcending meaning is not in the concrete thing or event. After all, meaning does not adhere to the thing, as it were, but is attributed to it from somewhere else. But the transcending meaning is not in the soul either. This could mean that it is not simply a matter of an already existing image in the soul, an inner psychic fact analogous to the outer concrete thing. It is much more an *ad hoc* meaning ("God"), mediating between the things found in the world and the images of the soul. It is a symbolic reality *sui generis*, the "transcending meaning," which stands between things and images, world and soul, and transcends both. This symbolic reality is for Jung divine as it were, because it is profoundly creative and numinous. It expresses two things: on the one hand, a mysterious quality in this symbolic activity and its "magical," miraculous character; and on the other, the fact that it makes use of the artist and makes him a "servant" of this power.

Considering some further aspects of this transcending meaning ("*Übersinn*"), it is described as "the mediator of life, the way, the bridge, and the going across." What could this mean? The creative symbol-generating transcending meaning is a "mediator of life" in that it creates the symbolic world of images and words that emerge between the external world of things and events and the inner world of images. It thereby mediates life, for life means movement within changing forms and the creative production of new forms. Life always wants new birth. This association of creativity and life is more than a literary construction. It has real meaning. People atrophy mentally and physically in an environment that offers no creative space. For instance, children who grow up in a home where order and clean-liness are more important than playful expression and where adaptation to given rules and observance of norms count for more than free self-actuation and self-invention not only suffer from the suppressed pleasure of self-formation, but later also from serious deficits in self-initiative and from the feeling of meaninglessness. And this mental paralysis often causes physical difficulties.

"Transcendent meaning" is also "the way" in that it lets people experience a continuous narrative process, a coherent story. Symbolic designing does not only produce isolated figures. Rather, these are closely connected and convey the satisfying feeling of a meaningful process. *The Red Book* is a good example of the insight that symbolic imagining and creative expression unfold along a coherent path—in this case as a book, as a work of artistic value and as a process with different phases.

"Transcendent meaning" is also called a "bridge." It is characteristic of symbolic figuration to establish connections between opposing realities and to mediate between a here and a there, to transcend op-posites with a third. There has recently been an astonishing example of this bridging function of symbolic reality in the field of politics. North and South Korea, much to the surprise of the world, have recently decided to reestablish official contact and to discuss measures for peaceful rapprochement. This surprising development is generally believed to be due to their joint participation in the Pyeongchang Winter Olympics. These were, in addition to the sporting competitions, a great symbolic staging. Even such a worldly and economy-connected large event can mobilize the bridging spirit typical of symbolic reality.

"The going across" indicates that the symbol leads to another state. It transforms. This is probably its most amazing feature. For example, a person says that painting pictures changes something in him or her. They had a physical or mental discomfort, and after painting, this is changed, and the person understands something new or feels different. Here, the act of creating a symbol shows this amazing process of transforming a physical malaise into a new realization. It is as if a physical-energetic phenomenon were transformed into a spiritual meaning through the symbolic image. The symbol, in this sense, "goes across" from the physical level, where something manifests itself as a disturbance, through the level of transformation into a visual expression, and finally arriving at spiritual meaning contained in the symbol. It appears that the symbol is this amazing organ of transformation that wants to redeem a person from suffering and lead to new meaning and new understanding. What is astonishing about this is that the symbol has this finalistic orientation toward meaning, that it wants to "redeem" by leading out of the narrowness of being, especially when this narrowness is operative in illness and distress.

The symbol is able to realize the "going across" not only between layers and planes of being, but also as a forward movement from now to later, i.e., not only as a process of transformation but also as a revolutionary movement toward a new consciousness. "*Habentibus symbolum facilis est transitus*" (For those who have the symbol, the passage is easy").[30]

The Foundation of Spiritual Creativity in a New Image of God

On the path of his inner experiences, Jung finds himself forced to question the collective image of God. He realizes that this no longer meets the requirements of soul's creativity and no longer covers the conditions of life. He therefore feels compelled to develop a new, more adequate and more creative idea of God. That may seem quite presumptuous. Above all, one may get the impression of psychological hubris that quite casually calls into question time-honored notions that have been decisive for many people in many times. But this creation of a new image of God does not spring from an arbitrary act of an arrogant consciousness. Jung is compelled to do so from within. It is "the spirit of the depths" that demands it. In that sense, one can speak of a true prophetic calling.

Why is it so important, in the eyes of Jung's inner reality, to ask the question of the right image of God and to renew it? This inner voice argues that the image of God largely determines the life of the soul and the possible liveliness or nonliveliness of the human being. Even if the Zeitgeist does not attach importance to the question of the image of God and classifies it rather as a negligible private matter, it could still be the case that the modern unbeliever has, in the background of his mind, an image of God that ultimately determines the view of life and the attitude toward it. A conscious or unconscious conception of God ultimately shapes the basic attitude of every human being: to their times, to their values, and to life in general. Even atheists have an idea about something most important, supreme, about what is important in life, or what is ultimately effective as an agent behind everything. For example, they have the idea that it is important to do good, to be loving, or to be honest or successful, or to be successful or to enjoy life. In the final analysis, these are all reflections of images of God, and indeed of images of God according to the Zeitgeist and to a "heroic" mentality, namely, to exclusively goal-oriented concepts of perfection.

> I understood that the God whom we seek in the absolute was not to be found in absolute beauty, goodness, serious-ness, elevation, humanity or even in godliness. Once the God was there.[31]

There are always ideas aimed at higher goals, i.e. performance-inspired ideas oriented toward a qualitative optimum. For these, something always falls by the wayside: evil, weaknesses and limitations, the ego with its needs, or, conversely, altruism, the sense of other people. There are Calvinistic ideas that have in the past founded a power attitude, a dominant behavior toward oneself, toward other people and toward nature. These are attitudes that have led to repression, one-sidedness in values and actions, and one-sided success thinking. This image of God, which has ultimately promoted the linear, exclusive, upward-striving tendencies of belief in progress, idealism, and ambitious competitiveness, is a profoundly uncreative image of God. It is an image of God that has promoted the adult will and the masculine-heroic self-conquest and has suppressed childlike play and the feminine.

Jung recognizes in *The Red Book* how the conception of God, which stands behind the basic attitudes of our society, our time, and our world, has brought us progress and the great developments of technical possibilities but has caused a massive lack of inner creativity and humanity. The previous one-sided vertical conception of God, which aims at improvement and perfection, promotes progress but not creativity, power but not love, dominance over but not recognition of the weak and limited, negation but not affirmation. Ultimately, such an attitude does not promote life but is a program of nonlife because it sacrifices the duality and changeability inherent to life in favor of abstract one-sidedness.

> I understood that the new God would be in the relative. If the God is absolute beauty and goodness, how should he encompass the fullness of life, which is beautiful and hateful, good and evil, laughable and serious, human and inhuman? How can man live in the womb of the God if the Godhead himself attends only to one-half of him?[32]

The new image of God that Jung exposes in *The Red Book* is determined by opposites that can coexist and complement each other. It is an image of God that integrates opposing qualities in itself. With such an image of God created, the meaning of life can no longer be about striving for an absolute, for self-conquest, for combat and success and dominance. Rather, the challenge is to acknowledge the other, to recognize limits and weaknesses, to play creatively with contrasting possibilities and perspectives, and to give birth from the endured and affirmed opposites. Then it is not about perfection, but about completeness, and the dynamics are no longer aimed at the pursuit of progress but toward soul-inspired transformation.

Endnotes

[1] C.G. Jung, *The Red Book: Liber Novus*, ed. Sonu Shamdasani, tr. John Peck, Mark Kyburz, and Sonu Shamdasani (New York, NY: W.W. Norton, 2009), 237.

[2] Ibid., 233.

[3] Ibid., 234.

[4] Ibid., 233.

[5] Ibid., 253.

[6] Ibid., 240.

[7] Ibid., 245.

[8] Ibid., 253.

[9] Ibid., 243.

[10] Ibid., 247.

[11] Ibid., 254.

[12] Ibid., 263.

[13] Ibid., 233.

[14] Ibid., 234.

[15] Ibid., 235-236.

[16] Ibid., 239.

[17] Ibid., 251.

[18] Ibid., vii.

[19] Ibid., 260-261.

[20] Ibid., 234.

[21] Friedrich Nietzsche, *Thus Spoke Zarathustra*, trans. by Richard J. Hollingdale (New York, NY: Penguin, 1968), Chapter 6.

[22] Jung, *The Red Book*, 235.

[23] C.G. Jung, "General Problems of Psychotherapy," in *CW*, vol. 16 (Princeton, NJ: Princeton University Press, 1966), par. 99.

[24] Ibid., 239.

[25] In German: "*Bedeutung der Dinge*" = "meaning of things."

[26] In German: "*Übersinn*" = "transcendent meaning."

[27] In German: "*der nicht im Dinge ist*" = "that is not in the thing."

[28] In German: "*zwischen den Dingen*" = "between things."

[29] Jung, *The Red Book*, 239.

[30] C.G. Jung, *Psychology and Alchemy*, in *CW*, vol. 12 (Princeton, NJ: Princeton University Press, 1968), page 225.

[31] Jung, *The Red Book*, 243.

[32] Ibid.

The Red Book Today:
From Novelty to Innovation—Not Art but Nature

Joseph Cambray

In the chapter of *Memories, Dreams, Reflections* titled "Confrontation with the Unconscious," Jung reports a variety of inner experiences that accompanied his work on the fantasies and materials that would become his *Red Book*. In this essay, I will look at his use of his own graphic productions as a mean for psychologizing, of making psyche through visual transformations. To start, it may be useful to explore Jung's own struggle with the activity he was engaged in beginning, in his own words:

> When I was writing down these fantasies, I once asked myself, 'What am I really doing? Certainly this has nothing to do with science. But then what is it?' Whereupon a voice within me said, 'It is art.' I was astonished. It had never entered my head that what I was writing had any connection with art. Then I thought, 'Perhaps my unconscious is forming a personality that is not me, but which is insisting on coming through to expression.' I knew for a certainty that the voice had come from a woman. I recognized it as the voice of a patient, a talented psychopath who had a strong transference to me. She had become a living figure within my mind.
>
> Obviously what I was doing wasn't science. What then could it be but art? It was as though these were the only alternatives in the world. That is the way a woman's mind works.[1]

Clearly the act of recording and working on his fantasy life had preconscious elements unbeknownst to Jung's conscious mind at the time. The question "What am I really doing?" holds the therapeutic exploration that lyses this emerging awareness, transforming it from what Christopher Bollas might call the "unthought known" into a conundrum deserving reflection.[2]

Unable to identify his activity as a form of science, as he understood it, the question echoes more strongly, gathering intensifying affect. Out of the growing tension emerges a voice that astonishes: It is "other" in its dissociative, not-self qualities, including its femininity, and declarative, aesthetic orientation. This can be seen as a fascinating moment of meeting inducing a radical rupture in ordinary egoic functioning and opening up imaginative possibilities. This is an aspect of soul, but felt as a sly deceiver with a clever, psychopathic streak, capable of seductive misleadings—the claim of "art" being chief among them.[3]

Jung's scientific rationalism initially guides his reflective interpretations. He recognizes the unconscious as potentially forming a not-I personality. This is reminiscent of his observations about his cousin the medium and her multiple personalities. Is there an individuation urge manifesting in this anima figure? Perhaps a future aspect of the self, the unconscious forming a homologue of the figure of Ivenes in cousin Helly? Multiplicity of personality is directly entering into Jung's own psychological experience, an inner, subjective reality that he is trying to frame against his earlier objective, scientific observations. Here I believe he is breaking psychological ground, opening to the emergent possibilities in his fantasy work, beginning to find an internal ecology of autonomous figures who populate his inscape. This finding is surely one dimension of the contemporary resonance to the publication of *The Red Book*.

As we move ever deeper into the worlds of virtual, augmented, and mixed realities, we find proliferation of personalities at our playful edges, enchanting, entertaining but also at times terrifying us with Artificial Intelligence horrors. Jung's pioneering discoveries provide a psychological frame for our fascination with avatars, cinematic and online. Jung's *Red Book* serves as the precursor of our cyber, postmodern, distributed identities. However, this is laden with shadows and cannot be reduced to idealistic escapism. The psychological work necessary to forge relationships with the figures of the imagination, understanding their symbolic meaning and compensations for our lives, is skipped over or avoided at our peril. Jung did champion the need to integrate the material arising from the unconscious, and this is often lacking in contemporary culture.

In particular, psychopathic dangers arise here, souls lost in cyber networks, where empathy for others can erode and even disappear. Children are especially susceptible to this. Fortunately, much of the loss is reversible if attended to and measures are taken—for example, see Sherry Turkle's *Alone Together* and *Reclaiming Conversation*.[4] In attuning to potential psychological danger, Jung's identifies the inner voice as that of a woman he finds disturbed and with a strong transference to him. This launches him into a process of discernment, learning to identify the "spirits" whom he is engaging as well as activating his suspicions and fears of the feminine.[5] The sexist reductionism of his understanding of "the way a woman's mind works" as if solely through rigid oppositions, such as art *or* science as the only possibilities, has a distinctly defensive feeling to it as well as reflecting the historical, patriarchal period in which it occurred. Feminine "logic," especially when employing the feeling function and valuing artistic productions, seems precarious to Jung and capable of leading his masculine, truth-oriented ego into error. This echoes his mistrust of women stemming from his childhood abandonment experiences.

Remarkably, just at this moment Jung catches himself in the act of suppression, internally silencing the voice with his denial and rejection of the proposal regarding "art." Instead, he proceeds to a confrontation, an *Auseinandersetzung*, with this feminine voice:

> I said very emphatically to this voice that my fantasies had nothing to do with art, and I felt a great inner resistance. No voice came through, however, and I kept on writing. Then came the next assault, and again the same assertion: 'That is art.' This time I caught her and said, 'No, it is not art! On the contrary, it is nature,' and prepared myself for an argument. When nothing of the sort occurred, I reflected that the 'woman within me' did not have the

speech centers I had. And so I suggested that she use mine. She did so and came through with a long statement.

I was greatly intrigued by the fact that a woman should interfere with me from within. My conclusion was that she must be the 'soul,' in the primitive sense, and I began to speculate on the reasons why the name 'anima' was given to the soul. Why was it thought of as feminine? Later I came to see that this inner feminine figure plays a typical, or archetypal, role in the unconscious of a man, and I called her the 'anima.'[6]

While he is able to relinquish some control, letting "her" use "his" speech center, it is for the sake of debate. Unfortunately, we do not have the "long statement" delivered by this figure, just the sense that he was able to vanquish this after hearing it out. I am, however, left with the sense that this was treated in a combative fashion, heightened by the perceived dark cunning of the figure. There seems to have been a collapse of curiosity about the telos of the voice. Was it solely a contest of wits in a divided self, or was there something more that this figure was hinting at?

Jung's counter of "not art but nature" is complex and self-challenging. By the time he was working on the fantasies of the *Red Book*, Germanic culture had already recognized and strongly embraced the power and vitality of biomimetic art, including that graphic source underlying some of Jung's own mandalas in the *Red Book*, Ernest Haeckel's *Art Forms in Nature*.[7] As if to undo his own "victory," Jung ends this passage with the recognition of the exchanges as ultimately having been with his own soul. Again, curiosity about the *telos* of the exchange is lost in favor of theorizing about the abstract archetypal nature of such a figure. While presumably accurate, this move is also a bit disappointing and leaves us with the original question of how to more deeply understand the activity he is engaging in while working on his fantasies. To the soul they are art, to consciousness they have become an expression and representation of nature, though exactly what aspects are left indeterminate. Are they expressions of Jung's own nature, of human nature, or of the world of nature manifesting through Jung's imagination, or perhaps all of these and more?

Visual Psychologizing

My focus in this essay will be narrower than the question of the artistry of the whole of *The Red Book* but will instead look at the visual, graphic aspects of the book and what this may be seeking to accomplish. To go further, I turn again to *Memories, Dream, Reflections,* where Jung discusses his move into painting mandalas:

> It was only toward the end of the First World War that I gradually began to emerge from the darkness. Two events contributed to this. The first was that I broke with the woman who was determined to convince me that my fantasies had artistic value; the second and principal event was that I began to understand mandala drawings. This happened in 1918-19. I had painted the first mandala in 1916 after writing the *Septem Sermones*; naturally I had not, then, understood it.
>
> In 1918-19 I was in Château d'Oex as Commandant de la Région Anglaise des Internés de Guerre. While I was there I sketched every morning in a notebook a small circular drawing, a mandala, which seemed to correspond to my inner situation at the time. With the help of these drawings I could observe my psychic transformations from day to day. One day, for example, I received a letter from that esthetic lady in which she again stubbornly maintained that the fantasies arising from my unconscious had artistic value and should be considered art. The letter got on my nerves. It was far from stupid, and therefore dangerously persuasive. The modern artist, after all, seeks to create art out of the unconscious. The utilitarianism and self-importance concealed behind this thesis touched a doubt in myself, namely, my uncertainty as to whether the

fantasies I was producing were really spontaneous and natural, and not ultimately my own arbitrary inventions. I was by no means free from the bigotry and hubris of consciousness which wants to believe that any halfway decent inspiration is due to one's own merit, whereas inferior reactions come merely by chance, or even derive from alien sources. Out of this irritation and disharmony within myself there proceeded, the following day, a changed mandala: part of the periphery had burst open and the symmetry was destroyed.[8]

The darkness from which Jung is emerging has to do with the relationship between the inner and outer worlds. For him, it is the discovery of psychic reality not only as a personal experience but valid for collective experience as well. As we know, this will be most fully articulated for him in the synchronicity hypothesis.

By implication, the impediment to these realizations was the seduction of seeing himself as doing art. The notion of art he identifies here would seem *not* to more deeply reveal the world; and the works of the modern artists of the time were taken by him as not genuinely spontaneous and natural but tinged with a corrosive narcissism, which he feared he would find in himself. However, when he was able to surmount this anxiety, the perspective on what he was doing changed, shifting from his ambivalence about himself as artist to becoming the psychologist of the collective, which was one of his most important contributions. Therefore, this warrants further examination. The fears about art should be tempered by recognition of his personal anxieties rather than become a critique of modern art.

In the act of freeing himself from doing "art" as he was conceiving it and simultaneously escaping the lure of the dangerous woman, a profound disruption occurred. The broken symmetry of his mandalic containment captured in his drawing (shown in Appendix A in *The Red Book*) reflected a psychological rupture and the onset of a process of transformation. Previously, I have discussed this in terms of a phase change yielding significantly increased complexity leading to the synchronicity hypothesis.[9] Here, I would like to reexamine this in terms of the work being done through the visual representations of these experiences.

Jung is able to pursue the rupture into a cosmological revisioning of the world. This is already thematic in what has come before in *The Red Book* with his repeated use of the symbolism of the cosmic egg. Since we know the *Red Book* was constructed chronologically in terms of page numbers, the explicit reference to the cosmic egg (Hiranyagarbha) held between horns on page 59 and the egg reappearing on subsequent pages up to its fiery opening on page 64 well precedes the mandala sequence, with its response to the woman's letter on page 84. However, as can be seen, perhaps reflecting anticipatory anxiety, on page 83, the powerful eruption from below into the mandalic space was already on the way a day or so before the letter actually arrived.

The culmination of this cycle of rupture and repair leading to a new cosmic egg, or new cosmology, is captured by the last image in the mandala series on page 97. Here, a much richer egg has been arrived at, multilayered in the midst of the four elements. I believe this visually represents a new vision of the nature of reality, which Jung, with the help of Wolfgang Pauli, struggles to articulate some years later. The implications of the hypothesis are that synchronistic processes were fundamental to the formation and evolution of the universe—as I've discussed elsewhere.[10] Jung's formulations of the hypothesis explicitly used the language of contemporary cosmology of his day, and his goal of linking inner and outer realities, psychology and physics, was pursued through the formulation of synchronicity.

Returning once more to the rupture from a slightly different vantage point, we can see that the break with the stubborn "esthetic lady" occurs at the same time as the artistic mandala breaks open. However, rather than just equating the two (art = dangerous woman), Jung may be looking for a new way to be in relationship with the images emerging from the unconscious. I would argue he is finding a deeper use for imagery, though the wholesale rejection of art seems excessive. Imagery can offer a way of thinking and even of doing psychological work through entering that imagery with full passion and wrestling with the truth of what is emerging.

The cognitive work that imagery and art is capable of was not well-articulated during this period of Jung's life. A key inaugural text on the topic was published in 1969 (eight years after Jung's death) by Rudolf Arnheim, the Gestalt psychologist and Harvard professor of psychology. Arnheim's *Visual Thinking* went counter to the views of his time, basing cognition in perception rather than cognition structuring perception.[11] He also argued in this book that language follows rather than precedes imagery in the mind. Since that time, the value of visual thinking has been increasingly recognized and is regularly taught in introductory courses in art and design.

Some contemporary Jungians have begun to elaborate and surpass Jung's choice of images to illustrate ideas in terms of the cognitive work done by them. An excellent example of a critical approach to Jung's choice of alchemical imagery can be found in Angela Connolly's "Cognitive aesthetics of alchemical imagery." There, she notes that Jung

> fails to consider the role of aesthetics in the creation of alchemical images and as Paul Bishop says with reference to alchemical symbols: 'Placing emphasis on the importance of intuition *(Anschauung)* Jung recognized the aesthetic appeal of such symbols, although he was reluctant to go one step further and regard this appeal in itself as central to their psychological function.'[12]

This underlines how the rejection of the psychopathic woman equated to art had some deformational impacts on Jung's psychologizing. As Connolly suggests, he does not consciously employ the aesthetic and sensuous aspects of the alchemical imagery in his choices of what to display in his publications. His choices focus solely on the symbolic meaning. Thus, the symbolism had to carry the freight, and the value of the sensuous and aesthetic aspects of the imagery remained unexplored. Obviously, it was present but remained preconscious at best.

As Connolly also notes, referencing the work of the historians of alchemy William Newman and Lawrence Principe and art historian Barbara Stafford, Jung did not consider the historical and cultural context of the imagery and ideas of alchemy. In this unconscious forfeiting of some of the nuanced reflections that might have arisen from including such considerations, Jung was able to articulate an archetypal base to the imagery. However, this tendency came at the cost of contextual understanding, and in turn this reveals a deficit in Jungian theory that we are still struggling to articulate in full. For example, the cultural aspects of Jung's theory are currently being discussed in an effort to move them from the implicit to the explicit domain—work begun by Joseph Henderson and carried forward by some of his protégés such as Tom Singer and Sam Kimbles as well as a growing number of others.[13] They work primarily out of a model of the complex, expanding theories of personal complexes into socio-cultural aspects. While a useful beginning, this is an enormous area, and there is much other material that remains to be integrated into such a view, especially from contemporary disciplines such as sociology, anthropology, neuroscience, evolutionary and epigenetic theories, complexity studies, cultural studies, intellectual history, and so on.

Despite these critiques, there was something extraordinary that Jung was able to extract from his work with alchemy and alchemical imagery. The outline of an entire model of coherent human psychological transformation across the life span of individuals and collectives, i.e., the notion of individuation, was captured in what he was able to synthesize in his alchemical studies. The hypothesis here is that his creative visual work in the *Red Book* was the prelude not only to his personal transformation but, as he realized by the end of that work, led to a general model of human maturation across the entire life span of the person. In particular, I would like to suggest that the series of images in *The Red Book* mentioned above form coherent trajectories of psychological states culminating in enhanced richness and complexity as Jung discovered in himself and in his dreams.

The *Red Book* culminates for Jung in several ways as he details in *Memories, Dreams, Reflections*. One path leads to the "Liverpool dream":

I found myself in a dirty, sooty city. It was night, and winter, and dark, and raining. I was in Liverpool. With a number of Swiss—say, half a dozen—I walked through the dark streets. I had the feeling that there we were coming from the harbor, and that the real city was actually up above, on the cliffs. We climbed up there. It reminded me of Basel, where the market is down below and then you go up through the Totengässchen ('Alley of the Dead'), which leads to a plateau above and so to the Petersplatz and the Peterskirche. When we reached the plateau, we found a broad square dimly illuminated by street lights, into which many streets converged. The various quarters of the city were arranged radially around the square. In the center was a round pool, and in the middle of it a small island. While everything roundabout was obscured by rain, fog, smoke, and dimly lit darkness, the little island blazed with sunlight. On it stood a single tree, a magnolia, in a shower of reddish blossoms. It was as though the tree stood in the sunlight and were at the same time the source of light. My companions commented on the abominable weather, and obviously did not see the tree. They spoke of another Swiss who was living in Liverpool, and expressed surprise that he should have settled here. I was carried away by the beauty of the flowering tree and the sunlit island, and thought, 'I know very well why he has settled here.' Then I awoke.[14]

Jung's focus was on the *beautiful* scene at the center. For him "the dream brought with it a sense of finality." He felt the goal of his strivings "had been revealed" and with this an archetypal experience of the self, which gave his life orientation and meaning, and held a "healing function." This encounter brought his personal visual and graphic experiment to a conclusion: "After this dream I gave up drawing or painting mandalas. The dream depicts the climax of the whole process of development of consciousness."[15]

In the present context, it is remarkable to realize that this achievement came with a numinous aesthetic experience embodied in the blossoming magnolia tree at the center. This illuminated philosophical tree with its glorious *rubedo* blooms stood at the acme of Jung's psychological journey through the realm of the unconscious. The sensuous aesthetic realm he has been rejecting becomes the source of confirmation for his own transformation, providing the affective assurance of the correctness of his years of wandering in pursuit of a new center. If this partial integration of the sensuous and the aesthetic into Jung's larger vision is linked back to the talented psychopathic patient, whom Sonu Shamdasani identifies as Maria Moltzer, then this may point to a refinement in Jung's intuitive function, for it was Moltzer who introduced intuition as a psychological function into Jung's typology.[16] The intuition of the self, accessed through the "Liverpool dream," is made more real through the aesthetic impact it had on consciousness. We could say Jung's visual thinking, which he was intuitively training during the years of craft work on the *Red Book,* reached its goal and, in this, freed him to find this in the world, in history, and in culture.

As he continues to discuss the dream, he notes it served as an orienting vision, replacing in a more profound way what he had lost "when I parted from Freud."[17] The juxtaposition of the new worldview, symbolically envisioned in the magnolia tree, together with the healing from his break with Freud, took a fascinating turn for me personally several years ago in China. I was part of a panel on dreams with a number of Chinese practitioners of various philosophies and arts. I had brought two origin dreams to discuss, Freud's Irma dream and Jung's "Liverpool dream." Each dream held key elements to the dreamer's views of the unconscious and launched their therapeutic methods. My hosts and fellow participants expressed more interest in Jung's dream as being closer to the kinds of transformational processes they were interested in. However, the surprise came from the comments of a doctor of Chinese medicine who observed the Mulan tree (*Magnolia Liliiflora*) can be used for nasal complaints (and for anemia)! Recall that Freud's dream was in response to his friend Fleiss' botched nasal operation on one of

Freud's patients—gauze left in by accident, with the patient nearly hemorrhaging to death and Freud's guilt over the matter. The doctor noted that the medicine from the type of tree in Jung's dream would have been helpful to Freud and his patient. This unexpected link between the origin dreams of psychoanalysis and Analytical Psychology delivered by a doctor of Chinese medicine was completely unanticipated but pointed to the larger archetypal themes that were at play. Jung's struggles to think visually using mandalas as the means of entry was indeed part of this healing arising from the unconscious. It was as if the essence of individuation activated by the transpersonal self was missing from Freud's inaugural approach, and with a turn toward China, the missing ingredient could be discovered.

The second related exit from the period of the *Red Book* is, as I have written about, the discovery of synchronicity. The secret link between the subjective and objective worlds of experience, the connection between psyche and soma, physical and psychological realities, emerged from Jung's receipt of the manuscript translation of the Chinese alchemical classic, *The Secret of the Golden Flower,* from Richard Wilhelm in 1928. At the very moment he received the manuscript with Wilhelm's request for Jung to write the foreword, he was working on the mandala on page 163 of *The Red Book* depicting a fortress with coloration that Jung felt was distinctly Chinese in feeling. Jung identified this as "the first event which broke through my isolation." He went so far as to write a commemoration underneath the picture and quotes this in *Memories, Dreams, Reflections*:

> In 1928, when I was painting this picture showing the golden, well-fortified castle, Richard Wilhelm in Frankfurt sent me the thousand-year-old Chinese text on the yellow castle, the germ of the immortal body.[18]

Now, an aesthetic experience was directly linked with a remarkable coincidence, and later that year Jung first employed the concept of "synchronicity" in a private seminar. From this, a whole cosmology was to flow as he articulated the concept in dialogue with Wolfgang Pauli as I have discussed elsewhere.[19]

A hitherto less examined link is that between aesthetic and synchronistic phenomena. Often more intense synchronistic experiences come with a sense of awe, and the uncanny aspects can evoke the sublime. These sorts of responses are characteristic of the synchronistic vignettes that Jung offers in his writings, which often have striking imagistic elements. For example, the patient with the "golden scarab" dream told this dream as a beetle sought to enter Jung's consulting room. The aesthetic dimension of the experiences are included but not often given a clear role in the psychological work beyond synchronistic, affective affirmation—in this case of opening up the patient's rationalistic defenses and allowing the analytic work to proceed. However, as with Arnheim and those who follow him, it may be that aesthetically induced affect is key to the transformational energies released for psychological work. I would encourage a rereading of Jung's cases from this vantage point, as I believe they do indicate a preconscious, intuitive valuation of aesthetics that has remained largely without a voice (as the "psychopathic lady" at the start of this process).

After the *Red Book*

In viewing Jung's artistic productions from childhood on through later life, as displayed at the Rietberg Museum in Zurich in 2011, it seems to me that after he stopped working on the *Red Book*, he moved more toward sculptural forms and did few or no paintings for manuscripts. Rather than pursuing graphic art on paper, Jung worked in wood and stone and painting the interiors of his tower at Bollingen. From this perspective his expression of psyche stayed close to his orientation as a highly skilled craftsperson—see Linda Carter's essay in this volume for a fuller study. The use of the illuminated manuscript format for the *Red Book* in the tradition of the skilled, religious craftsperson was most congruent with Jung's own nature and part of the soul he sought to recover during his *Red Book* period.

Jung used artistic forms as a way of thinking; his creativity was psychologically oriented rather than artistically focused. The artistry of the *Red Book* may be best conceived of as a tool to assist in giving substance and form to the psychological experiences that otherwise would have languished in silent subjective interiority. So, if the artistic productions of the *Red Book* were not done as art, as Jung himself adamantly insists, and I believe him, especially given his halting of these sorts of explorations after the Liverpool dream, what then shall we make of his psychological creativity emerging from that period?

As an innovator, Jung's gifts lay with opening up new terrains for psychology as it was conceived at the start of the 20th century. *The Red Book* is the testament of an intrepid explorer going into the psychological wilderness and charting new territory. This may be one of the more important legacies of *The Red Book*, including for our time. So how might we characterize his explorations?

Retrospectively looking at Jung's work, we can readily identify that his creativity could be now seen in terms of an ability to intuit the emergent edge of the psyche. He was a proto-complexity theorist in spirit before the notion was conceptualized. As I have written about previously, all of his methodology can be read as tools for discovering emergent phenomena, and his deepest cosmological-philosophical reflections point to a vision of the universe based in complexity.

Applying complexity theory to the study of creativity, the concept of "the adjacent possible" is becoming a valuable tool for exploring the pathways for development of novelty and innovation. One of the expansions in analytic thought that Jung's work might give rise to is the realm of a collective preconscious that becomes a fertile source of innovations—this is reflected in the often recognized near-simultaneous breakthroughs in various field by research groups working on similar problems spontaneously finding solutions to previously insoluble problems at nearly the same time, as if the solution were "in the air." At times these take on the quality of meaningful, noncausal overlaps, and hence the explorations of the *Red Book* can be viewed as paradigmatic.

The Adjacent Possible

The term "the adjacent possible" was coined by theoretical biologist and complexity scientist Stuart Kauffman.[20] This arose out of attempts to examine origins, especially the origins of life and how complexity evolves in our universe from points of origin. It is an evolutionary model (though not just of biology).

Using contemporary quantum mechanical arguments going beyond the standard model (the Copenhagen interpretation), Kauffman daringly argues that measurements of quantum systems do not simply collapse the wave function into one result (the observed). Instead, there is a more subtle decoherence of the manifold of possibilities resulting from measurement. Prior to contact/ measurement, quantum systems are considered to be in a holistic coherent state containing all possibilities. In decoherence, these possibilities are not lost due to collapse of the wave function (the standard view) but rather in this model remain in superposition of global coherence, yielding the many-worlds interpretation of quantum mechanics. The evidence Kauffman amasses for this is impressive, though still speculative and includes cogent arguments about reversibility of decoherence.

The decoherence model leads then to a new dualism, that of actuals (the observed) and possibles. Kauffman uses the quantum logic to reappraise the realm of possibles in relationship to actuals. The new dualism allows the realm of possibles to remain *ontologically real*. Furthermore, because the loss of (wave function) phase infor-mation in decoherence is acausal, these two realms, the actuals and the possibles, are acausally related. As Kauffman comments on our "open universe":

> The becoming of the universe can involve ontologically both the Actual and the Possible, where what becomes Actual can *acausally* change what becomes Possible and what becomes Possible can *acausally* change what becomes actual.[21]

With the ontological status of the realm of possibles established, Kauffman employs this result from quantum logic to look at evolution and innovative processes. This more practical focus brings into view another valuable distinction among possibles. The most salient for innovation are those possibilities near where a person or society currently is. The further from actuals, the more of a leap it is to instantiate a possible into a new actual. Even if the ideas can be grasped, often the technology to achieve them is lacking. For example, Leonardo da Vinci's screw-helicopter was a brilliant conception, but 15th century technology and materials science was not up to the task. Jung's *Red Book* may be a psychological version of innovation ahead of its time.

The adjacent possible holds what is potentially in reach if we can open up the imagination to it. In working analytically with unconscious material, there often appears in a dream a new room (sometimes several) that a person is finding in his or her current residence. This tends to come with the surprise of discovery. Kauffman shows how exploring this realm increases complexity—his examples include the step-wise evolution of increasingly complex molecules that can lead to accumulations of the precursors for life to emerge. The adjacent possible is the link between what is and what can be and brings these networks into engaged interaction. Steven Johnson, a popularizer of Kauffman's work, refers to this realm as "a kind of shadow future." He captures the expanding network quality of this in his book *Where Good Ideas Come From*:

> The strange and beautiful truth about the adjacent possible
> is that its boundaries grow as you explore those boundaries.[22]

Increasingly in the historical study of scientific discoveries, there is recognition of the importance of the role of serendipity in discovery. A well-trained, intuitive mind capable of recognizing when something unexpected occurs (often through a perceptual surprise stirring curiosity) may perceive a valuable new line of inquiry. For example, the story of Arthur Fleming's remarkable discovery of the antibiotic effects of penicillin through a series of extraordinary coincidences has been well-documented. As I discussed in my book on synchronicity, the serendipitous often seems to include a synchronistic element (the meaningful coincidence of this researcher at just this time and place).[23]

Recently the notion of the adjacent possible has been employed in broader studies of creativity in cultures. Physicist Vittorio Loreto and colleagues have looked at the way cultural networks are explored from the viewpoint of the adjacent possible.[24] They differentiate personal discoveries as novelty from the emergence of the new in cultures, or the world, which they term innovation. Using the Internet Movie Database to track innovations, they hint at a general model of the flow of innovation in the network of the possible. They track the movement of discoveries through stepwise expansion of the actuals into the possibles. Once a possible is chosen, a new node becomes actual and a new set of adjacent possibles is realized.

This research can be applied broadly. For example, similar network structures can be constructed for psychotherapy sessions, say the presentation of a dream as the actual with understandings, interpretations, and processing possibilities being realized in time among the participants as the flow through the adjacent possible. At times, these explorations yield something unexpected, such as synchronistic experience related to the content presented opening up a new pathway for the process—this would be in the realm of the novel. What would be exciting would be to develop a way of tracking these discoveries into the collective, recognizing when a shift from novelty to innovation is occurring.

Conclusion

One of the more remarkable accomplishments of Jung's *Red Book* for me is noticing how the novelties in his confrontation with the unconscious were in fact opening out into psychological innovations. While consciously focused on what he saw as an internal engagement but also carrying an echo of prophecy, Jung found his way to a methodology and ultimately a cosmology applicable for the contemporary world. In many ways, his model is more easily integrated and more palatable for the current age than they were at the time of his encounters that formed the core of the *Red Book*.

As complex systems with emergent properties become a new paradigm for knowledge in the 21ˢᵗ century, Jung's efforts take on great significance, clarity, and meaning. His prophetic powers were not individual but offer a vision for the way the psyche is ultimately inseparable from the universe. The objective aspect of the psyche can be discussed more readily today, in large part because of Jung's pioneering work. There remains much to be done.

Endnotes

[1] C.G. Jung, *Memories, Dreams, Reflections*, ed. Aniela Jaffé (New York, NY: Vintage, 1963), 185-186.

[2] Christopher Bollas, *The Shadow of the Object: Psychoanalysis of the Unthought Known* (New York, NY: Columbia University Press, 1987), 4.

[3] In *Cult Fictions*, Shamdasani hypothesizes based on impressive circumstantial evidence that the voice of the woman patient was that of Maria Moltzer; see Sonu Shamdasani, *Cult Fictions: C.G. Jung and the Founding of Analytical Psychology* (London and New York, NY: Routledge, 1998), 69.

[4] Sherry Turkle, *Alone Together: Why We Expect More from Technology and Less from Each Other* (New York, NY: Basic Books, 2011) and Sherry Turkle, *Reclaiming Conversation: The Power of Talk in a Digital Age* (New York, NY: Penguin Random House, 2015).

[5] In the *Memories, Dreams, Reflections* passage the identification of the voice is presented as the woman's; I prefer to read it as more metaphorical, as if it were her voice, underscoring how such a voice ultimately belongs to the larger personality of the author.

[6] Jung, *Memories, Dreams, Reflections*, 185-186.

[7] Joseph Cambray, "*The Red Book*: Entrances and Exits," in *The Red Book: Reflections on C.G. Jung's Liber Novus*, ed. T. Kirsch and G. Hogenson (New York, NY and London: Routledge, 2014).

[8] Jung, *Memories, Dreams, Reflections*, 195.

[9] Joseph Cambray, *Synchronicity: Nature & Psyche in an Interconnected Universe* (College Station, TX: Texas A&M University Press, 2009).

[10] Ibid., 18-21.

[11] Rudolf Arnheim, *Visual Thinking* (Berkeley and Los Angeles, CA: University of California Press, 1969).

[12] Angela Connolly, "Cognitive aesthetics of alchemical imagery," in *Journal of Analytical Psychology*, 2013, 58:1, 6.

[13] Thomas Singer and Joerg Rasche, eds., *Europe's Many Souls: Exploring Cultural Complexes and Identities* (New Orleans, LA: Spring Journal Books, 2016); Pilar Amezaga, Gustavo Barcellos, Axel Capriles, Jackie Gerson, and Denis Ramos, *Listening to Latin America* (New Orleans, LA: Spring Journal Books, 2012).

[14] Jung, *Memories, Dreams, Reflections*, 197-198.

[15] Ibid., 198-199.

[16] Nathalie Pilard, *Jung and Intuition. On the Centrality and Variety of Forms of Intuition in Jung and Post-Jungians*. (London: Karnac, 2015), 20, 209.

[17] Jung, *Memories, Dreams, Reflections*, 199.

[18] Ibid., 197.

[19] Joseph Cambray, "Cosmos and Culture in the Play of Synchronicity," in Stacy Wirth, Isabelle Meier, and John Hill, eds., *The Playful Psyche: Entering Chaos, Coincidence, Creation* (New Orleans, LA: Spring Journal Books, 2012), 135-138.

[20] Stuart Kauffman, *Humanity in a Creative Universe* (New York, NY: Oxford University Press, 2016).

[21] Ibid., 31.

[22] Steven Johnson, *Where Good Ideas Come From: The Natural History of Innovation* (New York, NY: Riverhead Books, 2010), 31.

[23] Joseph Cambray, *Synchronicity: Nature & Psyche in an Interconnected Universe*, 103-105.

[24] Pietro Gravino, Bernardo Monechi, Vito Servedio, Francesca Tria, and Vitorrio Loreto, "Crossing the Horizon: Exploring the Adjacent possible in a Cultural System," in *Proceedings of the Seventh International Conference on Computational Creativity (ICCC 2016)*, François Pachet, Amilcar Cardoso, Vincent Corruble, Fiammetta Ghedini (Editors). Paris, France, June 27-July 1, 2016. Publisher: Sony CSL Paris, France. ISBN 9782746691551.

"I am as I am not"[1]
The Role of Imagination in Construing the Dialogical Self

Velimir B. Popović

Introduction

The so-called "postmodern turn" has produced a sense of confusion in contemporary philosophy and the social sciences and humanities, undermining the Western mind and instigating doubt in its own existence, purpose, and sense of meaning. Guided by the credo "other than reason,"[2] it disputes basic tenets of modernity. It is usually considered to represent rejection or denial of many, if not most, of the cultural certainties on which the modern mind and cosmos have been based over a couple of centuries. Analytical Psychology and Jungian Analysis are offsprings of the modern mind, and consequently they became the target of caustic attacks by postmodern authors, who try especially to dispute or erase constitutive notions of those disciplines: the self, the subject, individuation, and imagination. Contrary to the modern notion of the subject, the postmodern subject is a decentered, multicentered, and fragmented being, lacking an essential core of identity. It is rather regarded as a process in continual flux, change, and disintegration. Postmodern psychotherapists are not inviting the subject to turn inward to inspect the self, for the reason that inside does not exist.[3] A "thinking and reflecting I" conceived as an interiorized entity that experiences, conceptualizes, and interacts with the world is an obsolete notion, hence the subject is nowadays advised to look outward at the ways it interacts with the social world through language, discourse, narrative, and action.[4]

Likewise, the notion of imagination is replaced by the phrase "the imaginary," which references an impersonal entity. While the former is subjective, always assuming an "author" or "creator" who produces or creates images (whether the "creator" is a conscious "I" or transcendent "Self"/"Soul"), the latter is nothing creative in itself; it simply stands for an "effect" of a technologically transmitted sign system over which the human subject has no control. The role of the image in postmodern philosophy and psychology—so precious a notion for our analytical theory and, even more, for our praxis—is essentially one of *parody*. The image is no more seen as something that refers primarily to some "original," either situated outside itself in the "real" world or inside human consciousness or in the personal or collective unconscious. Deprived of any fixed reference to an origin, the image appears to refer only to other images. At best, the postmodern image circulates in an apparently endless play of imitation. Each image becomes a parody of some other image that precedes it. The outcome is that in postmodern theory the imagination is no more seen as an "original" creator of meaning. In fact, postmodern theory renounces the very idea of "meaning."

Apart from the mentioned concepts that are exposed to reasonable yet sardonic criticism from the postmodern psychologists, the practice of analysis is targeted as well. The holy trinity of ψ disciplines[5]—the self, psychopathology, and psychotherapy—are all together, or one by one, exposed to serious, canny, even ironic de(con)structions, and the scraps that were left over after this procedure would serve as building blocks out of which *postpsychological therapy* will emerge.[6]

Yet Jungian psychologists, with a few exceptions, are heedless of how postmodern thought impacts its theory and practice. This lack of a response from the side of analytical psychologists begs to be analyzed, but this is not the intention of this paper. Nor is it my intention to revitalize the analytical conceptions of the self, but rather to accept the postmodern verdict and proceed onward. Instead of fighting for the modernistic/analytical notion of the self and subject, which would be a lost cause, I propose to try to build a *post-postmodern* notion of the self. In trying to accomplish this endeavor, it is not mandatory to look elsewhere, scrolling the postpsychological texts in order to find novel ideas, but only to delve into what is already there in our tradition. In Jung's *Red Book*, not the *Collected Works*, one may find the necessary material to build a post-postmodern notion of the self, since there it is narrated how the subject experiences itself and how a self is construed through dialogue and imagination.

**"Much has man experienced/since we are a dialogue/and can listen
to one another" (Hölderlin)**

"My life has been permeated and held together by one idea and one
goal: namely, to penetrate into the secret of the personality. Everything can be explained from this central point, and all my works relate
to this one theme,"[7] writes Jung in *Memories, Dreams, Reflections*.
Jung's central theme, variously and loosely labeled—personality,
personhood, individual, subject, subjectivity, self, or selfhood—and
the processes that lead either to its fulfillment or failure consume a
lot of space in his written works. Many of the essays found in *The
Collected Works* were written in an effort to offer a comprehensive
scientific discourse about self and its individuation (which Jung sometimes equates with the development or becoming of personality),
based on both his personal and his patients' experiences, and
amplified by the mythical stories from the collective cultural heritage.
These are voiced in an objective, unbiased, and, as much as possible,
impersonal way. The purpose was to offer a perspective on the self,
human nature, and the psyche, which was primarily based on his
subjective understanding yet written as a scientific discourse that
appears to impart objective knowledge.

Jung's *Red Book* stands in stark contrast to his other written
works in its unique nature, composition, form, and intention, and it
seems to me it challenges, changes, deconstructs, or reconstructs the
ideas he expressed in the writings contained in *The Collected Works*.
While creating the texts and images incorporated in the *Red Book*,
based on his "voluntary confrontation with the unconscious,"[8] Jung
was not hindered by its possible reception in the scientific circles, so
he freely reached for a quite peculiar narrative discourse to express
his encounters with the Unknown and Soul. He embraced narrative
and dialogue as principal forms by which his visionary experiences
are made meaningful. The compelling factor, which forced him to opt
for narrative discourse, was *fantasy*, which he could not, or chose not
to, translate into conceptual language. At the beginning, overwhelmed by doubt and disbelief when confronted with images that
personified themselves of their own accord, he tried to avoid any

conversation with them or at least to choose freely from among the plentitude of inner interlocutors, picking those who seem to be reasonable or more in accord with his conscious attitudes (better Elijah than Salome, for example), and, at first to listen to them and, second, to impose some meaning upon their verbiage. He was compelled, it seems, to subdue his conscious will and "to accept this way that forced me into dialogue with my soul."[9] After taking seriously what he was confronted with, Jung relinquished his resistance, since "in coming to terms with the unconscious, not only is the standpoint of the ego justified, but the unconscious is granted the same authority. The ego takes the lead, but the unconscious must be allowed to have its say *too —audiatur et altera pars.*"[10] When the voice of the "other" was distinctly heard, Jung tried to answer his own statements from the standpoint of his "I," consequently stepping into and creating a dialogue with it. "It is exactly as if a dialogue were taking place between two human beings with equal rights ..."[11] Later he would label those inner dialogues the "transcendent function," which arises from "the union of conscious and unconscious,"[12] where those two positions are "shuttling to and fro arguments and affects" that will eventually create a "living, third thing ... a living birth that leads to a new level of being,"[13] whose ultimate function is to widen the subject's consciousness.

It was an "ethical obligation" for Jung to confront "the images of the unconscious" and let them address him.[14] At any rate, "that was an experiment which was being conducted on *me* [Jung]," so he opened himself to "an incessant stream of fantasies, and ... everything in it seemed difficult and incomprehensible,"[15] but his strivings to find any meaning in his experiences with those fantasies were without success. Only when Jung altered his heroic stance for a more humble and passive one was he able to confront them on equal terms. "I wrote down the fantasies as well as I could, ... I had no choice but to write everything down in the style selected by the unconscious itself."[16] It was not just the style that those images forced upon him—they equally dictated the form, contents, stories, characters, and plots.

At first glance, the textual material, which starts to shape itself, bears a resemblance to mythical narratives. It seems that the mind is doing all the thinking, construing, and plotting stories that are not his own. Myths think, act, and voice themselves through human subjects rather than the other way around. They have no origin in any particular consciousness or individual human psyche, and they have no particular aim or end in view. Also, in myths the individual human being is not considered as the source or end of meaning. Like mythical narratives, Jung's written account in *The Red Book* seems to have autonomous existence, unfolding with its own logic in utter disregard for the peculiarities of his thought, and just reducing his conscious attitudes, opinions, and ideas to a mere function of those archetypal patterns. The reason is a simple one: In the realm of *mundus imaginalis*, "… the images have a life of their own and … the symbolic events develop according to their own logic …"[17] A genuine active imagination assumes that imaginal characters, which are taking part on an inner stage, possess self-consciousness, autonomy, agency, and freedom of will, judgment, and affectivity. It is as though we *see* or *hear* a certain imaginal character in and through particular ideas or perspectives that he or she embodies, and, the other way around, we may see or hear in and through him/her a particular image. However, Jung did not fall victim into the traps that archetypes were plotting for him, nor did he become a prey of their narrative plots. At first, he was prone to accept as a fact that he was confronted with the powers (i.e., the images) that were subduing him, but, as events were unfolding, he realized that he was "an acting and suffering figure in the drama of the psyche,"[18] which prompted him to take an active part in them.

> A chain of fantasy ideas develops and gradually takes on dramatic character: the passive process becomes an action. … The piece that is being played does not want merely to be watched impartially, it wants to compel [the imaginer's] participation. If [the imaginer] understands that his own drama is being performed on this inner stage, he cannot remain indifferent to the plot and its dénouement.[19]

The participation Jung had in mind means neither acting out nor concretizing the events that are happening on the stage of this inner theater. On the contrary, the sense of participation involved in active imagination is akin to that of the actants playing roles in a dramatic narrative.[20] There is an imaginative activity that is going on between himself and one or more of the characters on the stage. Activity, or, better said, interactivity, among of all actants is what makes the imagery into active imagination. As in theatrical plays, *dialogue* stands for this active ingredient that transforms fantasy into the genuine active imagination (or maybe it would be more accurate to call it *interactive imagination*). Addressing characters from his visions as well as letting them address him—the images want *to tell* themselves—was a crucial part of his stance toward them, and the outcome of this was neither premeditated nor disastrous for his psyche since the addressees were willing to converse with him. Above all, they invited him to enter into dialogues with them.

Once, when he was conducting an imaginal dialogue with his soul over the "dark solitude" that had befallen him, a nameless, white-bearded old man with a haggard face interrupted the conversation with, what at first glance, sounded "dreadfully meaningless":

> Never forget that you are a man and therefore you must bleed for the goal of humanity. ... You should become serious, and hence take your leave from science. There is too much childishness in it. Your way goes toward the depths. Science is too superficial, mere language, mere tools. But you must set to work.[21]

The old man was not coercing Jung to give up his psychological enterprises for projects in other disciplines that are more profound but to go for psychology of the depths. Previously in *Liber Primus,* "the spirit of the depths," during long conversations, undertook a similar line task of questioning Jung's belief in scientific psychology:

> He took away my belief in science, he robbed me of the joy of explaining and ordering things, ... took my under-

standing and all my knowledge and placed them at the
service of the inexplicable and paradoxical. He robbed me
of speech and writing for everything that was not in his
service ... [22]

Yet the ultimate purpose of divesting Jung of his epistemic tools—
explanations and understandings—was not for the sake of humiliating
or denigrating him but, on the contrary, to set him on the right track,
which resembles the apophatic stance vis-à-vis the Unknown. Those
two, as well other imaginal encounters with inner characters depicted
in narrative episodes of *The Red Book*, encouraged Jung to opt for a
"psychology with the psyche" (i.e., focused on the Other, the
Unknown, or the unconscious), one that is not based on *Erklärung*
but on *Verstehen*, i.e., a psychology that is a hermeneutical enterprise,
appropriating analogy, interpretation, and understanding as its
pivotal method (*Geisteswissenschaft*), and that incorporates subjectivity, irrationality, uncertainty, and synchronicity as feasible and
legitimate elements of scientific evaluation. The aim of Jung's
psychology of the depths (depth psychology), which starts to shape
itself in those dialogues, is not to soothe semantic anxiety, which
dominates scientific psychology, but to accept a humiliating truth that
psychology does not know anything essential about psyche. It takes
on epistemological insecurity as its starting point and from there
commences a dialogue with the unknown. In order to understand
the unknown, one has to enter into dialogue with it, as is stressed by
Jung: "This [is a] process of coming to terms with the Other." [23]

While in his other works this self-revealing and self-formatting
process is expressed in a *monological* mode, here in *The Red Book* it
is completely voiced in a *dialogical* mode. And dialogue seems to be
the most fitting container for images to express themselves *qua*
images. As we learned from dear old Socrates, at the heart of any
dialogue is the idea that what is exchanged has meaning. In his *Liber
Novus*, Jung offers a *dialogical* interpretation of image, which has its
subjective source (i.e., a human subject) and at the same time, its
trans-subjective (i.e., archetypal) significance. Implicitly, Jung
declares the primary function of the imagination to be a dialogue

between inside and outside, between self and other, between subjective and trans-subjective, between the subject that is in the world and the world that subject is in. That was wisdom bequeathed to him by "the spirit of the depths": "My speech is imperfect. Not because I want to shine with words, but out of the impossibility of finding those words, I speak in images. With nothing else can I express the words from the depths."[24] In that sense, the image emerges as a world of dialogue between intentional subjects, who also appear as images. In addition to this, a dialogue seems to be a true *topos* where images restore their subjectivity, strength, agency, intentionality, fullness, and, above all, their trans-subjectivity.

Assuming inner persons to be on a par with him, letting them embody and express themselves freely in imaginal dialogues, actively questioning, arguing, opposing, and disputing with, challenging and, most important, contradicting them, Jung was granted a rich yet unexpected reward—more images! As it was proclaimed to him by his serpent-soul: "You are entitled to a reward for what has been accomplished so far. ... I give you payment in images."[25] Instead of receiving some understanding of what is going on that would eventually lead to meaning lying hidden below those images, he was granted additional images—more of the same. Yet, this award was a most appropriate one, since Jung learned his lesson well as it was depicted in his previous conversation with "the spirit of the depths": "The spirit of the depths ... took away my belief in science, he robbed me of joy of explaining and ordering things, ... took my under-standing and all my knowledge and placed them at the service of the inexplicable and the paradoxical,"[26] in which "the supreme meaning" is contained. After musing on what "the spirit of the depths" has said to him, Jung concluded: "The supreme meaning is ... image."[27] It was not Jung but the image of "the spirit of the depths" that proclaimed the supremacy of images.

We are here confronted with yet another important issue: The imaginal encounters he had with various characters, in *Liber Primus* and *Liber Secundus,* or in "Scrutinies," such as Philemon, Salome, Izdubar, the Red One, and the Anchorite, are entirely presented in *dialogical* form. Moreover, dialogue is not just a matter of form; it is the essence of his epistemology. This is in contrast to his writings in *The Collected Works*, which are predominantly written from a *monological* perspective, i.e., from the point of view of an assumedly neutral and objective observer who meticulously describes inner psychic experience that would be transformed into concepts, then explained and eventually wrapped into a coherent narrative or scientific theory, and whose instrumental role is to strengthen the individuation process whose purpose is to create human being as a centered subject. In *The Red Book*, Jung's perspective vis-à-vis psyche is dialogical.[28] Jung's "I" is not an unbiased, detached observer whose task is to puzzle out meaning that lies hidden in the products of his own fantasy, but an interested and involved participant in conversation who strives to uncover meaning through dialogue with other subjects, which are in his narrative depicted as imaginal yet autonomous persons and equipped with their own perspectives, attitudes, ideas, emotions, and not requiring his "I" as an external agency to be voiced. In order to acquire some understanding, Jung first of all had to acknowledge the position or perspective of those to whom he was speaking, and a crucial element for acquiring some understanding in dialogues is *difference*. In a dialogue, both partners are different from each other, and the utterance each makes is always different from the others, and yet all these differences are held together in the context of dialogue. A dialogue is a proper place for understanding to appear, which is effected through an affective and cognitive correspondence and difference between Jung's perspective of understanding and that of his imaginal interlocutors. In dialogues Jung has had with them, this correspondence is achieved through the interplay of speaking and hearing, through posing questions and listening to the answers, agreeing or disagreeing with the perspective of other interlocutors in the conversation.

In addition to difference, the authentic dialogue is characterized by *lack of structure and completeness*. We speak of "being caught in," "entrapped in," or "falling into" conversations, insinuating that they are not planned in advance, merely happening. And that was what was going on through all the conversations Jung had with his inner interlocutors—no one knows what they will bring about or where they will lead since they are not regulated by any set of rules or guidance, and yet they seem to possess a kind of structure of their own. What emerged from those dialogues was neither Jung's nor theirs and hence so far transcends the interlocutors' subjective perspectives and attitudes that even Jung, who was at first of the opinion of having control over the content of the conversations, was perplexed by the autonomy, unpredictability, and inscrutability of the spoken words. The whimsical, autonomous, and unpredictable makeup of those conversations is what makes a true dialogue. A genuine dialogue is characterized by its openness towards *the possible.*

The fact that there are at least two interlocutors in the dialogue means that each of them brings a different perspective to it. Therefore, we may assume that dialogue as such always possesses more than one meaning. At first glance, it seems that all of those dialogues Jung had were composed of two elements: an utterance and a reply. As a matter of fact, it is more true to say that those dialogues are of *triadic* composition, i.e., they are of an utterance, a reply, and a *relation* between the two. The third element—the relationship—is the most important, for without it the other two elements would have no meaning. This represents the hermeneutical act, and at the same time it represents the basis of *the ethical* postulate of the active imagination: a person conducting it is, by taking an active stance toward psychic images, affirming and confirming their autonomy, agency, consciousness, and subjectivity. By means of an active stance toward images, they are acknowledged as rightful subjects. It is the dialogue, in other words, that provides the framework within which Jung and the inner characters become attentive to one another and to him. After recognizing their autonomy, Jung had to fight with them over various thorny issues. Now and then he would try to impose his own ideas, sometimes he would acknowledge what they were saying to him without disputing a word, occasionally he would comply after long discussions, and sporadically his questions would affect either ideas or actions of those who were speaking with him. Dialogical imagination was used by Jung to keep otherness from slipping back into silence. Jung's intention to understand his visions involved entering into dialogue, and entering into dialogue involved both bravery and humility on his part. It was the bravery to put forward his own views and—when it was timely and appropriate—to persuade his inner interlocutors of the right-mindedness of those views, and it was the humility to listen to their views and—when it was timely and appropriate—to learn from those views and thereby to extend his own consciousness, sense of the self, and his own perspective *vis-à-vis* psyche. Out of those imaginal dialogues with inner characters, a different notion of the human being starts to emerge—the human being as a decentered subject, beyond conventional notions of subject and object, whose consciousness emerges as an outcome of dialogue with the other (i.e., dialogue is a source of consciousness), and who is nourished by a poetic power of imagination, which transcends its control.

I find a concept of imaginal dialogue is a more fitting expression for the processes that are going on between Jung's conscious "I" and the other, or the unconscious, which were depicted in *Liber Novus*, than "the transcendent function" that he had proposed, since the latter connotes there is one subject (the conscious "I") who appropriates for itself—as understanding—what was previously unknown. As an idea, the transcendent function, whose purpose is to widen the consciousness, that will be more elaborated in his *Seminars* and *Collected Works*, assumes there is only one active subject or agency in any kind of inner dialogue or active imagination. It is a prerogative of the ego (the active subject)—after interacting with inner images—to cast a meaning on those psychic contents that are seen *as if* alive but are actually inert or dead objects (images), because a true meaning is not contained in them but solely in this agency. This way of knowing is in fact a self-oriented or self-contained form of understanding (i.e., self-enclosed epistemic acquisition)—in the service of ego—while the perspective of "the other" is objectivized, overshadowed, or abolished:

> It is not too much of a stretch of the imagination to
> personify them, for they have always a certain degree of
> separateness. This separateness is a most uncomfortable

thing to reconcile oneself to, and yet the very fact of the unconscious presenting itself that way gives us the means of handling it. It took me a long time to adapt to something in myself that was not myself—that is, to the fact that there were in my individual mind parts that did not pertain to me.[29]

Jung's initial impulse was to impose his conscious control over those autonomous images: "… if you can isolate these unconscious phenomena by personifying them, that is a technique that works for stripping them of power"[30] in order to find in them some previously unrevealed meaning that will increase his conscious mind. After differentiating oneself from the other, which is not part of itself, one could assimilate it into oneself. This implies that the real birth of meaning happens *after* the interlocutors—Jung's "I" and inner images—have participated in a dialogue but not *during* their encounter and conversation. This form of knowing, which assumes strict differentiation between subject and object is not the knowledge gleaned by participating actants in a dialogue, but a way of knowing where subject embraces knowing after revisioning what has happened in a dialogue. In fact, it was Jung's intention to hush multiple voices and subdue them within the single utterance or monological discourse. The purpose of the monological imagination, which prevails in his *Collected Works*, was to control or replace other discourses, other utterances or texts—to quiet their elocution and halt their further circulation by the help of denial or dismissal. It seems that Jung's monological imagination was based on his assumption that it could stand apart and look on from an external and superior perspective that would not be affected by the voices from below. Also, as we have learned from Jung, monological imagination is a principal way to individuate or to develop an integrated, unified, centered, coherent self. Yet, if we focus our attention on Jung's experiences in his *Red Book* and the way he narrated them, not how he described and explained them afterward in his written works and in seminars, it would be more fitting to call them imaginal dialogues. The reason is obvious and displayed plainly in the pages of *The Red Book*: The dialogue reveals something about its participants *while* they are communicating one with the other. The real birth of meaning happens *in* the dialogues Jung had, *while* he was talking to inner interlocutors and listening to what they were saying, but not in him as a self-reflexive, introspective, monological subject.

In a genuine dialogue, the interlocutors are changed as their initial assumptions, perspectives, or attitudes are disputed, ridiculed, tested, modified, scrutinized, approved, or acknowledged in the dialogue itself, as we have learned by reading Jung's *Liber Novus*. To gain understanding in a dialogue is not a matter of imposing one's own ideas and successfully asserting one's own perspective, but of being transformed by the material and perspective that the other one brought into the dialogue. A "real dialogue" relies on difference and disagreement between interlocutors. Even more, it relies on the participants' intention to explore those differences and disagreements together.

Another thing, as well, turns an ordinary conversation into a "real dialogue"—tacit agreement among the participants as to what the conversation is about—its subject matter—and a willingness to listen to the ideas or views of others. And that's what we have in the pages of *The Red Book*. To conduct a real dialogue meant that Jung allowed himself to be guided by the subject matter to which he and other participants in the dialogue are oriented. Hence, meaning, whatever it might be, emerges from dialogue. What emerged, as it is displayed in *The Red Book*, was neither his nor theirs (Soul, Philemon, Salome, etc.) and therefore far surpasses the interlocutors' subjective attitudes and perspectives. Understanding is not a question of an active subject (Jung) construing meaning of an inert and dead object. Quite the opposite, both interlocutors have perspectives that may productively be brought together, changing them both. But every conversation presupposes a common language or, better said, construes a common language. Something is set in the middle, as the ancient Greeks would say, which both sides in dialogue share, let us say a common language, by which they can express and exchange ideas with one another. Consequently, reaching an understanding on the subject matter of a conversation necessarily means that both sides in dialogue must, at first, agree whether they share a common language and, if not, to work one out. Also, a condition of every dialogue is to grant another interlocutor authority. Jung was not willing at first to acknowledge this as mandatory; however, he was forced to comply: "... the spirit of the depths forced me to speak with my soul, to call upon her as a living and self-existing being. ... Hence I had to speak to my soul as to something far off and unknown, which did not exist through me, but through whom I existed."[31] But what was the common language that both Jung and his soul used in *The Red Book*?

Jung took pains to find or accept a proper language, one that is, on the one side, dialogical and metaphorical and, on the other, conceptual and differentiated. Was it a conceptual language where a particular word or phrase is used to express or describe a specific idea or concept? From the conversation he had, Jung was urged not to believe in conceptual language: "Guard against being a slave to words."[32]

> You believe in your idols of words ... [and his soul was quite emphatic about it]: Words, words, do not make too many words. Be silent and listen ... Have you noticed that all your foundations are completely mired in madness? ... There are hellish webs of words, only words, but what are words? Be tentative with words, value them well, ... do not spin them with one another so that no webs arise, for you are the first who is ensnared in them. For words have meanings. With words you pull up the underworld. Word, the paltriest and the mightiest. In words the emptiness and the fullness flow together.[33]

It was very hard, humiliating, and painful for Jung to accept a language in which something comes to speak that is not a possession at the disposal of one (him) or the other of the interlocutors (inner characters). Eventually, a common language was found but not because either side adopted itself to the other, but rather because it was worked out in the conversation they had. This common language was the language of imagination, which consists of images, which are spoken *before* they are seen. The dialogues Jung had with his soul made him conclude: "I speak in images. With nothing else can I express the words from the depths."[34] At the same time, those images out of which this language was made were a common denominator for both sides (Jung and inner characters): Their subjectivities are expressed in images, and as well their common substrate or *subjectum*—that which stands under them or is thrown under them— were images. "The wealth of the soul exists in images," and images are "speech of my soul ... the guiding words of the soul."[35] If one intends to address soul or invite her into dialogue, one must speak her language—a language of images. "My friends," says Jung, "it is wise to nourish the soul,"[36] to feed her with spoken images.

Jung was, after all, commanded to "be silent and listen" to the images he confronted in his visions, not to observe and look at them. To say that images are spoken before they are seen is to give up a dominant Western fantasy that assumes them to stand for second-rate entities (εἰκαςία),[37] which are used as the cloth in which we dress up our abstract ideas and which (as images) visibly appear in a mental theater in front an internal observer. Jung, at least in the pages of *The Red Book,* is made to appreciate the opposite perspective: "The wealth of the soul exists in images,"[38] which represents "the supreme meaning."[39] Also, "whatever the nature of the psyche may be, it is endowed with an extraordinary capacity for variation and trans-formation."[40] Those insights eventually led him to the conclusion that soul as such and image as well are *polysemic* when either uttered, construed, or questioned in dialogue, which as mentioned above is the proper place where new meanings start to emerge. Every image has a story to tell. Here, it is obvious that Jung considers imagination less in terms of vision than of language. Imagination, upon which those dialogues stand, represents the capacity to question previous meanings, the capacity to open and construe new meanings by means of suspension of beliefs in earlier meanings. It has the power to create that which would otherwise not be present. In brief, imagination gives an image to an emerging meaning, which starts to unfold in dialogue. In that sense, imagination is the power to structure and restructure semantic fields. Therefore, at least in the pages of *The Red Book*, those spoken images (εἴδωλα λεγόμενα, *eidola legomena*)— emerging meanings—are not of *pictorial* but of *semantic* essence. The imagination operates here on the verbal level, producing new configurations or patterns of meaning. Later in life, Jung will stress this phenomenological and noetic aspect of images:

> Image and meaning are identical; and as the first takes shape, so the latter becomes clear. Actually, the pattern needs no interpretation: it portrays its own meaning.[41]

With those words Jung encapsulated the phenomenological account of imagination as *portrayal* (or as appearance), with hermeneutic account as *meaning*. Portrayal captures the essence of image as that which is portrayed *as* it is portrayed—that is, in the very mode, form, or shape in which it is portrayed. In that sense, image portrays itself in itself. And this particular portrayal is not random or accidental; the portrayal goes with a precise meaning, which is depicted in the very portrayal. If I am right, what Jung referred to as the image could be understood as a mode of presentation (portrayal) more than as a content of the process of imagination. And the mode of presentation or portrayal is essentially something at variance and therefore possible: A given mode of portrayal is always just one of several possible modes. In each new portrayal, with every new image, new meaning is expressed. After all, it is the soul that is polysemic— consisting of images—as it was inferred by Jung: "... the world of my soul [is] the many-formed and changing."[42]

From the pages of *Liber Novus*, we may infer that Jung recognizes in imagination the capacity for letting new images shape (portray) his understanding of (him)self and of the other. This power was not conveyed by visual images, but by spoken messages—the emergent meanings—in and through language and in dialogue. By replacing a visual model of the image with a verbal, Jung affirms the *poetical* role of imagination: that is, its ability to say one thing in terms of another, or to say many things at the same time, thereby construing or creating (ποίησις, *poesis*) something new.[43] This poetical imagination comes into play when a new meaning emerges from the literal meanings or from ossified interpretations and understandings. In a certain sense, this is a two-way process: What is unknown to present consciousness becomes known and familiar, and what is known and familiar becomes foreign. In appropriating other or new meaning into one perspective, one is also misappropriating a previous perspective in order to open oneself to another meaning. Here again, let us remember that the poetical imagination is above all a dialogical imagination—open-ended, paradoxical, open-minded, polysemic, erratic, versatile, and prepared to dialogue with what is not itself, with its other, greeting the difference in order to learn from it, as it is hinted in the etymological sense of *dia-legein* (δια-λέγειν): welcoming and embracing the difference in order to learn from it. The emergence of new images and patterns of meaning is an activity of the permanent yet never-ending "othering" of any self as well as of others. Those aspects of imagination—that it is uttered rather than seen and in a process of producing semantic innovations—certainly represented a healing factor that helped Jung to cope with his inner daimons. Inner interaction with (spoken) images could represent crucial aspects in analysis if it is seen as a dialogical interaction between the imaginative intentionality of a patient and of an analyst. Let me put it this way—analysis involves a dialogue (intersubjective process) whereby a self (the analysand) comes to know itself better by narrating itself to another (the analyst) more comprehensively and truthfully than it had narrated itself before.

Instead of saying that it was either Jung or some psychic image that was conducting a conversation with the other side, it seems more appropriate to say that dialogue conducted itself. As such, dialogue becomes a happening that takes place between embodied subjects who know no certainty as to the outcome of their conversation. The genuine dialogue is conversation that is not conducted by the intention or the will of either actant, and therefore it is never the one they wanted to conduct. The understanding of the self and the other has its own meaning beyond the conscious, conceptual language and its intentional acts, and this is based on a dialogical hermeneutic and understanding of spoken images of which not only soul but even the conscious "I" is one. In dialogical encounters, the sense of oneself, of the other, or of the world, is challenged and disputed, producing the effect of forcing one to see oneself and the other differently and from a new perspective—as the *self-as-other-than-itself* and the *self-in-relation-to-others*—and in this lies the transformative power of imaginal dialogues, whose purpose is to create self and subjectivity. This is, in my opinion, what is narrated in the pages of *The Red Book*.

Let me underline once more, in *Liber Novus* imagination is seen as a permanent interaction (dialogue) between the human subject (i.e., Jung), who imagines, and the images themselves.[44] Later on, in *Psychological Types*, Jung will keep on underlining this perpetual activity of the psyche: "This autonomous activity of the psyche ... is ... a continually creative act. [Imagination is] the creative activity from which the answers to all answerable questions come ..."[45] Imagination, especially one that is going on in dialogue, is assumed to be conscious of something other than itself, which prompts, inspires, and transforms it. And what is this *something other*? The answer is: *the world of possibility*, which is at once created and discovered by dialogical imagination. The "possible" is homogenous with the soul, the unknown, the unconscious, the other. The "possible" is also a factor that makes a dialogue productive—a productive dialogue has the effect of forcing human subjects to "see" or to "hear" things differently, from a novel perspective and in a new light. We learn from Jung that imagination is "the mother of all possibilities ... which fashions the bridge between the irreconcilable claims of subject and object ..."[46] The role of dialogical imagination could be apprehended as a space for exploring possibilities; it is only the realm of imagination that offers the freedom to reflect on possibilities. Each image one confronts in dialogue brings new perspectives—novel possibilities to explore. Thus, the possible world, possible self, or possible other that is intimated is always possible in relation to the actual, i.e., the actual offers resources for prefiguring the possible, and it is imagination that contemplates the possible guided by these given resources. And, the other way around, it employs the possible to revision the actual. When one has freedom to imagine new possibilities in dialogue, one can create new images of oneself and the other. Even more, new possibilities create new realities. "The psyche creates reality every day,"[47] says Jung. It creates reality *ex nihilo*, from nowhere, and it is not bound by an original or previous reality of which it is only a weak copy.[48] Because imagination does not copy a previous reality, it is free to produce a new reality "every day." In that sense, it alters, expands, and augments one's sense of reality and reality's possibilities. In this realm of imaginal dialogues, "to be possible *is* to be, and since it is imagination that envisages what is possible, it becomes the arbiter of experience, determining and directing its course."[49] Moreover, each new image represents yet another possibility to apprehend the unknown. This productive power of imagination lies in its ability to create something that would otherwise not be present.[50] It is imagination that keeps otherness from slipping into the unsayable or unknown. The otherness both invites to dialogue and prompts the self (or subject) to engage in dialogue, as Jung learned from "the spirit of the depths":

> I thought and spoke much of the soul. I knew many learned words for her, I had judged her and turned her into a scientific object. I did not consider that my soul cannot be the object of my judgment and knowledge; much more are my judgment and knowledge the objects of my soul. Therefore the spirit of the depths forced me to speak to my soul, to call upon her as a living and self-existing being ... I had to speak to my soul as to something far off and unknown, which did not exist through me, but through whom I existed.[51]

Jung's discourse with the soul in the pages of *The Red Book* seeks to show that the imagination (as dialogue, narrative, and poetry) is the basis of subjectivity and selfhood. For Jung, a psychological hermeneutics of subjectivity has to begin with the soul rather than the individual. The individual is always contained in the soul—we are steeped in a world that was created by our own psyche:

I do not contest the relative validity either of the realistic standpoint, the *esse in re,* or of the idealistic standpoint, the *esse in intellectu;* I would only like to unite these extreme opposites by an *esse in anima,* which is the psychological standpoint. We live immediately only in the world of images.[52]

The soul is articulated primarily as a basis for addressing psychological, personological, and anthropological aspects of subjectivity by way of imagination, and it opens at the same time a complementary perspective on humanity, groups, and society. *Esse in anima* marks a creative split in the imagination for Jung in that it consists of the two mutually irreducible poles of the dialogical imagination of the individual subject on the one hand and the dialogical imagination of group subjects or the other.

It is the case that only through some transfer from self to other— *via* imagination—that the other, which is alien and unvoiced, is brought closer. At the same time, by doing this otherness becomes the heart of selfhood. Ability to converse with the soul (or unknown) is beyond the rational mind and directed thinking, which both operate with concepts. In the world of *anima mundi,* imagination is the only viable means for communicating with images. The primary datum of Jung's psychology in *The Red Book* is the image, and the image is identified with the soul/psyche.

… image *is* psyche.[53] The wealth of the soul exists in images. He who possesses the image of the world, possesses half the world …[54]

If equipped with the imaginative sources, which allow the dialogue to happen, the human subject can transform into *homo imaginator—* someone able to create and explore those imaginal possibilities that emerge into existence at the crossing—dialogue—between self and the other/world/soul, and who is intentionally directed toward the other more than to the self. In *Liber Novus,* Jung shows that he has learned this lesson well. The main virtue of self-other (selfhood-

otherness) dialectics is to prevent the self from claiming the place of
psychological birth to be exclusively its own. This does not mean that
this place is taken by the *other*, which would thus seek to usurp the
self's birthright. The psychological birth of the subject is represented
by the imaginal dialogue between the two.

I wish in conclusion to stress once more Jung's tacit claim, as he
elaborated it in *Liber Novus*, that understanding—as self-understanding, or between individuals, group subjects, or cultures—is the
outcome of dialogue. It is especially true when a person wishes to
inspect, comprehend, or analyze oneself. In order to understand
oneself, one has to communicate with the Soul, the Other, the
Unconscious, or the Unknown. That is to say, with the otherness of
oneself and the otherness of the other, with the otherness of the past
or what-is-no-more and the otherness of the future or what-is-not-
yet. Therefore, one has to enter into dialogue with all of those
modalities of otherness and with their possibilities, which are
expressed in images, as images, or through images. The images are
the self's or subject's stepping-stones to the other-than-oneself, as
Jung learned from "the spirit of the depths": "You are an image of the
unending world, all the mysteries of becoming and passing away live
in you."[55] But for Jung, the hermeneutic circle debars any direct route
to immediate self-understanding. The human subject, the one that
starts to appear from the dialogues with the soul, can only come to
know itself through the hermeneutic detour of interpreting images—
via dialogue—that is, decrypting the meanings contained in visions,
dreams, myths, and symbols as produced by imagination. In short,
as Richard Kearney has said, "the shortest route from the self to itself
is through the images of others."[56] I would add: The images of the self
and of the other that come face to face with each other in the realms
of dialogue make the shortest route to the self, which is more than
itself and less than oneself.

Endnotes

[1] Heraclitus, *Fragments* (New York, NY: Penguin Classics, 2003), Fragment 40.

[2] Calvin Schrag, *The Self after Postmodernity* (New Haven and London: Yale University Press, 1997), 8.

[3] Amia Lieblich, Dan P. McAdams, and Ruthellen Josselson, *Healing Plots. The Narrative Basis of Psychotherapy* (Washington, D.C.: American Psychological Association, 2004); Dan P. McAdams, Ruthellen Josselson, and Amia Lieblich, *Identity and Story. Creating Self in Narrative* (Washington, D.C.: American Psychological Association, 2006); Michael Guilfoyle, *The Person in Narrative Therapy. A Post-structural, Foucauldian Account* (Houndmills, Basingstoke: Palgrave Macmillan, 2014); Hubert J. M. Hermans, and Giancarlo Dimaggio, eds., *The Dialogical Self in Psychotherapy* (Hove and New York, NY: Brunner-Routledge, 2004).

[4] The most prominent examples of such attitude one may find in books by Rom Harré, *The Singular Self* (London: Sage, 1998), and *Social Being* (Oxford & Cambridge: Blackwell, 1993); Kenneth J. Gergen, *Social Construction in Context* (London: Sage, 2001); *Relational Being. Beyond Self and Community* (Oxford: Oxford University Press, 2009); and Theodore Sarbin, ed., *Narrative Psychology: The Storied Nature of Human Conduct* (Westport, CT: Praeger, 1986).

[5] More on this issue one may find in Nikolas Rose, *Inventing Our Selves. Psychology, Power, and Personhood* (Cambridge: Cambridge University Press, 1996); *Governing the Soul. The Shaping of the Private Self* (London/New York, NY: Free Association Books, 1989); and in Hubert J. M. Hermans, and Agnieszka Hermans-Konopka, *Dialogical Self Theory* (Cambridge: Cambridge University Press, 2010).

[6] The concept "postpsychological therapy" was introduced by John McLeod, "Counseling as a social process," in *Counseling*, 10 (1999), 217-226.

[7] C.G. Jung, *Memories, Dreams, Reflections*, ed. Aniela Jaffé (New York, NY: Vintage, 1963), 232.

[8] Ibid., 202.

[9] C.G. Jung, *The Red Book: Liber Novus*, ed. Sonu Shamdasani, trans. John Peck, Mark Kyburz, and Sonu Shamdasani (New York, NY: W.W. Norton, 2009), 336.

[10] C.G. Jung, "The Transcendent Function," in *CW*, vol. 8 (Princeton, NJ: Princeton University Press, 1969), par. 185.

[11] Ibid., par. 186.

[12] Ibid., par. 97.

[13] Ibid., par. 189.

[14] Jung, *Memories, Dreams, Reflections*, 218.

[15] Ibid., 201-202.

[16] Ibid.

[17] C.G. Jung, "The Tavistock Lectures," in *CW*, vol. 18 (Princeton, NJ: Princeton University Press, 1976), par. 397.

[18] C.G. Jung, *Mysterium Coniunctionis*, in *CW*, vol. 14 (Princeton, NJ: Princeton University Press, 1963), par. 753.

[19] Ibid., par. 706.

[20] "actant"—an actant is not only a character in the story, but it plays a pivotal/structural role in the narrative that unfolds. Let us say, in *The Red Book*, each character plays an integral role (not only "Jung" as character) in the story, or, narrative. Without the contribution of the other actants the story of Jung's encounters with the unconscious would be incomplete or it would sound unconvincing. The relationship between the actants is what makes a narrative credible. Those relationships are creating conflicts or problems within a narrative that have to be overcome. Yet, a given actant could embody different characters within a story, therefore it may reside in the function of more than one character in respect.

[21] Jung, *The Red Book*, 336.

[22] Ibid., 229.

[23] Jung, *Mysterium Coniunctionis*, *CW* 14, par. 706.

[24] Jung, *The Red Book*, 230.

[25] Ibid., 323.

[26] Jung, *The Red Book*, 229.

[27] Ibid., 230.

[28] If, in its broadest sense, dialogue could be described metaphorically as a kind of conversation, the purpose of which is to facilitate a birth of truth to occur *while* interlocutors are discoursing, therefore helping them to see a given thing in a new light or from a novel perspective, then monologue features a subject's intention to use speech as a means for minimizing or preventing the possibility that it will be inspected or transformed in uptake. Other interlocutors (a subject's others) in the latter kind of conversation are not meant to revision or revoice

utterances but to embrace them with no hesitation, acknowledge them silently, or replicate them accurately.

[29] C.G. Jung, *Introduction to Jungian Psychology: Notes of the Seminar on Analytical Psychology Given in 1925* (Princeton, NJ: Princeton University Press, 2012), 49-50.

[30] Ibid., 49.

[31] Jung, *The Red Book*, 232.

[32] Ibid., 268.

[33] Jung, *The Red Book*, 298-299.

[34] Ibid., 230.

[35] Ibid., 233.

[36] Ibid., 232.

[37] Εἰκασία—*eikasia*—from the same root as εἰκών (*eikon*) or image, is a phantom or pseudo-knowing, playing an utterly passive, imitative, unreflective, mimetic role in Plato's philosophy and which represents the lowest rank of mental faculties, subordinated to higher forms of knowing—διάνοια (*dianoia*—discursive reasoning), ἐπιστήμη (*epistēmē*—scientific knowledge) and, at the top, νόησις (*noēsis*—rational intuition), which represents the most advanced form of knowing.

[38] Jung, *The Red Book*, 232.

[39] Ibid., 230.

[40] C.G. Jung, "Psychological Factors Determining Human Behavior", in *CW*, vol. 8 (Princeton, NJ: Princeton University Press, 1969), par. 235.

[41] C.G. Jung, "On the Nature of the Psyche," in *CW*, vol. 8 (Princeton, NJ: Princeton University Press, 1969), par. 402.

[42] Jung, *The Red Book*, 237.

[43] The question of the imagination clearly becomes a central one, and on the pages of *Liber Novus* there are many instances that indicate Jung was aware that this power is in a shambles, which begs to be rehabilitated. And for him this rehabilitation of the imagination presupposes a break from the conception of the imagination as an "image of something," "mirror image," or as a "mental image." That is, the problem was how to transform reproductive imagination into the productive power. The imagination, which would be productive or poetical, is what enables meaning to become "visible," comprehensible, the otherness expressible, and action doable and, above all, it is the *vas hermeticum* where the subject and selfhood could be forged.

[44] Contrary to monologue, a genuine dialogue is perpetual, which means it has no beginning and no end, and it is characterized by its very lack

of structure and completeness. We speak of "falling into," "brought into" or "forced into" conversation, suggesting that they are never planned, premeditated, and just happen. No one knows in advance where they will lead, as they are not regulated by norms and agreements, and yet they have a sort of structure of their own.

45 C.G. Jung, *Psychological Types*, in *CW*, vol. 6 (Princeton, NJ: Princeton University Press, 1971), par. 78.

46 Ibid.

47 Ibid.

48 In *The Red Book*, Jung is not a follower of Plato and other exponents of the reproductive theory of imagination, as he is in most of his other works, as it is expressed in his *Introduction*: "… we can never perceive anything but the image that is formed in our minds. We never see an object as such, but we see an image which we project out upon the object. We positively know that this image is only imperfectly similar to things as they are." (Jung, *Introduction to Jungian Psychology: Notes of the Seminar on Analytical Psychology Given in 1925*, 144). However, in *The Red Book* the images are the works of imagination, which creates them *ex nihilo*. Maybe it would be more appropriate to say imagination creates them *out of itself*. Therefore, the image is not a mirror image of something, nor it is a copy nor, at best, derivative from the original. The imagination of which is Jung speaking here is not an image *of* something. It is ceaseless and essentially undetermined (psychological and socio-historical) creation of images/metaphors/symbols, on the basis of which alone there could ever be a question of "something." In that sense, what he calls "reality" is its product, not an undisputed opponent. Despite his efforts to uncover the archetypal background of the images with which he was in a dialogue, he did not find one. The message he learned from those conversations is that the images did not represent anything, they are not images of something or pointing to something more profound; they are, simply, presenting and showing themselves. No archetype-as-such is standing behind the archetypal image.

49 Edward S. Casey, "Toward an Archetypal Imagination," in *Spirit and Soul: Essays in Philosophical Psychology* (Dallas, TX: Spring, 1991), 16.

50 The imagination at work—in *The Red Book*—is not reproductive imagination, in the sense of representation in its absence of something that already exists; its creations (narrative episodes of the *Liber*) cannot be deduced from antecedent conditions from Jung's life. It is productive

and creative, because it invents meanings that have never existed and that are not preformed in something that already exists.

51 Jung, *The Red Book*, 232.

52 C.G. Jung, "Spirit and Life," in *CW*, vol. 8 (Princeton, NJ: Princeton University Press, 1969), par. 624.

53 C.G. Jung, "Commentary on 'The Secret of the Golden Flower'," in *CW*, vol. 13 (Princeton, NJ: Princeton University Press, 1967), par. 75.

54 Jung, *The Red Book*, 232.

55 Jung, *The Red Book*, 230.

56 Richard Kearney, *Poetics of Imagination: Modern and Post-Modern* (Edinburgh: Edinburgh University Press, 1998), 149.

The Spirit of This Time:
"No One's Child," a Postmodern Fairy Tale

Žanet Prinčevac de Villablanca[1]

Selfish desire ultimately desires itself. You find yourself in your desire, so do not say that desire is vain. If you desire yourself, you produce the divine son in your embrace with yourself. Your desire is the father of the God, your self is the mother of the God, but the son is the new God, your master. ... But now, if you are in solitude, your God leads you to the God of others, and through that to the true neighbor, to the neighbor of the self in others.[1]

C.G. Jung

The Red Book, along with *Aion, Answer to Job,* and *Mysterium Coniunctionis*, is definitely among Jung's most profound works. In this work his "confrontation with the unconscious," or the process of individuation, is obvious and, as in the other works, named the purpose of humans in the coming New Aeon or Platonic Month, namely the Age of Aquarius, is shown to be self-realization. Unfortunately, scholars are not sure if we are still in the Age of Pisces or if the Age of Aquarius has already begun, but all of us are witnesses of the fact that the "ensuing chaos calls forth in compensation the birth of a new central psychic dominant. What will it be? Antichrist? ... It is the loss of our containing myth that is the root cause of our current individual and social distress, and nothing less than the discovery of a new central myth will solve the problem for the individual and for society. Indeed, a new myth is in the making and C.G. Jung was keenly aware of that fact."[2] Or, as Jung wrote in *Aion*:

The dechristianization of our world, the Luciferian development of science and technology, and the frightful material and moral destruction left behind by the second World War have been compared more than once with the *eschatological* events foretold in the New Testament. These, as we know, are concerned with the coming of the Antichrist: 'This is Antichrist, who denieth the Father and the Son.' 'Every spirit that dissolveth Jesus ... is Antichrist ... of whom you have heard that he cometh.' The Apocalypse is full of expectations of terrible things that will take place at the end of time, before the marriage of the Lamb. This shows plainly that the *anima christiana* has a sure knowledge not only of the existence of an adversary but also of his future usurpation of power.[3]

In this essay, I will focus on the search for soul under postmodern conditions. It is clear that humanity at this time is in crisis. But I am interested, as C.G. Jung was in the previous century, in what we can do about it. Jung certainly did his best. It follows that we should do the same in our time. A *depressive position* is not enough. One can go further via *active imagination*. It is important not to confuse this with "quasi-awakening," however, which is increasingly common even among experts on the psyche.

Postmodern people are in a hurry. They do not read a lot. They fail to make a distinction between fantasy and imagination. The world is full of terrorism, alienation, corrupt politicians, wars and destructions, pollution, economic crises, false prophets, and reality shows mostly of no value. Ethics and aesthetics have new outfits without a body to wear them. The body is lost, and all postmodern people can do is to find the naked body of no one's child somewhere deep in the forest and to offer it a brand-new "handmade" axiological coat. As Murray Stein writes: "In our time, Christianity has little to contribute to culture because it is out of touch with the unconscious and *Zeitgeist*. The only solution is to undertake a transformation process, like that of individuals who enter therapy and rediscover themselves in depth. Out of this engagement with the unconscious comes the impetus for new life, based on transformed inner world and a new sense of identity."[4]

It seems that Jung and Stein are of a similar opinion regarding "the way of what is to come," but I will take another approach here and look at postmodern man as an abandoned child. More precisely, I will use the image of the main character from the movie *No One's Child* because he is the product of our time and our culture and is part of all of us. I will consider him as "the spirit of this time," as one who needs to be found, or rather to be recognized. To go further, I will rely on Edinger's attitude: "Since the phenomena of synchronicity imply a fluid boundary between inner and outer reality, the unconscious can come to us from without as well as from within."[5]

No One's Child is a postmodern fairy tale based on a true story. An abandoned child was found in the forests of ex-Yugoslavia in the late 1980s. The movie was made in the second decade of 21st century and received a lot of awards all around the world (the Venice Film Festival in 2014 and Audience Award from International Critics Week, among others), probably because it accurately depicts the spirit of our time.[6] Audiences are left with niggling anxieties after watching the movie. The dreadfulness emanates from the screen in the cinema's darkness. From the first to the last scene, the main character of the film, a mute wild-boy, is alone, even in the presence of others. Spectators in the cinema share with him the same experience of *abandonment*. This could be a good start if one is to approach "the spirit of the depths."[7]

The desire to confront atrocities and beauties and finally to embrace them is necessary. For some, it could be the "happily ever after" of crises we are living in, which is not the case for the majority. But this could be a chance for those interested to involve themselves in an adventure in order to find the moral in Jung's *Red Book*, i.e., to discover the method he used to refind his Soul and to discover his own path and to show others a possible way to their own individuation. What he did in *Liber Novus* was self-experimentation on one hand and a direct response to existential questions in order to create a new psychological method on the other.[8]

Jung was searching for symbols and their meaning, but Elijah and Salome confronted him: "We are real and not symbols."[9] That was the beginning of Jung's encounter. Jungians, in collaboration with artists, writers, and members of the humanities, have been trying to bring Jung's work closer to the general public for years. One of their aims is to make it possible for a person to reach out to get *in touch* with the images (real phenomena!) from the unconscious and to find his/her own way, who he/she is and what his/her myth is. It is obvious that Jung had words that described what he knew deeply. That made it possible for him to contemplate the meaning of his experience. He wasn't just moved by images from the depths; he was also able to listen to, recognize, and differentiate the voices and figures and to be in dialogue with them.[10] Postmodern man should step into the *mundus imaginalis*[11] in the same way, but before that he has to come out from chaos, *pleroma, prima materia.* "The spirit of the depths" has to address *someone*, but we are afraid that postmodern man is not available.

We will return now to *No One's Child* to look closely at it, as closely as possible, as "the spirit of this time." Why? Because we have found that postmodern man is no one's child and is lost in the forests of "isms," without Father and Mother, left to rely on his basic instincts, abandoned and frightened, without belief, naked and vulnerable, with no language or only with language full of empty words. He is on the way to losing his sex (gender is lost, luckily not yet in languages) and to remain without offspring, without Other. The solution may be to meet the abandoned feral child. He is the same One in all of us. He is deep in the *forest.* Are the *forest and a feral child* places where we can find ourselves to meet "the spirit of the depths" later? Is the forest the place where "the spirit of this time" meets "the spirit of the depths"?

Plot of the movie *No One's Child*

In the winter of 1988, a team of hunters stumbles across a mute boy-child (Denis Muric) living among wolves deep in the forests of Bosnia-Herzegovina, which was then part of Yugoslavia. Randomly assigned the name Haris, the foundling is shipped off to an orphanage in the capital, Belgrade, despite being unable to speak or even walk on two legs. Inevitably, this freakish new arrival is cruelly bullied by the other boys. But over the next four years, he slowly learns human speech and behavior under the protective gaze of the kindly teacher Ilke (Milos Timotijevic) and fellow inmate Zika (Pavle Cemerikic), who takes Haris on exciting forays into the city center.

Just as Haris seems on course for a relatively normal adolescence, history conspires against him. Zika abruptly quits the orphanage, ditching his new friend for the shaky promise of a reunion with his own deadbeat father. Meanwhile, the off-screen collapse of the old Eastern Bloc fractures Yugoslavia into warring nations, flooding the orphanage with refugees and ethnic tensions. Belgrade is reborn as the Serbian capital, its streets awash with crime and violence. As Serbia and Bosnia are now at war, Haris is put on a train and sent back home, where he becomes enmeshed in the bloodshed almost by accident. The final scenes, shot in snowy woodland, neatly echo the film's opening. He is all alone, lying on the ground, gazing in the front of himself, with no contact to anyone. He is left by humans and left by wolves.

The abandoned, sacrificed, or rejected child had a different nature, a different life path *in illo tempore* (Mircae Eliade's expression) than in this time (both modern and postmodern). *In illo tempore* we speak about the Divine Child, a god. In the last four centuries, more than 100 feral children were found all around the world. *No One's Child* is the story about a feral child, mute, moving on all fours, and hairy from the deep forest, moved to civilization to find himself in the same forest on the end of the movie. All alone, lying on the ground, gazing in front of himself, he has no contact with anyone. Left by humans, left by wolves. In solitude, perhaps with a chance to give life to his incapacities? Is that his attempt to find his own path? Or is he going to die? What is the future of mankind?

James Hillman repeatedly quoted W.H. Auden's verse: "We are lived by powers we pretend to understand," and it seems that verse is reserved for people who are interested in thinking about the powers or to imagine them. The second step should be to try to connect with them (the powers), to confront them, to try to reach something, to solve the riddle, to play. To be in dialogue, even if we speak about "outside powers" (political systems, economic crises, political leaders, etc.) or "powers from inside" (God, archetypes, etc.). At least, it is important to know that it is all about pretending to understand. Or could we find other suggestions in Jung's *Red Book*? Most people in our time live by powers they are not interested in understanding. Is this incapacity? Is there a way out from incapacity? *Liber Primus* stated: "But the nameless spirit of the depths evokes everything that man cannot. Incapacity prevents further ascent. Greater height requires greater virtue. We do not possess it. We must first create it by learning to live with our incapacity. We must give it life. For how else shall it develop into ability? We cannot slay our incapacity and rise above it."[12] We have to enter into our incapacity.

One should learn to live with personal incapacity, to be close enough both to it and to banality. How can we apply that to the postmodern fairy tale we are talking about? Does a socio-realistic kind of black-minimalistic style of movie, not rich with symbols, intentionally impoverished, with modest narrative, try to hit the audience directly in its Achilles heel? Haris (the main character, the feral child) appears barefoot in the first and last scenes of the movie. In the first scene, he happened to be barefoot, but in the last scene, it was his choice. He removed the army boots himself. What will be the choice of a postmodern audience? Will they hide their Achilles heel from others and themselves, or will they confront their own wounds, their incapacity?

As is well-known, *The Red Book* begins with a biblical quotation of prophetic nature, and according to C.G. Jung, there are two principles: "the spirit of this time" and "the spirit of the depths":

> If I speak in the spirit of this time, I must say: no one and nothing can justify what I must proclaim to you. Justification is superfluous to me, since I have no choice, but I must. I have learned that in addition to the spirit of this time there is still another spirit at work, namely that which rules the depths of everything contemporary. The

spirit of this time would like to hear of use and value. I also thought this way, and my humanity still thinks this way. But that other spirit forces me nevertheless to speak, beyond justification, use, and meaning. Filled with human pride and blinded by the presumptuous spirit of the times, I long sought to hold that other spirit away from me. But I did not consider that the spirit of the depths from time immemorial and for all the future possesses a greater power than the spirit of this time, who changes with the generations.[13]

Concerning this passage of *Liber Novus,* Sonu Shamdasani refers to Goethe's Faust: "What you call the spirit of the times / is fundamentally the gentleman's own mind,/in which the times are reflected."[14] The spirit of the times when Jung was a "modern man in search of a soul," over a hundred years ago, has now changed for the postmodern man in search of a soul, therefore for all of us. The starting point is completely different. On the one hand, thanks to Jung and other scholars and artists from the beginning of the last century, we have been given the opportunity to apply new techniques and methods in search of the (lost) soul. On the other hand, "the spirit of this time" is like a Stuck Child. Therefore, the way to search for a soul is completely different.

We speak about a Divine Child *in illo tempore,* a rejected child who will not just survive but will have a heroic role. A feral child as *the spirit of this time* does not have a heroic role; a feral child is a rejected child, a victim. His purpose is to survive, but actually what is needed is to go further, not just to survive but rather to become part of a community, an equal member of society, to become an adult. A feral child is a real human-born child and a "wild animal's child" (Lat. *fera*—wild animal) at the same time. This child is something between human and animal, having a possible capacity for ego consciousness, although relying on instincts and the basic need to survive on the boundary of forest and an urban area. The feral child is stuck betwixt and between. The main problem of the Stuck Child (an image of "the spirit of this time") is the inability to go further. He is trapped in an eternal childhood.

Returning to the image of the feral mute boy in *No One's Child*, we see that he was abandoned, rejected, and left in the forests. Hunters find him and take him to social services, who send him from Bosnia to an orphanage in Serbia. The war starts, and Yugoslavia falls apart. The boy who was randomly named Haris (a Muslim name) leaves the Serbian orphanage to go back to Bosnia, which comes at the request of the Bosnian authorities. In Bosnia, he is lost again and found by Muslim soldiers. Again, he is left alone when the soldiers die in a battle. His life is full of constant, repeated abandonment. We might say that he is stuck in abandonment. The last scene of the movie shows him lying on the ground in the forest all alone and barefoot. So, this is the image of postmodern man. After all these centuries, humans are lost in nature and out of touch with community, or lost in community and out of touch with nature. We could also say lost in thinking and out of touch with imagination, lost in "the spirit of this time" and out of touch with "the spirit of the depths."

What has really happened with Haris Pućurica is not known. All traces of him were lost during the breakup of Yugoslavia. The movie deals with the atrocities of our time, with a Stuck Child as an image of "the spirit of this time," without meaning. The meaninglessness of abandonment, of war, of ethnicity are all evident in this image. The *need* is known to a Stuck Child, but *desire* needs to be found in the Stuck Child himself: "if you desire yourself you produce the divine son in your embrace with himself. Your desire is the father of the God, your self is the mother of the God, but the son is the new God, your master."[15]

If we speak about crises, whether individual, social, or economic, the way out is the same: To get out of it, one must go into it. That was exactly what Jung did in *Liber Primus* and *Liber Secundus* and especially in "Scrutinies." He was encountering the unconscious, and at the same time he had to struggle with himself and to argue with figures from the depths. Later, he would put the images, imaginations, dreams, and visions in order, after which he would try to translate all of that into "scientific language." Just as Dante wrote *The Divine*

Comedy in a vernacular language, which was a huge step in times when Latin was used by educated people, Jung left to the next generations "the key" for better understanding his theory, the spirit of (t)his time and "the spirit of the depths" in *The Red Book*. Their feats are in accordance with their personalities, while we are left to translate and transmit their images and thoughts and to find our own way.[16]

Just a little over a hundred years ago, when Jung started his encounter, the First World War knocked on the door. Since then, a lot has happened on the world scene: World War II, the Cold War, the collapse of the Eastern Bloc, financial and economic collapses all over the world, Middle Eastern wars, social turmoil in Muslim countries, increasing terrorism, global warming, climate change, and huge migrations. Technology has dominated people, much more than the other way around, as it seems. Politically correct speech hides various horrors, children can change sex without adequate medical and psychological examinations, and adults can do the same even at the expense of the state in countries of Eastern Europe. Some women fight against men more than for their own rights. To shorten further listing, we can use the words of a contemporary poet:

> There is a menace in the air
> Of tragedies in the making.[17]

It could be a description of "the spirit of this time." But luckily, beauty is still present, beside all these atrocities. All we have to do is keep on looking.

First, postmodern man has to see, feel, and register the meaning of "the spirit of this time." In other words, it is necessary to make order, inside oneself, then outwardly. The movie *No One's Child* or the Stuck Child is not able to do that without *mirroring*. Someone must put him before an audience. The next step would be that this child is recognized and accepted by the audience as part of themselves. Apparently this happened. The director and screenwriter put him on a screen before audiences, and he was taken up by the audiences, judging by the awards. However, it seems to me that the audiences were merely touched, and I am not sure that they will know exactly what has moved them, except for superficial sympathy of an abandoned child in the forest all alone, etc.

What is really needed is to deal with that image of a Stuck Child in the way Jung explains in the following lines: "I took great care to try to understand every single image, every item of my inventory, … and above all, to realize them in actual life. That is what we usually neglect to do. We allow the images to rise up, and maybe we wonder about them, but that is all. We do not take the trouble to understand them, let alone draw ethical conclusions from them. This stopping-short conjures up the negative effects of the unconscious."[18] We suppose that the postmodern society we are part of has a small number of individuals ready for a confrontation with the unconscious in the way Jung experienced himself, but there is a possibility for an encounter "with the unconscious from without," i.e., from products of culture: films, literature, paintings, etc. But still we need translators or mediators for the wider audience to discuss with them the meaning of the offered images and phenomena that represent "the spirit of this time." That would be the task of Jungian scholars, analysts and nonanalysts in this postmodern time.

We are all "the spirit of this time," and "the spirit of the depths" is in all of us. But as long as the ego/self-axis is broken for most of the population in this period, we are alienated, and most of us are the Stuck Child and can't go further. Jung spoke about the future, and what he expected in the next millennium, but in the meantime all we have to do is to spread our experience of human self-realization, or better to stay tuned to confrontation with the unconscious during our process of individuation: with the purpose *to know*, and not *to believe*. "When I was a child, I spoke like a child, I thought like a child, I reasoned like a child; when I became an adult, I put an end to childish ways. For now we see in a mirror, dimly, but then we will see face to face. Now I know only in part; then I will know fully, even as I have been fully known."[19]

During the seminars on Kundalini-Yoga in 1932, Jung "… provided a comparative history of active imagination, the practice that formed the basis of *Liber Novus*."[20] In his second lecture of his seminar, he spoke about the state of modern European consciousness, but it seems that in this postmodern time, the situation is even worse.

> Another very important attribute is that the gods are asleep; the *linga* is a mere germ, and the Kundalini, the sleeping beauty, is the possibility of a world which has not yet come off. So that indicates a condition in which man seems to be the only active power, and the gods, or the impersonal, non-ego powers, are inefficient—they are doing practically nothing. And that is very much the situation of our modern European consciousness. ... If you look at the symbol of the *mūlādhāra* in such a way, you understand the purpose of the yoga in the awakening of Kundalini. It means to separate the gods from the world so that they become active, and with that one starts the other order of things. From the standpoint of the gods this world is less than child's play; it is a seed in the earth, a mere potentiality. Our whole world of consciousness is only a seed of the future. And when you succeed in the awakening of Kundalini, so that she begins to move out of her mere potentiality, you necessarily start a world which is a world of eternity, totally different from our world.[21]

The following picture is a painting by a patient in her late 30s, divorced recently, with two children. She is interested in Jungian psychotherapy because she was told that Jung was of the opinion that "life starts in the second half of life." The last few years of her marriage had not satisfied her, she had an affair with a married man, and her husband found out and left her. She continued her affair for six months, but finally her partner left the relationship. In that period of time, she started to believe that her thoughts could be controlled by some "strange men" and that she was being stalked by someone. All she wanted was to find unconditional love, her *animus* (her words), and to become herself and to change her profession. All she had found in several relationships was a *puer aeternus* kind of man. She decided to start psychotherapy and if possible to remarry her ex-husband. We began to work together twice a week, and she brought her paintings to the fifth session. The paintings were made in the period when her ex-husband and lover left her. This is one of those paintings:

As we see, a woman is floating in a lotus position, and the first three chakras are merged into one in this picture. We can notice hands with stigmata as well. The eyes of woman are closed, while her hair is wild and scattered everywhere. According to Jung, symbolically, the *mūlādhāra*, the first chakra, is our conscious earthly personal existence: "… *mūlādhāra* is characterized as being the sign of the earth; the square in the center is the earth, the elephant being the carrying power, the psychical energy or the libido. Then the name *mūlādhāra*, meaning the root support, also shows that we are in the region of the roots of our existence, which would be our personal bodily existence on this earth."[22] Unfortunately, we can conclude on the basis of my patient's painting that she is unrooted and inflated:

Now if, as I say, you succeed in completing your *entelechia*,
that shoot will come up from the ground; namely, that
possibility of a detachment from this world—from the
world of *Maya*, as the Hindu would say—which is a sort
of depersonalization. For in *mūlādhāra* we are just identical.
We are entangled in the roots, and we ourselves are the
roots. We make roots, we cause roots to be, we are rooted
in the soil, and there is no getting away for us, because we
must be there as long as we live. That idea, that we can
sublimate ourselves and become entirely spiritual and no
hair left, is an inflation. I am sorry, that is impossible; it
makes no sense.[23]

The second chakra, *svādhistāna* has the all attributes that characterize
the unconsciousness, it is the second center, the water region. One
who has really done the night sea journey, has wrestled with the great
monster. That would mean one had been in *svādhistāna*.[24] According
to Jung, the way out of our *mūlādhāra* existence leads into the water.
There is a danger, of course, of one being swallowed by a monster,
but that is the only way to attain the higher development: "*mūlādhāra*
is darker, the color of blood, of dark passion. But this vermillion of
svādhistāna contains far more light,"[25] which is not visible at all in my
patient's painting. Actually, the first three chakras are mixed into one
in the area of the abdomen. The third chakra, *manipūra*, "is the center
of identification with god, where one becomes part of the divine
substance ..."[26] We can see that there are no boundaries between
chakras on the painting, which means there is no differentiation
between conscious, unconsciousness, and divine substance. The
woman is floating, her eyes are closed, she is not able *to see*, she is in
pain, her hands with stigmata are bleeding, and at the same time,
according to my patient, she is divine. Before she came for psychotherapy, and in the period when she made this painting, she had a
psychotic break and was prescribed antipsychotic medication. And
again, we will cite Jung and his view on self-realization (individuation):

You see, it is utterly important that one should be in this world, that one really fulfills one's *entelechia*, the germ of life which one is. Otherwise you can never start Kundalini; you can never detach. You simply are thrown back, and nothing has happened; it is an absolutely valueless experience. You must believe in this world, make roots, do the best you can, even if you have to believe in the most absurd things— to believe, for instance, that this world is very definite, that it matters absolutely whether such-and-such a treaty is made or not. It may be completely futile, but you have to believe in it, have to make it almost a religious conviction, merely for the purpose of putting your signature under the treaty, so that trace is left of you. For you should leave some trace in this world which notifies that you have been here, that something has happened. If nothing happens of this kind you have not realized yourself; the germ of life has fallen, say, into a thick layer of air that kept it suspended. It never touched the ground, and so never could produce the plant. But if you touch the reality in which you live, and stay for several decades if you leave your trace, then the impersonal process can begin. You see, the shoot must come out of the ground, and if the personal spark has never gotten into the ground, nothing will come out of it; no *linga* or Kundalini will be there, because you are still staying in the infinity that was before.[27]

In the first part of this essay, I tried to argue that postmodern man is not just without the awareness of transpersonal reality (God), but is more regressed and stuck, unrooted in this world, because he is no one's child and is lost in the forests of "isms," without Father and Mother, relying solely on his basic instincts, abandoned and frightened, without belief, naked, and vulnerable. I used the image of the main character in the movie *No One's Child* to speak of this condition. In the second part, I illustrated the same situation with the material from my practice. We believe that *The Red Book* may be of use to present and future generations of people who are disoriented and in need of psychological guidance for themselves, individually and culturally. This could be assisted at this time with great effort by Jungian scholars, analysts. and non-analysts, who would be translators and mediators between Jung's *oeuvre* and the wider population, so that the state of mythlessness, "the spirit of this time," can be recognized, opening the possibility to the way of "the spirit of the depths." I will conclude with the words of one Jungian scholar who dedicated his professional life to this task:

> It is evident to thoughtful people that Western society no longer has a viable, functioning myth. Indeed, all the major world cultures are approaching, to a greater or lesser extent, the state of mythlessness. The breakdown of a central myth is like the shattering of a vessel containing a precious essence; the fluid is spilled and drains away, soaked up by the surrounding undifferentiated matter. Meaning is lost. In its place, primitive and atavistic contents are reactivated. Differentiated values disappear and are replaced by the elemental motivations of power and pleasure, or else the individual is exposed to emptiness and despair. With the loss of awareness of a transpersonal reality (God), the inner and outer anarchies of competing personal desires take over. The loss of a central myth brings about a truly apocalyptic condition and this is the state of modern man.[28]

Endnotes

[1] C.G. Jung, *The Red Book: Liber Novus*, ed. Sonu Shamdasani, trans. John Peck, Mark Kyburz, and Sonu Shamdasani (New York, NY: W.W. Norton, 2009), 245.

[2] Edward F. Edinger, *The Creation of Consciousness: Jung's Myth for Modern Man* (Toronto: Inner City Books, 1984), 11.

[3] C.G. Jung, *Aion. Researches into the Phenomenology of the Self*, in *CW*, vol. 9/II (Princeton, NJ: Princeton University Press, 1959), par. 68.

[4] Murray Stein, *Jung on Christianity* (Princeton, NJ: Princeton University Press, 1999), 19.

[5] Edinger, *The Creation of Consciousness*, 68.

[6] https://www.imdb.com/title/tt3059656/awards?ref_=tt_awd.

[7] "The spirit of the depths is pregnant with ice, fire, and death. You are right to fear the spirit of the depths, as he is full of horror." In Jung, *The Red Book*, 238.

[8] Sonu Shamdasani writes in his Introduction to *The Red Book*: "Thus we see that the self-experimentation which Jung undertook was in part a direct response to theoretical questions raised by his research, which had culminated in *Transformations and Symbols of the Libido*." See ibid., 197.

[9] "I: 'What my eyes see is exactly what I cannot grasp. You, Elijah, who are a prophet, the mouth of God, and she, a bloodthirsty horror. You are the symbol of the most extreme contradiction.' E: 'We are real and not symbols.'" See ibid., 246.

[10] "As a result of my experiment I learned how helpful it can be, from the therapeutic point of view, to find the particular images lie behind the emotions. ...The essential thing is to differentiate oneself from these unconscious contents by personifying them, and at the same time to bring them into relationship with consciousness. That is the technique for stripping them of their power." C.G. Jung, *Memories, Dreams, Reflections*, ed. Aniela Jaffé (New York, NY: Vintage, 1963). 177.

[11] "A *second postulate* results: spiritual imagination is indeed a cognitive power, an organ of true knowledge. Imaginative perception and imaginative consciousness have their function and their *noetic* (cognitive) value within their own world, which is—as pointed out earlier—the

'*alam al-mithal*, the *mundus imaginalis*, the world of the mystical cities such as Hûrqalyâ, where time is reversed and where space, being only the outer aspect of an inner state, is created at will." In Henry Corbin, "Mundus Imaginalis or the Imaginary and the Imaginal," in Spring 1972, Zürich, 10.

[12] Jung, *The Red Book*, 240.

[13] Ibid., 229.

[14] Johann Wolfgang Goethe, *Faust*, Pt. 1, lines 577-579.

[15] Jung, *The Red Book*, 245.

[16] "The way is within us, but not in Gods, nor in teachings, nor in laws. Within us is the way, the truth, and the life. ... There is only one way and that is your way. You seek the path? I warn you away from my own. It can also be the wrong way for you. May each go his own way. I will be no savior, no lawgiver, no master teacher unto you. You are no longer little children." See ibid., 231.

[17] Charles Simic, *The Voice at 3:00 A.M.: Selected Late and New Poems* (Orlando, FL: Mariner Books, 2003), *Late September* poem.

[18] Jung, *Memories, Dreams, Reflections*, 182.

[19] *Corinthians 13*, New Revised Standard Version, Third Edition (Oxford University Press, 2001).

[20] Sonu Shamdasani, "*Liber Novus*: The 'Red Book' of C.G. Jung," in Jung, *The Red Book*, 220.

[21] C.G. Jung, *The Psychology of Kundalini Yoga: Notes of the Seminar Given in 1932 by C.G. Jung* (Princeton, NJ: Princeton University Press, 1996), 23-26.

[22] Ibid., 23.

[23] Ibid., 29.

[24] Ibid., 16.

[25] Ibid., 17.

[26] Ibid., 31.

[27] Ibid., 29.

[28] Edinger, *The Creation of Consciousness*, 9-10.

Reading and Rereading Jung as a Muslim: From Traditionalist Critique to the New Possibilities of *The Red Book*

Samir Mahmoud

C.G. Jung was one of the 20th century's most sympathetic exponents of both Eastern and Western spiritual traditions. He believed that these traditions enshrined the richest repository of wisdom and knowledge. It is particularly in the writings and the traditions of the alchemists and Gnostics Jung found documentations of the descents into Hades, the rebirths, the ascent narratives, and the various ordeals along the way. It is in describing the topographies of this journey and reviving this science of the soul—"modern man in search of a soul"—that he dedicated the last 20 years of his life.

The alchemists and Gnostics on whom Jung drew knew very well the dangers and fear associated with such a journey. The descent was to achieve a rebirth of the soul so that it would be saved from the evil compulsions of the material world, the "lower soul"; life has no meaning without it, for it is our destiny, our fate, the *summum bonum* of life, its *telos*, its *eschaton*. And yet it is something we hear little about today.

Jung, that brilliant diagnostician of the modern soul, was well aware that the modern experience is vexed by a profound incoherence—the duality of reason-revelation, sacred-profane, and religion-science, subject-object, inner-outer, man-world, social sciences-natural sciences—and has yielded unbearable consequences for the human psyche: disenchantment, alienation, anomie, neurosis, psychosis, dissociation, etc. Jung gives a clue to the source of this deep schism in the Western psyche and our modern problems: "... the daemon of the scientific spirit compelled the forces of nature to serve man to an extent that had never been known before."[1] This was announced by Nietzsche's famous pronouncement "God is dead," and it is here that one is to find "the true roots, the preparatory processes deep in the psyche, which unleashed the forces at work in the world today."[2] It seems the Gods have retreated to Olympus, as Heidegger later put it.[3]

In the meantime, we have lost our ability to establish a direct connection with the realm of the spirit. The rupture began when heaven was severed from earth, and revelation was demoted and substituted by reason. Left to fend on our own by means of the rational ego, we were cut off from the hierarchy of degrees of reality or the "Great Chain of Being."[4] This is very evident in the loss of our sense of the imagination,[5] of which Kathleen Raine, in reference to William Blake, had this to say: "Imagination is the ladder on which angels forever ascend and descend."[6]

The balance between God and man is a decisive one, for the compulsions and excesses of the modern world, the false delusions of grandeur and mastery, are born of the schism between nature/man and God, knowledge and revelation, heart and reason. Autonomous man, the ego without the possibility of a balance from above, is a recipe for inflation and dementia.[7] Equilibrium is crucial for maintaining a healthy tension between the opposites of the psyche. Herein, according to Jung, lies the root problem of the modern psyche. For Jung, modern man has lost this balance and has become victim to a host of unconscious compulsions that have driven him away from his true self into blind collectivisms (consumerism, nationalism, fundamentalism) from which he needs to be liberated.

As Jung explained: "… when God is in the soul, i.e., when the soul becomes a vessel for the unconscious and makes itself an image or symbol for it, this is truly a happy state. The happy state is a *creative state* …"[8] Jung was convinced this was the only future for religious traditions: God must become a living reality within the creative unfolding of modern consciousness. This is what he found lacking in the Christianity he grew up with.

Jung also knew that for some people the structure of the synagogue and church was still an adequate psychic container, and he was content to end a therapy if a patient decided to return to or join a religious community.[9] For those for whom Christianity or Judaism was no longer a "living option," i.e., those who were modern subjects born under the full light of modern consciousness, an entirely different approach to the numinous was required, a process he called individuation. Therefore, although the journey toward actualizing the self was once the preserve of religious traditions, Jung proposed that this lifelong process could be followed along two different paths: analysis (individuation) and religion. Jung rightly recognized the inner drive propelling us toward a divine *archē*, toward a divine wholeness, and it is around this that his entire psychology revolves.

But this raises a number of questions, to which Jung and Jungians have yet to provide satisfactory answers: If Jung was primarily writing for a Western audience, is his path of individuation equally valid for non-Western subjects? Have non-Western religious traditions like Islam become as impotent as Christianity has for modern consciousness?

PART I: Traditional Muslim Psychology or Jungian Psychology?

I have been reading Jung and using his ideas within a Muslim cultural and therapeutic context for over 10 years, and the most frequent question I get asked is this: Why should a Muslim read Jung? Does the rich Islamic spiritual tradition not suffice the Muslim soul? Why even bother with a figure who died more than 60 years ago, who developed his ideas within a European cultural context and who is barely known in the Muslim world? After all, he has been severely criticized within his own European context, so why read him in an entirely different cultural context?

The 20th century suspicion of Western psychology in general is a result of the failure of modernism in the Islamic world and the subsequent rejection of Western cultural ideas associated with it, especially psychology, which is seen as one of its most dangerous and corrosive forces. For conservative Muslims, as was the case with conservative European Christians in the early 20th century, modern Western psychology is a heresy propagated by the ideologues of modernism to undermine and ultimately destroy religion. Therefore, it is argued that Jung's work, like that of Freud, constitutes an affront to any religious sensibility and a manifestation of atheistic hubris (in the case of Freud) or at best agnostic confusion (in the case of Jung).

The traditional perspective is that the spiritual path to God can only be rooted in tradition.[10] The word "tradition" provides *the* key to the difference between Jung's psychology and Traditional Psychology. For the etymology of the word "tradition" (from *tradere*, "deliver," "transmit") gives it the following meaning: Tradition is not what humanity invents or produces, but what it receives.[11] Thus "tradition," in the final analysis, is of superhuman origins. Each of the world's religions possesses such a tradition, which was given to humanity at the beginning of time and constitutes its primordial origin. Thus, the existence of a tradition, embodying a set of metaphysical principles in forms determined by a particular revelation, is fundamental to any traditional account of the human being and his/her destiny, including Traditional Psychology. No human effort can understand the human condition and the divine without it, and it is evident that to return and to ascend back to the heavenly abode is to be guided by a divine source.[12]

For the Muslim traditionalist, Jung seemed to place too little value in the authority of tradition and scripture in general, let alone the Islamic tradition and scripture in particular, to warrant any serious attention from them. Some readers of Jung have interpreted him as calling for a new God and a new religion with him as its new prophet.[13] His often-arcane language and idiosyncratic terminology (the collective unconscious, synchronicity, the psychoid, etc.) and guru status among his followers are often cited as proof by his critics that he was calling for a new religion or religion after religion.[14] Jung's criticisms of established religious traditions, especially Christianity, and his development of a new symbolic language for understanding the unconscious may suggest as much. René Guénon, the Muslim traditionalist author of the early 20th century, described the psychotherapeutic movements emerging in Europe, which included Freud and Jung, as expressions of a "pseudo-spirituality."[15] Guénon considered Jung more dangerous than Freud because the latter was openly hostile to religion, but the former mimicked it. Even a modern follower of the psychoanalytic tradition, Philip Rieff, concluded something similar when he said: "Better an outright enemy [Freud] than an untrustworthy friend [Jung]."[16]

Therefore, I propose in Part I to offer the reader in general and the Muslim reader in particular a critical reading of Jung from the perspective of Traditional Psychology. This is important if it is to be of value to imams, Muslim psychologists, and Muslim intellectuals on the one hand and to the general reader who is interested in the critical reception of Jung in the Muslim world on the other.[17] I am convinced Jung offers, in his own way, a genuine response to the rise of secularism and the decline of religiosity in the modern world. His was an attempt to rescue religion in general and the numinous in particular from modern skepticism.

Given such a scathing critique, one legitimately wonders whether Jung can still speak to the Muslim world. In a previous book chapter on *The Red Book,* I documented how Jung had helped me rediscover the numinous in my own Islamic tradition, and I concluded there that "if Jung is to have any therapeutic value for Muslims it would have to be in the critical dialogue between Jung and Islamic spirituality."[18] Therefore, there are several major questions that need answers.

Is salvation possible outside a living religious tradition? What is the difference between Traditional Psychology on the one hand and Jungian psychology on the other? These are the meta-questions to which we need answers. In what follows, I shall summarize the major Muslim traditionalist critiques of Jung under four headings:[19]

1. The autonomy of the psyche and the denial of metaphysics: Is liberation possible without metaphysics?
2. Consciousness and the collective unconscious: The confusion of the spiritual and the psychic?
3. The *coincidentia oppositorum* and the shadow: Is the union of the angelic and the demonic possible?
4. Individuation and self: The god-image within and the God without?

1. The Autonomy of the Psyche and the Denial of Metaphysics: Is Liberation Possible Without Metaphysics?

For Jung, the psyche was the most powerful metaphor through which he formulated his understanding of human existence.[20] Although its exact nature eluded him, he believed that whatever it is, there is no point outside of the psyche from which to look at things "objectively," for we "are hopelessly cooped up in an exclusively psychic world." As such, it is only the psyche as subject that can take psyche as object. "The object of psychology is the psychic; unfortunately it is also its subject."[21] The epistemological implications, for Jung, of the psyche as both subject and object are that there is no direct access to the real world except as that world is reflected as psychic images, which may or may not be accurate representations of the world.[22]

Jung is not questioning the actual existence of a reality beyond the psyche; what he is denying is our ability to gain any access to this reality except through its effects on the psyche.[23] In this move, Jung eschews metaphysics and cosmology because of their claim to objective truth, claiming instead that all assertions about reality "come from the psyche and are necessarily subjective, conditioned, and relative." In his Commentary on *The Secret of the Golden Flower*, Jung admits: "... I am content with what can be experienced psychically, and reject the metaphysical ..."[24]

One is justified in asking why Jung, who was preoccupied with the archetypes, world mythologies, the psychoid, the *unus mundus*, and religions repudiated metaphysics, which seems to be quite intrinsic to the realm of his explorations. The answer, perhaps, lies in his commitment to the scientific method.

Jung's method, it must be understood, had several advances over those of his mentor Freud. The rationalist-materialist assumptions of the Freudian approach were soon quickly undermined by the assault on the so-called objectivity of the scientific approach, to which Freud was too closely allied. On the other hand, Jung's psychology remained unwittingly much more resilient, perhaps due to the antiscientific and mystical charges laid at it. Moreover, Jung was "metaphysically more flexible than Freud" and thus was able to posit the idea of the collective unconscious, the mythological substratum of the human mind, the archetypes, the significance of dream symbolism, etc.

Jung engaged a lot with the gnostic, alchemical, hermetic, and Eastern religions. In this, he shares the Romantic interest in the mystical and belongs to that line of Romantic philosophers, especially of German Romanticism, like Herder, Goethe, Schelling, Fichte, Schopenhauer, and even Nietzsche, who had a significant influence on him. The Romantics were well aware of the limitations of the scientific method and the Kantian method. It is in this Romantic move and other moments that he often showed signs of moving beyond scientific empiricism, as when he states that the "step beyond science is an unconditional requirement of the psychological development I have sought to depict, because without this postulate I could give no adequate formulation of the psychic processes that occur empirically."[25] However, even in his "step beyond science," Jung's critics accused him of not making the necessary step beyond a scientific psychology. Accordingly, Jung appears to capitulate to modernism, and his psychology remains at that psychological level and does not reach those high points of the spirit of which the mystics speak.[26]

As such, although Jung was "metaphysically more flexible than Freud," he was "epistemologically more exacting" with an explicit reliance on the Kantian critical tradition. His method was a scientific-empirical one for the understanding of what can be psychically experienced. This in itself is a major step beyond Kant, for Jung gave to the "internal" experience or phenomena what Kant had given to "external" experience or phenomena. His empiricism extended beyond the sense data to include all human experiences. But in the Kantian spirit, Jung denies psychology any claim to the *noumenal* world. The value of depth psychology remained in discovering the *phenomenal* psychic archetypes, structures, and mechanisms.

Jung's insistence that the psychic is the only supramaterial reality that we can explore and *know* was the source of the term "psychologism" with which his account was criticized.[27] It is also at odds with Traditional Psychology. From the viewpoint of traditional metaphysics, Jung's notion of the psyche and his rejection of metaphysics amounts to nothing less than a denial of the Intellect, that faculty by which Absolute Reality can be apprehended, and to which all traditional wisdoms testify. In denying the possibility of intellection and of absolute certitude concerning metaphysical realities, Jung, completely and with one broad sweep, seems to reject Traditional Psychology and all that it entails: metaphysical reality, its hierarchical "degrees of existence," "the manifest and the non-manifest," and "the multiplicity of states of being."

Jung, it seems, had tried to present depth psychology both as a rigorous science and a spiritual discipline of salvation. However, are their methods compatible? Jung establishes a clear distinction between the "metaphysical" and the "empirical." Is such a distinction possible from a traditional point of view?[28]

Traditional accounts of the psyche, the human being, and the soul are at once doctrines of salvation, which take for granted that life is a means to an end beyond itself. The understanding of psyche, thus, is "unintelligible without consideration of [its] metaphysical foundations."[29] As such, Traditional Psychology is not concerned with so-called positivistic scientific observation, but with subjective experiential participation in the divine reality. Its truth is not susceptible to positivistic verification but only to a self-contemplative experiencing.[30]

The traditional metaphysical foundation of the psyche/soul is best expressed by the symbolism of the cross.[31] On the one hand, the vertical axis represents the hierarchical states of the soul, which extend from the lower souls (vegetative and animal souls) to the rational soul, which is at the limits of the spiritual realm, to a higher soul of the transcendent spirit.

On the other hand, there is a horizontal axis, which represents possibilities along a moral/ethical and psychological horizon. This horizontal axis usually comprises the individual but in such a way that the individual is attached to the higher orders by the vertical axis. Both the horizontal and vertical dimensions constitute the totality of the "integral individual," that is, the individual in its manifest and unmanifest possibilities of being, the latter being represented by the vertical axis of the cross along which the individual realizes higher orders of being that culminate with the divine self.

To Jung's critics, his notion of the psyche seems to remain at the level of the rational soul and does not admit the multiplicity of possibilities represented by the vertical dimension of being.

2. Consciousness and the Collective Unconscious: The Confusion of the Spiritual and the Psychic?

Having maintained the autonomy of the psyche and eschewed metaphysics, Jung set out to discover empirically the structures and mechanisms of the human psyche. Like Freud, Jung derived much of his primary data from self-analysis and an introspection of the inner nuances and movements of his own psyche. It was from the analysis of his dreams that Jung developed his theory of the "collective unconscious."[32]

Jung, the empiricist-scientist, envisages the psyche as a multi-layered structure, the topmost layer being the conscious, beneath which is the "personal unconscious," and deeper still the "collective unconscious" to which he also added an evolutionary-historical dimension. Thus, Jung's notion of the unconscious is made to include the primitive and mythical substratum of the human psyche, "the ancestral heritage of possibilities of representation ... common to men and ... animals ..."[33] Thus, not only was the depth of the psyche extended downward into the recesses of the "unconscious," but also diachronically to suggest that the successive layers of the psyche correspond to the successive stages of the evolutionary development of the human race.[34] This leads to Jung's later notion that there are successive stages in the Western development of the god-image extending from animism to matriarchy, patriarchy, tribal monotheism, universal monotheism, and modern consciousness.

With the discovery of the unconscious, Jung had opened up the entire world of interiority and had significantly expanded the frontiers of knowledge. Like the Gnostics, alchemists, mystics, Sufis, and Romantics before him, Jung had turned attention inward to discern the hidden dimensions of the human soul in order to explore its mysteries, to render conscious the unconscious, and to intimate the infinite. Jung felt that he had finally put the modern Western psyche in touch with its most primordial being, the eternal divine within. For he thought that to ignore the demands of the unconscious, as modern man does, is to court disaster. It is to let loose that which is irrational, bestial, the "lower soul," the vegetative and animal mode of existence. Equilibrium must be maintained between consciousness and the unconscious. In this Jung and Traditional Psychology are agreed.

However, upon closer inspection, Jung's notion of the unconscious, as the "ancestral heritage of possibilities of representation" seems to refer to something other than that realm of interiority referred to in the various spiritual traditions. The evolutionary theory of the psyche is inconsistent with the traditional notion of "degrees of reality." For the traditionalist, although Jung embraces the entire person, the "whole" person and not only the material or terrestrial, he posits a multilayered structure for the unconscious that extends downward, and thus his notion of the psyche does not admit of those realms that belong to the subtle regions of an extension upward. In other words, it does not penetrate to the higher degrees of reality, the "higher soul." Jung's denial of metaphysics and cosmology, as we saw earlier, leads him at worst to deny or at best to ignore the vertical evolutionary sequence originating not in the depths of time but in the heights of the divine ideas or forms in which the human psyche is not only influenced by the residues of its historical evolutionary development, the vegetative and animal soul, but also by the essential residues of its emanation from the divine ideas.

It is quite intuitive to conceive the unconscious as a realm at the margins of individual consciousness that goes unnoticed by the empirical ego and consisting of memories, archetypes, dispositional tendencies, repressions, and images. However, to conceive of this realm as the only realm beyond individual consciousness, the contents of which are known only indirectly through their "eruptions" through the surface of consciousness, goes against Traditional Psychology's claim of a realm of direct vision over and beyond the consciousness of the empirical ego. From the point of view of Traditional Psychology, Jung is confounding that which is beyond individual consciousness but accessible to it with that which is beyond the reaches of individual consciousness altogether. Jung, it seems, spoke of the unconscious as "a definite entity" instead of a "relative modality of the soul."[35]

It seems, then, that Jung allocates to the collective unconscious what is usually reserved for the transcendental realm. For Traditional Psychology, the lower soul, both vegetative and animal, is subordinate to its principle, the self, which is a definite substance beyond the realms of the human psyche and exists in the intelligible realm of ideas/forms. A traditional phenomenology of the soul would thus suggest a tripartite psycho-spiritual realm. According to this traditional "psycho-cosmic structure," *consciousness*, i.e., that which is studied by depth psychologists, is on an intermediary plane between the luminous *superconsciousness* above and the dark *unconsciousness* below.[36]

Superconsciousness

⇕

Consciousness

⇕

Unconsciousness

This tripartite structure of the soul allows for the descent from ego-consciousness into the unconscious, Hades, the darkness of the shadow, the lower soul, and then the ascent into the superconscious, the higher soul, the spirit. This is to recognize an ascent after the descent.

Thus, from a traditional point of view, to deny the transcendental modalities of the lower soul is to reduce the entire journey to that of a descent. This multiplies the dangers of the spiritual journey because the "infernal" influences of the psyche, the lower self of the unconscious, are taken for the "divine inrushes" of the transcendental spiritual order, which inevitably happens when a "superconscious" over and above consciousness is denied. Also, it is important to remember that traditionally, inasmuch as there are symbols whose origin is the suprahuman, the Divine, there are symbols whose origin is the demonic. Hence, without a proper knowledge of the topographies of Hades, one is liable to mistake the diabolic for the angelic. The collective unconscious, however, seems made to include both the lower chaos and the higher states. This is to confuse the psychic realm and the spiritual realm.[37]

3. The *Coincidentia Oppositorum* and the Shadow: Is the Union of the Angelic and the Demonic Possible?

For traditionalists, the confusion of the psychic and the spiritual leads to another problem in Jung's psychology. The ego, lower self, shadow, and the sensual desires are all conditioning components that must be overcome along the journey of individuation.[38] Jung agrees that they must be overcome and states that a new center, a new balance between consciousness and the unconscious, must be achieved: "… if the … conscious and unconscious demands are taken into account … then the centre … might be called the self."[39] However, for Jung, this self is not one where the demands of the unconscious and the conscious are absent, as in Traditional Psychology, but balanced.

In Traditional Psychology, the goal is the isolation or separation of the soul from shadow, not the integration of both. For without positing the "superconscious" or the "higher consciousness," which is not rational but suprarational and is the ultimate goal of the initiate, the "unconscious" is made to include "both lower chaos and the higher states"[40] and, consequentially, in the process of individuation, where the opposites are integrated, the shadow, the demon, for Jung, is not overcome, as it is in Traditional Psychology, but carried with the initiate to a higher state of being, the angelic.[41] This position can be no farther from that of Traditional Psychology, where humans are both potential demons and potential angels but not a union of both. The goal of initiation, or wholeness so to speak, is an ascent from the less real to the really real, a spiral movement upward of purification of the "body of light," which is imprisoned in the "body of matter."

Often Jung compares this journey or process to "the descent into Hades." However, the comparison seems to fall short for the simple reason that a "descent into Hades" that is not followed by a "reascent" into "higher consciousness" is a "fall into the mire," according to the symbolism of the ancient Mysteries, and is consequently a failed initiation from a traditional point of view.[42] For without a proper knowledge of the structures of the soul and the "subtle realm," nothing can guard the soul against the dangers of the "descent into hell." The integration of shadow and Jung's suspicion of his father's faith and Christ's dictum, "be ye perfect, even as my Heavenly Father is perfect," led him to posit "wholeness" as opposed to "perfection." Jung, perhaps under the influence of Nietzsche, considered the struggle for perfection to be an ill-considered pursuit of a false moral elevation that is conducive to psychic disequilibrium and psychological problems. As a result, he recommended the integration of all psychic tendencies (even sometimes the pathological/shadow ones). Without a clear metaphysical/cosmological framework and hierarchical structure for the psyche, and by confusing the psychic with the spiritual, Jung eschewed the entire path of moral perfectibility that is a concomitant of all paths of individuation. From a traditional perspective, perfection and wholeness are two names for the same thing. As one critic and admirer of Jung recently put it:

> A *vertical* psychic hierarchicalization that does not produce a broad enough base of character and self-knowledge cannot establish any stable degree of spiritual elevation; likewise, any *horizontal* 'wholeness' that effectively represses the aspiration to spiritual elevation has cut itself off from the very influences that can order and purify the psyche. The center of the mandala of the integrated psyche is a projection upon the horizontal plane of the *peak* of the psyche where it touches the Spirit; if there is no peak, there can be no *center.*[43]

According to Jung's critics, the difference between individuation as understood traditionally (vertical perfection) and as understood by Jung (horizontal wholeness) is that for the former individuation is supposed to serve a higher end, while for Jung individuation seems to be its own *raison d'etre*. In traditional cosmologies of the soul, individuation is only a means and not an end because it is the transcendental self that is the goal and not the individual.[44] Jung rightly points out that:

> Individuation means becoming an 'individual,' and, in so far as 'individuality' embraces our innermost, last, and incomparable uniqueness, it also implies becoming one's own self. We could therefore translate individuation as 'coming to selfhood' or 'self-realization.'[45]

Jung also insists that becoming an individual has nothing to do with being individualistic or individualism. He exhorts the initiate to become conscious of his/her unique individuality, and in this his notion of individuation bears a resemblance to the process of spiritual liberation in Traditional Psychology. Individuation is the process of attaining "wholeness" or a balance between the opposites, which is a freedom from compulsion. However, this freedom is not a freedom for the ego to do what it desires, for this is a failed initiation and a case of "inflation," which has become the hallmark of our frenzy-driven technological civilization.[46] On the contrary, it is a freedom to freely submit to "wholeness" as represented by the archetype of the self or the image of God within.

Thus, Jung presciently posits a dual aspect of our liberation from compulsion: the first is liberation *from*, the second liberation *to*.[47] Compulsion appears as either a "consuming fire," in which case it is a liberation *from*, or a "life-giving warmth," in which case it is a liberation *to*.[48] In either case, it is a cause of lack of freedom. In the instance that it is a "consuming fire," it is the unconscious compulsion of our inferior side or the shadow that tends to surface and "has affinities with the devil."[49] The goal here is the withdrawal of projections and the liberation of the soul from such tyranny. In the

instance that the compulsion is a "life-giving warmth," it is an unconscious yearning toward "wholeness." This latter compulsion is a
compulsion *to*; a drive *toward*; the movement of the soul toward its
summum bonum, its *telos*.

But whereas for Traditional Psychology the ultimate goal is an
overcoming of the "I," for Jung its development seems to be the
ultimate goal: "To us consciousness is inconceivable without an ego;
... The Eastern Mind, however, has no difficulty in conceiving a
consciousness without an ego. ... I cannot imagine a conscious
mental state that does not relate to a subject, that is, to an ego."[50]
Liberation is the realization of unity with the source, and unless one
leaves the impurities of the lower soul behind, it is questionable, from
a traditional point of view, whether such a unity and attainment of
the Divine Self is possible. It seems then that the freedom that Jung's
psychology envisions is a freedom *for* individuality, while for Traditional Psychology it is a freedom *from* individuality.

4. Individuation and Self: The God-Image within and the God Without?

Individuation is the pride of Jung's psychology.[51] In fact, it is the
ultimate guarantee against the compulsions of the unconscious. For
Jung, individuation proceeds by way of increased differentiation of
the ego and the contents of the unconscious, which then makes it
possible for the ego to integrate those differentiated contents of
opposites to form the self. The self, for Jung, is the integrating factor,
expressed by the emergence of quaternity or mandala symbols. Without this process of differentiation, unconscious processes, projections,
and complexes constantly threaten the ego. Thus, the goal of the
individuation process is to achieve the "self," or the total personality,
also called the individuality. The ego becomes subordinate to the self,
which is the center for the personality, encompassing the conscious
and the unconscious. So the process of individuation begins with
an unconscious that lacks individuality and ends with a highly

differentiated consciousness, or self, which is a state of greatest freedom from compulsion.

The self, for Jung, is divine in nature, and it "might equally well be called the 'God within us.'"[52] However, bearing in mind the autonomy of the psyche discussed earlier and Jung's denial of metaphysics, the God Jung refers to is the *imago dei*, or the imprint, the image, in the psyche, and by no means is Jung referring to a referent beyond it.[53] Jung's initial encounter with God as a child was with the God of his Christian father. As he described it later, it was an encounter with an abstract God.[54] Successive personal visions unfolded a more personal God, not in the abstract, but in concrete reality as it touched and moved him in his soul. The abstract God "beyond all human experience leaves me cold," says Jung. "We do not affect each other. But if I know that he is a powerful impulse of my soul, at once I must concern myself with him ..."[55] He found precedents for this experience of God dwelling *within* in Meister Eckhart, for whom God was identical to the human soul, quoting him approvingly as saying: "For man is truly God, and God is truly man,"[56] and "So much ... is God in the soul, that his whole divine nature depends on her."[57]

The term "god-image" derives from the Christian *imago dei* of the early Church fathers. However, it is from alchemy, Gnosticism, Vedantic conceptions of the *Atman* or Self as *Brahman,* and Meister Eckhart that Jung discovered the notion of the god-image. Meister Eckhart had already intimated it when he referred to the unknowable aspect of the Divine as "the naked essence of the Godhead." The Godhead (*Gottheit* in German, meaning Godhood or Godliness, state of being God) is the substantial impersonal being of God, ultimate underlying unity, as opposed to the multiplicity of the individual persons of the Trinity (Father, Son, and Holy Spirit). In other words, *the Godhead* refers to the "what" or essence of God, and *God* refers to the "who" of God. Therefore, the god-image refers to the imprint of God within the psyche but not the divinity itself. The divinity itself is God "*an sich*" and the God within the psyche is the *god-image.* The distinction between God and the god-image is crucial, and using them interchangeably, as Jung often does, can be confusing.

Jung was not alone in making the distinction between an immanent divinity and a transcendent divinity, to use a more theological language. This is a fundamental principle in traditional metaphysics. Meister Eckhart and other mystics had already made this crucial discovery. The Islamic tradition, too, meditated on this question at length, distinguishing between the divine *essence qua essence* and the divine insofar as it manifests in the cosmos. The divine has, as it were, two faces: one turned toward itself within the silence of its own primordial solitude and the other turned toward its creatures.

Islam denied the possibility that we could ever know the divine essence. Indeed, Islam rejected the possibility that human beings could ever be privy to knowledge of the divine essence (or God *qua* God). Rather what humans can know is the aspect of God turned toward creation in general and the individual's soul in particular. The divine, which is infinite, cannot be encompassed by any finite or delimited idea, and so naturally any representation of the divine (whether an idea, concept, belief, or image) is an idol that must be shattered at some point.

The distinction between the divine as essence and the divine as creator is crucial because it safeguards God. An excessive emphasis on divine immanence leads to the dangers of idolatry (the confusion of God as only immanent in Christ exclusively); an excessive emphasis on divine transcendence leads to an abstract God that one cannot experience or relate to (like the God of Jung's father). Where Jung parts way with Traditional Psychology is his stance on divine transcendence.

Edward Edinger, arguably Jung's most devoted disciple, considered the distinction (between God and the god-image) to be a Copernican revolution in psychology comparable to Kant's epistemological revolution. In a typical Kantian move, Jung insists that the image we have of God within the psyche is knowable; the God beyond the psyche is not. What we can know as humans is only the god-image *within*, not God *without*.

As such, Jung insists that we cannot make inferences from our psychic experience (of the god-image) about a transpsychic divine reality (*noumenon*) that may lie behind the image (*phenomenon*).

Needless to say, this aspect of Jung has caused considerable consternation among orthodox theologians of most religious traditions because Jung seems to suggest that we are forever doomed to never know the divine beyond but are forever cooped up within our own psyche.

Therefore, despite the evident similarities with the traditional notion of Christ, the Buddha, or Khidr as self/Anthropos, there are significant differences.[58] In traditional religions, it is problematic, to say the least, to equate Christ, God, Atman, or the Buddha with the self in psyche. God is a real and objective reality beyond the psyche, which can be directly accessed through the faculties of the heart, inner vision, and the ascent of the soul through the veils of matter into the light of the intelligible realm. That part of the soul that does not belong to the higher modes of existence belongs to the corruptible realm of matter, the lower soul of the vegetative and animal soul, which inevitably corresponds as we have seen to the collective unconscious. In Jungian psychology, God is relativized as merely one "archetype" within the sphere of the subjective psyche (personal or collective).

Concluding Part I: Jungian Psychology or Traditional Psychology?

Jung no doubt made an invaluable contribution to 20th-century thought and to the expansion of our intellectual horizon. His great achievement lies in his ability to show the inexhaustible richness of the spiritual traditions of both East and West. But his work also raised fundamental concerns for adherents of traditional religion, particularly his early Muslim readers, concerning the status of the living religious tradition of Islam and the Holy Scripture of the Quran. As we mentioned in the introduction, from a traditional point of view, without divine guidance, which is enshrined in the sacred knowledge invested in the world's great traditions, no real emancipation from the unconscious compulsions is possible, and thus the possibilities for modern man are still open for the catastrophes of inflation, dementia, idolatry, nihilism, anomie, and alienation.[59]

This perhaps may explain why for Jung's critics, though Jungian psychology had and still has a large following and is a powerful therapeutic force, it remains quite ineffective as a collective means of salvation. Part of the reason perhaps can be found in its Janus-faced nature: It aspires to be both an empirical science and a means of spiritual salvation akin to the Gnostic or mystical traditions. Jung, in contrast to Freud, did not display hostility toward religion and the spiritual in the name of a materialist/rationalist science. However, most have taken the empirical, Kantian, and often positivist Jung at his word, and the tension in his work between the scientific and the mystical is evident.[60] In the final analysis, for his Muslim critics, Jung chose to overcome the schism between both at the cost of the truth-claims of the living religious traditions of his time.[61] Is this the final word on Jung?

I think Jung's Muslim critics were too harsh on him. I have always felt there is much more in Jung that exceeds what his early critics were willing to see in him, and this is how I have been reading him for years. Jung's vast corpus and his phenomenological insights offer much to the Muslim reader who is interested in patiently reading him. Charles Upton, a traditionalist himself, recently summarized quite succinctly the criticism of Muslim traditionalists and endorsed them but followed it with a several-page rereading of Jungian themes (archetype, ego, shadow, *anima*) within a traditional metaphysical framework in his essay titled: "Can Jung Be Saved?" The result was a brilliant "saving" of Jung, or at least a partial salvaging of his legacy.[62] While such attempts at "saving" Jung are honest and insightful, I think another approach is more fruitful. Years ago, Paul Ricoeur performed the remarkable feat of rescuing Freud's legacy from Freud's idiosyncrasies by believing quite firmly that Freud had opened up a new field of investigation and developed a new method that was of immense value.[63] Roger Brooke did the same when he provided a much-needed phenomenological reading of Jung.[64] I think something similar can be done with Jung from a Muslim perspective. In 1945, Yusuf Murad engaged with Freudian psychology, becoming the first to develop an Islamic variant of psychoanalysis, earning him the title of the "Arabic Freud."[65] How long will it be before we have the first "Arabic Jung"? In any case, the first post-Jungian was Jung himself.[66]

A contemporary Muslim reader of Jung has an advantage that perhaps early Muslim readers of Jung did not: None of them look at Jung from the perspective of *The Red Book*, which reveals Jung as a shaman, a mystic, and a magician. The critique presented above in Part I, while still valid at a certain level, may yield to a more nuanced reading of Jung *in spite of Jung himself*. *The Red Book* offers a fresh perspective on Jung and new interpretations unencumbered yet by the accretions of Jungian commentaries and countercommentaries. We have the hindsight of knowing what Jung experienced on the one hand and how he chose to interpret the data of his experience on the other. One must accept the experience but one need not always accept the interpretation Jung or Jungians proffer.

There is much work to be done by Muslim scholars who want to seriously engage with Jung and "reimagine" his psychology, to borrow a term from James Hillman. In the little space that I have left, I would like to focus on one possible pathway into Jung that *The Red Book* opens up for a contemporary Muslim reader, which reveals a convergence between the fundamental spirit of Islam and that driving Jung's investigations.[67]

PART II: *The Red Book* and the Return *of* and *to* the Primordial — An Islamic-Jungian Convergence on the Centrality of the Imagination

The Red Book caused a sensation when it was first published in 2009. Many Jungians opposed its publication, arguing that it was a diary of his personal experiences that should not have been made public. But without it, the "real Jung" would have faded into obscurity occluded by the "isms" and "schools" that his followers have created in his name, and the Muslim engagement would probably not have gone beyond the initial critique. Sonu Shamdasani, the editor of *The Red Book*, highlighted the importance of knowing *The Red Book* for properly understanding Jung when he stated:

If one does not place Jung's confrontation with the unconscious in a proper perspective, or understand the significance of the *Red Book*, one is in no place to understand fully Jung's intellectual development from 1913 onwards, and not only that, but his life as well: it was his inner life which dictated his movements in the world. ... For Jung's work on his fantasies in *Black Books* and the *Red Book* formed the core of his later work, as he himself contended. The *Red Book* is at the center of Jung's life and work. [Understanding Jung] without an accurate account of it would be like writing the life of Dante without the *Commedia*, or Goethe without *Faust*.[68]

Looking at Jung's *Collected Works* through the lens of *The Red Book,* one finds new pathways into the Jungian corpus. For Muslims, *The Red Book* can open up a new conversation. I have already discussed at length how I have traveled with Jung and how *The Red Book* has influenced me personally in a previous publication.[69] There, I described *The Red Book* as a visionary recital that reflects Jung's deepest encounter with his inner guide. One aspect of Jung that I have always found extremely appealing to my Muslim sensibility, which *The Red Book* highlights vividly and with a highly personalized language, is the absolute necessity of *experiencing God within at the most primordial and personal level through the imagination*. This question of primordiality and imagination is key to both the spirit of Islam and Jung.

The Primordial

In the midst of a disenchanted world in which religion was on the wane in the West, Jung sought to revive the spirit of religion by reconnecting it to its primordial roots—its creative experiential roots—from which the images, symbols, and beliefs of theology sprang so that the encounter with the divine was always a living one. Jung was after that "supreme meaning" that never dies even when the

Gods are killed. "The other Gods died of their temporality, yet the supreme meaning never dies, it turns into meaning and then into absurdity, and out of the fire and blood of their collision the supreme meaning rises up rejuvenated anew."[70] But the Gods never really die, for they are ever reborn. Contra Nietzsche, Jung states: "One used to believe that one could murder a God. But the God was saved, he forged a new axe in the fire, and plunged again into the flood of light of the East to resume his ancient cycle."[71] One senses an apocalyptic urgency in Jung's language and tone.[72] However, this urgency is not a forward-looking one into a distant future (modernism) nor a back-ward looking one into the past as some have suggested but rather one into the primordial depths of one's being.

In *The Red Book* in particular, we see Jung drinking from the archetypal wellsprings whence all numinous experiences pour forth. His *Red Book* is a spring of images rising up from the deepest levels, uncoagulated and not yet hardened by concepts. It is a text intended for the soul that defies the intellectual constructs of ego-consciousness and mundane daily experiences, its objective being to elevate and raise the soul to a higher plane, from ego consciousness to *superconsciousness,* from "the spirit of the times" to "the spirit of the depths," and from the physical world to the *imaginal world,* as we shall see shortly. Thematically and chronologically speaking, it is a text that defies the canon of narrative.

Accordingly, for Jung the only adequate approach to God is one where the relation is a perpetually living one in which the fount of god-images that flows forth from the unconscious is never interrupted. He was convinced that the only path for modern consciousness to the unconscious/God is a direct one through individuation and believed that the traditional religiously mediated paths no longer sufficed.[73] More importantly for Jung, at this deepest universal and primordial level of the unconscious, whence these images have their origin, the unconscious is neither Buddhist nor Christian nor Jewish. For those Christian theologians who accused him of undermining centuries of Christian theology, Jung pointed out in several places that we cannot Christianize the unconscious because it is autonomous.[74]

Jung was convinced that this more direct and personal experience had to become the norm for a modern consciousness, for ours is an age in which the god-image is undergoing a radical transformation due to a more radical transformation of consciousness. The God that Nietzsche declared dead is our historically inherited collective god-image that must undergo a metamorphosis if it is to survive. Whereas in the past, it may have sufficed to believe in Christ as individuated, as a symbol of the self, to attain salvation, this is no longer enough today for two reasons: First, in a highly pluralistic world in which cultural boundaries have collapsed and god-images are interchangeable, it no longer suffices to cling to a single manifestation of the unconscious; second, the god-image must be a highly individuated and personalized one. According to Jung: "we must all do what Christ did. We must make our experiment ... we must live our own vision of life ... then only does God become man in ourselves."[75] Jung places the burden of Christ on every individual, for this is the only way forward. Although Jung was addressing a Western audience—many of whom were still nominally Christian in an increasingly de-Christianized society—he was also addressing their heirs who would no longer identify as Christian at all.[76]

It is not entirely clear how other religious traditions fit into his theory. Most Muslims would not be comfortable with Jung's dismissal of Islam from the family of "Western" religions or the Abrahamic Judeo-Christian historical trajectory. Jung writes in his *Red Book* that "every subsequent form of religion is the meaning of the antecedent."[77] Why Jung did not see Islam as the meaning of Christianity, its antecedent, is an interesting question. Muslims certainly do see Islam as the meaning of Christianity, its natural successor and culmination.

In his discussion of the evolution of the god-image in the West, Jung described Christianity as the stage of "universal monotheism," i.e., the stage of "tribal monotheism" of the Jewish people being made available to the other nations (Gentiles). Yet in Jung's opinion Christianity remains incomplete because of its repressed "shadow of God." That is why, Jung insists, there remains a further stage beyond Christianity. From an Islamic perspective, Christianity is just another community-bound revealed message that was not intended as a universal dispensation. For Muslims, Islam is the primordial revelation, the return to the pure monotheism of Abraham.

As Louis Massignon has written, the Islamic imagination should be seen as the "product of a desperate regression, back to the primitive, the eternal pagan substrate of all religions—that proteiform cubehouse the Ka'ba—as well as to a primitive pre-Mosaic monotheism of Abraham. The Dome is built on the Rock."[78]

This "desperate regression" to a "primitive pre-Mosaic monotheism of Abraham" is how I choose to understand Jung's statement in his essay *Concerning Rebirth* that the Prophet Muhammad had a "primitive cast of mind."[79] While Jung's Muslim critics have rejected such a description, in the context of his understanding of Chapter 18 of the Quran, I have always read it as Jung actually praising the Prophet!

The fundamental principle at the heart of the Islamic message is Oneness, or *Tawhid*. It is Islam's declaration of faith. Yet it is neither a doctrine nor a specific god-image like Christ or the Buddha. In its infinitive form, *Tawhid* denotes a process of *making*-One, i.e., seeing the many manifestations of God (in the cosmos, in various cultures, religions) as essentially derived from a single origin, the One. Therefore, Islam does not just present yet another god-image alongside that of animism, Christianity, or Buddhism; rather, it claims to be the primordial substratum or archetypal principle of them all. Is this not what Jung had been searching for and struggling with in *The Red Book*?

Both Jung and Islam strove for the substratum of religious experience deep within a primordial ground at a depth that was universal and beyond the surface distinctions of particular god-images. Universality and primordiality can only mean this, and from this perspective, Christianity simply does not qualify as a "universal" or a "primordial" religion. What qualifies a religion as primordial and universal from a Jung-Islam perspective is that it contains within it, *in potentia*, all previous and all possible future god-images because it is a process that operates at the deepest levels of the archetypal realm, at a level of the unconscious that belongs to no tradition but is the source of them all. Only Islam, for Muslims, fulfills these criteria. Yet this is, it seems, what Jung was striving for. Islam is the "meaning" of its predecessor, Christianity. Is Islam the perspective that Jung has been looking for all along? Muslims are certainly justified in raising this question. The convergence between Jung and Islam becomes even more apparent when we turn to the centrality of imagination in both.

Creative or Active Imagination

The faculty that both Jung and Islam emphasize for plunging into the primordial depths for a living numinous experience is the imagination. Both Jung and the Muslim mystics struggled against the rationalisms of their times to defend the integrity of the imagination. The Islamic scholar Henry Corbin translates the Arabic word for imagination (*khayal*) as "creative imagination" in reference to how it was used in the Arabic mystical sources he worked on, and Jung called it "active imagination," deriving it from the practice of the alchemists.[80] Though they have been used quite differently by both traditions, in essence they are pointing to the same process and essential truth, namely, that the only means of access to the primordial level of being, of the numinous within and without, is through the use of imagination.

Islam placed immense importance on the imagination, parti-cularly for the path of knowing and arriving at God. There is the prophetic tradition that says: "Worship God *as if* you see Him." For the great Muslim mystic Ibn 'Arabi, everything hinges on the "as-if" because it announces the central role of the imagination in the knowledge and vision of God. The god-image is a product of the imagination. While both Jung's and Ibn 'Arabi's position is that man creates the god-images through imagination, such creation is not a false fabrication in order to fulfill an infantile wish, as Freud would have it, but rather a spontaneous creative act arising from the deepest and most primordial recesses of the collective unconscious, or, as Jung would call it later, the "objective psyche." The key function of imagination here is *creation,* not creativity. The artist employs creativity to innovate or design; the initiate *creates the new,* i.e., the ever-renewed images that well up from the primordial fount. The former is false fabrication while the latter is spontaneous creation. As such, one would need to distinguish between them. Accordingly, both Jung and Ibn 'Arabi distinguished between two types of imagination: The first we may call *fantasy,* and the second we shall call *imagination* proper.[81] The former is bound to the psyche (psychosomatic constitution) of the individual and does not operate beyond it. The other is not bound by the psyche even though it may operate through its mechanisms to open up to the "psychoid."

Imagination transcends the ego and has its source beyond the psyche. It is the means by which the soul experiences God and participates in the creative manifestation of the divine. Fantasy, on the other hand, never transcends the ego, its needs, desires, and conceptual concretions. Though fantasy may reflect the contribution of complex and archetype, it nevertheless centers on ego, rather than on anything transcendent. As such, there is no higher experience, reality, or truth in fantasy but merely the playing out of one image after another that titillates, amuses, or glorifies the ego. There is nothing intrinsically wrong with fantasy. It is necessary for the healthy function of the ego, but it does not grant access to the god-image. However, fantasy falsely deployed along the spiritual path creates illusion and folly while imagination creates reality and truth.

Therefore, anyone who endeavors to enter the inner world will have to confront the issue of fantasy and delusion. While imagination opens one to a higher ontological plane of reality or profound experiences of the self, fantasy moves in the opposite direction downward and leads to inflation and illusion. It is not always easy to distinguish between them, which is why criteria with which to discern are vital for the spiritual life. Quite damaging is mistaking other inner voices for that of the self/god-image. Jung struggles with this issue in *The Red Book.*

The individual listening to the inner voice and receiving images created by it may in fact be dealing with an autonomous complex or archetype and not the self/god-image at all. Turning inward can often release a rush of uncontrollable images. This is common on the path of individuation. The desert fathers of early Christianity who went into the wilderness to find God met hordes of demons instead.

Another way of putting it is to say that images either originate from fantasy (psychosomatic) or imagination (psychoid). The latter are as real as the things of the so-called objective world around us. Imagination belongs to the soul while fantasy belongs to our psychosomatic constitution. Imagination unfolds the self/god-image and leads to its manifestation. The ego that follows the imagination is in harmony with the self/god-image and will redeem itself; the ego that indulges in fantasy is divorced from the self/god-image and is destined to live an illusory existence.

The self/god-image for Jung and Ibn 'Arabi is not a purely psychological reality. God can only be known in and through the act of creation itself—an act incommensurate with any abstract concept, assertion of faith, or dogma. The true initiate (on the path of individuation) never professes a full and complete knowledge of God. Jung, in a statement that may have been written by a Muslim theologian, insists that the unknowable God cannot be known completely, i.e., any knowledge of God is really provisional. As Jung explains:

> [No] man can know God. Knowing means seeing a thing in such a way that all can know it, and for me it means absolutely nothing if I profess knowledge which I alone possess.[82]

Instead, the initiate's knowledge of God is always only by way of provisional images. However, the relativity of the images does not preclude the divinity from shining forth in them and even shattering them.

Jung did not develop a whole metaphysics or cosmology of the imagination. This is expressed by Sonu Shamdasani: "… whereas Dante could utilize an established cosmology, *Liber Novus* is an attempt to shape an individual cosmology."[83] *The Red Book* and Jung's *Collected Works* reveal, nonetheless, lineaments of several cosmological perspectives. In Appendix C of the *The Red Book*, Jung clearly develops a hierarchical division of the soul, which Shamdasani describes as "a preliminary sketch of cosmology of the *Septem Sermones*." Here is how Jung formulates this soul-cosmology:

> Something in me is part animal, something part God, and a third part human. Below you serpent, within you man, and above you God. ... Above you comes the dove or the celestial soul, in which love and foresight are united, just as poison and shrewdness are united in the serpent. ... If I am not conjoined through uniting of the Below and the Above, I break down into three parts: the *serpent* ... the *human soul*, ... and the *celestial soul*, as such dwelling with the Gods ... appearing in the form of a bird.[84]

While not a complete cosmology, it does not necessarily conflict with traditional Islamic cosmology *per se*. I have always been convinced that the Muslim mystic Ibn 'Arabi provides a remarkable metaphysics of the creative imagination within which Jung's active imagination can be comfortably situated.[85] The Islamic mystical tradition makes a clear distinction between three different ontological levels of existence: Spirit World, Imaginal World (*mundus imaginalis* or *interworld*), Sensible World.

Ibn 'Arabi sees the *mundus imaginalis* as the place where the world of pure immutable ideas from the spirit world meets with the world of the objects of the sensible world.[86] Its location between the two worlds of the intelligible and the senses gives it a mediating role; it is intermediary because it mediates between the two places and by so doing it assumes the character traits of both places much like an isthmus.

The important thing to bear in mind is that it is a real, concrete, ontological order of reality just as real as the spirit world and just as concrete as the sensible world. It takes on the qualities of both worlds. On the one hand, the *mundus imaginalis* is a place "where the spiritual takes body," corporealizing the intelligible forms to which it gives form. On the other hand, the *mundus imaginalis* is where

"the body becomes spiritual," dematerializing perceptible forms into
their spiritual essences. Because "spirits are embodied and bodies
spiritualized," the *mundus imaginalis* is a vast spiritual topography of
image-forms. It is from this world that the god-images have their
provenance.

The *mundus imaginalis* is a "precise order of reality" to which
there corresponds a precise mode of perception"[87]: intellect (for
perceiving in the spirit world); imagination (or the heart for perceiving
in the *mundus imaginalis*); sense perception (for perceiving in the
physical world). Therefore, corresponding to the threefold ontological
levels of existence, there is a threefold division of knowledge. To the
"subtle and immaterial" quality of the *mundus imaginalis* there
corresponds the subtle organ of the heart, "imaginative perception,"
or the eye of inner vision that is responsible for the perception of
visionary events where suprasensory realities, the forms and figures
of the *mundus imaginalis*, present themselves to the contemplative or
imaginative consciousness. This subtle organ of vision is none other
than the (active/creative) imagination itself, which has its own "noetic
or cognitive function" because it "gives us access to a region and a
reality of being," without which it would be impossible to penetrate.[88]

However, in a rational and scientific world, an independent
"noetic or cognitive function" that provides access to a region of
being/reality unavailable to the senses, and thus to rational and
scientific methods, is anathema. For such a rational and scientific
worldview, the imagination is nothing but the imaginary, the
fantastic, the unreal. Jung struggled with this in the face of "the spirit
of the times" as he was trying to articulate to the world the way of the
symbol and "the spirit of the depths."

Therefore, the imagination does not produce an arbitrary
construct obstructing our view of reality but acts as an organ of
knowledge just as real as—if not more real than—our senses. It is
an organ *sui generis* and not derived from sense perception; its
power is by "effecting a transmutation of sensory data," resolving
them into the "purity of the subtle world," so that they may be
restored as "symbols to be deciphered," the key for such a cipher being
"imprinted in the soul itself."[89]

The images are not those of fantasy. They are concrete, real images or forms that the *mundus imaginalis* makes possible because of its transmutation of sensible and intellectual forms into imaginal forms. If the schemas of the sensible world and the intellectual world were not "dematerialized" and "spiritualized," they would be disconnected. While we encounter in other philosophies or systems a trust of the image, which is a degradation of all that properly belongs to the imagination, the *mundus imaginalis* is its exaltation because it is the link in whose absence the schema of the worlds is put out of joint.[90]

Islam insists on the realm of the imagination in the worship of God and resists the urge to concretize the image or allow it to descend to the ontological plane of the sensible world (iconoclasm). That is why Muslims scrupulously observe the prohibition on creating physical images of God. It is not a negative prescription but a positive one. The treasuries of conventional imagery that aid the soul's worship of God simultaneously cripple the soul and starve God. Paradoxically, an iconoclastic disposition destroys images to allow for the as yet unrevealed god-images to shine forth on the screen of the heart in a continual cascade of ever-changing images. The images are that much harder to destroy if they have become concretized in physical form. While they still remain in the flux of the imagination (the *mundus imaginalis*), a shattering of the image is that much easier.

What guarantees that these images are produced by the imagination and not by fantasy? In the Islamic tradition, it is the elaborate conditions and configurative power of the prayer that comports the worshipper in such a way that the way is barred for fantasy and opened up for the imagination through the disciplining of the body, the practice of virtue, the concentration of the heart on God, and the recitation of the Holy Text of the Quran. The worshipper's prayers definitely follow the contours of the theological truths and metaphysical notions he has of God (this is what we have called, following Jung, the god-image), but these truths or delimitations, as Ibn 'Arabi would call them, catalyze rather than strictly limit the imaginative process. God certainly precedes all existent things and their prayer, but the god-image does not preexist these prayers; the latter is a living presence that unfolds through them. Therefore, God, insofar as he can be known and wants to be known, can be known through the human being's imagination and the dialogue that creative prayer initiates.[91]

Without an entire cosmology and metaphysics in which the imagination occupies an ontological position clearly distinguishable from fantasy, it is difficult to see how one can safely distinguish between the images of fantasy and those of the imagination without a guide, a clear path, or a map of the terrain. The Jungian tradition does not seem to provide criteria by which one can discern or differentiate between these images and their sources other than the advice given in therapeutic practice to stay with the images, for their numinosity is enough to announce their divine source. But is this enough? Jung may not have given much thought to an elaborate cosmology, however, he did make a clear distinction between what we have been calling "fantasy" and "imagination."

By insisting on the plane of the *mundus imaginalis* as the only ontological plane for imagining the divine (the god-image), Islam maintains the perpetual balance between the coming-forth of god-images from the unconscious and their resorption. The One God who is manifest in the many god-images is never lost sight of. Islam preaches a *god-imaging process* (with the imagination at the heart of it), not a specific god-image (which is one among an infinity of possible images). Therefore, Islam has always grasped all "god-images" as intrinsic moments of itself! There is considerable overlap between Jung and Islam, and much work yet lies ahead for the would-be scholar to fully develop this promising line of research.

Endnotes

[1] C.G. Jung, "Paracelsus as a Spiritual Phenomenon," in *CW*, vol. 13 (Princeton, NJ: Princeton University Press, 1967), par. 163. For more on the relation between Nietzsche's "God is dead" see C.G. Jung, "Psychology and Religion," in *CW*, vol. 11 (Princeton, NJ: Princeton University Press, 1969), pars. 138-149.

[2] Ibid.

[3] Martin Heidegger, "'Only a God can save us': The *Spiegel* Interview," in Thomas Sheehan, ed., *Heidegger: The Man and the Thinker* (Chicago, IL: Precedent, 1981), 57.

[4] Arthur O. Lovejoy, *The Great Chain of Being: A Study of the History of an Idea* (Cambridge, MA: Harvard University Press, 1964).

[5] See "Active Imagination in Ibn Arabi and C.G. Jung," in J. Marvin Spiegelman, *Sufism, Islam, and Jungian Psychology* (Scottsdale, AZ: New Falcon Publications, 1991), 104-118. See also Henry Corbin, *Alone with the Alone: Creative Imagination in the Sufism of Ibn Arabi* (Princeton, NJ: Princeton University Press, 1997).

[6] Kathleen Raine, *Golgonooza City of Imagination: Last Studies in William Blake* (Ipswich: Golgonooza Press, 1991), 6.

[7] Nietzsche is a case in point of such inflation, which, in its mildest sense, reflects the situation of modern man in general: "The tragedy of *Zarathustra* is that, because his God died, Nietzsche himself became a god; ... It seems dangerous for such a man to assert that 'God is dead'; he instantly becomes the victim of inflation." See Jung, "Psychology and Religion," *CW* 11, par. 142. Such is a malaise of the collective psyche as well as the individual psyche.

[8] C.G. Jung, *Psychological Types*, in *CW*, vol. 6 (Princeton, NJ: Princeton University Press, 1971), par. 425.

[9] See Margaret Clark, *Understanding Religion and Spirituality in Clinical Practice* (London: Karnac Books, 2012), 12-14.

[10] Hence the term "Traditional Psychology."

[11] Jacob Needleman, Antoine Faivre, *Modern Esoteric Spirituality* (New York, NY: Crossroad, 1992), 340-341.

[12] The traditionalist view is summarized by Frithjof Schuon thus: "Outside tradition there can assuredly be found some relative truths or views of partial realities, but outside tradition there does not exist a doctrine that catalyzes absolute truth and transmits liberating notions

concerning total reality." Frithjof Schuon, "No Activity Without Truth," in Jacob Needleman, ed., *The Sword of Gnosis: Metaphysics, Cosmology, Tradition, Symbolism* (Baltimore, MD: Penguin Books, 1988), 36.

[13] This is certainly the opinion of Richard Noll, *The Jung Cult: Origins of a Charismatic Movement* (Princeton, NJ: Princeton University Press, 1994).

[14] Steven M. Wasserstrom, *Religion After Religion: Gershom Scholem, Mircea Eliade, and Henry Corbin at Eranos* (Princeton, NJ: Princeton University Press, 1999).

[15] The critique by the Muslim traditionalist René Guénon has had a devastating effect on the reception of Jung among traditional Muslim intellectuals, especially in Egypt, Turkey, and Iran. See René Guénon, *The Reign of Quantity and The Signs of The Times*, trans. Lord Northbourne (Hillsdale, NY: Sophia Perennis, 2001). See the follow-up critique by the other influential Muslim traditionalist Titus Burckhardt in his *Mirror of the Intellect: Essays on Traditional Science & Sacred Art* (New York, NY: State University of New York Press, 1987).

[16] Philip Rieff, *The Triumph of the Therapeutic: Uses of Faith after Freud* (New York, NY: Harper & Row, 1966), 91.

[17] The initial reception of Jung has been quite a critical one, and any dialogue must address the issues raised by these critics.

[18] Samir Mahmoud, "Henry Corbin and Jung's Visionary Recital: A Personal Journey with Jung," in Thomas Arzt, ed., *Das Rote Buch: C.G. Jung's Reise zum "anderen Pol der Welt." Studienreihe zur Analytischen Psychologie*, Bd. 5 (Würzburg: Königshausen & Neumann, 2015).

[19] For a detailed study of traditional metaphysics by Muslim traditionalists, I refer the reader to the works of René Guénon, Frithjof Schuon, Titus Burckhardt, and S.H. Nasr. See also the works of the Indian traditionalist Ananda Coomaraswamy who refers to Traditional Psychology as pneumatology, which is a metaphysical science. "Whereas the empirical science is only concerned with the man himself 'in search of a soul' (this is in reference to the title of a book by Jung, S. M.), the metaphysical science is concerned with this self's immortal Self, the Soul of the soul. Hence we call the traditional psychology a pneumatology rather than a science of the 'soul' … we shall take for granted the distinction of 'soul' from 'spirit.'" A.K. Coomaraswamy, "On the Indian and Traditional Psychology, or rather, Pneumatology," *Coomaraswamy Vol 2. Selected Papers: Metaphysics*, Roger Lipsey, (ed.) (Princeton, NJ: Princeton University Press, 1977), 335-336.

[20] For an exposition of the ambiguity in Jung's use of the term "psyche," see Roger Brooke, *Jung and Phenomenology* (London: Routledge, 1991), especially chapter 5.

[21] C.G. Jung, *Psychology and Religion* (New Haven, CT: Yale University Press, 1938), 62.

[22] "We are in truth so wrapped about by psychic images that we cannot penetrate at all to the essence of things external to ourselves. All our knowledge consists of stuff of the psyche which, because it alone is immediate, is superlatively real." See C.G Jung, "Basic Postulates of Analytical Psychology," in *CW*, vol. 8 (Princeton, NJ: Princeton University Press, 1969), par. 680. Similar claims can be found throughout his writings. "The psychic alone has immediate reality," elsewhere he makes the most bold of his statements: "Only psychic existence is immediately verifiable." See C.G. Jung, "Psychological Commentary on 'The Tibetan Book of the Great Liberation,'" in *CW*, vol. 11 (Princeton, NJ: Princeton University Press, 1969), par. 769.

[23] "I am and remain a psychologist. I am not interested in anything that transcends the psychological content of human experience. I do not even ask myself whether such transcendence is possible." Interview with Mircea Eliade for *Combat*, in C.G. Jung, *C.G. Jung Speaking: Interviews and Encounters,* eds. W. McGuire & R.F.C. Hull (Princeton, NJ: Princeton University Press, 1977), 229.

[24] C.G. Jung, "Commentary on 'The Secret of the Golden Flower,'" in *CW*, vol. 13 (Princeton, NJ: Princeton University Press, 1967), par. 82. In this way, Jung had "dismissed the theoretical rights of metaphysics and theology." See James W. Heisig, *Imago Dei: A Study of C.G. Jung's Psychology of Religion* (London: Lewisburg Bucknell University Press, 1979), 122. Jung states his most quintessential position on metaphysics in the following manner: "Psychology treats ... all metaphysical ... assertions as mental phenomena, and regards them as statements about the mind and its structure that derive ultimately from certain unconscious dispositions. It does not consider them to be absolutely valid or even capable of establishing metaphysical truth. ... Psychology therefore holds that the mind cannot establish or assert anything beyond itself." See Jung, "Psychological Commentary on 'The Tibetan Book of the Great Liberation,'" *CW* 11, par. 760. Also see Philip Novak, "C.G. Jung in the Light of Asian Psychology," in *Religious Traditions: A Journal in the Study of Religions,* vol. 14, 1991, 68.

[25] C.G. Jung, "The Relations between the Ego and the Unconscious," in *CW*, vol. 7 (Princeton, NJ: Princeton University Press, 1966), par. 405.

[26] For an analysis of the similarities and differences between Jung's depth psychology and traditional mysticism see R.C. Zaehner, "Integration and Isolation," in *Mysticism: Sacred and Profane* (Oxford: Clarendon Press,1957), 106-128.

[27] Jung sounds most positivist in his essay "Spirit and Life." See C.G. Jung: "Spirit and Life," in *CW*, vol. 8 (Princeton, NJ: Princeton University Press, 1969), pars. 601-648. See also for an account of this debate Brooke, "Psyche and Experience" in *Jung and Phenomenology.*

[28] Compare Jung's notion that we "are hopelessly cooped up in an exclusively psychic world" and that the cause of religious experience "lies beyond human knowledge" with this kind of claim from the traditionalist Frithjof Schuon: "The distinctive mark of man is total intelligence, that is to say an intelligence which is objective and capable of conceiving the absolute ... This objectivity ... would lack any sufficient reason did it not have the capacity to conceive the absolute or infinite." Frithjof Schuon, "To be Man is to Know," *Studies in Comparative Religion*, 13:1-2, 1979, 117-118. "The prerogative of the human state is objectivity, the essential content of which is the Absolute. There is no knowledge without objectivity of the intelligence." From Frithjof Schuon, *Esoterism as Principle and as Way* (Bedfont: Perennial Books, 1981), 15ff. "This capacity for objectivity and absoluteness is an anticipated and existential refutation of all the ideologies of doubt: if man is able to doubt, this is because certitude exists; likewise the very notion of illusion proves that man has access to reality." Frithjof Schuon, *Logic and Transcendence* (London: Perennial Books, 1984), 13. Thus Frithjof Schuon, referring to modern science's claim to truth, writes that: "Modern science ... can neither add nor subtract anything in respect of the total truth or of mythological or other symbolism or in respect of the principles and experiences of the spiritual life. ... We cannot be too wary of all these attempts to reduce the values vehicled by tradition to the level of phenomena supposed to be scientifically controllable. The spirit escapes the hold of profane science in an absolute fashion." Frithjof Schuon, "No Activity Without Truth," 36-37.

[29] One Indian psychologist put it thus: "There is no empirical psychology in India. Indian psychology is based on metaphysics." See Jadunath Sinha, *Indian Psychology: Perception* (London: Kegan Paul, Trench, Trubner & Co., 1934), xvi.

[30] Ibid.

[31] For a detailed discussion of the symbolic significance of the cross see René Guénon, "Metaphysical Symbolism of the Cross," in René Guénon, *The Symbolism of the Cross* (London: Luzac and Company, 1958).

[32] Of direct relevance here is Jung's personal dream of the multistory house in 1909. See C.G. Jung, *Memories, Dreams, Reflections*, ed. Aniela Jaffé (New York, NY: Vintage, 1963), 160-161.

[33] C.G. Jung, "The Structure of the Psyche," in *CW*, vol. 8 (Princeton, NJ: Princeton University Press, 1969), par. 321.

[34] "If the unconscious is anything at all, it must consist of earlier evolutionary stages of our unconscious psyche. ... Just as the body has an anatomical prehistory of millions of years, so also does the psychic system. And just as the human body today represents in each of its parts the result of this evolution and everywhere still shows traces of its earlier stages—so the same may be said of the psyche. Consciousness began its evolution from an animal-like state ..." See Jung, *Memories, Dreams, Reflections*, 348.

[35] Titus Burckhardt's following comment is typical of such criticisms: "Consciousness is capable of gradation like light and is similarly refracted in contact with the media it meets. The ego is the form of individual consciousness, not its luminous source. The latter coincides with the source of the intelligence itself. In its universal nature, consciousness is in a sense an existential aspect of the intellect, and this amounts to saying that basically nothing is situated outside it. Whence it follows that the 'unconscious' of the psychologists is quite simply everything, which, in the soul, lies outside ordinary consciousness. ...This 'unconscious' is made to include both lower chaos and the higher states. Many of the errors of 'depth psychology', of which Jung is one of the chief protagonists, result from the fact that it operates with the 'unconscious' as if it were a definite entity." Burckhardt, *Mirror of the Intellect*, 63-64.

[36] Henry Corbin, *Man of Light in Iranian Sufism* (New Lebanon, NY: Omega Publications, 1994), 6-7.

[37] René Guénon offers the following critique: "Obviously, this term 'unconscious' is quite inept and what it serves to designate, in so far as it can be said to have any reality, is what psychologists more commonly call the subconscious, that is, the whole range of the lower reaches of consciousness ... the supra-conscious escapes completely by its very nature from the domain in which psychologists deploy their in-

vestigations, they never fail, when they happen to come across some of its manifestations, to attribute them to the subconscious … the productions of the sick, observed by psychiatrists, stem from the subconscious." Guénon, *The Reign of Quantity and The Signs of the Times*, 71. In fairness to Jung, his notion of the psyche is more nuanced. Murray Stein quite rightly understand it as a "spectrum with the archetype at the ultraviolet end and the instinct at the infrared." In other words, "the psyche is a region that is located in the space between pure matter and pure spirit, between the human body and the transcendent mind, between instinct and archetype." See Murray Stein, *Jung's Map of the Soul: An Introduction* (Peru, IL: Open Court Publishing, 1998), 102-103.

[38] Ananda Coomaraswamy reiterates the traditional view on this matter when he says that: "… in so far as [man] identifies himself with his experiences and passions, he fetters himself …" and [the] "'Self'is overcome by causality, good and evil, and all the 'pairs' of contradictories …" A. K. Coomaraswamy, "On the Indian and Traditional Psychology, or rather, Pneumatology," in *Coomaraswamy, Vol 2, Selected Papers: Metaphysics*, 342-343.

[39] Jung, "Commentary on 'The Secret of the Golden Flower,'" *CW* 13, par. 67.

[40] Burckhardt, *Mirror of the Intellect*, 64.

[41] Henry Corbin, referring to Jung's shadow and *coincidentia oppositorum*, says: "The man of light's ascent causes the shades of the *well* where he was held captive to fall back into themselves. Hermes does not carry his shadow with him; he discards it." Corbin continues: "… one has to affirm that the relationship of Christ to Satan, Ohrmazd to Ahriman, is not complementary but contradictory. Complementary elements can be integrated, but not contradictory ones." Corbin, *Man of Light in Iranian Sufism*, 47.

[42] See Guénon, "The Misdeeds of Psychoanalysis," in *The Reign of Quantity and the Signs of the Times*. According to Guénon, in the "descent into Hades" one, as it were, exhausts all inferior possibilities of being in order "to be able to rise thereafter to superior states." The fall into the "mire" represents the inability to rise out of the inferior possibilities and to be totally consumed by them.

[43] Charles Upton, "Can Jung Be Saved?," in *The Greater Jihad: Essays in Principial Psychology* (San Rafael, CA: Sophia Perennis, 2011).

[44] Hans Jacobs, a Jungian who had undergone the Hindu path of salvation, *sādhanā*, says: "Individual being and universal being appear as separates only to our senses; in reality, they are indissolubly tied up, the individual receiving his justification and position through cosmic determinants which must be understood and consciously assimilated in order to be ultimately transcended. It thus becomes the proper task of spiritual development to lead the individual beyond his conditioning components." Hans Jacobs, *Western Psychotherapy and Hindu Sadhana* (London: Allen and Unwin, 1961), 118-119.

[45] C.G. Jung, "The Relations between the Ego and the Unconscious," in *CW*, vol. 7 (Princeton, NJ: Princeton University Press, 1966), par. 266.

[46] "... we could say with Nietzsche, 'God is dead.' Yet it would be truer to say, 'He has put off our image, and where shall we find him again?' The interregnum is full of danger, for the natural facts will raise their claim in the form of various –isms, which are productive of nothing of anarchy and destruction because inflation and man's hybris between them has elected to make the ego, in all its ridiculous paltriness, the lord of the universe." See Jung, "Psychology and Religion," *CW* 11, par. 144. For a detailed discussion of inflation see Jung, "The Relations between the Ego and the Unconscious," *CW* 7, par. 227.

[47] "Compulsion, therefore, has two sources: the shadow and the Anthropos." See C.G. Jung, *Mysterium Coniunctionis*, in *CW*, vol. 14 (Princeton, NJ: Princeton University Press, 1963), par. 153.

[48] Ibid., par. 151.

[49] Ibid., par. 153.

[50] Jung, "Psychological Commentary on 'The Tibetan Book of the Great Liberation,'" *CW* 11, par. 774.

[51] See endnote 45.

[52] Jung continues, "The beginnings of our whole psychic life might seem to be inextricably rooted in this point, and all of our highest and ultimate purposes seem to be striving towards it." See Jung, "The Relations between the Ego and the Unconscious," *CW* 7, par. 399.

[53] "We experience 'symbols of the self' which cannot be distinguished from 'God symbols'. I cannot prove that the self and God are identical, although in practice they appear so. Individuation is ultimately a religious process which requires a corresponding religious attitude = the ego-will submits to God's will. To avoid unnecessary misunderstandings, I say 'self' instead of God." See Jung's letter to Hélène Kiener from 15 June, 1955 in Gerhard Adler, *C.G. Jung Letters*, trans. by R.F.C.

Hull. Vol. 2, 1951-1961 (Princeton, NJ: Princeton University Press, 1975), 265. Elsewhere he says, "the religious point of view ... puts the accent on the imprinter whereas scientific psychology emphasizes the *typos*, the imprint—the only thing it can understand." See Murray Stein, *Jung on Christianity* (Princeton, NJ: Princeton University Press, 1999), 194.

54 As when he describes his experience at the age of 12 of walking through the Münsterplatz in Basel and the vision he had of God seated on his throne unleashing a turd on the city cathedral, shattering its new roof and destroying the cathedral. He described it as an experience of the "direct living God, who stands omnipotent and free above the Bible and Church." The experience prompted him to seek a direct and immediate experience of the "living God," who stands outside both church and Bible, an experience his father never had. Jung, *Memories, Dreams, Reflections*, 57. His numinous experiences in Africa were particularly moving. Jung's extraordinary visions would accompany him for the rest of his life, *The Red Book* being its most powerful.

55 Jung, "Commentary on 'The Secret of the Golden Flower,'" *CW* 13, par. 74.

56 Quoted in Jung, *Psychological Types*, *CW* 6, par. 416.

57 Ibid., par. 418.

58 "Living in the West, I would have to say Christ instead of 'self', in the Near East it would be Khidr, in the Far East atman or Tao or Buddha, in the Far West a hare or Mondamin, and in cabalism it would be Tifereth." See C.G. Jung, "Flying Saucers. A Modern Myth of Things Seen in the Skies," in *CW*, vol. 10 (Princeton, NJ: Princeton University Press, 1964), par. 779.

59 Consider the following evaluation of psychology as a whole by A.K. Coomaraswamy: "While nineteenth century materialism closed the mind of man to what is above him, twentieth century psychology opened it to what is below him." See A.K. Coomaraswamy, quoted in W. Perry, "Drug-Induced Mysticism," *Tomorrow* 12:2, 1964, 196.

60 There are a number of formidable obstacles to coming to terms with Jung's psychology. He is an extremely difficult author to pin down because although he was a "prolific writer" he was never a "systematic one." Philip Novak, "C.G. Jung in the Light of Asian Psychology," in *Religious Traditions: A Journal in the Study of Religions*, 66. This may be a result of the tension between his knowledge and experience and may have resulted in a "conceptual eclecticism" that reflected his "dis-

satisfaction with his own formulations." This "conceptual eclecticism" means that Jung never treats a subject from a single perspective. See Brooke, *Jung and Phenomenology*, 2-3.

[61] Referring to a trip to India, Jung has this to say: "I studiously avoided all so-called 'holy men.' I do so because I had to make do with my own truth." See Jung, *Memories, Dreams, Reflections*, 275.

[62] Charles Upton, "Can Jung Be Saved?," in *The Greater Jihad: Essays in Principial Psychology* (San Rafael, CA: Sophia Perennis, 2011).

[63] Paul Ricoeur, *Freud and Philosophy: An Essay on Interpretation*, trans. Denis Savage (New Haven, CT: Yale University Press, 1970).

[64] Roger Brooke, *Jung and Phenomenology* (London: Routledge, 1991).

[65] Omnia El Shakry, *The Arabic Freud: Psychoanalysis and Islam in Modern Egypt* (Princeton, NJ: Princeton University Press, 2017).

[66] It would pay enormously to revisit Jung's entire corpus from the perspective of his notion of the *unus mundus*, for example. I hope to do so in the near future. Andrew Samuels, *Jung and the Post-Jungians* (London: Routledge & Kegan Paul, 1985); and Jeffrey Satinover, *The Empty Self: C.G. Jung and the Gnostic Foundations of Modern Identity* (Westport, CT: Hamewith Books, 1996).

[67] I am hoping to dedicate an entire study to such a convergence between Islam and Jung in the near future.

[68] Sonu Shamdasani, *Jung Stripped Bare: By His Biographers, Even* (London: Routledge, 2018), 102-103.

[69] Samir Mahmoud, "Henry Corbin and Jung's Visionary Recital: A Personal Journey with Jung," in Thomas Arzt, ed., *Das Rote Buch: C.G. Jungs Reise zum "anderen Pol der Welt." Studienreihe zur Analytischen Psychologie*, Bd. 5 (Würzburg: Königshausen & Neumann, 2015).

[70] C.G. Jung, *The Red Book: Liber Novus. A Reader's Edition*, ed. Sonu Shamdasani, trans. John Peck, Mark Kyburz, and Sonu Shamdasani (New York, NY: W.W. Norton, 2012), 120.

[71] Ibid., 296.

[72] In Hamann's essay "*Aesthetica in nuce*," which Jung was familiar with, Hamann writes, "Poetry is the mother-tongue of the human race; even as the garden is older than the ploughed field, painting than script; as song is more ancient than declamation; parables older than reasoning; barter older than trade. A deep sleep was the repose of our farthest ancestors; and their movement a frenzied dance. Seven days they would sit in the silence of deep thought or wonder;—and would open their mouths to utter winged sentences. The senses and passions speak

and understand nothing but images. The entire store of human knowledge and happiness consists in images. The first outburst of creation, and the first impression of its recording scribe;—the first manifestation and the first enjoyment of Nature are united in the words: Let there be Light! Here beginneth the feeling for the presence of things. ... Speak, that I may see Thee! This wish was answered by Creation, which is an utterance to created things through created things. ... The fault may lie where it will (outside or within us): all we have left in nature for our use is fragmentary verse and *disjecta membra poetae*. To collect these together is the scholar's modest part; the philosopher's to interpret them; to imitate them, or—bolder still—to adapt them, the poet's. To speak is to translate—from the language of angels into the tongue of men, that is to translate thoughts into words—things into names—images into signs." In Johann Georg Hamann, "Aesthetica in nuce," edited by H.B. Nisbet, in *German Aesthetic and Literary Criticism: Winckelman, Lessing, Hamann, Herder, Schiller, and Goethe* (Cambridge: Cambridge University Press, 1985), 141-142.

[73] I don't think Jung was against religious traditions or a religiously mediated god-image but he was convinced that we had entered into an Aeon where more and more people could no longer follow such a path.

[74] Jung, "Psychology and Religion," *CW* 11, pars. 40-44.

[75] Jung, *C.G. Jung Speaking: Interviews and Encounters*, 98.

[76] A recent statistic published in Europe has shown that the majority of Europeans no longer identify as Christian, which makes Jung's work all the more relevant today.

[77] Jung: *The Red Book: Liber Novus. A Reader's Edition*, 258.

[78] Norman O. Brown, *Apocalypse and/or Metamorphosis* (Berkeley and Los Angeles, CA: University of California Press, 1992), 92.

[79] C.G. Jung, "Concerning Rebirth," in *CW*, vol. 9/I (Princeton, NJ: Princeton University Press, 1968), par. 258.

[80] In his early works on Avicenna, Henry Corbin uses Jung's term "Active Imagination" as synonymous with the Arabic *khayal*.

[81] I am using "fantasy" and "imagination" in a non-Jungian way here. Jung often uses fantasy to refer to the work of active imagination and refers to his experiences in *The Red Book* as "fantasies." I am making a clear distinction between two types of imagination, which for convenience sake I am referring to as fantasy and imagination,

respectively. Although the terms are not strictly used by Jung in this way the definitions I have given to each are consistent with Jung's distinction between two types of imagination: the former illusory the other real and creative. See C.G. Jung, *Psychology and Alchemy*, in *CW*, vol. 12 (Princeton, NJ: Princeton University Press, 1968), par. 219 and par. 393ff.

[82] Quoted in Edward F. Edinger, *The New God-Image: A Study of Jung's Key Letters Concerning the Evolution of the Western God-Image* (Asheville, NC: Chiron Publications, 2018), xiv.

[83] Sonu Shamdasani: "Introduction," in: Jung, *The Red Book: Liber Novus. A Reader's Edition*, 31.

[84] Jung, *Appendix C*, in: *The Red Book: Liber Novus. A Reader's Edition*, 577. This tripartite division of the soul is commonly found in many traditional cosmologies, including the Islamic tradition. The symbolism of the bird also figures quite prominently in Islamic sources.

[85] I have been reading Jung in this manner for years, and it has been extremely enlightening.

[86] Henry Corbin, *Temple and Contemplation*, trans. by Philip Sherrard and Liadain Sherrard (London: KPI & Islamic Publications, 1986), 266.

[87] Henry Corbin, *Swedenborg and Esoteric Islam*, trans. by Leonard Fox (West Chester, PA: Swedenborg Foundation, 1999).

[88] Henry Corbin, *Spiritual Body and Celestial Earth: From Mazdean Iran to Shi'ite Iran*, trans. by Nancy Pearson (Princeton, NJ: Princeton University Press, 1977), I.

[89] Ibid., 11.

[90] Ibid., ix.

[91] It is worth reading Henry Corbin's *Alone with the Alone: Creative Imagination in the Sufism of Ibn Arabi*, trans. by Ralph Manheim (Princeton, NJ: Princeton University Press, 1998). This text illustrates the conditions that guarantee and catalyze the imagination as opposed to fantasy. The Islamic ritual prayer pre-supposes praying at certain times of the day (governed by the movements of the sun across the sky), the performing of ablutions, concentrating the heart on God, reciting the Quran, and fixing the eye on a single point to "open" up the imagination or the eye of the heart. These conditions, once fulfilled, protect the worshipper from the function of fantasy and whim.

From Internal to Open Psyche: Overcoming Modern Consciousness?

Toshio Kawai

Evaluation of *The Red Book*

Before I give my impressions and ideas in this essay, I would like to consider how to read and evaluate *The Red Book*. There are several possibilities to be taken into account for its evaluation.

First of all, *The Red Book* without doubt is important from a historical point of view. It provides a clear and extensive documentation of how Jung developed and came to his main psychological ideas. The second layer was full of such ideas, which were based on his personal experiences presented in the first layer. Moreover, *The Red Book* provides important resources not only concerning theories but also materials. It was surprising for me that many of the images Jung dealt with in his writings are based on his personal experiences in his *Red Book*. For example, in Chapter 5 of *Liber Secundus*, Jung encountered a scarab whose symbolism was discussed in Jung's paper on synchronicity. In this sense, *The Red Book* offers precious, historical documentation for research.

But it is still an open question whether this work is important as a psychological work. The question is whether it brings any more new ideas to Analytical Psychology than were previously known through Jung's *Collected Works*. Then we can ask ourselves whether this book is not only important but also interesting. To put it differently, does the book have value as a work? Is it good art or literature? As is well-known, Jung was against the idea of seeing his work as art. But especially the second book, *Liber Secundus*, can be read as an experimental novel or a collection of short novels. Is *The Red Book* selling well only because Jung wrote it, or is it interesting even without knowing the author? These will be future questions after the initial enthusiasm.

As I am a psychologist, I will not go into the question of whether this book is good as art or literature. I have to confess that it was not interesting at all when I was translating the whole book into Japanese. However, I read it anew to study it and found it quite interesting. Therefore, we may need some distance.

From a psychological point of view, I would like to distinguish the formal aspect from the substantial aspect, the content. We can call them structure and content or, to use the term of Giegerich, the semantic and the syntactic.[1] What is meant by content is probably clear. It means the stories, materials, motives presented in the book. The death and rebirth of God, killing of the hero, mandalas, snakes, birds, and sun are such materials. The pictures Jung painted in his *Red Book* belong to this category as well. Concerning this aspect, classical symbolic interpretations of materials are common approaches. The formal aspect has to do with how Jung is related to the material, how Jung expresses it, how the materials are connected. Then we have to investigate the psychological structure and movement of *The Red Book*. In this essay, I would like to focus more on the formal aspect of *The Red Book*. In this way, I would like to show how the *Red Book* was written from modern perspective despite its archaic and premodern content and then how it tries to overcome the modern framework.

Position of the Ego or Vision Ego

When my father, Hayao Kawai, the first Jungian analyst in Japan, came to the C.G. Jung Institute in Zurich in 1961 and started his training, Marie-Louise von Franz said to him, rather proudly: "You must be impressed by the power of the unconscious psyche." He answered, with a bit of humor and irony, that he was not so much impressed by the power of the unconscious as by the power of consciousness. After 50 years, this impression seems to be still valid. Namely, concerning *The Red Book* I was not so impressed by the rich content out of the unconscious, but by the strong consciousness holding its place. I will explain this in reference to several aspects.

In the first book, *Liber Primus,* overwhelming images and visions are depicted. There was a famous initiating vision where the northern part of Europe was covered by a flood. After two weeks, the vision returned. Jung thought his "mind had gone crazy."[2] He expressed at various times the anxiety of becoming psychotic. But we have to notice that all these images and visions, however tremendous they might be, are very clearly seen and grasped. Moreover, the clearness of images must be due to a stable standpoint of the observing ego. That is why Jung could have images and visions that are not contaminated but very clear. Such a clear distinction does not indicate a psychosis at all. The content could be extraordinary and overwhelming, but the syntactic structure is unshaken and still intact. This is why it is important to distinguish the syntactic aspect from the semantic.

The characteristic feature of schizophrenic thought consists not in its bizarre contents but in the passive mode of being seen, being observed. Schizophrenics often paint many eyes in their pictures— they feel observed. They do not have visions but rather acoustic hallucinations. This is not to be understood as a difference in sensory modes between visual and acoustic, but as a difference in mode of being. German humanistic psychiatrist Jürg Zutt explained in his classic paper "Blick und Stimme" ("The Gaze and the Voice") that the voice of the schizophrenics is the expression of being spoken to and seen instead of seeing.[3] We can speak here about the loss of subjectivity: the "other" is overwhelming the subject and destroying its functioning so that the subject is replaced by the "other." So Jung did not need to be worried about the onset of psychosis, since he could keep the observing subject safe.

I would like to make a cultural side remark that there are very few reports of people having visions in Japanese history. There are some Buddhist stories in *Nihon-Ryoiki* (ninth century) that have the features of visions, but they could be imitations of Indian or Chinese works. The lack of visions is due to the ambiguous differentiation of subject and object in the Japanese psyche and culture.

The second point has to do with the function of emotion. Jung was overwhelmed by the images, which produced strong emotions,

These emotional reactions are very often mentioned in *Liber Primus*. For example, at the beginning, Jung says: "From then on the anxiety toward the terrible event that stood directly before us kept coming back."[4] In the third chapter, he writes: "I follow, but it terrifies me."[5] At the beginning, anxiety and fear are especially remarkable. The style and atmosphere are really dramatic.

Later the feeling of anger comes up, too, for example in Chapter 6: "But I was indignant at him and said ("Ich aber empörte mich gegen ihn und sprach"), 'How can I sink? I am unable to do this myself.'"[6] In this chapter, the rage of the ego is strongly noticeable. The emotion has, so to speak, a dialectic function. It is, of course, caused by the surprising invasion of the unconscious and so proves the dominance of the unconscious and confusion of the consciousness. On the other hand, it underlines and reinforces the existence of the ego, which is centered and highlighted due to the emotional reactions. You can have anxiety because you are aware of yourself and afraid of losing yourself. Very often one starts to have an anxiety dream of being chased or persecuted in adolescence when the ego is going to be established. So anxiety proves and strengthens the ego. Strong emotional reactions in *Liber Primus* do not necessarily confirm the dominance of the unconscious but rather the existence of the ego as a solid reference point.

The stable position of the ego can also be noticed in the conversation with the soul or psychic other. In Chapter 3 of *Liber Primus*, "On the Service of the Soul," Jung says to his soul: "I should give myself completely into your hands ... "[7] There is a total devotion to the soul and self-abandonment. Nevertheless, he continues: "... but who are you?" This question makes it clear that there is a position from where the question can be posed. The more important and overwhelming the soul is, the more significant the position of the ego who stands vis-à-vis to the soul. Jung never forgets the position of the ego.

The position of the ego is not only discernible in relation to the figures with whom it interacts but also is not lost even in the utmost crisis. The experience of hell was surely terrible. Jung wrote: "No one knows what happened during the three days Christ was in Hell. I have experienced it."[8] But on the other hand, Jung said: "He who journeys to Hell also becomes Hell; therefore do not forget from whence you come."[9] Therefore, he has never lost sight of the position of the ego. This was not a total loss.

Despite the overwhelming contents of visions and emotional reactions, then, the standpoint of the ego is never lost. This is a striking, formal characteristic of *The Red Book,* to which we have to pay more attention.

From Tragedy to Comedy

As we have seen, in *Liber Primus* the stable position of the ego is noticeable, despite and because of the overwhelming experiences and images. The more the ego suffers, the more it proves its existence: I suffer, therefore I am. We can call it proof of the ego via tragedy.

In *Liber Secundus,* Jung seems to gain more distance from the images. The images are no longer as threatening as they were in the first book. There is also a historical distance from the images. For example, when Ammonius tried to attack Jung, he could not reach him: "He jumps up incensed and wants to lunge at me. But I am far away in the twentieth century."[10] Similarly, in front of the powerful God, Izdubar, Jung knows quite clearly that he lives in the world of science, where the ancient worldview is not valid anymore.

In *Liber Secundus,* Jung is not overwhelmed by the figures and images but is even rather superior to them. For example, one of the lowly in Chapter 3 was a person who came out of prison and was very poor and weak. Jung had to pay for the dinner and the night's accommodation. The God Izdubar, bull-man, collapses and sobs like a child after he was taught by Jung that he was not immortal. Philemon was not a powerful and spiritual person like Elijah in *Liber Primus.* And even Elijah is powerless in the *Liber Secundus.* After having heard that his serpent was stolen by Jung, Elijah tried to curse him, but Jung replied: "Your curse is powerless. Whoever possesses the serpent cannot be touched by curses."[11] These scenes remind us of dreams in which the dream ego is not overwhelmed and threatened by other figures.

With such changes, the story is not serious and tragic anymore but rather comical. The freedom and confidence of the ego lead to comedy. Every story in *Liber Secundus* is somehow comical. In *Liber Primus*, Jung expressed a real concern about going mad. But in the *Liber Secundus*, Jung was sent to a psychiatric clinic in his dream. The conversation with the Professor evokes humorous feeling because there is no real danger.

In the medical consultation, Jung said to the Professor: "But Professor, I'm not at all sick, I feel perfectly well." The Professor answered: "Look, my dear. You don't have any insight into your illness yet. The prognosis is naturally pretty bad, with at best limited recovery."[12]

So the ego manifests itself in *Liber Secundus* with more distance and via comedy. But it is important to notice that the ego insists on its existence throughout, whether by way of tragedy or comedy.

Doubled Opposites

Throughout the whole of *The Red Book*, the structure of contrasts and opposites is striking. It starts with the opposition of "the spirit of this time" and "the spirit of the depths." We can point out many contrasts and opposites, like sense and nonsense, high and deep, Elijah and Salome, the Red One and the Anchorite, the librarian and his daughter, snake and bird. But not only are there these contrasts or opposites, but Jung regularly intervenes with them. So there are also oppositions between Jung and Salome, Jung and the Red One, Jung and the old man's daughter. The opposites are therefore formed not only in the unconscious, in the image, but also between the ego and the unconscious. And both opposites derive from the establishment of the ego because ego produces its vis-à-vis and discerns the difference there. The so-called way of individuation is rather understood as a relationship between the ego and the unconscious that involves their integration. So Jung says in the *Liber Secundus*: "I have united with the serpent of the beyond. I have accepted everything beyond into myself."[13] However, *The Red Book* seems to stress differentiation rather than union. Concerning the devil, Jung writes in the following way: "Taking the devil seriously does not mean going over to his side, or else one becomes the devil. Rather it means coming to an understanding. Thereby you accept your other standpoint."[14]

In "Scrutinies," the third book, Jung says concerning the soul: "Shield men from her, and her from men."[15] He emphasizes repeatedly the importance of distinguishing himself from his soul. I add another citation: "Why? Because you can't distinguish yourself from your soul. But you are distinct from her, and you should not pursue whoring with other souls as if you yourself were a soul, but instead you are a powerless man who needs all his force for his own completion."[16]

The point consists in keeping one's distance rather than being identified with the other. I have to add that the individuation process described in Jung's work "The Relations between the Ego and the Unconscious" also emphasizes the aspect of differentiation. Then the question arises concerning how union and differentiation relate to each other. In *The Red Book,* there are some poetic suggestions on this point in Philemon's Sermons to the Dead. While the Pleroma is nothingness or fullness and has no differentiation, the Creation is differentiation.

The psychology of opposites takes place not only between the ego and the unconscious but also in the unconscious. So Jung says to Satan: "… we have united the opposites. Among other things, we have bonded you with God."[17] Then we would like to ask how both contrasts relate to each other. This remains somehow unsolved in *The Red Book* and has to wait for Jung's studies in alchemy. In alchemy, there is a *soror mystica*, a female assistant to the adept. But in alchemy, union between king and queen in the alchemical retort is more important than the relationship between adept and *soror mystica*, or that between adept and the material. This double differentiation leads to the schema of the "marriage quaternio" in "The Psychology of the Transference."

Internalization

Internalization is another key aspect of the formal point of view. Jung seems to be aware that he does not live in the premodern world. He confesses, for example, that he does not know how to pray to the sun: "I should not forget my morning prayer—but where has my morning prayer gone? Dear sun, I have no prayer, since I do not know how one must address you."[18] He invented some afterward. But the emphasis seemed to be laid on the loss of the prayer.

In this sense, there is no God anymore because God appears in a concrete prayer or ritual based on its tradition. Jung's experience of the Elgonyi in Uganda is a good example. The indigenous people there praise the sun when it comes up, as described by an old man who said: "In the morning, when the sun comes up, we go out of the huts, spit into our hands, and hold them up to the sun." This old man could not explain the meaning of the ritual, but said: "We've always done it."[19] Then Jung had to realize that religious experience consists not in the symbolic meaning but in the pure performance carried out by the community. Therefore, without a ritual or prayer based on the tradition there is no God anymore.

While the death and rebirth of the God were seriously and literally made a theme of *Liber Primus*, the rebirth of God was realized in *Liber Secundus* as the internalization of God. After Izdubar had collapsed, Jung had to transport him. In order to carry him, Jung made Izdubar into a mere fantasy. "I am basically convinced that Izdubar is hardly real in the ordinary sense, but is a fantasy." Because the fantasy "takes up no space" and Jung can "squeeze Izdubar into the size of an egg and put him in the pocket," he can transport him easily.[20] When Izdubar came out of the egg again, this was understood as the rebirth of God.

But for us, it is more important to notice that the rebirth of God became possible by way of internalization. As Jung writes, God "did not pass away, but became a living fantasy." "If we turn the God into fantasy, he is in us and is easy to bear."[21] The literal death and rebirth of God in *Liber Primus* is realized in *Liber Secundus* more psychologically through the idea of internalization. This is the achievement of *The Red Book*. Due to this internalization, Jung could establish his psychology, which deals with God and rituals as an inner reality of fantasy. So the rebirth of God was for Jung not a literal rebirth, but rather the birth of psychology, which is based on the idea of internalization and the reality of fantasy. In *Psychological Types,* Jung states his famous motto, which is quoted often by James Hillman: "The psyche creates reality every day. The only expression I can use for this activity is *fantasy*."[22] This is the basis of Jung's psychology, which was achieved in the second part of *The Red Book*.

If I may make another cultural side remark, this clear-cut differentiation of inner and outer reality is also something foreign to Japanese culture. There is a long tradition in Japan of expressing the soul as a concrete thing or art for which Ikebana (flower arrangement) and Japanese gardens are typical examples. To put it precisely, in the art of the garden, the soul resides. That is why sandplay therapy is very popular in Japan. So the clear internalization is admirable, but for the Japanese psyche, it remains a foreign achievement.

From Symbol to Directness: Sacrifice

Despite the mythological and premodern contents of *The Red Book*, it was clearly based on the modern understanding of psyche with the idea of a central ego, self-relation, and internalization. In this sense, *The Red Book* shows clearly how Jung could establish his psychological and psychotherapeutic methodology: Jung emphasized the meaning of a mythological layer of the psyche, which was, however, approached by the modern way of self-relation and internalization.

But *The Red Book*, especially its third part of "Scrutinies," has an aspect that goes beyond the modern understanding and structure of psyche. This aspect appears firstly as physical experiences, at least as physical metaphors. *The Red Book* tried to show premodern cults that were still alive as fantasy. And premodern Gods and images are mostly experienced as visions and understood in terms of symbolism. However, for me this is somehow not so convincing because of the distant and analyzing attitude. As I pointed out, taking distance is a way to establish the ego, which can weaken the reality and the presence of the unconscious. I am rather more impressed by several scenes of sacrifices in *The Red Book* where the body seems to play a central role. Then Jung is no longer aloof from the vision. For example, the chapter "The Sacrificial Murder" in *Liber Secundus* is very impressive. Jung was compelled to eat a piece of liver from the dead girl. A woman who is supposed to be the soul of this girl asks Jung: "Step nearer and you will see that the body of the child has been cut open; take out the liver." She asks further: "Take a piece of the liver, in place of the whole, and eat it."[23] Jung was reluctant, but finally he ate a piece of liver:

> I kneel down on the stone, cut off a piece of the liver and put it in my mouth. My gorge rises—tears burst from my eyes—cold sweat covers my brow—a dull sweet taste of blood—I swallow with desperate efforts—it is impossible— once again and once again—I almost faint—it is done. The horror has been accomplished.[24]

I would like to mention one more scene of sacrifice. This is a scene of self-dismemberment, which reminds me of the vision of Zosimos. Jung trampled upon himself using a winepress machine:

> I have trodden the winepress alone and no one is with me. I have trodden myself down in my anger, and trampled upon myself in my fury. Hence, my blood has spattered my clothes, and I have stained my robe. For I have afforded myself a day of vengeance, and the year to redeem myself has come.[25]

These scenes are, of course, tremendous. But I have the impression that they are much more real for me and familiar. They remind me of many novels of the Japanese writer Haruki Murakami. In his stories, violent and cruel scenes are frequently described that could be connected with premodern cults and rituals. For example, in *Kafka on the Shore*, the character Johnnie Walker, who may be the father of the protagonist, a boy named Kafka, must take out the heart of a cat and eat it, then cut off the head of the cat.[26] This act is not only perverse and cruel but evokes some ritualistic associations and meanings. The extraordinary popularity of Haruki Murakami's books in Japan shows that such violent scenes can appeal to modern Japanese people, to the Japanese psyche. And as Murakami's novels are popular all over the world, not only in Japan but in the contemporary world in general, the numinous can probably no longer appear in either a ritual or through the symbolic, but in direct violence and sexuality. The numinous used to be mediated by rituals and symbols that were carried out by the community and tradition. But because rituals and symbols have lost their power in the community, the numinous can only appear directly through violence and sexuality, which however have no clear meaning.[27]

As Jung's failed experience with the church in his youth made clear, he was aware of the death of rituals and symbols. These scenes of physical sacrifices may try to find a direct access to the numinous in the age of loss of symbol and ritual.

From Internal to Open Psyche

Physical experiences in sacrifice were one way to go beyond the internal, self-reflecting modern psyche. This is a trial to go out of internal psyche to reality as body, but it remains with the personal, limited body. The third part of *The Red Book* shows another possibility of overcoming the internal psyche.

The third part consists mainly of sermons of Philemon to the Dead, which are similar to the *Septem Sermones ad Mortuos,* which Jung published privately after his crisis and was included later in his autobiography, *Memories, Dreams, Reflections.*

In confrontation with his mental crisis, Jung finished his experiment as recorded in *Liber Primus* and *Liber Secundus* of *The Red Book* in 1914. But he started to write again in his diary, *The Black Books,* in 1915. This may indicate that his attempt to find his own myth was not sufficient and he needed to go a step further.

At the beginning of 1916, Jung experienced a mysterious event in his house, which led to *Septem Sermones ad Mortuos* and the third part of *The Red Book*, "Scrutinies." Jung reported: "There was an ominous atmosphere all around me. I had the strange feeling that the air was filled with ghostly entities. Then it was as if my house began to be haunted. My eldest daughter saw a white figure passing through the room. My second daughter, independently of her elder sister, related that twice in the night her blanket had been snatched away; and that same night my nine-year-old son had an anxiety dream."[28] We can notice that "an ominous atmosphere" was not only limited to Jung's personal, internal psyche but was shared by his children. The following morning, on Saturday, his son drew a picture of his dream. Strange things continued:

> Around five o'clock in the afternoon on Sunday the front doorbell began ringing frantically. It was a bright summer day; the two maids were in the kitchen, from which the open square outside the front door could be seen. Everyone immediately looked to see who was there, but there was no one in sight. I was sitting near the doorbell, and not only heard it but saw it moving. We all simply stared at one another. The atmosphere was thick, believe me! Then I knew that something had to happen. The whole house was filled as if there were a crowd present, crammed full of spirits. They were packed deep right up to the door, and the air was so thick it was scarcely possible to breathe. As for myself, I was all a-quiver with the question: 'For God's sake, what in the world is this?' Then they cried out in chorus, 'We have come back from Jerusalem where we found not what we sought.' That is the beginning of the *Septem Sermones*.[29]

Just before reporting this peculiar happening, Jung emphasized how important it was for him to have a family and his work as psychiatrist. He "needed a point of support in 'this world.'" When Jung was writing the first and second book of his *Red Book*, he saw his patients during the day and spent family life normally. Only during the night did he continue his self-experiment with active imagination. It was held only within his internal space, so there was no contact and contamination with outer reality, though Jung understood his terrible visions at the beginning in connection with the onset of World War I.

But now the Dead flowed out from internal space to external space. The difference between dead and alive was not kept anymore. Not only he but also his children noticed the presence of the Dead. According to modern psychological paradigm, the Dead should represent the unconscious of Jung. But the paradigm of internal and self-reflecting psyche is not valid anymore here. The understanding of psyche here is open psyche shared with community, his children, even with the Dead. This experience led Jung to coin the concept of "synchronicity," which goes beyond the understanding of inner, enclosed psyche.

Difference from the Premodern Worldview and a New Psychology

The idea of sharing with community and the Dead may remind us of the premodern understanding of psyche, which is not limited to an individual: The psyche was an open system, which spread out to the community, nature, and the world of the Dead. But we can notice some differences from the premodern worldview. Firstly, the Dead in Jung's experience could not find what they sought in Jerusalem and came back to this world. This means that they could not find their redemption, their mythological place. Secondly, Philemon teaches the Dead in the case of Jung's experience, while in the traditional ritual and worldview, the Dead are treated and welcomed by offerings. For example, in Japan, the ancestors are gods who return to the world regularly. The equinoctial day in spring and autumn and the Bon Festival in summer are occasions on which the ancestors come back. It is striking how these festivals appear and play a decisive role in dreams, even if the dreamer does not pay much attention to those festivals. People live in touch with the Dead, or the Dead continue to live in touch with living people. As another example, I can mention the habit on the eve of Celtic new year, the Samhain, on the 31st of October. This habit is transformed to All Saints Day in Christianity and Halloween. Originally, this meant the end of summer and the beginning of winter, when the boundary between this world and another world become unclear and the Dead return to the villages and are treated by offerings. The original idea is still noticeable in the habit of Halloween. It would be interesting to examine Jung's experiences, such as this one and his dream after his mother's death, in connection with the Samhain.

Unlike the Dead and ancestors in the premodern cultures, the Dead in "Scrutinies" or *Septem Sermones* seem to have lost their mythological place. We do not have any offerings for them. Such a situation may have to do with the First World War, which caused not only more than 16,000,000 dead, but also destroyed the traditional worldview regarding the Dead.

If we think about the onset of Jung's psychological crisis, it started with the anticipation of the First World War as the outer reality. Jung worked out this crisis as an internal one through active imagination, which led to *Liber Primus* and *Liber Secundus*. But again, Jung was forced to go beyond the internal psyche. Although Jung's experience with the Dead has similarities with the premodern worldview, it is very different. This is why Jung thought it necessary to revise his theory and to create such concepts as synchronicity and the psychoid.

In this essay, I cannot go into the possibility of this new psychology, as I would like to focus on the formal characteristic and structure of *The Red Book*. I would like to suggest that the interpretation of the Sermons of Philemon is important for understanding the essence and direction of this new psychology. The first Sermon to the Dead begins: "I begin with nothingness. Nothingness is the same as the fullness. In infinity full is as good as empty."[30] In these phrases, the way to put and substantiate the ego as starting point is totally negated. Even the idea of substance is negated because it starts with nothingness. For the future of Analytical Psychology, it is worth thinking what kind of psychology can open up from here.

Endnotes

[1] Wolfgang Giegerich, "Psychology – The Study of the Soul's Logical Life," in A. Casement, ed., *Who Owns Jung?* (London: Karnac Books, 2007), 247–263.

[2] C.G. Jung, *The Red Book: Liber Novus*, ed. Sonu Shamdasani, tr. John Peck, Mark Kyburz, and Sonu Shamdasani (New York: W.W. Norton, 2009), 231.

[3] Jürg Zutt, "Blick und Stimme," in *Nervenarzt*, 28, 350–355, 1957.

[4] Jung, *The Red Book*, 231.

[5] Ibid., 235.

[6] Ibid., 240.

[7] Ibid., 235.

[8] Ibid., 243.

[9] Ibid., 244.

[10] Ibid., 272.

[11] Ibid., 324.

[12] Ibid., 343.

[13] Ibid.

[14] Ibid., 319.

[15] Ibid., 343.

[16] Ibid.

[17] Ibid., 319.

[18] Ibid., 271.

[19] C.G. Jung, *Memories, Dreams, Reflections*, ed. Aniela Jaffé (New York, NY: Vintage Books, 1963), 266.

[20] Jung, *The Red Book*, 282-283.

[21] Ibid., 283.

[22] C.G. Jung, *Psychological Types*, in *CW*, vol. 6 (Princeton, NJ: Princeton University Press, 1971), par. 78.

[23] Jung, *The Red Book*, 290.

[24] Ibid.

[25] Ibid., 300, citing *Isaiah 63:3-4*.

[26] Haruki Murakami, *Kafka On The Shore*, trans. P. Gabriel (London: Vintage, 2005).

[27] Toshio Kawai, "The experience of the numinous today: from the novels of Haruki Murakami," in A. Casement and D. Tacey, eds., *The Idea of the Numinous: Contemporary Jungian and Psychoanalytic Perspectives* (London & New York, NY: Routledge, 2006), 186–199.

[28] Jung, *Memories, Dreams, Reflections,* 190.
[29] Ibid., 190-191.
[30] Jung, *The Red Book,* 346.

The Golden Seed: The Hidden Potentiality within the Vile and the Misshapen

Patricia Michan

I would like to kick the garbage away from me, if the golden seed were not in the vile heart of the misshapen form.[1]

C.G. Jung

Introduction

Jung's writings about his personal experiences in *The Red Book,* in conjunction with key theoretical ideas that he developed over time, create an armature correspondent to psychic patterns and processes that I encounter in my work with analysands. In 1916, some two years after having begun his researches into his own psyche as expressed in *The Black Books,* Jung wrote his essay "The Transcendent Function." He was in his own process of being pressed to the necessity of accessing and relating to the unconscious through developing a dialectical relationship between ego and non-ego.[2] This requires tapping into and developing a working relationship with the encompassing arc of provisions in both ego and non-ego, while simultaneously navigating the given endangerments, including failure to access embedded provisions, getting caught in the "sterile circle"[3] of negative psychic entanglements, and being overwhelmed by unconscious contents. In his writings during the period of his *Red Book* and continuing throughout his life, Jung articulated the value and necessity of the encompassing field of the provisions of psyche.

My emphasis in this essay is on the functional importance of those provisions that I map within the arc of the psychically negative: distortions, activations, emotional outbursts, and pathologies that attend upon expressions of false imagination, symptom, complex, projection, defense, constellations, waking dreams, all of those ego dystonic "fateful detours and wrong turnings"[4] that function as placeholders, but which, if potentiated, support movement toward wholeness.

The entire arc of this unwelcome function of psyche manifests through seemingly worthless ways in which "psyche creates reality every day."[5] Jung's valuing of the negative is the radical territory expressed in Christ's exhortation in the end of "Scrutinies," claiming that anyone who welcomes the worm, i.e., the devil, and can bear the worm will receive the gift, "the beauty of suffering."[6] All of these manifestations are part of psyche's creative function that we indeed need to welcome in the clinical hour. We see this, for example, in the concept of the "projection-making factor" in the psyche.[7] Projection is one of the many methods through which psyche makes the inaccessible accessible. The functional "making" potential embedded within psychic agency is, for good or ill, the key to accessing deeply important and inaccessible unconscious material and hence to the enlargement of the personality. Both ego and non-ego contribute to the "making" of psychic reality. This territory, often dismissed as one-sidedly negative, tends to express itself with a compulsive quality. Jung states that the compulsion itself has a twofold source: the shadow (unlived life potential, positive or negative) and the Anthropos (the source level).[8] In clinical practice, compulsive expression points to embedded agency. Jung, in contending with compulsive energies, engages the psychic agency within both shadow and Anthropos. In *The Red Book,* he distilled gold from the *prima materia* of his own process, and he participated in furthering that gold through the articulation of his ideas both at that time and throughout the course of his life. The complex and dynamic theoretical material emerging in his *Red Book* came to flower over decades. I am deeply invested in presenting, with clinical specificity, the way in which I have been informed by Jung's engagement in *The Red Book,* as well as by the later flowering of these ideas.

The distinction Jung makes over time between true and false imagination provides an interesting lens regarding the relative values of the negative and the positive. In 1911, prior to his *Red Book,* in his

chapter "Two Kinds of Thinking,"[9] in *Symbols of Transformation* Jung
values directed thinking over the lesser value of fantasy.[10] In 1913,
however, Jung states: "The psyche creates reality every day. The only
expression I can use for this activity is *fantasy*. ... It is the mother of
all possibilities, where, like all psychological opposites, the inner and
outer worlds are joined together in living union."[11] Fantasy then joins
the inner and the outer in living and thereby potentially accessible
form. Jung further expresses the positive potential embedded in false
imagination claiming that the so-called useless fantasies must
undergo a process. In fact, they must have to be made valuable and
"[i]n order to unearth the treasures they contain they must be
developed a stage further."[12] These ideas are in reference to both the
creative aspects within the arc of false imagination and the
dependence on the relational/dialogic for mining both true and false
imagination's preeminent value, albeit a value that hinges on the
participation of the ego. In the same paragraph, Jung recognizes, "It
is therefore short-sighted to treat fantasy, on account of its risky or
unacceptable nature, as a thing of little worth. It must not be forgotten
that it is just in the imagination that a man's highest value may lie."[13]
I highlight Jung's use of the word "may" here because the value
embedded within the positive and negative aspects of imagination
may not and often never does come to fruition. The duplicity and
duplexity of the mercurial are rampantly at work in psychic
expression. In particular, the territory of false imagination provides
an elucidating lens applicable to the understanding of the inherent
richness in negative psychic manifestations in general.

It serves here to explore the complex layered nature of imagination. Imagination does not produce anything in concrete external
reality. It does, however, in mercurial fashion borrow from the
concrete. Thus, imagination expresses, through a rather mysterious
amalgam of the invisible but real, psychic experiences rooted in
concretely known reality, visually expressed as images and ideas. The
image relies on the specific for the presentation of the immaterial
(source level, the unlimited, the illimitable). This constitutes a paradoxical conjunction of opposites par excellence. It resonates to the
energies and forms Jung maps as the "double nature of Mercurius."[14]

It is expressive of the pervasive mystery of the relationship between the one and the two underlying psychic process. It serves analytic work to recognize and value that the arc of psychic expression includes, like the mercurial, the highest of the high and the lowest of the low.[15] In "The Magician" (Liber Secundus) drafted in Black Book 7 on January 27, 1914, Jung reflects this reality: "I would like to kick the garbage away from me, if the golden seed were not in the vile heart of the misshapen form."[16] The high and the low both partake of the archetypal and the visually concrete, i.e., the duplex. In the instance of complexes, for example, there is a structural twofold quality composed of an archetypal core and what is sometimes referred to as a personal shell. The latter is resonant to the limited and the specific and provides adequate or inadequate housing, so to speak, for the archetypal provision at its core. Working with their duplex nature is an example of the necessary and valuable work with the negative in order to redeem the positive, i.e., the gold seed. The vile and the misshapen in clinical work are of the deepest value both implicitly and directly throughout Jung's writings. This can be deeply challenging for both analysand and analyst. Jung himself in 1915, while writing "The Magician," struggled with the necessity of valuing the low, the contradictory, the paradoxical, in short, the challenging territory of the "mercurial serpent." In his conversation with the serpent in Liber Secundus, he states: "We stand in the vastness, wed to the serpent, and consider which stone could be the foundation stone of the building which we do not yet know."[17] He further states: "The most ancient? It is suitable as a symbol. We want something graspable. ... The devil is probably supposed to create it ..." and further, "[the devil] emerged from the lump of manure in which the Gods had secured their eggs."[18] This passage expresses the essential contradiction in one-sidedly regarding the negative/false as useless. The gold seeds/eggs that are buried/gestated within the manure may be extracted. Interestingly, manure gives off heat, which is essential to gestational/ripening processes. The agency of renewal inherent in both the eggs and the manure are in evidence in the statement of an anonymous alchemical commentator: "Thus the Word of renewal is invisibly inherent in all things ..."[19] In addition, the devil him/herself specifically emerges from the manure. The function of the mercurial, the daimon/demon, the two/one, sponsors movement extending from unconscious predifferentiation through separation, equilibration, and ultimately to varying degrees of synthesis, including preparation for subsequent rounds of process.

Returning to the informing lens of Jung's theoretical treatment of fantasy/imagination, it should be noted that 21 years later, Jung's conception shifted again. In 1935, in Tavistock Lecture V, he forgoes the valuing of the encompassing arc of imagination so central to his thought in the intervening years. His focus turns to active imagination as a technique. In this lecture, Jung states: "I really prefer the term 'imagination' to 'fantasy,' because there is a difference between the two which the old doctors had in mind when they said that 'opus nostrum,' our work, ought to be done 'per veram imaginationem et non phantastica' ... In other words, ... fantasy is mere nonsense, a phantasm, a fleeting impression; but imagination is active, purposeful creation."[20] He says further that fantasy is "more or less your own invention, and remains on the surface of personal things and conscious expectations," while "active imagination, as the term denotes, means that the images have a life of their own and that the symbolic events develop according to their own logic—that is, of course, if your conscious reason does not interfere."[21]

At the heart of active imagination as a technique is the dialogue between ego and non-ego, ego as the noninterfering but sometimes challenging voice that stands separate face-to-face with the voice of the inner other. A genuine vis-à-vis is achieved when these paradoxically unequal opposites stand as functional equals.

In Jung's shift of 1935, false imagination was discarded as one-sidedly negative. In keeping with this perspective, in his Eranos lecture of 1936 Jung states that, "imaginatio... [is] the real and literal power to create images ... the active evocation of (inner) images *secundum naturam*, an authentic feat of thought or ideation, which does not spin aimless and groundless fantasies 'into the blue' ... but tries to grasp the inner facts and portray them in images true to their nature."[22] False imagination becomes fantastical, "a mere 'conceit' in the sense of insubstantial thought," "something ridiculous."[23] False imagination then becomes something to "kick away." It is no longer of value.

The shifts and contradictions woven into Jung's expression of his developing thought attest to his dedication to remaining true and alive to his experiences of and researches into psyche. These statements regarding the complex and paradoxical positive potential of the entire arc of imagination characterize Jung's thinking from 1913 until 1935. In retrospect, this arc of valuing is applicable to positive and negative manifestations in psyche as well.

I posit the usefulness and necessity of deeply valuing the entire arc of psychic expression of both negative and positive as it manifests in clinical work. In fact, in any analytic hour we as analysts "stand in the vastness, wed to the serpent."[24] This reflects moment to moment in clinical process the necessity, the monumental task, of reading and valuing the dual meaning of all expressions of psyche that form the *prima materia*, including those in the form of the stone of little worth. Doing so supports recovery of the discarded inherent value embedded in the negative.

The conjunction of the gold seed and the garbage is profoundly expressed in myriad permutations in Jung's treatment of ideas, including that of the *paradoxa*,[25] the unity of the opposites, the Pleroma, the figure of Abraxas, the figure of Mercurius, the "mercurial serpent,"[26] the paradoxically existent-nonexistent, the *coincidentia oppositorum*, and the circular distillation (processes of differentiation/integration). Each of these territories profoundly maps both the structural and dynamic provisions essential to the use of both positive and negative psychic expressions as they are brought into clinical process. Because of the limitations in the scope of this paper, I will restrict myself to exemplifying these understandings, theoretically and clinically, through the ideas of *paradoxa*, the Pleroma, Abraxas, the figure of Mercurius, and the daimon/demon.

For example, in Jung's treatment of the *paradoxa*, he shines light on the predifferentiated unity of the opposites (two-in-one) through his understanding of the mysterious transformative arcane substance: "Characteristically, the paradoxes cluster most thickly round the arcane substance, which was believed to contain the opposites in

uncombined form as the prima materia, and to amalgamate them as
the lapis Philosophorum."[27] The arcane substance contains the
opposites in undifferentiated form as *prima materia* or *lapis exilis* (the
stone of little worth) at the beginning of any round of process and
shifts to an amalgamated form as the *lapis philosophorum* at the end
of any round of transformative process. The *lapis* as *prima materia* is
both "base and noble, or precious and *parvi momenti* (of little
moment)."[28]

Jung describes this state of preexistence/potentiality in the "First
Sermon to the Dead," published privately in 1916, through naming
pairs of predifferentiated opposites (the two in one) that characterize
the Pleroma: "… the effective and the ineffective, the fullness and the
emptiness, the living and the dead, the different and the same, light
and darkness, hot and cold, force and matter, time and space, good
and evil, the beautiful and the ugly, the one and the many, etc."[29] The
potentiality therein is realized through processes of separation and
synthesis. The contradictory formulation of the pleromatic essence
(both one and two, existent and nonexistent) permeates the unfolding
of Jung's thought. It lies as a treasure within *The Red Book*, both on
the seed level and in Jung's heroic rounds of engagement with it.

The predifferentiated energy underlying any pair of opposites
is also expressed in the paradoxical figure of Abraxas, the representation of the all-encompassing God in *The Red Book*, a paradoxical
unity of the "*summum bonum*," and the "*infinum malum*."[30] Jung's
statement, "Abraxas produces truth and lying, good and evil, light
and darkness, in the same word and in the same act"[31] is an early
dramatic expression of his structural emphasis on the *coincidentia
oppositorum*[32] and the implicit dynamic sponsorship of psychic
process implied in the phrase "Abraxas produces."

Almost three decades later, in the essay titled "The Spirit
Mercurius," we see a reverberation of the psychic realities expressed
by the figure of Abraxas in Jung's articulation of the figure of
Mercurius. Both unite the opposites, can be destructive or creative,
and are the highest of the high the lowest of the low.[33] Jung writes that
Mercurius is "undoubtedly akin to the godhead; …[and] … is found
in the sewers."[34] Further, Jung states that "the 'heart' of Mercurius is

at the North Pole" and is the "true fire". That is "the heavenly spirit within."[35] This corresponds to the *stella maris* which "stands for the fiery center in us from which creative or destructive influences come."[36] This position of the "heart of Mercurius" expresses his/her importance as a guiding, orienting agency. Mercurial bivalence is endemic to psychic material. Understanding this pervasive truth provides a primary tool in clinical practice. Clinical material, like Mercurius, is also "the process by which the lower and material is transformed into the higher and spiritual, and vice versa."[37] This corresponds to the alchemical process of the circular distillation (processes of differentiation/integration).[38] Viewing clinical material through this lens serves the effort of being consciously in the presence of "the devil, a redeeming psychopomp, an evasive trickster, and God's reflection in physical nature."[39] The arc of Jung's thought thus casts the complex figure of Mercurius as an exemplar of structural wholeness and dynamic sponsorship of wholeness. The core aspect that allows the neutral potentiality of Mercurius and its magnetic heart of ambiguity to function as a bridge between the pairs of opposites is that of having qualities that are both the same (or similar) and different. This supports processes of linking and equilibration which further differentiate and lead toward integration.

The bivalent potentiality of mercurial energy is likewise expressed by the likeness and the difference between the figure of the daimon/demon, expressive of the split between the negative and positive, between the high and low poles of Mercurius. The division of the one into the two is expressly descriptive of a psychic stage following separative processes. In the history of Western thought, Christianity split the *duplex* nature of Mercurius,[40] reducing the demon to the one-sidedly negative. The flattened Christian view of the paradoxical, creative, mercurial psychic provisions reverberates in how profoundly ego-dystonic analysands tend to experience the rich provisions accessible to the work through the psychic factors that allow for the making of projection, complex formation, defense, etc. One of the challenges in clinical work is containing and working with the *materia* in such a way that the dross as well as the gold is accessed, accepted, challenged, and potentially transformed. As Jung says in

Chapter XI of *Liber Secundus*, "You are entirely unable to live without evil."[41] Psychic process depends on the double nature of psyche. In *Liber Primus*, Jung refers to this bivalence, this "terrible ambiguity,"[42] in terms of the relativity of the new, more encompassing God that comprises both poles of the opposites. He engages in a deep and troubled reflection: "How can man live in the womb of the God if the Godhead himself attends only to one-half of him?"[43] "That is the ambiguity of the God ... Unequivocalness is simplicity and leads to death. But ambiguity is the way of life."[44]

The terrible negative aspect of the twofold nature of psyche does provide all of those psychic expressions I map within the arc of the negative. The negativizing of the myriad expressions of the source level/the divine as caught in matter—i.e., made manifest in the limited and lived—is necessary for expression. The mismatch between the unlimited and the limited, between the spiritual and the concrete lived, requires psychic suffering. However, the mismatch itself, the conjunction of opposites in psyche (including good and evil), is what allows for process and ultimately for the realization of the paradoxically existent-nonexistent in realized form, albeit a form characterized by a dual nature. This reality supports processes of individuation. On a radical level, it reverberates to the realization of the living God, the whole man, even though this is never fully achieved. Clearly, the valuing of all of those expressions that conform to the pole of the common, the mundane, the evil, and the false must be accorded their place in clinical practice. As the alchemist Gerhard Dorn exhorts "transform yourselves into living philosophical stones!"[45]

Clinical Material: The Case of Mara

Understanding the paradoxical twoness in oneness in clinical material is at the heart of tapping into the mystery of the mercurial psychic provision. Although it is easy to get hopelessly mired in the psychic "dung-heaps," the hands-on understanding of the conjunction of gold and dross in psychic *materia* serves as a reliable compass for orienting to the mercurial complexity and provision in the clinical hour. The key concepts at work in *Liber Novus* and elaborated throughout Jung's life provided a clinically applicable lens in the analytic process of a 62-year-old woman I am calling Mara.

When Mara entered analysis, she was in crisis, in utter despair, following a radical mastectomy necessitated by breast cancer. Although a professional artist, she had stopped painting a year before. She is the second wife of a wealthy older man with whom she had been having an affair for five years until his wife divorced him. They married and had three children. His first four children, fearing they would lose their inheritance, bullied Mara. Mara attempted to ingratiate herself to his children in an unconsciously manipulative way. Her conscious position that all seven children be treated equally was consonant with her consciously committed spiritual ideas. She attempted to win her stepchildren's love while being blind to her shadowy self-manipulation and manipulation of the other. The positive value and negative means formed an unconscious conjunction (the gold seed and the "manure"/dross).

Although loathed and sadistically, tyrannically controlled and abused by both her parents, Mara idealized and blindly submitted to them. As a consequence, Mara internalized both the imprints of neglect and compensatory accommodation to abuse and abusers. At the same time, she reacted against the resultant inner and outer restrictions. Her reactivity manifested symptomatically, compulsively, self-destructively. As an adolescent, she had endless destructive affairs and chronically abused alcohol and cannabis. Her reactivity was dangerous, defensive, and demonic, truly a "false turning." However, it also daimonically preserved the pathway to self-respect and self-assertion in seed form.

In her marriage, she was one-sidedly submissive, denying, and naively idealizing her husband's neglect and abuse. She persisted in a pattern of devotedly waiting with dinner for him late into the night while he partied without informing her. As we focused on her patterns, her delusions gave way to consciousness of her desperate efforts to create harmony and to protect herself and her children. This also challenged her long-held, distorted narrative of being loved and protected by her parents. Her genuine adherence to positive values was embedded in an ego-syntonic unconsciously distorted sense of personal power. The gold seed of her values was embedded in the "manure" of wrong-order self-sacrifice and an illusion of personal power.

Through careful processes of circumambulation and resultant awareness of the disjunction between the positive and negative aspects of this pattern, Mara realized that both her core values and the destructiveness of her denials and manipulations protected no one. She gradually came to see the embedded value of this long-held twofold pattern for her psychic survival. This opened her to being able to tolerate and value in a differentiated way the hitherto unconscious conflation of positive and negative. In her initial material, the proverbial "hand of God ... in the shit"[46] is in ample evidence.

Jung further articulates the unconscious as an entry point to accessing the embedded gold. In his conversation with the serpent in *Liber Secundus*, he speaks about the necessity of the devilishly graspable.[47] The graspable stone, psychically speaking, is all that lies within the arc of expression of the *lapis exilis*. The "fateful detours" scripted by the dynamic relationship between the gold and the dross (daimon/demon) must be valued in clinical process. The paradoxical state of the *prima materia* as a predifferentiated unity carries within it the agency of differentiation. In part, this sponsorship is accessed through support of dual mercurial agency.

The mysterious complex roots of the figure of the devil (daimon/demon) warrant an examination of the figure itself as well as the etymology of the word. The structure and dynamic within this figure provide a key to tapping into processes of psychic agency. The figure of the devil, like Mercurius, is of the highest and the lowest. At the root level, the devil and the Divine have the same origin: It is the bifold predifferentiated source level that thereby sponsors process. We see this mysterious and paradoxical agency in clinical work at every turn. Etymologically, the arc of words, including demon, daimon, devil is expressive of agencies resonant in critically important separative processes. Many words beginning with di-, de-, dis-, dai-are related to the twofold, the double, the twice, the false, the separative, the dismembering, the ego dystonic, and psychically pertain to the processes of coming apart and back together essential to individuation. In clinical process, the "negative" aspect of this duplex agency manifests through the limited and concrete. Manifestation in this form is necessary to the realization of the Divine in lived life. Working with the pervasively present "lump of manure" taps into the agency of its heat/energy and accesses the embedded gold seed.

Typically, clinical material is presented in predifferentiated form, a kind of monolithic yet unconscious layering in which the opposites lie as one. The "compulsive" magnetic energies, richly and energetically supplied by emotion support direct focus in the clinical hour to the provision within the "negative." In my experience, despite the reality of what Liliana Wahba calls "expressions of … incurable, unalterable evil,"[48] the presence of the positive within the negative is nearly ubiquitous. As analysts, we labor to "… draw the arcane substance to the surface in order to prepare from it the *filius philosophorum, the lapis.*"[49]

Mara's conjoint forms of the positive and the negative (including the monstrous form of the conjunction) underwent successive changes. Through valuing emotional expression, including the hot gestational "manure" in which we find both the smelly, repulsive mercurial energies as well as the hidden eggs of the gods, we were able to tap into the twofold psychic provisions at each successive stage of differentiation.

When we encounter a paradoxical unity of the opposites, whether in predifferentiated or conflated form, the inherent provisions for process within the psychic structure and dynamic lie dormant.

In the initial sessions, Mara described a long repetitive search for meaning, which she had pursued through attending, by her own description, an "endless cycle of self-help workshops." I was informed by her use of the word "endless" that her one-sided defensive mode of attempting to take care of herself was fraying. After the mastectomy, she desperately increased her attendance at these workshops, but it had not helped. It was clear that the emotional heat of her suffering was overriding her defensive adaptation.

The "hand of God" was visible both in her devastating suffering as well as her attachment to spiritual values. Her suffering echoed Jung's expression in "Descent into Hell in the Future": It was an "infernal poison and agonizing death."[50] This suffering in Mara's journey carried a connection to the sacred through the dark side of the daimon/demon twinship. The dynamic between the daimon/demon, the positive and the "negative," the true and the false in psychic expression is complex, often frightening, and deeply challenging. In citing the Ebionites, Jung states: "Two, they assert, were raised up by God, the one Christ, the other the devil."[51] The structural and dynamic provisions within the two-and-one provide a hands-on clinical tool. This understanding guided me in the delicate back-and-forth work between symbol and symptom, image and activation. It further supported the process in the navigation of danger and positive potential. Mara brought the following initial dream into the fifth session:

> I dream that I go into the sea. I can see that at the bottom of the deep sea there is a bottle. A snake is trapped inside the bottle. It is badly hurt with wounds and sores on its skin. It seems like it has been there for a long time. The bottle has a hole in it through which the snake can creep out. There is a hand with a small stick. This hand—I don't know if it is yours or mine—seeks to guide the snake so it can come out through the hole in the bottle.

My initial and tentative response was to see the dream as a confirmation of the deep wounds and entrapment of the energy expressed by the figure of the mercurial serpent, a process-supporting provision that presses purposively for wholeness although frequently in an as yet undifferentiated, threatening, or threatened form. The image of the serpent pictures Mara's psyche, both historically and in the present. Despite the power of her defensive idealization, I tentatively saw the dream as prognostically positive. The dream expresses energies of guidance, possibility of escape, and the ambiguous dual efficacy in Mara's association to the guiding hand as "yours or mine," expressive of a mercurial provision. It suggested both the positive potential in the transference and her latent internal reverberant capacity for guidance. Further agency is also expressed through the ambiguity/contradiction in the image of the trapped serpent that is able to creep out.

In circumambulating the dream material, Mara thought it expressed that she was on the verge of profound immediate magical healing and renewal, rather than as information about potential process. Her unconsciousness of the wounds and entrapment of the serpent image informed the necessary focus on the "negative."

In both the dream text and Mara's associations, psyche presents critically important expressions of the mercurial: ambiguity, contradiction, and paradox. This mercurial sponsorship thus implicitly expressed is essential to the making of the "spagyric medicine"[52] and its meaning of taking apart and putting back together. The activation and healing of the shape-shifting capacity of the wounded mercurial agency was to be of primary importance in the process. This gradually supported her to forgo her reliance on her defensive pattern of idealization and further potentiate the dialogic relationship between ego and non-ego resources. The operational denial of personal agency, the projection of God entirely outside, so in evidence in the *prima materia*, is thus countered in the dream text. The work initially focused on ego consolidation and differentiation, shadow, and defensive structures. Murray Stein's statement regarding shadow, i.e., that "the seeds of psychological renewal and of possible future directions for life lie hidden within it"[53] apply equally to the broader arc of negative psychic expression.

As we circled the material, my task was to support Mara's emerging ability to tolerate and even to value the manifestations of the negative. This was the beginning of a challenging new dynamic between ego and non-ego. Jung's dialogue in *The Red Book* models this challenge. For Mara, this would be a lengthy process. Her ego investment in an immediate transformation and her assumption that I was to be a magical healer was temporarily useful. She had hope, which I protected while gently supporting process opening to the value of the limited and the illimitable, the positive and the negative, the demonic and daimonic within her. Her idealizing transference provided the space for her to shift the complex relationship between ego and non-ego.

Bearing this in mind, I will turn now to the dream text and the multiplicity of patterns and dynamics expressed through the symbolic/archetypal.

In the dream text, the ego enters into the realm of the unconscious and is afforded a view of the bottom of the sea without putting her at risk. This gave me a perspective for which she, at this point, was unprepared. This dual perspective (albeit carried in the analytic relationship) maps the beginning for Mara of the in-between mercurial space essential to separative processes. Mara's first steps toward a genuine and ego syntonic connection between ego and non-ego were expressed through the field. Although separative processes must sometimes, as in Mara's case, be initially carried by the analyst, they are primarily accessed through expressions of "false imagination" ranging from simple differentiation to horrific dismemberment.

In the dream, a grievously wounded serpent is trapped in a transparent glass bottle. Mara's defensive structures left her blind to the serpent's woundedness. In *The Red Book*, Jung links separation and unification as functions of the archetypal energy of the serpent[54] to both Mercurius and the devil. He/she is "the serpent that fertilizes, kills, and devours itself and brings itself to birth again."[55]

It was left to me to hold the monstrous conjunction of the horrifically wounded serpent and Mara's idealizations. The activated, painful internal sparks of emotion resulting from her illness and dismemberment as well as from her suppressed unconscious knowledge of the endangerment to her children released in her a provision, a burning desire (*vinum ardens*), that was still ensnared in her pattern of denial.

As the darkness in her unconscious defensive structures started to differentiate, she experienced loss of the illusion of protection and a blow to the idealized sense of self. I was heartened at that point in the process by Jung's words in *Liber Primus*: "Therefore on your journey be sure to take golden cups full of the sweet drink of life, red wine, and give it to dead matter, so that it can win life back. The dead matter will change into black serpents. Do not be frightened, the serpents will immediately put out the sun of your days, and a night with wonderful will-o'-the-wisps will come over you."[56] In Mara's process, the mercurial agency did not immediately extinguish the previously ruling principle of consciousness. The fragrance of the "sweet drink of life" intermingled with the still great pain of her as yet unfulfilled desires to be whole, to hold, and to protect. Jung's injunction to not be frightened, to be prepared for the difficulties that lie ahead, is germane here at this point of shift in process. "Will-o'-the-wisps," a light that magnetically draws travelers in the dark from the safety of the established path, also known as *ignus fatus,* meaning foolish fire, is an apt reference to the stage at which the energy of the daimon/demon becomes accessible.

For Mara, this form of the mercurial energy was both threatening and guiding. She needed to be pulled from the old "fateful path" into the unknown toward the positive value embedded within the previously relied-upon negative.

The mercurial magnetic attraction to wholeness within Mara had been suppressed by the patterns of endangerment and compensatory defensive structures. As these structures were becoming conscious, the resource of her desires burst through their preserved state within the constrictive established defenses. The conjunction of the aliveness and the woundedness in the mercurial sponsorship became available for differentiation in the work. With further ego consolidation, we began to mine the positive embedded value and to appreciate the protection of the previous defense.

One of the core meanings of the energies of Mercurius, like that of Hermes, is the ability to shape-shift, to serve the goal of wholeness whether through good or ill. According to the text, the dreamed serpent has the ability to come out of the bottle. However, psychically speaking, the serpent was trapped. The mercurial agency had to be inactive in order to protect her.

At this point, it was clear that the agony and threat Mara was experiencing was in part responsible for this activation of the mercurial capacity to shift. At this early point, Mara was simultaneously experiencing intense demonic, emotional pain and the stirrings of accessible, positive psychic provisions.

The entrapment of the wounded serpent within the bottle guided me to focus on the containment and restoration of the provisions of the mercurial agency. The reverberation to the alchemical *vas* as *bene clausum* emphasizes the function of containment.

To further this process, I suggested that Mara should draw the dream. She enthusiastically drew a bottle containing a serpent. As in the dream, the bottle had a hole in it. It was perfectly round and evenly cut and so small that despite the extreme skinniness of the wounded serpent, it could not make its way out of the hole. Even with the help of the "guiding hand" the restoration of the shape-shifting capacity of the mercurial sponsorship would be necessary.

In discussing the drawing, Mara made no mention of the serpent's wounds. I read this as a necessity to work with and honor her complexes and defenses, while at the same time being informed of the capacities within the still wounded mercurial agency. I gradually and carefully reflected points of shadowy psychic dimensionality in the narrative while supporting her genuine spiritual values.

Her association to the guiding hand holding a small stick in the drawing was the same as in the dream text: She did not know if it was my hand or hers. This informed me that the availability of the provisions of the duplex mercurial within the field was more ego-near than in the contradictory gap between the imprisonment of the serpent and its ability to exit the hole (shape-shifting function).

These early expressions of mercurial provision mapped a foundational precursor and pathway to the development of a genuine and safe dialogue between conscious and unconscious. Her current extreme distress paradoxically pushed her to forgo the no longer sufficient defenses toward a greater potentiality for wholeness.

A first-order task with Mara was to hold within myself the reality of the embeddedness of the gold seed within the dross. I focused on both the blocks and the capacities expressed in the wounds to her ability to tolerate a realistic scope of wholeness as well as to release and develop the inherent mercurial support for process. Our focus alternated between reflections of both the ego syntonic positive aspects as well as tapping into and differentiating the resources within the dross itself. The value of that which Mara typically "kicked away" was now pressing into accessibility.

Thus the dream, the drawing, and the analytic process both strengthened her ego and opened the potentialities embedded within the "wrong turnings." Mara was challenged to develop the ability to tolerate and even embrace the unwelcome and difficult. She gradually came to see and value the positive within the negative, and to engage in the work of both extracting the gold from the dross and working the material of the dross. She was gradually able to find/make a psychic center within which she could tolerate the demonic and the daimonic within her patterns.

At the beginning of our work together, she had self-identified one-sidedly as highly spiritual and ideal, yet mysteriously subject to mistreatment and victimization. She gradually developed under-standing and compassion for herself. She became increasingly able to discuss, face, and even value the negative in herself. For example, she began to realize her own unconscious manipulative behavior in her attempts to relate to her stepchildren. Step-by-step, her denial, distortion of reality, and one-sided identification with her ideals became clear. Mara realized both that she had unconsciously been attempting to manipulate her stepchildren in order to protect her own. She also admitted to consciousness the clear evidence that her stepchildren hated her and wished to manipulate their father in order to disinherit her. Although these realizations shocked her, she nonetheless was able to own her desire to protect her own children and still extend fair treatment to her stepchildren. In the realization of her denial of their hatred, she began to take responsibility for her role in the patterns of victimization in her life. Mara sacrificed her naïveté and grounded her differentiated values in concrete, dis-criminated action. She resumed painting and went back to exhibiting her artwork in galleries. She stopped inviting the stepchildren, and confronted and challenged her husband to treat all of the children fairly. She did not simply accept her husband's word regarding the will. She participated with a lawyer in crafting a document that would serve all fairly. She was able to extract the gold seeds of the loving protective energy toward her children as well as the spiritual value of integrity and fairness toward all from her previous unconscious shadowy trickster behavior.

It was a suffering for her to realize that she had been unconsciously living out of behaviors and attitudes that were so deeply contrary to her values. She also came to understand and differentiate the negative form to which she had been subject and the embedded value within the negative. She developed a receptive humility. She forwent even residual false obeisance.

Understanding the unconscious conjunction of the dark and the light in her prior position allowed her to realize her pattern of shadowy, destructive self-manipulation and manipulation of others, as well as to redeem the embedded gold seed of her core spiritual values. The result was a gradually enriched, though challenging, dialectical relationship within both the analytic and intrapsychic field. The sufficient holding in the analytic relationship (clinical *vas*) supported her dimensionality to accept and work with the complex mercurial psychic provisions without injury or reactivity. After eight years of analysis, Mara had attained to a mature capacity to self-regulate. She achieved a secure ground from which to embrace and work with the ongoing ups and downs of life with support of a richly internal capacity for dialogue between ego and non-ego.

Conclusion

Jung's recording in *The Red Book* of his psychic experiences has far-reaching expression in his articulation of theory. His profoundly meaningful and interrelated elaborations lay bare the encounter of his ego with various personifications of psychic energies and voices, both syntonic and dystonic to the ego. The expressions of this encounter experientially mapped the developing vis-à-vis between the ego and non-ego. The energies of multiplicity and unity, paradox, mercurial energies, the *lapis exilis/lapis philosophorum*, the daimonic/demonic, the arcane substance, the making of the "medicine," and circular distillation are in evidence in his process. Jung's experiences and his honing of them into theory have inspired me and informed my clinical work. The development of a dialectical relationship between ego and non-ego is supported by analytic technique based on the intricate structural and dynamic interrelationship of polarized (valuable and valueless) aspects of life and psyche. Key to this process is the recognition and reconnection with the profound value of gold seed embedded within the negative as well as in the energetic value in the mercurial heat of the "manure" itself. This is laid bare in Jung's early and rueful acceptance of the necessity of valuing the negative as reflected in his statement of 1916, "I would like to kick the garbage away from me, if the golden seed were not in the vile heart of the misshapen form." The heart of Jungian technique is informed by the inclusion and use of these dark aspects of psychic means. Psychic realization of the inner divine in life hinges on the all-important dance between the purely psychic and the concrete lived (including emotion), between the material and the immaterial, between the limited and the unlimited. Valuing psychic material as presented in the clinical hour in its totality, approaching pre-differentiated material with an understanding of its paradoxical twofold nature, and supporting differentiation into discrete related or opposing energies requires standing in a clinical attitude of accepting and valuing all psychic manifestation from a stance of attuned discrimination. This method is designed to access the gold seed in the "manure" and to utilize the energetic value in the mercurial heat of the "manure" itself.

Endnotes

[1] C.G. Jung, *The Red Book: Liber Novus*, ed. Sonu Shamdasani, trans. John Peck, Mark Kyburz, and Sonu Shamdasani (New York, NY: W.W. Norton, 2009), 320.

[2] Although the dance between the ego and the non-ego is complex and highly orchestrated, I include the entire arc of expressions coming dominantly from the source level whether through images, dreams, visions, synchronicities, constellations, or activation defenses, symptom formation, and projection. By non-ego, I refer to what we might think of as the source level provisions, sponsorships, and agencies, whether expressed closer to the archetypal pole of the instinct archetype arc or, on the other hand, nearer the instinct pole of that arc. I engage with the non-ego as that agency Jung refers as "immortal" (C.G. Jung, *Aion. Research into the Phenomenology of the Self,* in *CW,* vol. 9/II (Princeton, NJ: Princeton University Press, 1959), pars. 348-349) as that agency outside the conscious ego which prompts, directs, stirs us outside the province of the directed ego. I choose to use the term ego and non-ego in order to further a "working" differentiation between those agencies coming from nearer the pole of the unconscious from those coming from nearer the pole of the conscious ego.

[3] C.G. Jung, "The Transcendent Function," in *CW,* vol. 8 (Princeton, NJ: Princeton University Press, 1969), Prefatory Note.

[4] C.G. Jung, *Psychology and Alchemy,* in *CW,* vol. 12 (Princeton, NJ: Princeton University Press, 1968), par. 6.

[5] C.G. Jung, *Psychological Types,* in *CW,* vol. 6 (Princeton, NJ: Princeton University Press, 1971), par. 78.

[6] Jung, *The Red Book,* 359.

[7] C.G. Jung, *Aion. Research into the Phenomenology of the Self,* in *CW,* vol. 9/II (Princeton, NJ: Princeton University Press, 1968), par. 20.

[8] C.G. Jung, *Mysterium Coniunctionis,* in *CW,* vol. 14 (Princeton, NJ: Princeton University Press, 1963), par. 153.

[9] C.G. Jung, *Symbols of Transformation,* in *CW,* vol. 5 (Princeton, NJ: Princeton University Press, 1956), par. 4.

[10] Ibid., par. 20.

[11] Jung, *Psychological Types, CW* 6, par. 78.

[12] Ibid., par. 93.

[13] Ibid.

[14] Jung, *Aion, CW* 9/II, par. 234.

[15] The "Aurelia occulta" gives a graphic description of Mercurius: "By the philosophers I am named Mercurius; my spouse is the [philosophic] gold; I am the old dragon, found everywhere on the globe of the earth, father and mother, young and old, very strong and very weak, death and resurrection, visible and invisible, hard and soft; I descend into the earth and ascend to the heavens, I am the highest and the lowest … I am the carbuncle of the sun, the most noble purified earth, through which you may change copper, iron, tin, and lead into gold." See C.G. Jung, "The Spirit Mercurius," in *CW*, vol. 13 (Princeton, NJ: Princeton University Press, 1967), par. 267.

[16] Jung, *The Red Book*, 320. In the original in German: "Ich möchte mit einem Fußtritt den Unrat von mir stossen, wenn das goldene Korn nicht wäre im eklen Herzen der Missgestalt." Murray Stein provides an alternative translation from the German that expands the spectrum of meaning: "I would like to push the filth away from me, if the golden grain were not in the loathsome heart of the monstrosity."

[17] Jung, *The Red Book*, 320.

[18] Ibid.

[19] C.G. Jung, "The Spirit Mercurius," in *CW* 13 , par. 271.

[20] C.G. Jung, "The Tavistock Lectures," in *CW*, vol. 18 (Princeton, NJ: Princeton University Press, 1976), par. 396.

[21] Ibid., par. 397.

[22] Jung, *Psychology and Alchemy, CW* 12, par. 219.

[23] Ibid.

[24] Jung, *The Red Book*, 320.

[25] Jung, *Mysterium Coniunctionis, CW* 14, pars. 36-103.

[26] "The purified and nourished serpent in alchemy is the mercurial serpent, the Ouroboros, which is connected with the round thing. It is one of the basic symbols in alchemy and refers to Mercury, not as ordinary mercury or quicksilver, but to the god or spirit Mercury. The serpent is a Gnostic symbol for the spinal cord and the basal ganglia, because a snake is mainly backbone. Snakes are weird and strange, and on account of this, they have been used as a symbol for the unconscious since olden times. If the unconscious can be localized anywhere, it is in the basal ganglia, and it has the same uncanny character. The snake really represents the vegetative psyche, the basis of the instincts, if one may express it in that way. It is here (and in this place in the human being) that the greatest secret is to be found, the

panacea, the universal medicine; and, according to the text, fortunate indeed is the man who finds it." See C.G. Jung, *History of Modern Psychology: Lectures Delivered at ETH Zurich. Volume 1, 1933-1934*, ed. Ernst Falzeder, trans. Mark Kyburz, John Peck, and Ernst Falzeder (Princeton, NJ: Princeton University Press, 2018), 97.

[27] Jung, *Mysterium Coniunctionis, CW* 14, par. 36.

[28] Ibid.

[29] Jung, *The Red Book*, 347.

[30] Ibid., 350.

[31] Ibid.

[32] Jung, "The Spirit Mercurius," *CW* 13, par. 256.

[33] Ibid., par. 267.

[34] Ibid., par. 269.

[35] Ibid., par. 256, including footnote 8.

[36] Jung, *Aion, CW* 9/II, par. 212.

[37] Jung, "The Spirit Mercurius," *CW* 13, par. 284.

[38] "The alchemists were fond of picturing their *opus* as a circulatory process, as a circular distillation or as the uroboros, the snake biting its own tail" (see Jung, *Aion, CW* 9/II, par. 418).

[39] Jung, "The Spirit Mercurius," *CW* 13, par. 284.

[40] Jung, *Mysterium Coniunctionis, CW* 14, par. 117.

[41] Jung, *The Red Book*, 287.

[42] Ibid., 243.

[43] Ibid.

[44] Jung, *The Red Book*, 244.

[45] C.G. Jung, "Psychology and Religion," in *CW*, vol. 11 (Princeton, NJ: Princeton University Press, 1969), par. 154.

[46] Marie-Louise von Franz, "What Happens When We Interpret Dreams?" In L.C. Mahdi, ed., *Betwixt and Between. Patterns of Masculine and Feminine Initiation* (La Salle and London: Open Court, 1987), 434.

[47] Jung, *The Red Book*, 320.

[48] Liliana Liviano Wahba, "Imagination and Evil," in Murray Stein and Thomas Arzt, eds., *Jung's Red Book for Our Time: Searching for Soul under Postmodern Conditions*, Vol. 1 (Asheville, NC: Chiron Publications, 2017), 199.

[49] Jung, *Aion, CW* 9/II, par. 239.

[50] Jung, *The Red Book*, 238.

[51] Jung, "The Spirit Mercurius," *CW* 13, par. 271, footnote 21.

[52] Jung, *Mysterium Coniunctionis, CW* 14, par. 663.

[53] Murray Stein, *In Midlife: A Jungian Perspective* (Dallas, TX: Spring, 1983), 83.

[54] Jung, *The Red Book*, 247.

[55] C.G. Jung, "The Psychology of the Transference," in *CW*, vol. 16 (Princeton, NJ: Princeton University Press, 1966), par. 409.

[56] Jung, *The Red Book*, 244.

Troll Music in *The Red Book*

Gunilla Midbøe

My soul, where are you? Do you hear me? I speak, I call
you—are you there? … What words should I use to tell you
on what twisted paths a good star has guided me to you?
Give me your hand, my almost forgotten soul.[1]

C.G. Jung

On November 12, 1913, Jung wrote in the *Draft* of the text that would
become *Liber Novus*: "… at the beginning of the following month, I
seized my pen and began writing this."[2] From the first lines of *Liber
Primus* to the last word of "Scrutinies," one wonders: Where did this
narrative's language come from? Jung himself was overwhelmed by
the words and images. They reach out beyond time and space, and
he struggled to hold on to his "I," his ego, in order to keep his
experience and his writing contained within the frame of what would
become *The Red Book*.

My curiosity about how *The Red Book*'s narrative was born and
contained within musical rhythms and images grew even stronger
while reading *Trollmusik* by Selma Lagerlöf (1858-1940), the internationally known Swedish writer and first woman to win the Nobel
Prize in Literature in 1909. She wrote this remarkable text shortly
after her debut as a writer, but it was not published until after her
death. There are striking similarities between *The Red Book* and
Trollmusik regarding plot and themes. Both texts are deeply connected
to the importance of integrating shadow figures and experiences into
an individuation journey that never ends.

In this essay I will explore how the experience of a deep connection to dialogical language and "troll music"—a metaphor for

hidden and emergent language—can be connected to Analytical Psychology. To enter into a meaningful relationship with the question of how and why Jung's *Red Book* is a book for our time, I will start with the trolls and introduce them as they appear in Norse mythology and Scandinavian folklore. Then, I will continue with the connections between *Trollmusik* and *The Red Book* as an inspiring language for Jungian psychoanalysis today and finally conclude with a clinical vignette of integration described more extensively in my book *The Elliptical Dialogue*.[3]

Trolls and "the Spirit of the Depths"

The etymology of the Old Norse nouns *troll* and *tröll* developed from the Proto-Germanic neuter noun, *trullan* ("giant," "fiend," "demon," "werewolf"). The origin of this word is unknown.[4] In Scandinavian folklore, trolls became beings in their own right. They live far from human habitation and are, of course, not Christianized. Their appearance varies greatly: They may be ugly and slow-witted, or they may look and behave exactly like human beings. They are sometimes associated with particular landmarks, and in our modern popular culture, they are also depicted in a variety of forms—for instance as "internet trolls."

In this present context, I am referring to the trolls that are associated with mountains and forests where they live together in small family units, can grow very old—well over 100 years—and make gold like the alchemists. They also have language ability and know how to speak. They communicate with each other, tell stories, and express their desires and what they think about how we humans behave in different, remarkable, and surprising ways. I understand trolls as very transformative in their different ways of existence and their communication abilities.

In Nordic literature and musical composition, the most famous example of this is the individuation drama *Peer Gynt* by Henrik Ibsen. When Peer meets the trolls in the Hall of the Mountain King, the Mountain King wants him to live forever. By ripping out his left eye, he takes away Peer's human gaze and gives him troll sight, a tail, and the offer of eternal life. Peer accepts the tail and the troll's clothing, but he leaves the Mountain Hall when he is presented with the possibility of eternal life. He wants to remain human:

> I am willing to swear that a cow is a maid;
> An oath one can always eat up again: –
> But to know that one never can free oneself,
> That one can't even die like a decent soul;
> To live as a hill-troll for all one's days –
> To feel that one never can beat a retreat, –
> As the book has it, that's what your heart is set on;
> But that is a thing I can never agree to.[5]

In the musical composition by Grieg, one can readily imagine the trolls' dance and treading movements and Peer's flight from the Mountain King as he is asked to deny his finite nature. He chooses to live a limited life as a human being, albeit an exuberant one.

Through my mother's family, I am a descendant of the Forest Finns. They migrated from Savonia and Northern Tavastia in Finland and settled in forest areas of Sweden, especially in the province of Värmland, during the early 17th century. While walking in the forests of Värmland, I was told legends about the connection between the Forest Finns and the trolls. "Mieskuva" (the Forest Finn expression for magical images) trees communicate with human beings by way of images. If one looks carefully at the trunk of such a tree, it might be possible to catch sight of a face. It is said that trolls make this imprint for us to consider and contemplate. They make face carvings, according to the legend, if one had been deceitful in earlier relationships, inner or outer. To meet with and look into the eyes of this figure and to begin to talk with the emergent face in the "Mieskuva" tree is like an active imagination where light is on shed on the encounter with shadow. While strolling in the woods, I was also tuned into the sound and language of special trees, the "Kyöri" (English: curved, oblique, crooked). These are trees whose entangled branches make strange sounds when they rub together in the wind. This "troll music" language can be heard even today if one pays attention to the trees bending toward one another. When the wind makes them move together, one can hear a kind of humming, creaking, squeaking sound. "Kyöri" trees play troll music, which is a language for our imagination to understand.

What humans might see and hear in the woods can be found in the illustration by Theodor Kittelsen titled *Skogstroll.*

Theodor Kittelsen: *Skogstroll* (Forest Troll, 1906)

This image connects us with the dark side of our instincts and with nature. The lunar light emanating from the eye invites us to a dialogue with our own shadow figures. If we can tolerate their existence and meet with them, they can help us to individuate.

Magic Language

What is significant about the language in *The Red Book* and *Trollmusik*? The element of timelessness is what struck me most. The narratives remain relevant to our world today, and the language is full of life in a way that connects me to myself. When reading these texts, my imagination starts flowing. I connect to my inner self, and I can continue my dialogue with my spirit of the depths and with my spirit of this time. This feature of stimulating an inner dialogue contributes importantly, in my opinion, to making *The Red Book* a book for our time. The language of *The Red Book* is exceptional in Jung's writings. With his intuition he goes beyond the psychological language of his *Collected Works*.

When reading the works of Selma Lagerlöf, who was a student of depth psychology and Eastern wisdom, the same fascination as I find in Jung's *Red Book* appears for me. From where does all this fantastic language come? Both Lagerlöf and Jung write from the perspective and vision of inclusiveness. Wholeness is their shared vision.

In Lagerlöf's short story *Trollmusik*, published after her death in *Skilda Tider* (*Different Times*), a gifted organ player in a remote parish far from civilization is rehearsing the music for the early service on Christmas Day. At first, he does not understand what is happening to the organ. The organ is known for being untrustworthy because every now and then it begins autonomously to play false and dissonant chords. It misbehaves. This is what it is doing now in this rehearsal. Suddenly, every piece he plays sounds false. The more he practices, the weirder the organ sounds.

As he struggles on, he remembers the story of an ancestor of his who also had played this organ. The story was that this ancestor had denied the trolls the possibility to play their own music in the mountains by destroying their instruments. Ever since then, when the organ plays false, it is because of the spell of the trolls. The organ sounds as if it were screaming in protest from olden times. The trolls had not forgotten the insult and the injustice that had been done to them. The organ player now wants to make up for the injustice and to repair what his ancestor had done. He feels that he owes a huge debt to the trolls. He decides to step away from the organ and go out into the town. There he becomes strangely confused and gets lost, begins to act crazy and behaves as if he does not remember his otherwise usually polite and righteous persona. He spends the night in revelry and drunken madness. When he returns in the morning and sits down at the organ, the sounds it produces are more beautiful than ever before. It is as though magic has taken over and the music is transformed: "The music sent out from the organ on Christmas

Morning was magic (sv. *trolleri*), and the old parish clerk also said, 'Indeed, now all of us are included within the organ and in its tunes, everybody. No difference between trolls, thieves and heretics. We are all incorporated within the organ and finally the trolls also play their instruments as part of the wholeness.'"[6]

The presence of the trolls in the organ now enabled them to take part in the celebration of the birth of the Christ child. They want to be a part of this music even though they are considered to be pagans and pre-Christian heathens. When the organist is able to include their sounds in the music of the church, they become participants in the celebration of the birth of Christ. Now the organ starts to play in clean and melodious tones in a miracle of inspiration that connects heaven and earth and embraces the Mother Earth archetype. "It was a wonder, it was magic,"[7] Selma Lagerlöf writes.

Wherein lies the magic, the enchantment? It is that all is included, all are let in, and all are admitted. Trolls, thieves, and heretics—everyone has a voice, no one is left out. This is the key to the magic of this language.

In *The Red Book,* we also come upon the issue of "magic." What is it? It seems to bear a resemblance to the language of the trolls as Selma Lagerlöf writes about it in *Trollmusik.* It is not part of the normal rational vernacular. It is of a different psychic register.

In Chapter XXI of *The Red Book,* Jung enters into a dialogue with the Magician, Philemon. Strangely enough, I find that Jung's painting of the Philemon bears an uncanny resemblance to the painting of the Forest Troll by Theodor Kittelsen.

In this fascinating dialogue with Philemon, Jung is told that the language of magic is beyond his cognitive ability, rational understanding, and comprehension. Jung is, of course, nonplussed:

I: 'Well I must confess that that is new and strange. So nothing at all about magic can be understood?'
F: 'Exactly. Magic happens to be precisely everything that eludes comprehension.'
I: 'But then how the devil is one to teach and learn magic?'
F: 'Magic is neither to be taught nor learned. It's foolish that you want to learn magic.'[8]

Later, when Jung walks away somewhat dizzily from the small garden where Philemon and his wife Baucis live, he falls into a profound inner reflection. He concludes that one can only be silent about this and make magic into a way of living with the attitude that there is "a great other" that also operates in our lives. If we can remain open to it, then magical operations take place. "Stupidity too is part of this, which everyone has a great deal of, and also tastelessness, which is possibly the greatest nuisance."[9] This seems very similar to what the organist in Lagerlöf's story discovered.

The thought of the great philosopher Ludwig Wittgenstein (1889-1951) can be recognized here. By practicing silence, by animating objects outside oneself as possible communicating phenomena, a dialogue can be created between the "I" and the symbol: "It thinks, speaks."[10] Wittgenstein was contemporary both to Jung and Lagerlöf. In taking the perspective that language and the construction of language account for the creation of human consciousness, what cannot be brought into spoken language must be committed to silence: "What we cannot speak about we must pass over in silence."[11]

Magic and troll music appear to be searching for wholeness in the mode of silence and in openness to the "nonunderstanding," but one never knows with any certainty.

The Elliptical Dialogue

Now I come to the question of what conclusions can be drawn for Jungian psychoanalytical work today from the teachings and dialogues between Philemon and Jung and the metaphorical understanding of "troll music." Analytical Psychology as well as its clinical application, Jungian psychoanalysis, is relational and dialogical in its essence. It is also a fact of our time that professional Jungian groups and societies have developed worldwide. It is global. In South America, throughout all of Europe, in Asia, Australia and New Zealand, and in South Africa, we can find Analytical Psychology being taught and put into practice. The language of Analytical Psychology reaches out through cultural borders and is valid

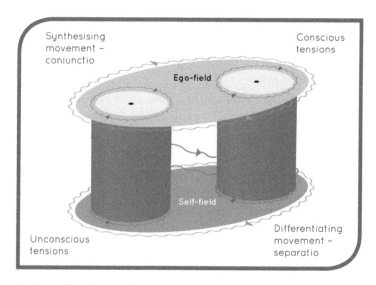

The Elliptical Dialogue in depth dimension (Figure created by Gunilla Midbøe)

regardless of nationality and identity. In a sense, it is timeless and yet it takes the position of making imprint on "the spirit of this time."

I am presenting here the Elliptical Dialogue as a model, based on Jungian theory and practice, for communication in all types of psychotherapy. The geometrical and archetypal form of the ellipsis as shown in the model below is always in movement, indicating the ongoing dialogue in intrapsychic and interpersonal dimensions as well as in unconscious fields of the psyche.[12]

Relational dynamics and language are, as I will show in the following, crucial for analytical work. The "troll music" of the unconscious (the repressed, the shunned, the neglected and forgotten past) has to be played, listened to, and made conscious. The model of the Elliptical Dialogue is grounded in Analytical Psychology and integrates as well the systems theory of Gregory Bateson and Ludwig Wittgenstein's way of seeing language.

Before illustrating the inclusion of "troll music" in the Elliptical Dialogue in a clinical vignette, I wish to indicate some important perspectives from Wittgenstein's conception of language.

Wittgenstein's World—"Now I can go on"

"Now I can go on."[13] What words touch us, move us, and make us go on in our everyday lives? This is where my curiosity takes me when reflecting on the language of *The Red Book* and when drawing implications for the analytical experience within the clinical relationship. In the figure of the Elliptical Dialogue, this is indicated by the elliptical form taken by unspoken and spoken language that passes back and forth between analyst and analysand. Wittgenstein's work can provide us with some resources that can be helpful when we try to grasp the meaning of the fleeting changeable relations and dialogues that we are part of in our daily lives but especially in our practices as psychotherapists and psychoanalysts.

In our analytical work, we are accustomed to taking the *experiences* of clients, as offered to us in the form of inner mental representations of individuals, as our starting point for dialogue and relationship. Maybe then, Wittgenstein's method can offer an important contribution for additional fruitful perspectives on communication because he is concerned with our *practices*: How we get on in everyday life and how we make sense to each other. Here, attention is given to the moment-by-moment changing circumstances surrounding our talk—in gestures, in tonality, in specific words, in rhythm and bodily expressions. These circumstances often are hidden from view and assume no more than a negligible part of our awareness, so we tend to overlook them. Wittgenstein offers ways of grasping our continuously changing sense of living relatedness, both to each other in a dyad and to the larger world around us.

According to Wittgenstein, we live in a flow of irreversible relational activity that ensures that everything we do in practice is a response to another or otherness in our surroundings, and this inevitably relates us to them in some way. The point of Wittgenstein's thought is to direct our attention to something not yet noticed, to point toward something actually present in our surroundings at the moment of use. In effect, he says: "Look at *this*"; "Look at *that*"; "Notice the *details* of these differences"; "Notice the *relations* or *connections* between these details." The purpose of this is, as he says, to give "prominence to distinctions which our ordinary forms of language easily makes us overlook"[14] and to change our "*way of looking at things*"[15] to influence our *styles* of looking and thinking, speaking and listening, reading, touching, remembering, and so on, and to attend to the ways in which we interact with, order, and reorder them. The aim for Wittgenstein in all this is, as I see it, to produce in us "just that understanding which consists in 'seeing connections.'"[16] This is to enable us to notice the links and relations between our talk and the rest of our activities and the environment and context that we have so far failed to notice. The aim of his investigations is to bring to light the very dialogical nature of our everyday communications and to see that something new is always created. It is only by reordering our relations to others and othernesses around us that we can change ourselves—and this is often not easy to do.

"Facing the Void"—A Clinical Vignette

Now, having taken part of in the experiences in *The Red Book* where Jung meets with Philemon and engages in a dialogue about the understanding of magic and with the help of the map of the Elliptical

Dialogue and some perspectives from Wittgenstein, I will describe the end of a rather turbulent analysis with "Björn" (my client) when he became able to say: "I can just go on and try to live as fully as I can."[17]

Jungian psychoanalytic dialogue, which engages in the exploration of liminal intrapsychic space and interpersonal inner and outer realities, and is here referred to as "troll music," is visually presented in the image painted by Björn and titled "Facing the Void."

Facing the Void

The calm night atmosphere in this image resembles that of the seventh Sermon to the Dead in *The Red Book*: "But when Philemon had finished, the dead remained silent. Heaviness fell from them, and they ascended like smoke above the shepherd's fire, who watches over his flock by night."[18] Reflecting on *The Red Book* is helpful for clinical understanding of analytical work today. The dead souls of the Seven Sermons who return from Jerusalem with unanswered questions and unfulfilled demands are unindividuated souls who had to wander the earth in order to complete their life's journey and finally be able to find release and ascend.

My client Björn had come to the end of our work together when he said: "Now I just can go on and try to live as fully as I can." The way to a calmer inner and outer atmosphere had been a long journey with many challenges and violations of the blue frame in the elliptical dialogue that were caused by passionate ruptures.

The analytical journey often includes turning from chaos to order, and the reverse, where openness to "nonunderstanding" ("magic") and levels of meaning beyond words are present. Keen attention is the key to the process of analysis. One of the first words from Björn that entered our dialogue was "fearful," which referred to his initial dream. When I asked him, "What do you mean with the word 'fearful'?" Björn told a story of abuse during childhood and of how he had consequently been caught up in a severe negative father complex all his life. This word, "fearful," set the stage for all that was to follow in the analysis.

Staying with the spoken and unspoken language within the Elliptical Dialogue (in the green elliptical line of the diagram) offers the possibility of transformation through interactive exchange. In Björn's life, the "law" was connected to the "word," and the "word" came from the father. He related that "in my inner world, the words went deep inside myself. My father's words, when I was a child. … And this was the 'given,' the world as my father had spoken it. And at the same time it was different. Something more, something else, and something that was not said. Something that was also true, but no one said that. It was in a place of its own, outside. It was as though it was nonexistent. But it existed, it was present." This reflection emerged in a session of retrospection and consolidation as Björn was weaving together words and images from our work with the father complex. I was able to offer my reflections (along the green elliptical line of the diagram): "But Björn, what kind of words were unpermitted words?" Björn replied: "What comes to my mind now are just words for obstinacy: 'No!' 'Will not!' They could not be spoken, because from these words represented rebellion, denial and commitment of sin. The words 'will not' were very dangerous because then I was in exile." I think that this dialogue was able to emerge due to the mutual experience and trust that Björn and I had developed while working with his images and the various interactions between us, which included connection, several painful ruptures, and subsequent reconnections.

The image titled "Facing the Void" (see above) can be seen as a transference image depicting our analytical relationship. The image portrays a seated couple, connected by their tails but with space between them, surrounded by nature in the form of birds, the moon, flowers, and trees. It is a safe place for looking into the openness of what is to come and what has passed. This image was also connected to the following words spoken by Björn: "We sit inside a deep forest, the forest is in darkness, yes, it is so dark that you can hardly see the path. It is dangerous, but not life-threatening if you are able to have a direction and a goal. If you have a goal and know where you are aiming, you are able to discover the path that leads forward. Now I can go on and try to live as fully as I can."

Conclusion

In this essay, I have explored parts of *The Red Book*, "troll music," and dialogical language in the Elliptical Dialogue with the aim of trying to understand what is common to the three perspectives and if they tell us something about the necessary conditions for "magic," as Jung learns about it from Philemon. Both Lagerlöf and Jung demonstrate the ability to master words and language into a form that builds a relationship with us readers. Jungian psychoanalysis is also firmly grounded in relational dynamics and in the mutuality of the partners in the psychoanalytical setting. When looking into our world of today we can be caught by a feeling of resignation. But no one can live without deep sympathy and compassion. To read Jung's *Red Book* is to become engaged and participate in a mutual dialogue from within.

Language focused on the spontaneous expressive response to growing and living forms, i.e., symbols, is powerful and carries potential for change. Symbols carried by "troll music" are both responsive and expressive to each other, *and* they are responsive to and expressive of the otherness in inner and outer reality, as Philemon is in Jung's life or the "troll music" included in the wholeness of the organ music in Lagerlöf's text. Significant for Analytical Psychology and its clinical application, Jungian psychoanalysis, is the dialogically structured language as shown in the dialogue taking place in the image "Facing the Void." By taking action in the language exchange and involving ourselves in it, we can engage in a living, flowing interaction where the direction of consciousness comes from deep inner levels of complexity in our individual and collective relational psyche. Perhaps we can then create the potential for lowering the center of gravity toward the spirit of the depths and away from nihilism, indifference, and resignation.

In conclusion, I would like to reference the last word inscribed by Jung in his *Red Book* near the end of his life, as a reminder that inner and outer reality are equally real and that openness to depth must inevitably form the ground for Analytical Psychology: *Möglichkeit* ("possibility").[19]

Endnotes

[1] C.G. Jung, *The Red Book: Liber Novus. A Reader's Edition*, ed. Sonu Shamdasani, trans. John Peck, Mark Kyburz, and Sonu Shamdasani (New York, NY: W.W. Norton, 2012), 127.

[2] Ibid., 127 n34.

[3] Gunilla Midbøe, *The Elliptical Dialogue* (Asheville, NC: Chiron Publications, 2017).

[4] Vladimir Orel, *A Handbook of Germanic Etymology* (Leiden, Boston: Brill, 2003), 410.

[5] Henrik Ibsen, *Peer Gynt* (Mineola, NY: Dover Publications, 2003), 36.

[6] S. Lagerlöf, *Trollmusik. En julberättelse.* In *Skilda Tider* (Stockholm: Albert Bonniers Förlag, 1949), 362. My translation.

[7] Ibid.

[8] Jung, *The Red Book*, 401.

[9] Ibid., 405.

[10] Ludwig Wittgenstein, *Tractatus Logico-Philosophicus* (London: Routledge and Kegan Paul, 1976), 6.522

[11] Ibid., 7.

[12] Figure created by Gunilla Midbøe. Included in *The Elliptical Dialogue* (Asheville, NC: Chiron Publications, 2017).

[13] Ludwig Wittgenstein, *Philosophical Investigations* (Oxford: Basil Blackwell 1953), 60.

[14] Ibid., 51.

[15] Ibid., 57.

[16] Ibid., 49.

[17] For a fuller account of this clinical case, see my book *The Elliptical Dialogue*.

[18] Jung, *The Red Book*, 535.

[19] Ibid., 191.

A Japanese Perspective on the Meaning of the Serpent in *The Red Book*

Mari Yoshikawa

When we open *The Red Book*, the small painting on the first page immediately attracts our attention. On the letter D, placed between the sea and the land, a two-toned colored serpent, black on the back and white on the belly, is stretched upward toward heaven. It wears a golden crown. Placed so prominently at the beginning, this indicates the importance of the serpent-image in this book. This forms a common element between *Liber Novus* and Japanese myth. In this essay, I will trace the presence of the serpent image in *The Red Book* and discuss some comparisons with the serpent in Japanese myths and ancient legends.

The Serpent in Ancient Japan

During the late Jōmon period (14,000-400 B.C.E) of prehistoric Japan, people lived by hunting and gathering. Later in this period, primitive farming began. We can find a design of the serpent on Jōmon pottery. The first figure shows a relic from the late Jōmon period and the second figure a serpent handle on a clay pot.

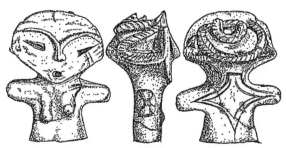

第2図　頭上にまむしを乗せた土偶　長野県藤内16号住居址発見（縄文中期前半）（宮坂光昭『蛇体と石棒の信仰』より転写）

Serpent on the head of a dog and a clay female figure from Jōmon period

Serpent handle on a clay pot found in the Nakappara ruins at Nagano prefecture

Since there was no alphabet at that time, we can only speculate about what this meant. It is presumed that this pottery was used in important rituals at that time. From this we may surmise that the image of the serpent was alive in the minds of the ancient Japanese. In a later period, ancient oral traditions were recorded in the collection titled *Kojiki*, the legendary "Stories of Old Japan," dating from the early eighth century (711–712 C.E.).[1] This work was composed by Ono Yasumaro at the request of Enpress Genmei.

How did the serpent appear in *Kojiki*? The first mention of the serpent image in *Kojiki* describes eight serpents entwined around the Goddess Izanami in the Underworld. When Izanami passed away, her husband, Izanagi, visited her in the Underworld in order to bring her back to the Upperworld. He found her body wound about with eight "thunders"—on her head, chest, belly, private parts, and around both hands and legs. "Thunder" is presumed by researchers to mean "serpent" in ancient Japanese.[2] The image of serpents around the dead Goddess seems to represent the destructive energy of death in the Underworld.

The mightiest serpent in the *Kojiki* is eight-forked and described as follows: "Its eyes are like red cherries and it has eight heads and eight tails. Covered in moss, cypress and cedar, it spans eight valleys and eight peaks, and when you look at its belly you see blood oozing cut everywhere."[3]

Later in the *Kojiki*, there is a story of a marriage between a maiden and Ōmononushi, who is known as a god of water and thunder and is one of oldest gods in Japanese mythology. He is associated with Mount Miwa and is worshipped at the Ōmiwa shrine there. The story suggests that his substance is a serpent and is told as follows: *Ikutamayori-hime* (meaning "The Lady Summoned Lively

Soul") was fine and noble. In the middle of the night, a man came to her repeatedly to join her in marriage. Soon the maiden became pregnant. When her father and mother asked her about the pregnancy, the maiden replied: "There is a handsome youth, I don't know his name or that of his family. Every night he comes to me, and in spending time with him thus it came to pass that I became pregnant."[4] Her father and mother, wishing to know who this person was, instructed their daughter: "Scatter red clay by your bed. Thread a needle with a bundle of hemp yarn and sew it onto the hem of his robe."[5] She did as she was instructed, and when they looked in the next morning, the needle had passed through the keyhole of the door and gone outside, leaving only three loops of thread behind. Following the thread, they reached Mount Miwa—"Three Loops"—where it stopped at the shrine of the spirit. So that is why he is known to be the descendant of a spirit.

It is suggested that this episode in the *Kojiki* is associated with a type of Japanese fairy tale about marriage with a serpent. There is *Odamaki* (a spool of thread type of tale) in which a strange youth comes to a young woman who puts a needle with thread into her partner's clothing to find out who he is. The other type of tale is known as the Rainmaking type, in which a young woman is sacrificed to a serpent god to make rain. These Japanese fairy tales suggested that the image of a sacred marriage with a serpent groom was prevalent in ancient Japan.

In another collection of old legends and myths called *Nihon Shoki*, there is a moving story of marriage of Ōmononushi with a princess, the daughter of the Emperor Yamato-totohi-momoso-hime-no-mikoto. This story clarifies that Ōmononusi is actually a serpent.

> Ōmononushi came to the princess Momoso-hime always at night. One day the princess asked him to stay until noon in order to find out about his appearance. He agreed on the condition that she would not show surprise when she saw him as he is. But the next morning when she found a beautiful small serpent in the box where he had indicated she would find him, she screamed in alarm. The god then

became a human being and felt great shame. He blamed her, saying: 'You made me feel shame because of not enduring, so I will make you feel shame by going back.' The god then went up in the air to mount Miwa ('Three Loops'). At that point, the princess felt great regret and took her life.[6]

This story reminds us of the fairy tale of Psyche and Cupid in *The Golden Ass*, the oldest Western novel written in the second century C.E. by Lucius Apuleius. Like Psyche, who wanted to see how her husband looked and then lost him, Momoso-hime, too, lost her husband, however not because she looked but because she couldn't endure the reality of what she saw. She had lived in unity with him in the dark night, but in the light of the day, she couldn't endure the sight of him and screamed in terror. From the point of view of Analytical Psychology, the marriage with Ōmononushi corresponds to the individual attempting to unite with the "Other" beyond ego-consciousness. Her curiosity destroys her union with Ōmononushi, the Serpent God of the unconscious. Her consciousness could not endure it.

The tragedy of Momoso-hime reflects a danger for us Japanese who are now living with the Western ego, i.e., modern consciousness. Can we endure the reality of that which is beyond the ego? It may not be the beautiful "Other" we expect to see. For our modern consciousness, it might seem awful, and we might throw it away screaming rather than endure and accept it. But we should gaze at it, and if possible endure union with it since it connects us to the source of life.

Images of the Serpent in *The Red Book*

I was surprised that the serpent has such important roles in Jung's *Red Book*. At the beginning of his active imagination experiences, he found the serpent to be a strange creature. Gradually, he approached it and had a vision of it being wound around him. Then he had several dialogues with the serpent and at last achieved unity with it. In obtaining the wisdom of the serpent, Jung changed. How did he change? In the following, I will trace the process of Jung's transformation through the serpent in *The Red Book*.

Liber Primus

The figure of the serpent first appears in Chapter V of *The Red Book*, titled "Descent into Hell in the Future." "The spirit of the depths opened my eyes," the Narrator writes, as he catches "a glimpse of the inner things, the world of my soul."[7] He goes down into a cave and removes the stone that covers an opening in a rock. Peering into the depths, he sees a wounded man and a large black scarab floating in an underground stream in which "shines a red sun, radiating through the dark water. There I see—and a terror seizes me—small serpents on the dark rock walls, striving toward the depths, where sun shines. A thousand serpents crowd around, veiling the sun."[8]

Following this vision, Jung tries to understand the serpent by associating it with ancient Egyptian myth. In Egypt, the snake/serpent god of the night, *Apep* or *Apophis*, confronts the sun god every night in a deadly cosmic battle. The ancient Egyptians believed that the *uraeus* (cobra) was the protector of the Pharaoh. Indeed, the essence of the divinity of the Pharaoh was attributed to *Shai*, the snake/serpentine embodiment of the Divine Creator.

The serpent appears repeatedly in *The Red Book*, which suggests that it has a unique meaning. It appears next in Chapter IX, "Mysterium Encounter": "An old man stood before me. He looked like one of the old prophets. A black serpent lay at his feet. Some distance away I saw a house with columns. A beautiful maiden steps out of the door."[9] The old man gives his name as Elijah and introduces his daughter as Salome. While Jung is annoyed by the strange matching of Elijah and Salome, he recognizes later that these two figures are personifications of Logos and Eros.[10] About the snake, Jung writes: "In myths the snake is a frequent counterpart of the hero … therefore, the presence of the snake was an indication of a heromyth."[11]

In Chapter IX of *The Red Book*, the discussion of the serpent continues: "Apart from Elijah and Salome I found the serpent as a third principle. It is a stranger to both principles although it is associated with both. The serpent taught me the unconditional difference in essence between the two principles in me."[12] Later: "The serpent is the earthly essence of man of which he is not conscious. Its character changes according to peoples and lands, since it is the mystery that flows to him from the nourishing earth mother."[13] The serpent as the third principle seems to be a dynamic element. As Jung concludes: "The way of life writhes like the serpent from right to left and from left to right, from thinking to pleasure and from pleasure to thinking. Thus the serpent is an adversary and a symbol of enmity, but also a wise bridge that connects right and left through longing, much needed by our life."[14] The serpent is an image of movement linking the two opposites, thinking and pleasure, Elijah and Salome.

In the Chapter XI, "Resolution," the narrator finds himself in front of a steep ridge in a wasteland. He is on the border between dark night and bright day. He sees a ferocious battle taking place between a black and a white serpent. In the course of the battle, the front part of the black serpent become white. The serpents curl about one another, one in the light, the other in darkness. The narrator suggests that this means the power of the light will become so great that even the darkness that resists it will be illuminated by it. Jung understands this vision of the battle between the black and white serpent as follows: "Before I ascend to love, a condition must be fulfilled, which represents itself as the fight between two serpents. Left is day, right is night. The realm of love is light, the realm of forethinking is dark. Both principles have separated themselves strictly, and are even hostile to one other and have taken on the form of the serpents. This form indicates the daimonic nature of both principles."[15] He recognizes this as "a repetition of that vision where I saw the struggle between the sun and the black serpent."[16]

Jung linked the vision of the struggle between the sun and the black serpent to the World War raging at that time, where "the loving light was annihilated, and blood began to pour out."[17] He thought that this struggle should be understood as "a conflict in every man's own nature."[18]

Jung presents another surprising vision that includes the black and white serpents: "I see the divine child, with the white serpent in his right hand, and the black serpent in his left hand. I see the green mountain, the cross of Christ on it, and a stream of blood flowing from the summit of the mountain—I can look no longer, it is unbearable—I see the cross and Christ on it in his last hour and torment—at the foot of the cross the black serpent coils itself—it has wound itself around my feet—I am helf fast and I spread my arms wide. ... The serpent has wound itself my whole body, and my countenance is that of a lion."[19] Salome tells him: "You are Christ," and the scene comes to a climax with Jung saying: "It is as if I stood alone on a high mountain with stiff outstretched arms. The serpent squeezes my body in its terrible coils and the blood streams from my body, spilling down the mountainside. Salome bends down to my feet and wraps her black hair round them. She lies thus for a long time. Then she cries: 'I see light!' ... The serpent falls from my body and lies languidly on the ground."[20]

At the end of *Liber Primus*, Jung reflects again on the serpent: "The serpent lurks behind the pure principle. Therefore I lost courage, until I found the serpent that at once led me across to the other principle."[21] The other principle is love. This indicates that the main theme of *Liber Primus* is the process of going across from one principle, forethinking, to another principle, love, with the guidance of the serpent. The goal is integration of the two principles: "If you go to thinking, take your heart with you. If you go to love, take your head with you. Love is empty without thinking, thinking hollow without love."[22]

Liber Secundus

In Chapter XIX of *Liber Secundus*, "The Gift of Magic," Jung's soul brings him a magical rod: "A black rod, formed like a serpent ..."[23] She tells him that magic demands sacrifice of solace, both the giving and the receiving of it. She says that magic is a gift from the darkness. About the nature of magic, she tells him that it is the working of men on men. The text seems to suggest that the secret power of psychotherapy is magic, which does not affect the client directly but first affects the therapist, and only if the therapist experiences it does an invisible effect pass on to the client. Psychotherapeutic power should never be used for the client's solace, or for the therapist's solace. The way for someone to use this magic, he describes as follows: "Raise your hand up to the darkness above you, pray, despair, wring your hands, kneel, press your forehead into the dust, cry out, but do not name Him, do not look at Him. Leave Him without name and form. What should form the formless? Name the nameless? ... The way is open to whomever can continue in spite of riddles. Submit to the riddles and the thoroughly incomprehensible. There are dizzying bridges over the eternally deep abyss. But follow the riddles."[24] These words seem to direct the psychotherapist in the quest for individuation, which demands suffering without easy salvation.

Chapter XX, "The Way of the Cross," begins with a vision of the black serpent: "I saw the black serpent, as it wound itself upward around the wood of the cross. It crept into the body of the crucified and emerged again transformed from his mouth. It had become white. It wound itself around the head of the dead one like a diadem, and a light gleamed above his head, and the sun rose shining in the east."[25] This vision of the way leads to the realization that "the way leads through the crucified, that means through him to whom it was no small thing to live his own life, and who was therefore raised to magnificence."[26]

In Chapter XXI, "The Magician," Philemon appears. An aged magician "who has not yet managed to banish old age," he lives with his wife Baucis: "Their interests seem to have become narrow, even childish. ... Philemon is old and has become somewhat feeble-minded."[27] Interestingly, Philemon is associated with the serpent: "You lie in the sun, Oh Philemon, like a serpent that coils around itself. Your wisdom is the wisdom of serpents, cold, with a grain of poison, yet healing in small doses. Your magic paralyzes and therefore makes strong people, who tear themselves away from themselves."[28] The narrator concludes: "Your kind is far more serpentlike."[29]

In this chapter, Jung is being prepared for the process of transformation. He learns about magic from Philemon and is armed with chain mail, a secret armor. He plans to deceive a great iridescent serpent with the wisdom of Philemon. The serpent, who is made to believe she is Jung's soul, reveals her secret to him. It is amazing what a trickster Jung is! Jung does not surrender to the serpent but takes advantage of her. How indomitable he is. That is Jung, who did not put his forehead to the floor even in his dream.[30] She reveals her secret as follows: "So, have you noticed that the becoming of the soul follows a serpentine path? Have you seen how soon day becomes night, and night day? How water and dry land change places? And that everything spasmodic is merely destructive?"[31] Then the serpent winds herself around Jung's feet, and Jung feels as if "all pots are on the boil."[32] The serpent replies that she is preparing a meal for a "union with all humanity."[33] Jung describes his experience of this vision with these words: "The opposites embrace each other, see eye to eye, and intermingle. They recognize their oneness in agonizing pleasure. My heart is filled with wild battle. The waves of dark and bright rivers rush together, one crashing over the other. I have never experienced this before."[34] While Jung succeeds in turning his pain into joy, the serpent tries to bite his heart to make him just suffer, but in vain because of the protection of his secret armor. Jung proves that he has learned the serpent's secret. He avoids entrapment "… because I have studied the art of stepping from the left foot onto the right and vice versa, which others have done unthinkingly from time immemorial."[35] Jung concludes: "The sinuous line of life could not escape me in the long run."[36] And he mentions the relation between love and the serpent: "But wherever there is love, the serpentlike abides also."[37] Then he has to acknowledge that his soul is a serpent.

He asks his soul, the serpent: "How will it be, now that God and the devil have become one? Are they in agreement to bring life to a standstill? Does the conflict of opposites belong to the inescapable conditions of life?"[38] The serpent then goes to the Beyond to bring Satan up to meet him. Satan speaks for himself: "My life bubbles and foams and stirs up turbulent waves, it consists of seizing and throwing away, ardent wishing and restlessness. That is life, isn't it?"[39] Satan objects to the absolute, to the unification of the opposites, and to including God and Satan in a single form, saying: "This smells of monism."[40] Further: "That is no life, it is a standstill or as good as a standstill, or rather: it lives interminably slowly and wastes thousands of years, just like the miserable condition that you have created."[41]

Satan's words enlighten Jung. He understands Satan's words, and so Satan is released back into his hole again. The unification of opposites is dissolved, and the symbol of the Trinity rises back to heaven.

After Jung strikes down the Cabiri with his sword, he declares: "Just as a tower surmounts the summit of a mountain on which it stands, so I stand above my brain, from which I grew. I have become hard and cannot be undone again. No more do I flow back. I am the master of my own self. I admire my mastery. ... I wait upon no one and no one waits upon me. I serve myself and I myself serve. Therefore I have what I need."[42] These are impressive words. Here he looks back on his process of transformation and declares: "I have united with the serpent of the beyond. I have accepted everything beyond into myself. From this I have built my beginning."[43] He was renewed through unification with the serpent.

How was Jung changed by this serpent vision? This question reminds us of an answer Jung gave to a similar question about the difference individuation makes in the personality of an individual: "The individuated human being is just ordinary and therefore almost invisible."[44] Continuing, he makes a reference to Zen Buddhism: "Nobody can have a vision and not be changed by it. First he has no vision, and he is the man A, then he is himself plus a vision = the man B; and then it might be that the vision may influence his life, if he is not quite dull, and that is the man C."[45]

Jung looked the same as before, but internally he had changed. The change is proved in the vision in the last chapter of *Liber Secundus*, where Elijah and Salome appear again. Elijah wants to give Salome to Jung. Jung rejects her decisively, even though she wants to be Jung's. He tells her: "You are like the serpent that coiled around me and pressed out my blood."[46] These words remind us that Jung's vision of becoming the Crucified related to his experiences of Salome. Here he tells Salome: "Be your own master and your own slave, do not belong to me but to yourself. Do not bear my burden, but your own."[47] Jung asks her to "give to me out of your fullness, not your longing ... If your harvest is rich, send me some fruit from your garden."[48]

Jung advises Elijah to set her on her feet. He confesses as well that he has the serpent that Elijah lost. Jung tells him that the serpent gave him hardness, wisdom, and magical power. He declares to Elijah that whoever possesses wisdom is not greedy for power. Jung recognizes that his rejection to Salome is a sacrifice. The serpent is now pulled upward and turns into a small white bird that flies up to the heavens and returns with a golden royal crown with lettering incised within it saying: "Love never ends."[49]

Here I would like to conclude this discussion of the serpent in the calligraphic volume of *Liber Novus*. We may assume that Jung's Salome experiences were the trigger for a series of active imaginations through which he achieved psychological transformation by working with the experiences in the making of the *Red Book*. As a result of these experiences, he got the wisdom and magic of the serpent. This seems to be associated with a belief in love and the sacrifice of solace, which is in other words the essence of psychotherapy. Jung found the secret of the sinuous line of life and that becoming the soul follows a serpentine path. It seems to be related to the art of stepping from the left foot onto the right and vice versa. What does this mean? I will examine Jung's investigation of the serpent after the *Red Book*.

Jung's Later Investigation of the Serpent

According to Jung in his late work *Aion*, the serpent symbolizes "coldblooded," inhuman psychic contents and tendencies of an abstractly intellectual as well as a concretely animal nature—in a word, the extra human quality in a person: "... the snake is the commonest symbol for the dark, chthonic world of instinct."[50] Further, he mentions the serpent as one of three symbols, along with water and the Logos, of the "phenomena of assimilation that are in themselves of a numinous nature and therefore have a certain degree of autonomy."[51] This phenomenon of assimilation must accompany the annunciation of the Christ-figure in order to make it effective in history. Jung writes that these symbols "represent the prototypes of the Christ-figure that were slumbering in man's unconscious and called awake by his actual appearance in history and, so to speak, magnetically attracted."[52] Jung continues: "This magnetic process revolutionizes the ego-oriented psyche by settings up, in contradiction to the ego, another goal or centre which is characterized by all manner of names and symbols; fish, serpent, centre of the sea-hawk, point, monad, cross, paradise, and so on."[53] He called this goal the self, "that indescribable whole consisting of the sum of conscious and unconscious processes."[54]

To summarize, the serpent is the symbol of Christ and the self. Jung explains the reason of the choice of the serpent as follows:

> It appears spontaneously or comes as a surprise: it fascinates; its glance is staring, fixed, unrelated; its blood cold, and it is a stranger to man: it crawls over the sleeper, he finds it in a shoe or in his pocket. It expresses his fear of everything inhuman and his awe of the sublime, of what is beyond human ken. It is the lowest (devil) and the highest (son of God, Logos, Nous, Agathodaimon). The snake's presence is frightening, one finds it in unexpected places at unexpected moments. Like the fish, it represents and personifies the dark and unfathomable, the watery deep, the forest, the night, the cave. When a primitive says, 'snake,' he means an experience of something extra-human.[55]

The serpent is something beyond the human, the ego, and rational thinking. For the ego, it is frightening, but it can guide the ego beyond rational thinking to the depths, where the source of love is that drives the soul to becoming whole through suffering.

In Jung's view the nature of the serpent connects to psycho-therapy and healing. The serpent in classical Greece is commonly associated with the staff of Asklepios. Thus the serpent became the symbol of the god of healing as the *caduceus* on which a serpent is entwined around a staff.

Conclusion

By exploring images of the serpent in *The Red Book*, we found that Jung's psychological transformation was achieved through gaining unity with the serpent through his suffering of crucifixion. In *Liber Secundus*, he acquired the serpent's wisdom and magic. This linked to the psychotherapeutic *opus*, which brought him to appreciate the giving of love and to reject the demanding of love from Salome.

It is surprising that there is some similarity of the function of the image of the serpent in ancient Japanese myth and the active imaginations of *The Red Book*, since Jung had never studied Japanese myths. In Jung's understanding, it would be due to the collective unconscious. That means that the images of the serpent derive from the deep layer of the psyche, which is common to all people and lies beyond the confines of time and space.

In both materials, unity with the serpent or marriage with the serpent has an important meaning. The serpent represents "the strange other," which seems to be so far from ourselves that unity with the serpent therefore leads to the growth of consciousness.

In Japanese myth and legend, a maiden gets married to the serpent in the dark, and then she tries to discover his substance. Another princess asked her husband to reveal his figure, but she screamed at his real figure so that her husband ran away from her.

I suppose that the ancient Japanese had a unity with the serpent in the dark, or in unconsciousness. They could live their bond with a great god in the dark and without consciousness. But as the conscious realm grew, it became difficult to unite with it because it is strange to the ego. When she discovered her husband's real figure, the Japanese maiden died because she was so astonished. Another Japanese princess was more active to negotiate with her husband to reveal his figure, but she couldn't endure his real figure, so the unity was dissolved.

On the other hand, Jung's approach toward unity with the serpent is more conscious. Only in the first vision in *Liber Primus,* when a thousand serpents crowded around, veiling the sun, was he seized with terror. After that, even when he was squeezed by the black serpent with blood streaming from his body, he kept his conscious position intact. It is his manner to confront and unite with the nameless one beyond the ego. In *Liber Secundus,* he becomes a schemer and a trickster. He even charms the serpent with his flute to manipulate it and convinces it that it is a part of his, Jung's, self. There is correspondence to these tricky ways toward the serpent in Japanese myth when the hero, Susano-no-Mikoto, defeats the eight-forked serpent by getting it drunk. As his reward, Susano-no-Mikoto acquires a maiden who should have been sacrificed to the serpent and a sword that was removed from the serpent's tail. In *The Red Book,* Jung becomes a hero when he gets the serpent's wisdom and magic without killing the serpent. Jung seems to be an evolved type of hero in his active imagination. As a man, he seems not to be patriarchal. After the dialogue with the serpent, he acquires the toughness to reject Salome and encourages her to stand on her own feet.

Following the serpent in *The Red Book,* in comparison with Japanese myth, it is apparent that Jung's quest for his soul brought him the self's wisdom and magic and the secret of the serpentine path. What is the serpentine path? It is said that "the becoming of the soul follows a serpentine path."[56] It involves "the art of stepping from the left foot onto the right and vice versa"[57] and "the sinuous line of life."[58] And it is said as well that "whenever there is love, the serpentlike abides also."[59] It seems to suggest the serpent's relatedness to the unthinking way of the body and to life and love. This is a kind of riddle of *The Red Book.*

We might be able to use this in our quest today to follow our self's serpentine path.

Endnotes

[1] Ono Yasumaro, *The Kojiki: An Account of Ancient Matters*, trans. Gustav Heldt (New York, NY: Columbia University Press, 1983).

[2] Eight thunders means eight serpents according to Akiho Fukushima, *A study of Japanese myth and legend in Kojiki* (Nihon-shoki: Rokko Shuppan, 1988) (福島秋穂著.-記紀神話伝説の研究-六興出版, 1988).

[3] Yasumaro, *The Kojiki: An Account of Ancient Matters*, 25.

[4] Ibid., 84.

[5] Ibid., 85.

[6] Anonymous, *The Nihon Shoki: The Chronicles of Japan* (日本書紀) (Library of Alexandria, 2012).

[7] C.G. Jung, *The Red Book: Liber Novus, A Reader's Edition*. ed. Sonu Shamdasani, tr. John Peck, Mark Kyburz, and Sonu Shamdasani (New York, NY: W.W. Norton, 2009), 147.

[8] Ibid., 148.

[9] Ibid., 174.

[10] Ibid., 204 n238.

[11] C.G. Jung, *Memories, Dreams, Reflections*, ed. Aniela Jaffé (New York, NY: Vintage, 1963), 182.

[12] Jung, *The Red Book*, 180.

[13] Ibid.

[14] Ibid., 181.

[15] Ibid., 199.

[16] Ibid.

[17] Ibid.

[18] Ibid.

[19] Ibid., 196-197.

[20] Ibid., 197-198.

[21] Ibid., 200-201.

[22] Ibid., 200.

[23] Ibid., 379.

[24] Ibid., 383.

[25] Ibid., 388.

[26] Ibid., 389.

[27] Ibid., 396-397.

[28] Ibid., 408.

[29] Ibid.

[30] Jung, *Memories, Dreams, Reflections*, 219.

[31] Jung, *The Red Book*, 414.

[32] Ibid., 415.

[33] Ibid.

[34] Ibid.

[35] Ibid., 417.

[36] Ibid.

[37] Ibid.

[38] Ibid., 418-419.

[39] Ibid., 423.

[40] Ibid., 421.

[41] Ibid., 423.

[42] Ibid., 429.

[43] Ibid.

[44] Gerhard Adler, *C. G. Jung Letters*. Trans. by R. F. C. Hull. Vol. 2, 1951-1961 (Princeton, NJ: Princeton University Press, 1975), 324.

[45] Ibid.

[46] Jung, *The Red Book*, 436.

[47] Ibid., 438.

[48] Ibid.

[49] Ibid., 446. This is a quotation from *I Corinthians 13:8*.

[50] C.G. Jung, *Aion. Researches into the Phenomenology of the Self*, in *CW*, vol. 9/II (Princeton, NJ: Princeton University Press, 1959), par. 385.

[51] Ibid., par. 295.

[52] Ibid.

[53] Ibid., par. 296.

[54] Ibid.

[55] Ibid., par. 293.

[56] Jung, *The Red Book*, 414.

[57] Ibid., 417.

[58] Ibid.

[59] Ibid.

Jung as Craftsman

Linda Carter

When I was writing down these fantasies, I once asked myself, 'What am I really doing? Certainly, this has nothing to do with science. But then what is it?' Whereupon a voice within me said, 'It is art.' I was astonished. It had never entered my head that what I was writing had any connection with art. Then I thought, 'Perhaps my unconscious is forming a personality that is not me, but which is insisting on coming through to expression.' I knew for a certainty that the voice had come from a woman. I recognized it as the voice of a patient, a talented psychopath who had a strong transference to me. She had become a living figure within my mind.

Obviously, what I was doing wasn't science. What then could it be but art? ...

I said very emphatically to this voice that my fantasies had nothing to do with art, and I felt a great inner resistance. No voice came through, however, and I kept on writing. Then came the next assault, and again the same assertion: 'That is art.' This time I caught her and said, 'No, it is not art! On the contrary, it is nature ...'[1]

We now know from the research of Sonu Shamdasani that the woman in question in the above passage was Maria Moltzer, a Dutch woman trained as a nurse with whom Jung was involved at the time.[2] Jung credits Moltzer with discovering the intuitive function, very important given that Jung's early system of typology consisted only of extraversion and its affiliation with feeling and introversion with its concomitant connection to thinking.[3] In her 1916 presentations to the Analytical Psychology Club in Zurich, Moltzer[4] expresses concern about Jungian reductionism into extraversion and introversion and suggests a third way of adaptation via intuition.[5]

From her point of view, intuition is the oldest function and emerges out of instinct, allowing for adaptation to life through *understanding*. She even implies that intuition operates to link the conscious with the unconscious and possibly thinking and feeling through art, visions, and religious practices[6] in a way that resonates with Jung's ideas about the "transcendent function," also written about in 1916 but not published until 1958.[7] One wonders, with hindsight, about the mutual influence between this doctor and a bright, highly intuitive patient whose ideas have been relegated to a mere mention in the history of Analytical Psychology. (Parallels can be found in the minimization of Spielrein's influence on Freud's concept of the death instinct.[8])

I offer this backdrop from Shamdasani's research in order to make the case that Jung was more a craftsman than an artist, a craftsman whose hands carried a kind of *natural* implicit body knowledge, as well as extraordinary *intuition* that could creatively transform spirit into matter. He was a man with a keen eye for detail and specificity as is evident in the precision of the lettering and images in *The Red Book*.[9] The large leather-bound volume provided a substantial container to give weight and validity to what could have been seen as ephemeral experiences. Laboring with deep concentration and seriousness, Jung profoundly engaged with the ink, vellum, colors, and at the same time with his imagination. Like a medieval monk, he worked within the medium of an illuminated manuscript, thus giving structure and method that could help hold the depth of his internal world. His remarkable skills were put to use as means to intuitively follow affects into fantasy experiences that brought together body, mind, and heart. He was crafting and being crafted by his own soul. In *Memories, Dreams, Reflections*, he speaks of his confrontation with the unconscious (1913-1919) as a scientific experiment whose outcome he was vitally interested in, but the endeavor was "… an experiment which was being conducted on me."[10] He himself was the stone being crafted, carved, shaped, molded into the *lapis*, the self.

Skilled craftspeople have developed a kind of "knowing" through their hands. They can tell when something "feels right" and may not be able to explain in words what they mean at a conscious level. They follow an ineffable thread through a labyrinth of possibilities working within the constraints of their medium, method, size of the project, level of experience, and time boundaries. In many ways, this process is not unlike the frame of analysis that has to do with time, fees, training of the analyst, and what each individual in the dyad brings to the engagement. The constraints of a craft project and the boundaries of analysis provide containment and a holding environment for creative possibilities to emerge.

When starting out to make mandalas in the internment camp at Château d'Oex as Commandant de la Région Anglaise des Internés de Guerre in 1918-19, Jung did not intend to improve his artistic capabilities or technique, nor was this a goal throughout the making of the *Red Book*. There was no intention to sell his work or show it in museums or galleries. Rather, he was using artistic dexterity within the style of illuminated manuscript lettering harking back to the Christian Middle Ages along with Asian-influenced circumscribed mandala paintings. These very specific modes were used as syncretic vehicles for manifesting the dissociated parts of himself. They were the tools of the trade for a craftsman mining his own unconscious for the precious metals that would later catch his interest in medieval alchemy, a metaphorical system that he used to further elaborate the human psyche. Although Jung saw his descent as very individually his own, he consistently looked to the past and to the future to find generalizability and a sense of belonging, something not securely established in his family of origin (to be discussed later in this essay).

The Jung family has in its possession drawings, watercolor landscapes, and childhood sketches that show some significant talent, but Jung's interests began to shift away from the *Red Book* sometime around 1920, when he undertook the building of the tower at Bollingen and then even further in about 1928 with the beginning of his alchemical studies. In building the tower, he felt that he

> ... had to achieve a kind of representation in stone of my innermost thoughts and the knowledge I had acquired. Or, to put it another way, I had to make a confession of faith

in stone. That was the beginning of the 'Tower,' the house which I built for myself at Bollingen.[11]

Again, we see a similar *modus operandi* to the one employed in the *Red Book*. Jung was not an architect, designer, landscaper, stone-mason, or sculptor. He was seeking the means to embody and materialize through craft and work with his hands a profound *knowing* that had been hard-won and that demanded continued evolution. In his essay on the transcendent function, Jung speaks of the intuitive wisdom not to be found by following the intellect but by following the instincts of the hands:

> Often it is necessary to clarify a vague content by giving it visible form. This can be done by drawing, painting, or modelling. *Often the hands know how to solve a riddle with which the intellect has wrestled in vain* (italics, mine). By shaping it, one goes on dreaming the dream in greater detail in the waking state, and the initially incomprehensible, isolated event is integrated into the sphere of the total personality, even though it remains at first unconscious to the subject.[12]

We see in this passage that the impulse for making is not art for art's sake but for what is already in *nature,* the inclination toward self-healing.

Like Jung, the alchemists were not honing skills as artists; they were experimenting with materials found in nature to *understand* (in Moltzer's sense above) and obtain something of meaning and value crafted through chemical interactions. Similar to monks who also used apprenticeship systems, the alchemists employed study, observation, note-taking, and drawing along with trial and error to creatively record their highly elaborate, detailed work that, as we can see in retrospect, *intuitively* resonates with Jung's own experiments in which he used the methods of craftsmanship, such as painting mandalas, building the tower, and sculpting stone. Perhaps the alchemists did not literally discover the *lapis,* but by following an implicit thread of truth running through their practices, they metaphorically found the philosopher's stone. Jung had the intuition and vision to recognize parallels with the individuation process and to articulate, albeit in convoluted ways at times, his psychological appreciation of the alchemical *opus.*

As can be seen here through his involvement with illuminated manuscripts and alchemy, Jung had a lifelong interest in the Middle Ages and in play with stones. He says:

> My first concrete memory of games dates from my seventh or eighth year. I was passionately fond of playing with bricks, and built towers which I then rapturously destroyed by an 'earthquake.' Between my eighth and eleventh years I drew endlessly—battle pictures, sieges, bombardments, naval engagements.[13]

Later, between seven and nine came the famous incident when Jung wonders, "Am I the one who is sitting on the *stone,* or am I the stone on which he is sitting?" At 10, Jung carved his secret manikin hidden in a pencil case and accompanied by a "smooth blackish stone from the Rhine, which I had painted with water colors to look as though it were divided into an upper and lower half, and had long carried around in my trousers. This was *his* [the manikin's] stone."[14] Later in life after a trip to England in 1920, Jung interpreted the manikin as a *kabir,* wrapped in a cloak and hidden in a *kista* "… with a supply of life-force, the oblong black stone."[15] In the same passage, he looks at the similarities between his childhood rituals and those that he witnessed while traveling, and says of the Africans: "… they act first and do not know what they are doing. Only long after do they reflect on what they have done."[16] By his own accounts, from early childhood through old age, Jung's play with natural materials and with art supplies opened him to a depth of feeling that, with time and some distance, could be analyzed with reflection and formulated into conscious thoughts and interpretations. (Experienced analysts often interact with patients through intuition or implicit knowing and only later, through self-supervision, come to a cognitive understanding and interpretation explicitly.)

Within the containers of the *Red Book*, the tower at Bollingen, and alchemy, Jung pursued a method important in his self-explorations called *active imagination,* which may or may not be part of a Jungian analytic process depending on where one trains. In brief, the term *active imagination* was used by him through the years interchangeably with a variety of other descriptors but was first presented as such in the context of the Tavistock Lectures in London in 1925.[17] Joan Chodorow notes that it is has to do with the natural healing of the psyche[18] and "... is a single method, but ... is expressed through many different forms"[19] including painting, drawing, writing, sculpting, dance, and a variety of other expressive modalities. Active imagination is a means for the conscious ego to invite and to come into relationship with a multiplicity of selves emergent from the unconscious, usually through intentional, daytime fantasy. Jung discusses different ways that the unconscious may communicate with a receptive ego such as through an audible voice or a visual image (nonpathological), depending on the personality of the individual.[20] Further, he notes that there are some people whose communication systems take a different route,[21] and the following description seems relevant to our topic:

> There are others, again, who neither see nor hear anything inside themselves, but *whose hands have the knack of giving expression to the contents of the unconscious* (italics, mine). Such people can profitably work with plastic materials.[22]

With the active imagination technique, a symbol is synthesized and comes into being through the conjunction of the conscious with the unconscious and emerges as the transcendent function.

At this point, it is worth reviewing the procedure that Jung recommended for engaging with active imagination. He saw the psyche, like the body, as a self-regulating system in which the irrational unconscious compensates the directed thinking of consciousness.[23] To bring the two together in a movement toward symbol formation and finding balance in a disrupted mind, Jung suggests entering active imagination by "eliminating critical attention, thus producing a vacuum in consciousness."[24] The starting place is the emotional state itself. Then, he recommends the following:

> [The individual] must make himself as conscious as possible of the mood he is in, sinking in it without reserve and noting down on paper all the fantasies and associations that come up. Fantasy must be allowed the freest possible play ...[25]

Jung goes on to emphasize that the fantasy must not leave the orbit of its object, namely, the affect. Further, he warns against distraction by what I believe he sees as Freud's more thinking or cognitive approach as it could lead away from the centrality of emotion. Jung clearly says here that fantasies are at the deepest level fueled by affects that can find expression in symbols or concretely in artistic products.[26] Additionally, he says: "The whole procedure [active imagination] is a kind of enrichment and clarification of the affect, whereby the affect and its contents come nearer to consciousness, becoming at the same time more impressive and more understandable," and a vitalizing effect is achieved.[27] The previously unrelated affect becomes an articulated idea with the assistance of consciousness, and this coordination is the beginning of the transcendent function.[28] Through play and giving the emotion visible shape in expressive modalities, "... a product is created which is influenced by the conscious and the unconscious, embodying the striving of the unconscious for the light and the striving of the conscious for substance."[29]

In the following, a case will be made that Jung's use of active imagination in unconscious fantasy was contained by the *Red Book*, the building of Bollingen, and researches into alchemy. Further, his intersubjective relationships, activities of daily life and skill development in multiple areas were critical for holding together a mind with the potential for dissociation and fragmentation due to early childhood trauma. These critical aspects emerged from the implicit procedural domain, different from the unconscious described by Freud as repressed trauma or the unconscious described by Jung as the personal realm of complexes and the collective where archetypes reside. Findings from neuroscience and infant research will help the reader to appreciate the subtle importance of the nonconscious in intersubjective relationships and in skill development as operating in the background to support Jung's confrontation with the unconscious through active imagination.

Jung generalized his own experiments with active imagination such that he saw the potential for healing of the psyche as a synthetic and prospective method with a focus on the purpose and meaning of symbols as they led the way into future individuation and psychic wholeness. Although interested in personal history, he turned to myth, stories and fairy tales to expand and elaborate an individual's experience within a larger cultural context. This was, of course, in contradistinction to Freud's reductive, causal approach leading back to childhood through free association. Critics have viewed Jung's model as defensive, evident in the historical data in his autobiography and in Deirdre Bair's research.[30] His personal anamnesis would lead most trained clinicians to imagine insecurity of attachment related to mother Emilie's depression. Prior to Jung's birth, she had two stillbirths and a third baby who lived only five days; following Jung's birth, Emilie had several lengthy stays in "rest homes."[31] By his own report in the autobiography, Jung suffered with multiple adverse events, traumatic incidents, and illnesses throughout his childhood. He was mistrustful when the word *love* was spoken, associated *woman* with innate unreliability, and *father* meant reliability but powerlessness.[32] He and his mother, along with members of previous generations on her side, were fascinated by ghosts, and his medical school research revolved around his cousin's mediumistic experiences, which he later saw through the lens of the Word Association Experiment as having to do with the dissociability of the psyche. Further, he revealed the peculiar internal splits that he and his mother had with daytime and nighttime personalities known as "Personality No. 1" and "Personality No. 2." So, through uncanny experiences in his family, interest in spiritism of the day, and as a result of findings from the Word Association Test, Jung created a theory of complexes, subpersonalities, or, in contemporary language, a multiplicity of selves.[33]

From a psychopathological perspective, we could say that Jung was susceptible to psychic fragmentation and dissociation (See Winnicott, Sedgwick and Meredith-Owen[34]). We now know from current neuroscience and infant research what Jung could not have known at that time in history: Dissociative symptoms and fragmentation in adulthood are correlated with what is called "early relational trauma," also referred to as "hidden trauma," which has to do with disruptions in the preverbal earliest phases of life.[35] Particularly problematic are disorganized attachment patterns that are thought to arise when parents who should be a source of comfort are both frightened and frightening.[36] On the other hand, some parents (due to their own attachment and/or trauma histories, psychopathology, etc.) may tend to withdraw from the infant's overtures for attachment at times of heightened arousal and present as helpless so that they do not or cannot provide essential comfort. Further, the infant may infer that he/she is frightening an already frightened parent. Internalization of these contradictory models may lead to failures in integration of strategies for seeking comfort and protection when under stress and lead to what Giovanni Liotti describes as vulnerability to dissociative processes in adult life.[37] From Karlen Lyons-Ruth and colleagues, we learn that this vulnerability has to do with limitations on the part of attachment figures to modulate fearful arousal through responsive dialogue on a day-to-day basis. Such ongoing and problematic affective interaction patterns can be subtle and hard to detect as they tend to be enacted nonverbally, out of conscious awareness well into adulthood. It is also true that specific traumatic events are significant but the nonconscious failures of parental soothing become woven into identity and stress regulation (fight/flight/freezing), consequently making underlying struggles less obvious, requiring a longer time in therapy to establish a trusting relationship.[38]

One can imagine, then, that Jung and patients who have similar histories, including internalized patterns of relational failures, early abuse, neglect, or ill-fortune related to natural disasters or war, would need to establish a secure base within a containing and empathic relationship before traumatic affects can emerge, be experienced, and eventually integrated. In 1912, given his family history, the break with Freud, and the loss of Sabina Spielrein, Jung's visions of Europe covered in blood and his worries about "doing a schizophrenia" are not surprising. With the onset of World War I, Jung came to understand this vision as precognitive of the collective cultural disaster that was about to unfold. However, anxieties about his own mental stability seem to be well-founded. Although Jung felt that analysis of what he called the "personal" or "Freudian unconscious" were relevant, I believe he knew that he could not survive regression into a black hole of pathology. Consequently, through collective mythologies, he creatively located alternative stories and characters displaying heroism and self-agency with whom to identify. Along these lines, Jung notes,

> The causal standpoint merely inquires how this psyche has become what it is, as we see it today. The constructive standpoint asks how, out of this present psyche, a bridge can be built into its own future.[39]

In an attempt to cross the bridge and move toward health and wholeness, given a childhood history of what sounds like fragmentation and possible early relational trauma, it is not surprising that Jung would seek synthetic models that could assist him in forming a coherent sense of self. He intuitively sought relationships and expressive arts methods to help mend the painful splits in his psyche. The unfolding constructive method gave hope to Jung (and now to us) for a new kind of future without condemning him (and us) only to repeating past pathological patterns through repetition compulsion, a psychodynamic concept, or put another way, through instantiated neural pathways that are hardwired. True engagement with almost any art form can help bring forward parts of the self not previously known to consciousness. If taken seriously, witnessed, and recognized, these new, emergent aspects can be fostered and encouraged so that they begin to form solid ground or substantial containers for holding the vulnerable and wounded elements that can sometimes dominate the psyche. With repetition, these constructive experiences open the possibility for alternative self-perceptions creating new networks in the brain.

Psychotherapists know very well the importance of structure and the value of the therapeutic relationship when patients are facing difficult aspects of inner turmoil. During the period between 1912 and 1919 when Jung was confronting the unconscious, he was, in fact, embedded within an organized lifestyle and substantial relational matrices.

During times of crisis, it is often said that the "activities of daily living" become essential and include eating well, sleeping, exercise, and good general self-care. Jung was not burdened by childcare or household duties as those were within Emma's domain and the couple had three servants to assist them. He was known to eat heartily and with gusto, and he gives credit to the regularity of family meals and work with patients as having had a stabilizing effect on him.

Jung's dependable routine included spending mornings on the lakeshore building villages, towers, churches, and walls with stones that he found nearby the Küsnacht house. Sometimes, his son Franz was permitted to join him. In a way, it could be seen as a kind of sandplay therapy in a natural setting. Such concentrated play can be extremely soothing and serve to calm a disrupted mind, as those experienced in work with children understand so well. This three-dimensional method of contact with sand, water, and miniatures in the consulting room, or in Jung's case, earth, waves of the lake, and found objects may have served to stimulate tactile sensations and allowed for the manipulation of solid materials in a given space where stories could naturally begin to unfold. This seemingly simple process of quiet play with the rhythm of tides, fresh air, and sounds of birds and animals was probably quite comforting and was an opportunity for the building of both external and internal structures as the stories of the tiny villages came into being. Here was another variety of active imagination through contact with the natural world.

From recent neuroscience literature, we have learned that involvement in play with metaphor and narrative helps to coordinate and integrate right and left hemispheric functioning. Regina Pally notes that both Fred Levin (1997) and Arnold Modell (1997) believe that the use of metaphor also serves bilateral integrative coherence. She continues: "By containing within them sensory, imagistic, emotional, and verbal elements, metaphors are believed to activate multiple brain centers simultaneously."[40] They are ways of perceiving, feeling, and existing. This simultaneity may be the neurophysiological correlate facilitating the transcendent function relating conscious to unconscious and affect to insight and cognition.[41] Dan Siegel notes that "coherent narratives are created through interhemispheric integration" and include the interpreting left hemisphere and the mentalizing right hemisphere."[42]

So, Jung's solid fund of knowledge based on a classical education gave him resources that spanned world religions and cultures, Greek, Roman, and European history, studies in science, philosophy, and languages along with writing skills that he put to use in letters and personal journals; this background founded in stories and the recording of narratives probably had not just psychological and emotional benefits but neurobiological benefits as well. He was sufficiently equipped with accessible metaphoric capacities and the training to articulate his thoughts in organized ways. (See James Pennebaker and Joshua Smyth on the healing value of narrative writing, trauma and the immune system.[43]) It seems safe to assume that Jung was intuitively making use of play with story and writing as means of self-healing outside conscious thought.

Earlier generations of Jungian analysts have tended to focus on Jung's intrapsychic descent while working on his *Red Book* or building Bollingen as if in monkish solitude, but the evidence presented in this essay argues for the essential importance of an interactive field. The healing power of intersubjectivity has become a central and controversial topic in contemporary psychoanalysis and resonates with neuroscience and attachment findings (some described above). There has been a shift away from a more traditional Freudian one-person psychology model within which analysis focused on the intrapsychic conflicts of the patient to a two-person psychology model that includes analysis of the internal world but also the interpersonal field dynamics of the co-created third as the relationship, or in Jungian parlance, the transcendent function. Along similar lines, Jung used the metaphor of an alchemical container as the vessel of analysis as a way to amplify the mutually co-constructed relationship. Sadly, Jung's prescient metaphor of mixing two chemical substances that he used to envision the bidirectional influence emergent in the doctor/patient relationship has not been referenced or included in the current psychoanalytic conversation even though it predates similar present perspectives by decades. In fact, a case can be made for Jung as a proto-intersubjectivist. (Further discussion of intersubjectivity is beyond the scope of this present essay.)[44]

So, on the one hand, we can say that Jung probably experienced the transcendent function through conjunctions in intersubjective lived relationships, and on the other, we can see Jung's *Red Book* as an embodied synthesis of his active imagination fantasies. It is in itself a *crafted object* including text and images that came into being through a process of *craft-making* from the engagement of his mind, materials, and hands. To achieve the proficiency in lettering and pictures that we now witness in the mass-produced book, Jung would need to have developed a significant level of skill through repetitive practice. Scribes and illuminators of medieval manuscripts were required to move through levels of apprenticeship that involved copying, pattern books, and sometimes tracing. According to Edward Bruce Robertson, Jung's abilities as an amateur artist could most likely have been achieved through the classical education within the institutions of his time. Like the monks, his printing skills could have been secured by copying from books readily available.[45]

The importance of the declarative and procedural domains within the context of the intersubjective field has been established, but it is also relevant to deepening our understanding Jung as craftsman. Any new skill, such as playing the piano, at first requires concentrated, conscious attention in the explicit domain known as declarative knowledge, discussed above. Once a certain level is mastered, the implicit domain of procedural knowledge comes into play and, for example, specific focus on where to find the keys and how to use the foot treadles is no longer necessary. Explicit, conscious concentration falls away and nonconscious knowing takes over. The jazz pianist plays through a feel for the music, his emotional state at the time, and the implicit knowledge of his hands in contact with the instrument. The Boston Change Process Study Group notes that "most of the literature on procedural knowledge concerns knowing about interactions between our own body and the inanimate world."[46] As *homo faber*, or "man the maker,"[47] we interact with the physical environment through *technique*, a French term derived from the Greek *technikos*, which has its roots in how to do or make things.[48] Howard Risatti notes that "for craft, practice is essential for the hand to acquire the necessary technical manual skill to process material into functional form."[49] He goes on to say:

> ... while the musician doesn't make a physical object, the acquisition of technique by musician and craftsman is essential because both must be able to perform so effortlessly that the mind is not engaged with problems of physical execution but is freed to concentrate on the more intellectual, abstract, and conceptual problems concerning form and expression.[50]

With implicit knowing, the hand as a sensing organ is much more than an appendage of the physical body; rather, it is a reflection of the entire human organism and an extension of the mind.[51] As John Ruskin said in 1859, we have in our hands, the "subtlest of all machines."[52] So, with manual dexterity (Latin root for manual is "by or of the hand"[53]), the craftsman can nonconsciously, outside explicit consciousness, enter a state of creative resonance or reverie that allows for conjunction between imagination and the material world. The result is an object that may represent a synthesized symbolic third.

In Jung's case, we might imagine that through education and practice he had remarkable skills accessible through procedural knowledge. The ability to work outside explicit consciousness may have freed him to engage in active imagination fantasies emergent from the personal and collective unconscious. The knowing hand in contact with materials such as ink, paper, and page, could lead the way for play with fantasy fueled by affect. Sonu Shamdasani quotes Erika Schlegel, who aptly noted in 1921 that Jung "had fallen into art as a manner of speaking. But art and science were no more than servants of the creative spirit, which is what must be served."[54] Impelled by spiritual necessity with access to well-developed procedural knowledge, Jung painted mandalas and carefully recorded fantasies that expressed a profound depth of meaning. Put another way, his intersubjective matrices and significant skills in multiple areas formed a scaffolding for Jung to enter different layers of the unconscious and recognize metaphorically represented aspects of himself that had never before been conscious. By crafting the *Red Book*, he was giving form and substance to his own psychological/religious myth, a bridge to the future.

In amazing ways, *The Red Book*, as we now experience it, conveys a depth of soul that spans time. Throughout history, books have been functional means for organizing information, recording history, transmitting cultural and religious practices, and as vehicles for connections between and among individuals and generations. Illuminated manuscripts have been thought to have perpetuated the Christian message despite invasions by non-Christian groups; they served to include a nonliterate public who could listen to story and appreciate beautiful pictures. The adornment and care that went into the making of illuminated manuscripts and their preservation over the intervening centuries informs us of the deep meaning that they have held. Jung's *Red Book* was brought into being with this kind of care, attention, and value.

By creating it as an illuminated manuscript, Jung bypassed the printing press and modern technology and reached back beyond his family of origin to what he may have envisioned as a more romantic time, a time of knights, castles, courtly love, chivalry, Arthurian legend, and the magic of Merlin. Bollingen can be seen as a castle and a return to the natural world and a simpler lifestyle; or as a much-needed maternal container; or as a defensive structure; or as a place of peace and solitude; or as a three-dimensional active imagination made by his own hands. Interest in the Middle Ages began in childhood, evident in drawings of knights and battles, and to this day, a stone castle that he built resides on the lake behind the Küsnacht house. Shamdasani quotes Jung as saying, "I must catch up with a piece of the Middle Ages—within myself."[55] Perhaps he was struggling to build bridges to this earlier period in history, going past his natal family so that he could give birth to a self within a different kind of story.

Moving from the personal to a cultural context, Jung was an Anglophile who would have been well aware of the influence of the Medieval Era on the Arts and Crafts Movement (1888-1920) put forward by John Ruskin and William Morris, among others. Ruskin wrote of his concern for workers in an industrialized society who, with division of labor, became separated from the meaningful process of transforming raw materials into finished products. He, too, had a longing for return to an idealized time when functional objects were handcrafted with quality and imbued with a different sense of value and meaning, unlike mass-manufactured items. Ruskin saw machines as a threat to the soul of the worker and to the very fabric of British life.[56] Ruskin and like-minded collaborators in the Arts and Crafts Movement placed "an emphasis on the true value in an object or building being derived from the pleasure in creating it ..."[57] Along with Ruskin and Morris, the Pre-Raphaelite Brotherhood was a loosely affiliated group of passionate and prolific artists committed to nature and spiritual goals. Like Jung, they were inspired by a soul connection to the romantic poetry and legends of the Middle Ages, and their artwork reflects the powerful influence of an idyllic, magical past.

However, in contrast to the Pre-Raphaelites, Jung was not a fine artist striving to develop his talent as a painter seeking acclaim for his aesthetic portrayal *of* nature. Rather, he was using well-honed skills as a craftsman to express what he found *in* nature—that is intuition, affect, imagination, and an inborn human inclination toward self-healing. Drawing, painting, writing, and sculpting served to embody and make manifest the complexities of the inner world as a world of nature, no different from the rain or stars. Jung's use of his hands and choice of modalities identified him with ancestors who employed similar skills during earlier periods in human collective development.

Amazingly, the word *craeft* "first appeared in written English over a thousand years ago."[58] To be distinguished from fine art, *craeft*, or craft, is an essential aspect of daily human existence, historically tied to functionality and usefulness, which springs from the timeless human struggle for survival when confronted with nature.[59] Therefore, craft has persistently carried a sense of purpose that is primordial and emergent from physiological necessity and is quite probably an essential innate human trait.[60] Jung sensed that his work was not art but nature's expression inborn from the beginning of time. Out of an intense psychological necessity for individuation, Jung used craft skills to bring together imagination and body with the material world. He was a man with a curious mind open to surprise and wonder who ventured to the edges of unknown territories. This sense of wonder is embedded in the Ancient Greek *poiein*, the root word for *making*.[61] And from Plato in the *Symposium*, we learn that "whatever passes from not being into being is a poesis," a cause for wonder.[62] At this moment, here and now, we can encounter the manifestation of Jung's imagination and find inspiration to follow our own threads that take us with faith and wonder into soul-making in communion with ourselves and the greater surround.

Endnotes

[1] C.G. Jung, *Memories, Dreams, Reflections*, ed. Aniela Jaffé (New York, NY: Vintage, 1963), 185-186.

[2] Sonu Shamdasani, "The Lost Contributions of Maria Moltzer to Analytical Psychology: Two Unknown Papers," in *Spring Journal of Archetype and Culture* (Woodstock, CT: Spring Publications 64, 1998), 103-106.

[3] Ibid., Sonu Shamdasani cites C.G. Jung, *Psychological Types*, in *CW*, vol. 6 (Princeton, NJ: Princeton University Press, 1971), par. 773.

[4] Maria Moltzer, "On the Conception of the Unconscious," first presented in German to the Psychological Club in Zurich and published in English with introduction by Sonu Shamdasani in *Spring Journal of Archetype and Culture* (Woodstock, CT: Spring Publications, 64, 1998), 114.

[5] Ibid., 116-117.

[6] Ibid., 117.

[7] C.G. Jung, "The Transcendent Function," in *CW*, vol. 8 (Princeton, NJ: Princeton University Press, 1969).

[8] Coline Covington and Wharton, B., eds., *Sabina Spielrein: Forgotten Pioneer of Psychoanalysis, Second Edition* (London: Routledge, 2015), 11.

[9] C.G. Jung, *The Red Book: Liber Novus*, ed. Sonu Shamdasani, tr. John Peck, Mark Kyburz, and Sonu Shamdasani (New York, NY: W.W. Norton, 2009).

[10] Jung, *Memories, Dreams, Reflections*, 78.

[11] Ibid., 223.

[12] Jung, "The Transcendent Function," *CW* 8, par. 180.

[13] Jung, *Memories, Dreams, Reflections*, 18.

[14] Ibid., 21.

[15] Ibid., 23.

[16] Ibid.

[17] Joan Chodorow, ed., *Jung on Active Imagination* (Princeton, NJ: Princeton University Press, 1997), 1.

[18] Ibid.

[19] Ibid., 4.

[20] Jung, "The Transcendent Function," *CW* 8, par. 170.

[21] Ibid., par. 171.

[22] Ibid.

[23] Ibid., par. 159.

[24] Ibid., par. 155.

[25] Ibid., par. 167.

[26] Ibid.

[27] Ibid.

[28] Ibid.

[29] Ibid., 168.

[30] Deirdre Bair, Jung: a Biography (Boston, MA: Little, Brown, 2003).

[31] Ibid., 18, 21.

[32] Jung, *Memories, Dreams, Reflections*, 21.

[33] Ibid.

[34] On Jung's splitting see the following review and articles: Donald W. Winnicott, Review of "*Memories, Dreams, Reflections* by C.G. Jung," in *International Journal of Psycho-Analysis*, 1964, 45, 450–455; also David Sedgwick, "Winnicott's dream: Some reflections on D.W. Winnicott and C.G. Jung," in *Journal of Analytical Psychology*, 2008, 53, 4, 543–60; and William Merdith-Owen, "Winnicott's invitation to 'further games of Jung-analysis,'" in *Journal of Analytical Psychology*, 2015, 60, 12-31.

[35] For additional references on "hidden trauma" see: Marcus West, *Into the Darkest Places: Early Relational Trauma and Borderline States of Mind* (London: Karnac, 2016), 61-62.

[36] Mary Main and Hess, E., "Parents' unresolved traumatic experiences are related to infant disorganized attachment status: Is frightened and/or frightening parental behavior the linking mechanism?" In Greenberg, M., Cummings, E., eds., *Attachment in the Preschool Years: Theory, Research and Intervention* (Chicago, IL: University of Chicago Press, 1990), 161-184.

[37] See Giovanni Liotti, "Disorganized/disoriented attachment in the etiology of the dissociative disorders," in Dissociation, 1992, 4, 196-204 in Karlen Lyons-Ruth, Dutra, L., Schuder, M., Bianchi, L., "From Infant Attachment to Adult Dissociation: Relational Adaptations or Traumatic Experiences?" In *Psychiatric Clinics of North America*, 2006, 29.

[38] Karlen Lyons-Ruth, Dutra, L., Schuder, M., Bianchi, L., "From Infant Attachment to Adult Dissociation: Relational Adaptations or Traumatic Experiences?" In *Psychiatric Clinics of North America*, 2006, 29.

[39] C.G. Jung, *The Psychogenesis of Mental Disease*, in CW, vol. 3 (New York, NY: Pantheon Books, 1960), par. 399.

[40] Regina Pally, *The Mind-Brain Relationship* (London and New York, NY: Routledge, 2000), 132.

[41] For specific references cited here, see Joseph Cambray and Carter, L., "Chapter 5: Analytic Methods," in *Analytical Psychology: Contemporary Perspectives in Jungian Analysis* (New York, NY: Routledge, 2004).

[42] Dan Siegel, *The Developing Mind, Second Edition: How Relationship and the Brain Interact to Shape Who We Are* (New York, NY: Guilford Press, 2012).

[43] See review article by Bridget Murray, "Writing to Heal," in *APA Monitor on Psychology,* June 2001, 33, 6, 1. Cites work of researchers James Pennebaker and Joshua Smyth who document immune system improvement with writing about trauma. Murray also cites literature to the contrary.

[44] Linda Carter, "Bidirectional Influence in the Matisse/Picasso Relationships and Clinical Practice," *ARAS Online* (2009). Also, Jung as proto-intersubjectivist was discussed as part of a panel with Andrew Samuels and David Sedgwick called "The analyst is as much 'in the analysis' as the patient: Jung as Pioneer of Relational Psychoanalysis," in *The Legacy of Stephen Mitchell Sustaining Creativity in Our Psychoanalytic Work, 10th Annual Conference,* sponsored by International Association of Relational Psychoanalysis and Psychotherapy, The Roosevelt Hotel. New York City, 2012.

[45] E. Bruce Robertson, Ph.D., Director of the Art Design & Architecture Museum, University of California at Santa Barbara (UCSB), personal communication, March 2018.

[46] D. N. Stern et. al., "Non-interpretative Mechanisms in Psychoanalytic Therapy: The 'Something More' Interpretation," in *The International Journal of Psychoanalysis*, 79, 904.

[47] Howard Risatti, *A Theory of Craft: Function and Aesthetic Expression* (Chapel Hill, NC: University of North Carolina Press, 2007), 78.

[48] Ibid., 99.

[49] Ibid., 101.

[50] Ibid.

[51] Ibid.

[52] John Ruskin as quoted in Alexander Langlands, *Craeft: Inquiry into the Origins and True Meaning of Traditional Crafts* (New York, NY: W.W. Norton, 2018), 24.

[53] Definition of the word *manual* from (www.vocabulary.com/dictionary/manual). Retrieved March 2018, 54.

[54] Erika Schlegel, March 11, 1921, Notebooks, Schlegel papers. Quoted by Sonu Shamdasani, *"Liber Novus*: The 'Red Book' of C.G. Jung," in C.G. Jung, *The Red Book: Liber Novus: A Reader's Edition* (New York, NY: W.W. Norton, 2012), 37.

[55] Jung, *The Red Book: Liber Novus: A Reader's Edition*, 78.

[56] Ruskin's views described in Langlands, *Craeft: Inquiry into the Origins and True Meaning of Traditional Crafts*, 32-33.

[57] Ibid., 28.

[58] Ibid., 9.

[59] Howard Risatti, *A Theory of Craft: Function and Aesthetic Expression*, 56.

[60] Ibid., 57.

[61] Richard Sennett, *The Craftsman* (New Haven, CT: Yale University Press, 2008), 211.

[62] Ibid.

Jung's *Red Book* and the Alchemical *Coniunctio*

Mathew Mather

Our age is seeking a new spring of life. I found one and
drank of it and the water tasted good.[1]

C.G. Jung

Liber Novus and Alchemy

On Friday, December 12, 1913, while at his desk deeply troubled,
Jung took the decisive step to "let himself go." Sinking into a
trancelike state, he entered an otherworldly imaginal realm that
would remind him of the land of the dead. Thus began his so-called
experiment as a confrontation with the unconscious.[2] He chronicled
the ensuing experiences over the next few months in what he called
his *Black Books*. Over the following years, he developed commentary
on the experiences and artistically reworked the material into
calligraphic text and exquisite images in the style of an illuminated
manuscript. This became his *Red Book*, which he titled *Liber Novus*.

Jung notes that December 12 was Advent.[3] That evening, in
1913, the moon was approaching a full moon in Gemini (sun in
Sagittarius). To be precise, it would be full moon the following night,
on the December 13. This is noteworthy, as Jung at this stage of his
life had already developed a keen interest in astrology.[4] Less certain,
though, was whether or not he knew that this portion of the sky,
being traversed by the sun, is also part of the "serpent-bearer"
constellation Ophiuchus (associated with the Greek Asclepius).[5] This
constellation has often been touted as the 13th sign as an alternative
zodiac to the Aristotelian-derived 12 signs, prevalent in popular
culture. The sun during this time of the year was also moving into

close conjunction (celestial longitude) with the brightest star in Ophiuchus, known as *Ras Alhague*. This star, on the forehead of Ophiuchus, as "third eye," is associated in astrological lore with intuitive vision.

In Greek mythology, Asclepius was taught by the wounded healer, the centaur Chiron. He had the power to not only heal but to bring the dead back to life. Such connotations have contributed to his serpent-entwined staff becoming the iconic sign for medicine and a prominent icon in Western alchemy. This serpent holder is also a starkly contrasting image to Christian iconography such as Saint George and the Dragon and Saint Patrick and the Snake. In Jungian parlance, Asclepius is an image that harmoniously unites, and thus heals, the "split archetype" of spirit and instinct.

Liber Novus, especially the aspect of it as an imaginal voyage, has its origin in this time moment that includes a 12-13 ambiguity and a divinatory focalization on Ophiuchus/Asclepius. Furthermore, esoterically considered, the numerological expansion from 12 to 13 implies the inclusion of feminine and shadowlike components that do not fit comfortably within traditional Christianity. These elements include: Judas, Mary Magdalene, Lilith, 13 lunar cycles, "serpent charmer." Not surprisingly, in biblical symbolism, the number 13 has been summarized as meaning "lawlessness and rebellion." In short, its inclusion would entail an adjustment of the Christian myth from a "split" toward more unitary formulations, as an integration of the shadow and the feminine.

However, nowhere in *Liber Novus* do we meet such personalities as Asclepius and Lilith. Instead, at the beginning, we meet the biblical figures of Elijah and Salome. The work is also far more informed by a Gnostic sensibility than alchemical ideas. This is not surprising, as Jung's serious interest in alchemy only began when most of *Liber Novus* had already been completed, in 1928. Understandably, there are precious few explicit references to alchemy in this work.

Based on this observation it may seem superfluous to bother with a consideration of this book from an alchemical perspective. We should, however, remember that in the final paragraph of *Liber Novus,* Jung wrote of how alchemy allowed him to integrate the experiences into a whole. Retrospectively, he also considered this work in terms of an alchemical *opus*, derived from the *Black Books* as a *prima materia* to be worked upon. In *Memories, Dream, Reflections* we read: "It has taken me virtually forty-five years to distil within the vessel of my scientific work the things I experienced and wrote down at that time. ... I hit upon this stream of lava, and the heat of its fires reshaped my life. ... the primal stuff that compelled me to work upon it."[6] A few pages on, we read: "the process through which I had passed at that time [1913-17] corresponded to the process of alchemical transformation."[7]

* * *

In what follows I consider a specific alchemical notion as the *coniunctio*. After clarifying Jung's understanding of this idea, I provide further context by locating it in terms of what could be considered his Aquarian myth. This "astro-alchemical myth" forms a conceptual framework to then consider a sample of *coniunctiones* that appear in *Liber Novus*. After this, I recount a synchronicity story as a return to the theme of Ophiuchus/Asclepius, proffered as an example of the value of *Liber Novus* for our times.

The Alchemical *Coniunctio*

Jung was embroiled in alchemical research for more or less the last three decades of his life (1928 up to his death in 1961). During this period the notion of the *coniunctio*, as a central concern, informed much of his mature works. Concerning this notion he stated: "the [alchemical coniunctio] ... usually consists in the union of two pairs of opposites, a lower (water, blackness, animal, snake) with an upper (bird, light, head, etc) and a left (feminine) with a right (masculine)."[8]

For example, these features are clearly seen in the 16th-century *Rosarium Philosophorum* woodcut series. We get a King (right) and a Queen (left), with a dove (above) and a "mercurial water" (below). Such a configuration can be considered as a compensatory archetypal image relative to the "Christian myth" with its privileging of only the transcendent above and the masculine. A chthonic below and the feminine are undervalued and often despised, mirroring the split myth, or *separation,* of Christianity (male-female, good-evil, spirit-matter, heaven-hell).

For Jung, medieval alchemy, as an esoteric undercurrent to a collective Christian consciousness, was not only compensatory but also prospective and visionary of a grand archetypal dynamic from *separatio* to *coniunctio.* More broadly, he believed there was an evolution from Gnosticism to medieval alchemy—and then his Analytical Psychology picking up the thread in the 20th century.

A major difference between the alchemical worldview and the post-Enlightenment scientific-materialist worldview is that the former adheres to the notion of a chain of correspondences that includes astrological and magical affinities.

To illustrate: the King has correspondences that include the sun, the substance gold, the alchemist, a sunflower, a bee, the zodiacal constellation Leo. The Queen's correspondences include the Moon, the substance silver, *soror mystica,* a moonflower, a spider, the zodiacal sign of Cancer. An attempt to achieve an amalgam of gold and silver (*coniunctio*) in the *vas* thus has "magical correspondences" that may correlate to the relationship (and transferences) between alchemist and *soror mystica.* A bee getting caught in a spider's web, during an attempt at a *coniunctio* of gold and silver during a solar eclipse, for instance, may synchronistically reflect the great difficulties inherent in achieving this operation.

* * *

Furthermore, associated with the *coniunctio,* especially in its more gendered male-female forms, is the consequential birth of a divine child as the *filius philosophorum* ("son of the philosophers"). In Analytical Psychology, this is the birth and growth of the self in the psyche, as a result of ego-consciousness in dynamic relation to the unconscious (individuation).

Jung's Aquarian Myth

Jung believed his life coincided with the transition of the Great Ages, from the Aeon of Pisces to the Aeon of Aquarius. Each Aeon, as the precession of the spring equinox through a zodiacal sign, takes about 2,165 years. In his reckoning, the Aeon of Pisces can be considered synchronistic with the "Christian myth" over the roughly past 2,000 years. The beginning of the new Aeon, according to him, may well have been coincident with his life (though precise timing turns out to be problematic).

In his volume *Aion*, Jung expands on the Age of the Fishes. Broadly, the Aeon of Pisces is characterized as a *separatio*. The early centuries of Christianity coinciding with the precession of the equinox traversing through the first vertical fish mirrored heavenly aspirations of overcoming instinctual nature (sins of the flesh). This characterized not only traditional Christianity but also the more esoteric Gnosticism with its myths of ascension. In this work, Jung further points out that the precessed equinox moving to the second (horizontal) fish coincided with an enantiodromian swing away from spirit and a greater valuation of matter and a preoccupation with the Antichrist. This sweep of time, in effect, had more clearly differentiated out a range of opposites such as spirit-matter, heaven-hell, Christ and the Antichrist.

The Age of Aquarius, the water-bearer, is composed of the symbol of a "cosmic anthropos" holding a *vas* (grail) out of which a "divine water" flows. The cosmic anthropos is sometimes represented as angelic, with wings.[9] This symbol can be considered especially in terms of the *coniunctio*.[10] The differentiation of opposites in the Aeon of Pisces can now become united in the Aquarian vessel, or *vas*, by means of an alchemical *opus* such as the individuation of Analytical Psychology. Out of this operation, a new being, as a new God, can hatch in the individual psyche (as opposed to a singular historical person, like Jesus).

A further observation is that the vertical and horizontal fishes of the Piscean Age are above the ecliptic. This could be interpreted as the Christian myth being a predominantly transcendent religion, in which God is largely a *deus absconditus*. In contrast, the constellation Aquarius intersects the ecliptic, signifying deity experienced as an immanence and as a state of grace.

In summary: The Christian Aeon, with its crucifix-like image of the sword, constellated a *separatio*. In contrast, the Aquarian Aeon, with its graillike vessel, constellates a *coniunctio*. The opposites of the Piscean Aeon, as the two fishes, find a variety of alchemical symbolic expressions: winged and wingless dragons, king and queen, red and white substances, stag and unicorn—requiring unification within the *vas*. Out of this *vas*/womb, a divine child can be born and fertility restored to a wasteland.

Such a meta-narrative, like Jung's "secret knowledge," forms an almost invisible structure that underpins his life myth. Understandably, he likened himself to Wolfgang Goethe, whom he considered was also "in the grip of that process of archetypal transformation which has gone on through the centuries ... what was alive and active within him was a living substance, a suprapersonal process, the great dream of the *mundus archetypes*."[11] *Liber Novus* (the *New Book*) can be understood within this esoteric context as a transition of the Ages from Pisces to Aquarius.

I now explore three successive *coniunctiones* evident in *Liber Novus*. The first appears in *Liber Primus*. The remaining two are in *Liber Secundus*.

The *Red Book* and Alchemical *Coniunctiones*

Toward the end of *Liber Primus*, there is a climactic moment that develops over three nights. On the third night, Elijah appears on a steep ridge, amid a wasteland. The scene is divided into daylight on the right and nighttime on the left, with a rock between. From the night, a large black serpent emerges and is met by a large white serpent emerging from the day. After a tumultuous battle, a unified, single white-black serpent emerges.

The scene then changes to Calvary, the mount on which Jesus Christ was crucified. Jung witnesses the cross, the removal of the cross, and the lamentation. Comforted, he then sees the divine child holding the two serpents, the white one in his right hand, the dark one in his left. Shortly after, he sees Christ on the green mountain, in the last hour of his crucifixion. Blood streams from its summit. Moments later, Jung finds himself in the place of Christ.

A black serpent, coiled around his feet, winds itself around his body. His head becomes that of a lion. The serpent then agonizingly squeezes him in its coils. Blood streams from his body and flows down the mountainside. Salome then wraps her black hair around his feet, at which she cries, "I see light!" Her blindness is gone. The serpent falls lethargically onto the ground. Jung then walks to Elijah, who is shining like a flame, and kneels at his feet. Soon after, the scene ends, and Jung reemerges from the mystery to everyday consciousness.

This event can be considered in terms of the alchemical *coniunctio*. In the system of correspondences the sun (Sol) corresponds to the lion, gold, king etc. The moon (Luna), corresponds to the serpent,[12] silver, queen, etc. In this visceral and torturous image, we get a coming together of these two principles. At the heart of this mystery is an apotheosis, as Jung's suffering identity with deity.

The image, as a Leontocephalus, can be amplified.[13] A similar image is found in the Mithraic mysteries as Zervan Akaruna or Aion—a lion-headed deity entwined by a python-like coiled serpent. The mythologist Joseph Campbell elaborates this image by identifying the lion as a solar symbol (eternity) and the serpent to a lunar symbol (time). He also points out that the name Zervan Akarana means "Boundless Time." A lightning bolt on its chest signifies "ultimate illumination" as an apotheosis at the core of the mystery.[14] It has also been linked to seven coils (chakra system, seven initiatory stages), with the serpent head appearing at the forehead, symbolic of ultimate illumination at the third eye. Notably, this image also has affinities with the serpent-holder constellation Ophiuchus/Asclepius.

It is this image of the Leontocephalus that Jung later chose as a frontispiece to his book *Aion,* which chronicles the symbolism of the self through the Aeon of Pisces.[15] This suggests that his apotheosis, as identification with this figure, represents an avatar-like experience of a Great Age as a recapitulation of the Piscean Aeon and anti-cipatory of the *coniunctio* of the coming Age of Aquarius. In the *vas* of his psyche, two "contrary substances" have amalgamated. The Hermes-like divine child, holding a tension of black and white ser-pents, is a further corroborative symbol.

Astrologer, Jungian analyst, and scholar Liz Greene writes about this image: "Jung's leontocephalus is an image of the polarity of Aquarius and Leo, the celestial Man and the celestial Lion conjoined and united: a kind of reversed image of the about-to-be-born 'rough beast' in Yeat's own prophetic poem ab out the changing of the Aions, *The Second Coming*, which has 'a shape with lion body and the head of a man.'"[16] Jung, as she so eloquently elaborates, was born with Aquarius rising and while the sun was setting in Leo.

* * *

The next *coniunctio* appears in *Liber Secundus*. The book begins with Jung in a medieval castle at the highest point in a tower, wearing green garments. Winding toward him along a road through forests is The Red One. In angst, Jung realizes he is headed toward him but is greatly relieved, upon meeting, that he is not "the devil" bent on harming him. They engage in a spirited dialogue. Jung tells him, "You're no real pagan, but the kind of pagan who runs alongside our Christian religion."[17] In further dialogue, The Red One comments about dancing through life and reflects on "some third thing for which dancing would be a symbol."[18] At this, The Red One changes into a more human reddish flesh color, and Jung's green garments sprout leaves. There has been a "chemical exchange" in which both have been transformed.

Later in the journey, Jung encounters an ascetic Christian anchorite called Ammonius. This character is in a solitary contem-plation in the Libyan desert, dedicated to a single holy book like the Bible. Ammonius introduces Jung to the profound scriptures but also to a deep appreciation for the desert and its timeless solar cycles. Jung, expounding a soliloquy on the sun as the deity, ends up seducing Ammonius into sharing his appreciation for "glorious Helios."

Ammonius, shocked, realizes something is amiss: "no, that is pagan—what's wrong with me? I'm confused—you are Satan—I recognize you—give way, adversary!"[19] Jung escapes and returns to his normal waking state, back in the 20th century. Later, he accuses Ammonius of hiding his evil behind his virtues and claims that he "locked Satan in the abyss for a millennium, and when the millennium had passed, you laughed at him, since he had become a children's fairy tale."[20]

A while later Jung finds himself walking in the countryside among hills and flowers with a green forest ahead and accompanied by The Red One and Ammonius. The Red One has become gaunt and shabby, and his hair has turned gray. Ammonius looks like a paunchy old monk. After some dialogue between them, Jung leaves.

Dreamlike, his situation then changes. He finds himself in the grip of a profound transformation amid darkness, death, drunkenness, and music. He is born from a woman and grows, magically, in a matter of hours. It is springtime. He further recounts "a strange being grew through me. This was a laughing being of the forest, a leaf green daimon, a forest goblin and prankster … utterly inconstant and superficial, and yet reaching deep down, down to the kernel of the world … within myself I had become one as a natural being … I was a hobgoblin."[21]

This scene represents another *coniunctio*. Ammonius can be understood as a personification of the first vertical (spirit, Christ) fish in the Age of Pisces as a heavenly aspiration and ascetic overcoming of bodily instinct. The Red One could then be a personification of the second horizontal (matter, Antichrist) fish of the Age of Pisces. These two "white and red substances" in the *vas* of Jung's psyche undergo an "alchemical transformation" to create a new vitality as a *viriditas*. In a kind of dynamic equilibrium, each is changed. Jung's ego-consciousness as "mercuriallike substance" is key toward catalyzing this transformation and undergoes radical experiences that culminate in him being born as a "divine child" and as a "hobgoblin."

Image 22, in *Liber Novus*, is embedded within the text of this narrative. The scarabs symbolize the dynamism behind a "new dawn" (a new Platonic month!). In a *circulatio* motion, they rotate symbols of Christ and the Antichrist (crucifixes) around a central *vas*, in which a blessed green-gold tree grows. This is a variation on the "two fishes" being united in the *vas* of Aquarius. The image also illustrates the integration of a (spiritual—violet) above and a (instinctual—earth colored) below. Compared to the previous *coniunctio*, this one is "higher" and more differentiated in that it involves humans and a more prominent "divine child."

* * *

The final *coniunctio* I consider appears in *Liber Secundus*. Here, Jung regresses to a much deeper mythohistorical layer of the psyche, prior to the "Christian myth," and restores a core of this experience into a contemporary and visionary context as "a new God for a new Age."

Traveling east, where the sun rises, he traverses a harsh terrain and eventually gets to a mountain ridge. Approaching the ridge, he hears a rhythmic mighty din, which turns out to be the approach of a giant called Izdubar. The giant has bull horns, a suit of armor on his chest, exquisite stones in a messy beard, and a bull-striking double-ax in his hand. Fortunately, Izdubar does not kill him but rather engages in a dialogue, as he is on a soul-searching journey to the west. Jung, as modern man, reveals a scientific and disenchanted worldview of the west, including a discrediting of the "immortal soul." Izdubar, the ancient one, is mortified and collapses.

Jung "magics" his fallen God, Izdubar, into an egg and returns home to the west. With "the magical warmth of his gaze," he incubates the egg on a sacred red rug, accompanied by Vedic incantations. In the first incantation, for instance, we read: "He is the eternal emptiness and the eternal fullness. Nothing resembles him and he resembles everything. Eternal darkness and eternal brightness. Eternal below and eternal above. Double nature in one."[22]

At the end of the third day he hatches the egg. Amid a fiery plume of smoke, a divine child as the new God, the Orphic Phanes, emerges. A sequence of shape-shifts of Phanes then ensue that include: Telesphorous (daimon of Asklepius); dragon-slayer; cosmic Anthropos (Image 123). The shape-shifts eventually settle as the iconic Philemon (Image 154) alongside a Priestess in a temple (Image 155).

* * *

The name Izdubar is a synonym for Gilgamesh, from ancient Sumeria (~ 2500 B.C.E.). Historically, this epoch coincides with the Age of the Bull (Taurus), ruled by the Goddess Ishtar, and associated especially with the planet Venus. In terms of Platonic months, Jung had regressed to the "dawn of civilization" when humanity was separating from its "animal nature." In the epic, the cultured king Gilgamesh and wild man Enkidu end up in a grueling fight but end up settling their differences and becoming inseparable friends.

Jung's unique depiction of Izdubar is an integration of the solar hero-king Gilgamesh (two-thirds god, one-third man) and his "twin brother" as the lunar wild man Enkidu, roaming like a gazelle (horns as crescent moon). Izdubar, with both Enkidu's horns and Gilgamesh's cultured beard and attire, also combines the earthy-red (infrared) instinctual polarity and the celestial-blue (ultraviolet) spiritual polarity of the archetype, evident in his blue and red attire. Based on these observations, Izdubar can be thought of in terms of especially a "sun-moon" *coniunctio*, at an animal and human level with intimations of a higher "royal" *coniunctio*.

This vital essence from prehistory, incubated in the egg, is surfaced to Jung's contemporary times. The Vedic incantations, as a more "feminine" spiritual wisdom tradition, allows for its nurturance and growth. Izdubar is effectively transmuted into a "bright ambiguity," hatched as the divine child and the newly appearing God as the Orphic Phanes.[23]

Phanes then shape-shifts. Eventually, we see him as monster-slayer and then as a kind of "cosmic Anthropos" (Image 123). As cosmic anthropos, we clearly see "a new god for a new Age" as the symbols now correlate to Aquarius. The slayed monster (Atmavictu) is fertilizing a "wasteland" with the help of the life-engendering cabiri and "magic water" pouring from the Anthropos as water-bearer. This "water" combines the red and blue (the instinctual and spiritual polarities of the archetype) and thus reinforces *coniunctio* symbolism, of having combined two substances in a *vas*.[24] Furthermore, a celestial temple in the sky associates with the square constellation Pegasus, located between Pisces and Aquarius.

Some pages later we get a further settling, with the images of Philemon (Image 154) and a Priestess (Image 155). The winged Philemon has a solarlike halo, whereas the veiled Priestess is depicted with the crescent Moon. In these images we finally get a more gender-balanced representation of the *coniunctio*, now represented at the highest level as celestial Sol-Luna illuminated and angelic.

Philemon is not an inaccessible and transcendent God of the Christian Aeon of the Fishes. Instead, Jung has enigmatic dialogues with him as his "psychagogue and guru" not only in imaginal trancelike states, but also during garden walks. In a dialogue, toward the end of *Liber Secundus*, he says to Philemon: "Oh Philemon, you are a man, and you prove that men are not sheep, since you look after the greatest in yourself, and hence fructifying water flows into your garden from inexhaustible jugs," and a bit further on "... you pour out living water, from which the flowers of your garden bloom, a starry water, a dew of the night."[25] Philemon is clearly depicted as an angelic water-bearer, and therefore as a new god-image of the approaching Aquarian Age.

* * *

In summary, we see that much of *Liber Novus* can be considered in terms of an alchemical *opus*, with its imagery of the *vas* and alchemical operations such as *separationes* and *coniunctiones*. I gave the gist of such an analysis by focusing especially on the *coniunctio* in light of a transition of the Ages from Pisces to Aquarius. As we witnessed, the narrative arc of *Liber Novus* reveals at least three *coniunctiones* that progress from the animal (lion and serpent) to the human (The Red One and Ammonius) and on toward the trans-human or angelic (Philemon and Priestess). As such, the progression depicts elements of a right (King), a left (Queen), an Above (wings, Sun, Moon) and a Below (serpents). A greater integration though continues beyond *Liber Novus* as informed by Jung's intense fascination with alchemy over the last three decades of his life. His

Bollingen tower, paintings and engravings as well as his written *magnum opus* especially embody such a development.

I now return to my opening image, as the serpent holder Ophiuchus, and relate a synchronicity story as a way of illuminating a contemporary resonance with *Liber Novus*.

Full Moon in Ophiuchus: A Synchronicity Story

In the early spring of 2014, I decided to put in a proposal to present for a Jungian interdisciplinary conference in Wroclaw, Poland, scheduled for June 12-14, 2014. With the recent publication of my book *The Alchemical Mercurius* (based on my Ph.D.), I decided to focus on the theme of *Saint Patrick and the Snake* approached through the lens of fine art. Living in Ireland, this would help with some much-needed contextualization of my project, in terms of the changing myth/s of our time, and especially in light of having spent the past few years in contemplation of an alchemical serpent! The relevance of Saint Patrick and the Snake is that he was supposedly responsible for initiating Ireland into the Christian faith. Mythically, he is famous for driving all the snakes out of Ireland, where "snakes" is thought to refer to the older pagan religions. Ophiuchus as serpent-bearer represents the opposite.

Although I had a broad idea, I still wasn't sure which artist/s to focus on. It was around this time that an email from our college library was sent around, as periodically it does, to enumerate recent additions to the library. One of the books that caught my attention was titled *Gone: Site-Specific Works by Dorothy Cross*. This reignited an old interest, having come across her *Virgin Shroud* in the Tate Modern some years prior. After a short perusal of the book, I was captivated. Without any doubt, I had found my artist.

Dorothy Cross kindly agreed to meet up for a discussion. She was also generous enough to share her astrological details, which revealed her sun in Aquarius and moon in the 13th constellation Ophiuchus. This lunar placement could be read as the myth of her life having something to do with a feminine "serpent-bearer."

Around this time (and earlier), the Irish news was replete with sordid revelations of the Catholic Church, such as child sexual abuse by the clergy. The tragic history of the Magdalen Laundries, of unwed mothers being separated from their babies and doomed to a life of slave labor cleaning dirty linen (to atone for their "carnal sins") was brought painfully to light by such award-winning films as *Philomena* (2013). Other Irish films such as *Calvary* (2014) depicted the pathos of an eroding faith in the Catholic Church, of a community "losing its myth." This mirrored the dire situation of a faltering religion and this particular aspect of Irish culture in crisis.

Taking such considerations into account, I finally devised a title for my conference proposal: *Saint Patrick and the Snake: interpreting contemporary Irish art through the lens of Jung's alchemical myth.* In light of my topic, I found it quaint that the conference program was first posted on the IAJS (International Association of Jungian Studies) discussion forum on Saint Patrick's day, March 17, 2014. According to this initial program, I was scheduled to present on Thursday June 12 (at the time, I wondered if this might be changed to the more symbolically loaded Friday the 13th).

Some days after the publication of the conference schedule an impressive e-publication of the program followed. I was still scheduled for June 12. The program also showcased the presenters by means of a short biography, their abstract, and an image. The picture chosen for me was a beautiful stained-glass image of Saint Patrick in his religious regalia holding a crozier in his left hand and a church close to his bosom in his right hand. Impressive as this was, I could not help but wonder about the other character in the title of my presentation: the Snake.

I acknowledged the exquisite image of Saint Patrick chosen for me by reproducing it on my introductory slide. I also decided though to rectify the missing Snake by including an image of a sensuous and erotic Eve and the Serpent in the garden of paradise, by placing this next to Saint Patrick.[26] The two images, side by side, allowed for a charged comparison: male and female, good and evil, spirit and matter, culture and nature, clothed and naked.

I was also intrigued when, a couple of weeks before the conference, my presentation was changed from Thursday, June 12 to

Friday, June 13 (without requesting this). In the aftermath of a busy academic year, I also had not expanded my research to include astrological considerations. I knew the conference would be during a full moon, though I did not pursue this any further.

It was only once I was in Wroclaw though, on the Wednesday evening, that I realized the upcoming full moon in the constellation Ophiuchus might also be near a significant fixed star. Having too small a screen on my smartphone and no astrological software, I texted my wife to ask if she could check on this. She texted back soon after with news that the full moon, taking place at 22 degrees Sagittarius, would be at the same celestial longitude as *Ras Alhague*, the star located on the "forehead" of Ophiuchus.

The symbolism of this, in light of not only my presentation but the conference theme as a whole, was astonishing. I briefly elaborated this anomaly at the start of my talk on Friday the 13th with rough pen marks on a flip chart, as I did not have time to include a slide. Ophiuchus/Asclepius could be considered, in many ways, as paradigmatic of the Jungian project and of what it has to offer other disciplines. The "feminine" lunar, though, highlighted a complement to the "masculine" solar that characterized the beginning of Jung's imaginal voyage (with the *Sun* in Ophiuchus) that resulted in *Liber Novus*.

A full moon in Ophiuchus invokes more of a *female* "serpent charmer" and so amplifies a greatly contrasting image to Saint Patrick and the snake. The serpent charmer implies a different myth, aligned to the alchemical *coniunctio*, offering a healing for the ailing myth of a wounded Christianity. Such a theme resonates with much of Dorothy Cross' creative project, as I touched on in the presentation.

In a literal sense she often uses the motif of a *cross* in her art, as a reworking of this most Christian of symbols. A dramatic example is a photograph of her lying naked on her back, in a crucifix-like posture, in a natural rectangular rock formation in the *Serpent's Lair* off the rugged west coast of Ireland, on Inis Mor on the Aran islands.[27]

Another example: one of Cross' site-specific installations, as part of the 1992 Edge Biennale in Madrid, occurred in a 12th-century convent that is still used as a nuns residence. Titled *La Primera Cena* (*The First Supper*) the enigmatic work features an abject-looking "milking maid" chair buttressed into a circle of 12 silver vessels (her

Twelve Apostles) that surround a rectangular table on which a cowhide is placed. Prominent udders, as if ready to be milked, point upward. Her inclusion of a 13th place as "milking maid" (or excluded other, or everyman/woman!) suggests a radical enactment toward a reconfiguring of the Christian myth—a *first supper*, perhaps, with the earthly Great Mother! Or Boann/Boinn, the Irish Cow Goddess!

Commentators agree on her bold project. One (non-Jungian) reviewer went so far as to write that "[whereas] St Patrick … drove the snakes out of Ireland; it would seem that Cross wants to re-introduce them."[28] Another (non-Jungian) writer states: "Cross … attempts to restore to Christian myth and iconography the powerful presence of the material body and desire."[29]

One might say her life's work has functioned, in part and in a visionary sense, to remove the oppressive shackles of Christian doctrine (concretized into secular law). Thanks to visionary artists such as her and the work of activists, progress has been made. The past few decades in Ireland has seen the legalization of: contraception (1980), divorce (1996), gay marriage (2015), and recently (on May 25, 2018) a repeal of the law that criminalizes abortion, the eighth amendment. Pressures are now also on for the inclusion of woman into the Catholic priesthood, as well as more separation between church and state in public institutions such as schools and hospitals.

* * *

In short, this *synchronistic happening* on Friday the 13th June 2014, precisely 100 years, six months and a day after Jung's imaginal descent on December 12, 1913, allows for a contemplation of changes unfolding within the cultural mythic landscape, of "dreaming the myth onward," by a witnessing of the work of one of Ireland's most acclaimed visual artists and of the Jungian project reaching out, more broadly, into a plethora of disciplines. These can be read as signs of a loosening myth and hopeful seeds of a new birthing emerging from the soulless clutter of broken images. In the words of Jungian scholar Thomas Arzt, "much would be gained if the planetary turbulences of postmodernity could be interpreted as a pregnant phase of initiation, as a *rite de passage*."[30]

Endnotes

This essay is based on themes in my book *The Alchemical Mercurius: Esoteric Symbol of Jung's Life and Works* (London and New York, NY: Routledge, 2014), with especial emphasis on chapter 5.

[1] Cited in C.G. Jung, *The Red Book: Liber Novus*, ed. Sonu Shamdasani, tr. John Peck, Mark Kyburz, and Sonu Shamdasani (New York, NY: W. W. Norton, 2009).

[2] C.G. Jung, *Memories, Dreams, Reflections*, ed. Aniela Jaffé (New York, NY: Vintage Books, 1963), 203.

[3] Advent is a holy day when the birth of Christ is anticipated, and also the anticipation of the Second Coming.

[4] See Liz Greene, *Jung's Studies in Astrology: Prophecy, Magic and the Qualities of Time* (London/New York, NY: Routledge 2018), 18-19.

[5] From his Letters, Seminars and Bollingen stone engravings we know that he had a great interest in the constellations, including those beyond the ecliptical zodiac of the twelve signs.

[6] Jung, *Memories, Dreams, Reflections*, 225.

[7] Ibid., 236.

[8] C.G. Jung, "The Philosophical Tree" in *CW*, vol. 13 (Princeton, NJ: Princeton University Press, 1967), par. 462.

[9] For a contemporary example, see French-Swiss painter and sculptor Niki de St. Phalle's *guardian angel* (1997) in the Zurich train station.

[10] Jung's *magnum opus*, *Mysterium Coniunctionis*, prospectively enacts this, as an elaboration of *Liber Novus*.

[11] Jung, *Memories, Dreams, Reflections*, 232.

[12] The serpents' ability to shed its skin, and renew itself, gives it Lunar associations: the Moon "dies but renews itself" every New Moon.

[13] See Liz Greene's contextualization of the Leontocephalus in Volume 1 of this series: "The Way of What is to Come: Jung's Vision of the Aquarian Age," 48-52. See Murray Stein and Thomas Arzt, eds., *Jung's Red Book for Our Time: Searching for Soul under Postmodern Conditions*, Vol. 1 (Asheville, NC: Chiron Publications, 2017).

[14] Joseph Campbell, *The Masks of God: Occidental Mythology* (Harmondsworth, England, Penguin Books, 1991), 263-266.

[15] Jung was a Leo. Just as in the Aeon of Pisces, the opposite sign of Virgo has great import, so in the Aeon of Aquarius, the opposite sign of Leo has significance.

[16] Liz Greene, *The Astrological World of Jung's Liber Novus: Daimons, Gods, and the Planetary Journey* (London/New York, NY: Routledge 2018), 168.

[17] Jung, *The Red Book*, 259.

[18] Ibid., 260.

[19] Ibid., 272.

[20] Ibid., 274.

[21] Ibid., 276.

[22] Ibid., 284.

[23] See Sonu Shamdasani's elaboration of this figure, and Jung's understanding of it, in Jung, *The Red Book*, 301 n211. Phanes is here described as having a united duality (four eyes, four wings etc.) and as a god of love, and as androgynous. For a more extensive elaboration, see Liz Greene's *The Astrological World of Jung's Liber Novus*, 129-139.

[24] Consider also a *sublimatio* of The Red One and Ammonius.

[25] Jung, *The Red Book*, 316.

[26] "The Temptation of Eve" by artist John Roddam Spencer-Stanhope (1829-1908).

[27] An internet image search using: "Dorothy Cross serpent's lair" should yield this image.

[28] Enrique Juncosa in *Dorothy Cross* (Irish Museum of Modern Art, Charta Publications, Dublin, 2005), 25.

[29] Robin Lydenberg (2005), *Gone: Site-Specific Works by Dorothy Cross* (McMullen Museum of Art, Boston College, University of Chicago Press) 29.

[30] Thomas Arzt in Volume 1 of this series: "The Way of What is to Come: Searching for Soul under Postmodern Conditions," 20; see Murray Stein and Thomas Arzt, eds., *Jung's Red Book for Our Time: Searching for Soul under Postmodern Conditions*, Vol. 1 (Asheville, NC: Chiron Publications, 2017).

The Red Book: A Journey from West to East via the Realm of the Dead

Megumi Yama

In this essay, I would like to bring Jung's cosmology in *Septem Sermones ad Mortuos* into contact with the concept of *kami* in Shintō. I hope this may present a new perspective on *Septem Sermones ad Mortuos*, especially with regard to "nothingness," which finally can lead to a deep understanding of similarities and differences between the West and the East. Why do I dare to struggle with such a challenging theme? I will answer this question later.

While Jung was confronting the unconscious during a period of inner disorientation, he encountered "the East" in his active imaginations. Since his childhood, he seems to have been attracted to things that compensate for what the West has devaluated and repressed for a long time in its history. Being engaged in a challenging inner journey, Jung drew many mandalas. Not until he received the manuscript of the German translation of *The Secret of the Golden Flower* from Richard Wilhelm did he think of them as an expression of the self. I would like to argue that Jung's journey was not merely in a horizontal direction from the West to the East but a long journey via descent in the vertical direction to the realm of the dead. That is to say Jung had to go through regaining contact with the dead before reaching the culture of the East. Because of globalization today, it is much easier to go around the world, and many people with various backgrounds have an opportunity to encounter different cultures for various reasons. We should keep in mind that when we cross the boundary between different cultures, inevitably we must also go through such an experience as Jung did, but for better or worse most people are unconscious of it.

In a series of conversations on *The Red Book* with Sonu Shamdasani, James Hillmann says at the very beginning: "... opening the *Red Book* seems to be opening the mouth of the dead."[1] I agree strongly. Then Hillman points out that the loss of contact with the dead is a collective symptom and that what matters is realizing there is a porous permeability between the living and the dead, between life and death. Shamdasani calls *The Red Book* Jung's "Book of the Dead" in the sense that this is his attempt to find a way of relating to the dead. As mentioned above, I would like to argue that crossing the boundary between different cultures entails such an experience of descent to the underworld.

I would like to answer the question of why I am writing on this topic. While reading *The Red Book,* I tried to experience what Jung went through for myself, and I came to realize that the source of the energy that urged me to involve myself with this challenging attempt was rooted in my personal life experience.

Because of my father's work, I lived in America with my family when I was 13 and 14 years old, which was the beginning of 1970s and, of course, long before globalization. At first I was embarrassed by the American clear-cut and rational way of thinking and speaking, but gradually I became well-adapted to such a different mode of thinking and communication. Although Japan was my native country, going back there after 15 months in America was quite difficult for me. Generally, Japan tends to be a homogeneous culture, and I, who had had a chance to live in a Western culture at the delicate time of adolescence, could no longer accept what other Japanese took for granted, without doubt unconsciously. I tried to be careful not to express myself clearly and directly, as this would go against the Japanese style of communication, where people are expected to express themselves in an implicit way and guess the intention and feeling of others without making anything clear.

Gradually, at least at the manifest level, I seemed to readapt to my former circumstances in Japan. On the other hand, at night I used to keep writing "I want something absolute" in my diary. I did not know what it meant in those days, but the desperate feeling of longing for the absolute at that time still comes back to me vividly after so many years. As is well-known, Japan is a Great Mother-dominated country, and after living in a Western country for a certain period of time, everything seemed to have felt to me so ambiguous that I had a sense of being dragged into a bottomless swamp, which may be compared to falling into the Pleroma. Japan's polytheistic culture may well be experienced as such after spending some time in Western monotheistic cultures. The former has no absolute center but non-fixed multiple perspectives, while the latter has one center. This is not only the matter of religion but also in the modes of living and thinking that are shaped in a long history of each culture. As I did not have enough knowledge to deal with this problem intellectually, what I experienced was the overwhelming feeling of longing for something absolute.

In *Septem Sermones ad Mortuos,* the text reads: "Differentiation is creation. It is differentiated. Differentiation is its essence and therefore it differentiates. Therefore man differentiates, since his essence is differentiation,"[2] and continues: "If we do not differentiate, … we fall into nondifferentiation … We fall into the Pleroma itself and cease to be created beings. We lapse into dissolution in nothingness. This is the death of the creature."[3] In Japanese culture, where everything is connected and homogeneity is unconsciously but forcibly valued, "discrimination" is the most difficult thing. I really wonder what the *principium individuationis* processes should be like in such a culture. I would like to argue that this is not a question for only Japanese but for people all over the world who are deeply and complicatedly influenced by each other because of globalization.

Anecdotally, I would like to add that it was the "Demian image" that supported me until my mid-20s. I read Hesse's *Demian* soon after I went back to Japan. A famous passage—"The bird fights its way out of the egg. The egg is the world. Who would be born must first destroy a world. The bird flies to God. That God's name is Abraxas"[4]—remained with me, although I knew nothing about Abraxas. As one now knows, in 1916-17 Hesse went through an analysis with Josef Bernhard Lang, a disciple of Jung. And later in 1921, after having analytical sessions with Jung, Hesse became very interested in Jungian psychology. *Demian* is considered to present Hesse's individuation process.

The Relationship with the Dead

One day in the beginning of 1916, Jung had a restless feeling, which was followed by a striking series of parapsychological events involving also his family members. In *Memories, Dreams, Reflections,* he writes of what happened:

> Around five o'clock in the afternoon on Sunday the front door bell began ringing frantically. ... The whole house was filled as if there were a crowd present, crammed full of spirits. ... I was all a-quiver with the question: 'For God's sake, what in the world is this?' Then they cried out in chorus, 'We have come back from Jerusalem where we found not what we sought.'[5]

With these words, *Septem Sermones ad Mortuos* commences. The subtitle of this work is: "... written by Basilides in Alexandria, the City where the East toucheth the West."[6] As soon as Jung took up a pen, he says, the whole assemblage of spirits evaporated, and the haunting was over. It seems to me that his writing itself worked as a consolation of the souls of the dead and settled Jung's soul, too.

The author was identified as Basilides, a famous Gnostic sage in Alexandria in the second century. At the same time, Basilides may mean a "man from Basel," who would be Jung himself.

I would like to point out one thing that may clearly show the difference between the West and Japan regarding the relationship between the living and the dead. When *Memories, Dreams, Reflections* was first translated in Japan in 1973, *Seven Sermons to the Dead* was included as an appendix. Hayao Kawai translated this title as "Shisha eno Nanatsu no Katarai,"[7] which literally means "Seven Talks to the Dead." *The Red Book* took over this translation when it was translated in 2010. When we use the word "talk" instead of "sermon," it is more natural to say "talk with the dead" rather than "talk to the dead." The latter suggests an interactive communication, but the former is a unilateral one. Needless to say, the original title feels severer than the Japanese title.

Why did Kawai choose "talk" instead of "sermon," despite the fact that "a talk to the dead" sounds somewhat strange? One of the reasons for it may be that generally Japanese prefer mild expressions to strong ones, especially if it is in reference to the dead. If *Seven Sermons to the Dead* were translated word by word, it would be "Nanatsuno Shisha eno Sekkyo," and perhaps many Japanese readers might feel something that does not fit well in their mind. While they do understand it intellectually, their indigenous sense as Japanese would feel somewhat unfamiliar with giving sermons to the dead. I am not sure if Kawai chose the word "talk" in order to be accepted by Japanese readers or not, but at least it is true that it feels much milder and that severity is weakened when we use "talk" instead of "sermon."

This may also have something to do with the relationship between the living and dead in Japan. In ancient times, when people died, their spirits were believed to ascend to the mountain. In those days the living and the spirit of the dead were thought to be living together without strict boundary. Hayao Kawai writes: "For Japanese the wall between this world and the other world is, by comparison, a surprisingly thin one."[8] Even today, Japanese occasionally tend to have a feeling that the dead are around us and watching us. Although Japan is one of the most highly developed countries in science, its premodern world may reappear in critical times such as unexpected natural disasters. After the Great East Japan Earthquake and Tsunami in 2011, so many strange stories concerning the sighting of spirits of deceased family members prevailed among survivors, especially in rural parts where the communities were expected to provide the function of protective containers. These stories were born in the ambiguous boundary between living and the dead. Some books report that at first these experiences were accepted among the survivors with surprise, but gradually they seemed to have brought deep healing to the people.[9]

Closeness to the dead may make Japanese prefer the word "talk," which implies mutual communication, rather than imagining the delivering of sermons. In any case, I would like to argue that lack of severity in Japanese culture in general is taken as either positive and negative.

The Concept of *Kami* in Shintō in Ancient Times

I would now like to introduce the concept of *kami* in Shintō in ancient times.[10] Since the concept is so fundamentally different from monotheistic Christian culture, I am afraid that it may look somewhat ambiguous or unclear. However, this is important because the ambiguous nature of *kami* seems to be not only unique in religious and cultural contexts but also noteworthy in terms of its deep fixedness in the Japanese psyche. I hope it presents another perspective when reading *Seven Sermons to the Dead*, especially with regard to Pleroma and Abraxas.

Although the Japanese word *kami* is usually translated into English with terms such as deity, god, or spirit, none of these words precisely captures its full meaning. What makes this concept more ambiguous is that due to the syncretism in Japanese religion, the term *kami* is used for both gods and goddesses in Buddhism and for the innumerable spirits of Shintō. Moreover, the word *kami* is not only used for Japanese *kami* but also for other religious deities such as Jesus Christ and all other gods and goddesses in religions and mythologies all over the world. Although Shintō is polytheistic as well as animistic, I am using the word "*kami*" instead of the plural "*kamis*" because plural and singular are not usually distinguished in the Japanese language. The *kami* of Shintō in ancient times are collectively called "*yaohorozu-no-kami*," literally meaning "eight-million-*kami*" in Japanese, and this is usually understood as an infinite number of omnipresent *kami*.

I would now like briefly to present some characteristics of ancient *kami*. In the ancient animistic world, *kami* were not separate from nature but were part of nature and possessed both good and evil characters without distinction. They were considered to be manifestations of the interconnecting energies of the universe and the energy of creation of all things. *Kami* are considered to reside in mountains, rocks, rivers, waterfalls, and other features of the landscape and in naturally occurring phenomena such as wind, lightning, earthquake, volcanic eruptions, and so on.

I would like to point out just two more important characteristics of the ancient *kami*. The first is the *kami*'s invisibility, the second is their mobility. Under the influence of the introduction of Buddhism in the sixth century, some *kami* were given form as statues or pictures, and permanent shrines were erected. But originally, according to Tetsuo Yamaori, a Japanese scholar of religion, invisible *kami* were believed to exist freely in the air, traveling from mountain to village, village to river, etc.[11] Yamaori writes: "*Kami* have transmigrated to de-individualized *kami* of the land of one's birth and the guardian *kami* of the land by sinking deeply into the internal part of the community."[12] They extinguished their personality by going into the inner part of the land. However, as the ages passed, certain objects and places began to be designated as the interfaces of humans and *kami*. There are natural sites that are considered to host unusually sacred spirits and therefore are considered to be places of worship. These venerated objects, together with the surrounding mountains or forests, gradually evolved into permanent shrines. Primitive Japanese *kami* hid themselves deep in the mountains where they resided, disappearing from view of the people. Through the medium of visual *shintai* (lit. *kami*'s body), people worship the accumulation of various *kami* (*yaohorozu-no-kami*) as one entity simply called *kami*.

As Shintō has no founder, no dogma, and no scriptures, it has been questioned whether it should actually be considered a religion. In general, Shintō has been regarded as Japan's indigenous belief, which traces its origins back to ancient animistic worship of nature and ancestors. Even after the major world religion of Buddhism arrived in Japan, the indigenous belief was not replaced or regarded as inferior. On the contrary, the primary beliefs of ancient Shintō are still today deeply imbued in Japanese culture and respected by people in everyday life. Many families venerate various household *kami*, such as the *kami* of fire and the *kami* of the kitchen, and these are still familiar even among young of this time. There used to be *kami* of mountains, *kami* of rice fields, *kami* of wells, etc., who existed all around. Although with the rapid economic development in 1960s and 1970s these *kami* seemed to have disappeared from modern society, I have realized that they still reside within people's deep psyche. The animistic beliefs seem to be somewhat alive in the undercurrents of society, in which inanimate items and objects are believed to have souls as do humans and animals. The popular Japanese phrase *mottainai* does not necessarily only mean "not wasting" but also the idea that we should respect even small things because spirits inhabit them.

In a similar vein, in the *Fourth Sermon to the Dead,* Philemon says: "Happy am I who can recognize the multiplicity and diversity of the Gods,"[13] to which the dead object that he seems to be teaching a raw form of superstition and polytheism. Philemon admonishes them: "Did they (the dead) do penance for the sacred ore that they dug up from the belly of the earth? No, they named, weighed, numbered, and apportioned all things. They did whatever pleased them. ... You saw the powerful—but this is precisely how they gave power to things unknowingly. Yet the time has come when things speak."[14] This seems to be similar to the thought that *kami* are felt to be omnipresent within everything in Japanese culture. It is also related to the Soul's words in a dialogue between Jung and Soul in *The Red Book* when she says: "You should become serious, and hence take your leave from science. ... Science is too superficial, mere language, mere tools."[15] I would argue that when the modern Western ego was introduced to Japan, it only superficially prevailed, and the old animistic beliefs were not totally excluded. People are living in a multilayered society, which can be seen as both positive and negative. Out of the denial of the modern Western ego, the new God Abraxas was born, who seems to have the similar characteristics to ancient Japanese *kami.*

Next, I would like to explore the Japanese attitude toward religion in general. Japanese people often visit Shintō shrines and Buddhist temples and pray to the *kami* at certain annual events, as well as at important life events, in order to convey gratitude and call upon them for protection. Nevertheless, what may seem strange is that most Japanese would not consciously identify themselves as either Buddhists or Shintōists. It is interesting that Yamaori notes:

> Our (Japanese) 'atheism' seems to be just a vague version
> and apparently different from the convinced atheism such
> as that which modern Western cultures produced. ... This
> is because we seem to have not necessarily performed the
> 'killing of God' as Dostoyevsky or Nietzsche have done.[16]

He mentions that the characteristic of the traditional Japanese
religious attitude lies not in the "either/or" but the "this and that."
Furthermore, he refers to Japanese atheism as "passive atheism,"
which was delineated from within a mental attitude of "this and that"
where the subject is extinguished. Therefore, Japanese tend to accept
and contain everything without excluding something because it does
not suit them.

On the contrary, at the beginning of the Second Sermon in
Septem Sermones ad Mortuos, the dead cry out, "We want to know
about God. Where is God? Is God dead?"[17] which sounds much more
earnest and serious than the Japanese attitude toward religion.
Philemon begins by answering, "God is not dead."[18] While remarking
that God's essence is "effective fullness," Philemon says: "Everything
that we do not differentiate falls into the Pleroma and is cancelled out
by its opposite. If, therefore, we do not differentiate God, effective
fullness is canceled out for us."[19] I would like to argue that there is an
important keyword, "differentiation," at the root of the difference
between Philemon's sermon and Japanese mentality.

Pleroma and "Nothingness"

I would now like to compare the notion of creation in Jung's cosmology
with that in Japanese mythology. First of all, it is interesting that the
First Sermon commences with "nothingness":

> Now hear: I begin with nothingness. Nothingness is the
> same as the fullness. In infinity full is as good as empty.
> Nothingness is empty and full. ... That which is endless
> and eternal has no qualities, since it has all qualities.
> We call this nothingness or fullness the *Pleroma*.[20]

Following this, descriptions of Pleroma continue on and on, which do not make much sense if we try to understand them according to rational thinking. It feels like a desperate effort to articulate the apparently contradictory characteristics of "nothingness" by all possible words. We must realize how laborious it is to describe "nothingness" with words and at the same time recognize that a logical dualism lies deep in the Westerner's psyche. Therefore, it was indispensable for Philemon to start by denying the dualism, that is to say, by dissolving the thick boundary between the opposites. I would argue that it was very meaningful for Jung to begin with "nothingness," even though it was a laborious process, because it finally led him to discover the self. Denying the existing rationality and trying to articulate "nothingness" with words as clear as possible is the first step toward the birth of Abraxas.

Hayao Kawai points out that a direct experience of "nothing-ness" is beyond human words and writes: "Positive and negative, subject and object are contained within the circle of nothingness beyond all differentiation, so that it becomes impossible to objectify it. Although we cannot verbalize it directly, we can do so with an interpretation of a part of its working, and a fairy tale may serve as that kind of interpretation."[21] I would argue that the Japanese creation narrative gives some suggestions, too. As Kawai pointed out, giving a full description of the Pleroma with words will not be successful no matter how one tries because the quality of Pleroma is to contain everything, even those things that contradict each other, while on the other hand, words are used to differentiate things. As Philemon teaches, "It is fruitless to think about the Pleroma, for this would mean self-dissolution,"[22] and then goes on to the next topic, "Kreatur." Later, he returns to the question: "But why then do we speak of the Pleroma at all, if it is everything and nothing?"[23] He answers his own question as follows; "I speak about it ... to free you from the delusion that somewhere without or within there is something fixed or in some way established from the outset. Every so-called fixed and certain thing is only relative."[24] It seems to have something to do with what the voice of his Soul said earlier: "You should become serious, and hence take your leave from science. There is too much childishness in it. Your way goes toward the depth. Science is too superficial, mere language, mere tools."[25]

It is noteworthy that during this time Jung began to draw mandalas. Of the first one he writes: "This is the first mandala I constructed in the year 1916, wholly unconscious of what it meant."[26] I understand his drawing mandalas as a compensation for what he was articulating with words. Words coagulate and fix, while drawing facilitates solutions. Through the experience of drawing mandalas, he obtained confirmation of his idea about the self. In *Memories, Dreams, Reflections*, Jung writes: "During those years, between 1918 and 1920, I began to understand that the goal of psychic development is the self. There is no linear evolution. There is only a circum-ambulation of the self. Uniform development exists, at most, only at the beginning; later everything points towards the centre."[27] Thus, he finally reached the understanding of the self as the goal of psychic development through both verbalizing and drawing, each compensating the other. I understand this as an integration of the West and the East in a deep sense.

Creation in *Seven Sermons to the Dead* and in Japanese Mythology

As mentioned previously, no particular scripture exists in Shintō, but the old Japanese mythologies contain a description of the earliest creation myth. There are two main sources: One is the *Kojiki*, the "Record of Ancient Matters," and the other is *Nihonshoki*, the "Written Chronicles of Japan." Both were written in the early part of the eighth century. My discussion is based on the *Kojiki* for the reason that the *Nihonshoki* was compiled as an official history in order to assert the independence and autonomy of Japan as a nation in the international area, while on the contrary the *Kojiki* is considered to contain more original indigenous Japanese myths. The beginning of *Kojiki* reads as follows:

At the time of the beginning of heaven and earth, there became in Takama-no-hara (the Plain of High Heaven) kami named Ame-no-mi-naka-nushi-no-kami (Master-of-the-Center-of-Heaven); next, Taka-mi-musuhi-no-kami (High-Producing-Deity); next, Kami-musuhi-no-kami (Divine-Producing-Deity). These three *kami* all became as single kami and they hid their bodies.[28]

The whole process before First Parents Izanagi and Izanami appear is illustrated in the following figure:[29]

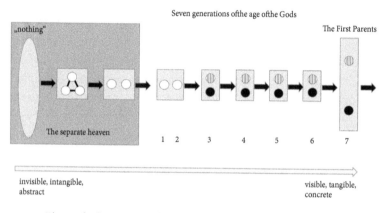

The gradual transition of "nothing" to the concrete First Parents

Considering the fact that *kami* appear suddenly one after another, the seeming "nothingness" at the beginning is likely to contain every possibility, which I would argue corresponds to the Pleroma. Surprisingly, the narrative begins with so few words that only time is identified in quite a vague way but nothing else is depicted.

Description with few words corresponds to "the principle of nonexpression,"[30] as Toshihiko Izutsu calls it. He writes: "(It) stems from the awareness of the expressiveness of non-expression,"[31] and "It applies to almost all forms of art that are considered most characteristics of far Eastern culture."[32] As I understand, non-expression is also one of the expressions of "nothingness." In general, it is considered that fewer words may leave more room for free imagination. Japanese poetry, *haiku*, which consists of only 17 syllables, may be a good example of this. Silence is not just literally silence but possibly pregnant with affluent unuttered words if we immerse ourselves in the imaginative world that develops between the written lines. It goes without saying that in such a case the reader's commitment is necessary.

When is the "beginning of heaven and earth"? What do we imagine from this brief phrase? Where is "the plain of high heaven"? Nobody can tell where it is. At least, however, we can realize that the setting is in an extraordinary and special time and space. Probably we are expected to imagine this specialness, which implies also that something very special is going to take place afterward. (On the contrary, there is no description about time and space in the Sermon.) The vagueness in the *Kojiki* text may have something to do with Japanese high-context culture, where context is usually taken into consideration in many situations. In Japanese society people are expected to use a different word even for the first person according to each situation.

Master-of-the-Centre-of-Heaven

At the very beginning of the *Kojiki*, it seems that suddenly three single *kami* come out of what is seemingly nothing one after another. These first three *kami* are called "Three Kami of Creation." According to Kawai, they make up the first important triad, which consists of one central deity, Master-of-the-Centre-of-Heaven, who is very important but does nothing, and the other two who are both producing deities.[33] This states the completion of the foundation for spiritual producing power to work in the Separate Heaven, which also implies that the future generation is being prepared. I would like to point out a similarity between the "Three Kami of Creation" and Abraxas, since the appearance of the former is a manifestation of potential energy and possibility that make *kami* then appear one after another, while the latter is called "effect."[34] In his commentary to *The Secret of the Golden Flower*, Jung states: "… the mandala is not only a means of expression but also produces an effect."[35] I would argue that, while drawing mandalas, Jung found the characteristic feature of Abraxas, which is effect. Circumambulating is not just being in a situation of self-dissolution. If some special energy works there, such as spiritual producing power, circumambulating may take us into the inner part of the psyche.

Hayao Kawai also points out that Master-of-the-Center-of-Heaven's name suggests his centrality, although he never appears in the myth narrative again, while the other two *kami* play important roles afterward.[36] Where did Master-of-the-Center-of-Heaven go? I would like to suggest that he/she hid himself/herself deep in the innermost place of the universe and never appeared again. As a result of what we have seen regarding the ancient *kami* in Shintō, I understand Master-of-the-Center-of-Heaven as the prototype, as well as the core, of Japan's innumerable *kami*. As humans, we can never see or have direct contact with this *kami*; all we can do is to have an indirect contact through worshipping the medium. Japanese *kami* in Shintō are considered to refer to phenomena that inspire a sense of awe and wonder in the beholder. This can be compared to Rudolf Otto's famous description of the numinosum, a *mysterium tremendum et fascinans*. It is quite similar to the view of Norinaga Motoori, the preeminent scholar of Shintō and Japanese classics of the 18th century, who defined *kami* as "a being or a thing which bestows a sense of awe."[37] According to him, anything, high or low, good or evil, could possibly be a *kami* if a person experiences it with a sense of awe.

As shown above, there is a long history before the First Parents appear in the *Kojiki*. If we understand the birth of them as the appearance of something embodied and visible, the story predating their appearance can be understood as that of seeming nothingness, which is often skipped even in Japan. As I have shown above, as several generations of *kami* come into being one after another, they gradually take *kami* form. Although each embodies a separate *kami*, ultimately they show orientation as a whole. From within this orienting flow, the first parents "become." Through this process of connecting seemingly fragmented images an important thread may emerge. Such a concept may finally lead to the Buddhist idea of *jinen*—a state in which everything flows spontaneously, just as it is.

Although this idea basically comes from Buddhism, what we have seen implies that it has something to do with ancient *kami* in Shintō.

The First Sermon reads: "In the Pleroma there is nothing and everything. It is fruitless to think about Pleroma for this would mean self-dissolution."[38] On the contrary, in Japanese creation myth being dissolved in the Pleroma and staying within it seems to be much more valued. As mentioned above, something from within himself drove Jung to draw mandalas, which made him circumambulate the self and finally brought him to the center—the self, which is considered to be not the center of consciousness but the center in the innermost part of the psyche. And I would argue that the center that Jung encountered is equivalent to the Master-of-the-Center-of-Heaven who became and appeared as the first *kami* but then went hidden and never appears again.

Jung began articulating "nothingness" with words, and then by drawing mandalas, he encountered Abraxas and reached the self. On the contrary, although Japanese seem to know "nothingness" from the beginning, they should not be conceited, as they are not at all good at differentiating and they do not know about it in a true sense. As Jung warned Westerners against becoming pitiable imitators of Eastern spirituality, Japanese should be aware that they introduced the modern Western ego only superficially and are living with a multilayered psyche in a multilayered society.

To conclude, Master-of-the-Center-of-Heaven, who came into being as the first *kami* is hiding himself/herself in the center of universe. He/She is an invisible *kami*, who does "nothing." As we cannot have direct contact with this *kami*, all that we can do is to try to have a relationship with Master-of-the-Center-of-Heaven as a whole through the channels of multiple *kami*. This relationship depends upon whether or not we have a sense of awe and respect toward *yaoyorozu-no-kami*. As Japan has been a Great Mother dominant country, "establishing a subject" is an important topic in our field of psychotherapy. It may give us hints with regard to alternative ways, which is leaving oneself in the flow of "*jinen*"— doing nothing. But this does not necessarily mean literally doing nothing, but rather waiting for the time to come when one senses a sign of connection with the hidden *kami,* Master-of-the-Center-of-Heaven.

Jung writes in *The Red Book*: "I understood that the God whom we seek in the absolute was not to be found in absolute beauty, goodness, seriousness, elevation, humanity or even in godliness. Once the God was there. I understand that the new God would be in the relative."[39] On the contrary, I would like to state that Japanese should know that the new *kami* would be in the absolute, one *kami*.

Endnotes

[1] James Hillman and Sonu Shamdasani, *Lament of the Dead: Psychology after Jung's Red Book* (New York, NY: W.W. Norton, 2013), 1.

[2] C.G. Jung, *The Red Book: Liber Novus, A Reader's Edition*. ed. Sonu Shamdasani, tr. John Peck, Mark Kyburz, and Sonu Shamdasani (New York, NY: W.W. Norton, 2009), 511.

[3] Ibid., 511-512.

[4] Hermann Hesse, *Demian* (London: Penguin Modern Classics, 1919/2017), 73.

[5] C.G. Jung, *Memories, Dreams, Reflections* (New York, NY: Vintage Books, 1961), 190-191.

[6] C.G. Jung, Appendix V, *Septem Sermones ad Mortuos* (1916) in *Memories, Dreams, Reflections*, 378.

[7] C.G. Jung, trans. Hayao Kawai et al., *Yungu Jiden—Omoide, Yume, Shisou* (Tokyo: Misuzu shobou 1973).

[8] Hayao Kawai, *Mukashibanashi to Nihonjin no Kokoro* (Tokyo: Iwanami Shoten, 1982), 167-168. (*The Japanese Psyche: Major Motifs in the Fairy Tales of Japan*, tr. Gary Snyder (Dallas, TX: Spring Publications, 1996), 103).

[9] Shuji Okuno, *Tamashii, demo iikara soba ni ite: 3 El lgo no reitaiken o kiku* (Tokyo: Shin-yo-sha Publishing Ltd, 2017). (*Be with me even if you are a spirit: Listening to a ghostly experience after 3.11.*). Also: Kiyoshi Kanebishi, eds., "Shishatachi ga kayou machi: takushi doraiba no yurei genshou," in *Yobisamasareru Reisei no Shinsaigaku: 3.11 Sei to Shi no Hazama de* (Tokyo: Shin-yo-sha publishing Ltd., 2016) (*Awakening spirituality in disaster studies: 3.11 between death and life*).

[10] This idea was originally presented at the Conference on *Holism: Possibilities and Problems* at University of Essex, 2017.

[11] Tetsuo Yamaori, *Kami to Hotoke: Nihonjin no shukyoukan* (*Kami and Buddha: Japanese view on religion*) (Tokyo: Kodansha, 35th edition, 2014), 2.

[12] Ibid., 30.

[13] Jung, *The Red Book*, 525.

[14] Ibid., 527.

[15] Ibid., 473.

[16] Tetsuo Yamaori, *Kindai Nihonjin no shuukyou ishiki (Modern Religious Consciousness of Japanese)* (Tokyo: Iwanami-shoten, 2007).

[17] Jung, *The Red Book*, 515.

[18] Ibid., 516.

[19] Ibid.

[20] Ibid., 509.

[21] Hayao Kawai, *Mukashibanashi to Nihonjin nno Kokoro* (Tokyo: Iwanami Shoten, 1982), 30. (*The Japanese Psyche: Major Motifs in the Fairy Tales of Japan*, tr. Gary Snyder (Dallas, TX: Spring Publications 1996), 20).

[22] Jung, *The Red Book*, 510.

[23] Ibid., 510.

[24] Ibid., 511.

[25] Ibid., 473.

[26] Ibid., 42.

[27] C.G. Jung, *Memories, Dreams, Reflections*, 196-197.

[28] Y. Takeda, ed., *Kojiki* (Tokyo: Kadokawa-shoten, 1995); my translation.

[29] Megumi Yama, "Ego consciousness in the Japanese psyche: culture, myth and disaster," in *Journal of Analytical Psychology*, vol. 58, 2013, 52–72.

[30] Toshihiko Izutsu, *Toward a Philosophy of Zen Buddhism* (Boulder, CO: Prajna Press, 1982), 234. Originally, 1977 by the Imperial Iranian Academy of Philosophy published by arrangement with the author.

[31] Ibid.

[32] Ibid.

[33] Hayao Kawai, "Japanese mythology: balancing the Gods," in *Dreams, Myths & Fairy Tales in Japan* (Einsiedeln: Daimon, 1995).

[34] Jung, *The Red Book*, 517.

[35] C.G. Jung, "Commentary on 'The Secret of the Golden Flower'," in *CW*, vol. 13 (Princeton, NJ: Princeton University Press, 1967), par. 36.

[36] Kawai, "Japanese mythology: balancing the Gods," 78.

[37] Norinaga Motoori, *Kojikiden* (*Commentary on the Kojiki*) (Chikumasshobo Motoori Norinaga zenshu, vol. 9, 126); my translation.

[38] Jung, *The Red Book*, 510.

[39] Ibid., 166.

The Red Book and the Black Swan: The Trickster as a Psychological Factor Behind the Boom and Bust Cycle

Anna Milashevich

Introduction

This paper aims to demonstrate manifestations of the trickster archetype in the business domain. I will use Jung's *Red Book* to show that the dynamics of business life are in many ways a reflection of collective unconscious factors, which the trickster brings to the surface with its disruptive art of chance occurrences. I will begin by stating the relevance of *The Red Book* for my arguments, followed by a brief outline of the trickster concept in Jungian psychology and the introduction of the notion of the "progressive trickster." I will then argue that the trickster manifests in business in so-called "black swan" events, such as the 2008 financial crisis. I will explain the implications of trickster dynamics for the consideration of meaning and economic policies. The paper concludes by claiming that the trickster is an essential energy that makes a complex system such as the business domain "antifragile."

The Relevance of *The Red Book*

The Red Book, through its many characters, teaches us about the autonomy of the collective unconscious. It is an account of Jung's own struggle to come to terms with the fact that there are factors that influence us on both personal and collective levels, yet do not arise from or depend on us in any significant way. The collective unconscious is alive and active: There is a constant emergence out of it of forms and processes that are beyond our rational understanding. Following his *Red Book* experiences, Jung in his further work argued for the need to separate the collective unconscious from the personal[1] and thus attempted to present the collective unconscious as something different and to consolidate the contents of it as psychological realities on their own right, i.e., the archetypes.[2] The appearance of the trickster is the consolidation of one of these realities. This differentiation between the personal and the impersonal levels is needed, as otherwise a person is seen a "puppet of the archetype."[3] This insight constitutes the essence of Jungian psychology, which while honoring the numinous as the organizing force behind personal and social dynamics and structures, is careful to do so at a distance.[4]

Following Jung's proposition, I will argue that the business domain shows evidence of unconscious contents and patterns, which are not put there by repression but exist because business is a domain that rests on human thought and activities, which in turn rest on collective unconscious dominants/archetypes. The trickster, as we will see, plays a particularly important role in this domain. When we understand this psychological "dominant," we enrich our ways of engagement with it.

Trickster in Jungian Psychology

The trickster figure is common across diverse mythological traditions, epochs, and cultures. There are African tricksters (Ananse and Eshu), Native American tricksters (Coyote and Wakdjunkaga), Asian tricksters (Susa-no-o and Sun Wuk'ung) and European tricksters (Loki and Hermes). Trickster characters embody a wide range of characteristics, which makes it difficult (particularly for the modern Western mind) to imagine them as embodied in a single phenomenon.[5] Amid this diversity, we meet such characteristics as the thief, shepherd, magician, healer, educator, spiritual guide, fool/clown, wise old man, youthful hero, evildoer/antihero, to name but a few.

As stated above, in Jungian psychology the trickster is a vital part of psychological reality and, in Jungian terminology, constitutes an archetypal figure or personification. The trickster's role is that of the pattern-breaker, disrupter, and boundary-crosser. Its disruptive acts release psychic tensions and thus link and balance the dynamics of consciousness and the unconscious. Illuminating these "transformative and generative aspects" of the trickster, Andrew Samuels regards it as a "yardstick and spur to consciousness."[6] Joseph Campbell notes: "The trickster hero represents all those possibilities of life that your mind hasn't decided it wants to deal with. The mind structures a lifestyle, and the fool or trickster represents another whole range of possibilities. He doesn't respect the values that you've set up for yourself, and smashes them."[7]

Jung writes that in its pure form the trickster is a "reflection of an absolutely undifferentiated human consciousness, corresponding to a psyche that has hardly left the animal level."[8] However, he points out that the appearance of the trickster signifies the possibility of transforming the meaningless into the meaningful.[9] While stressing the trickster's low intellectual and moral level,[10] Jung also states that the trickster is capable of progressive development, gradually learning to control his bodily functions and sexual impulses.[11]

As a prelude to the next section, it is useful to differentiate between what could be termed "classic" and "progressive" tricksters, which represent different levels of consciousness yet share the same nature and archetypal functioning, i.e., they are pattern-breakers and disturbers. Progressive trickster is characterized by a high level of consciousness and is what could be called a "literate" trickster: that is, its interference is based on its ability to "read" conscious and unconscious patterns. In contrast, the "classic" trickster simply acts out the imbalance and subsequent tension between consciousness and the unconscious. In *The Red Book*, Philemon is such a progressive trickster, who appears in the form of a magician, educator, and spiritual guide, and whose task throughout Jung's journey is linking and balancing the unconscious and conscious dynamics. Philemon's presence in *The Red Book*, as with all trickster figures, is ambiguous: He is in and out of the picture, appearing at some crucial moments/ turning points, particularly when Jung attaches more value to one opposite than to the other. More so, it was Philemon who prompted Jung to write *The Seven Sermons to the Dead*: Jung "was compelled from within, as it were, to formulate and express what might have been said by Philemon."[12] The *Sermons* present Jung's version of gnostic wisdom, and later Jung spoke of them as a "prelude to what [he] had to communicate to the world about the unconscious."[13] In particular, his interest in Gnosticism led Jung to a certain interpretative understanding of alchemy, which further supported and enriched his ideas.[14]

Within this context, it could be argued that Philemon, among other things, led Jung to the discovery of the whole range of trickster figures. In his later work, Jung was particularly intrigued by the alchemical trickster figure of Hermes/Mercurius, referring to him, as he did somewhat similar to Philemon, as a spiritual guide.[15] Samuels, drawing on Jung, states that the alchemical Hermes/Mercurius could be taken to represent psyche itself.[16]

Just as Philemon was Jung's spiritual teacher in his *Red Book* journey, the mythical figure of Hermes can be kept in mind as a guide into the psychological terrain of the business world. Among many of his roles and functions (such as messenger between gods and people and guide of souls to the underworld), Hermes is the guardian of trade and commerce and could even be considered the symbol of the business domain and business creativity in particular.[17] Hermes, whose high levels of intelligence and trickery are elevated to the level of an art, is an example of the progressive trickster. As seen in mythology,[18] Hermes is very precise with his disruptive surprises; he is playful and spontaneous, yet strategic and manipulative. Trickster-fools, such as Tom Thumb or Coyote, do not function at this level of sophistication: Their surprises are instinct-driven and idiotic. Both types, however, are effective communicators between consciousness and the unconscious. These distinctions and convergences are important, as this chapter will argue that high levels of intelligence lie behind certain disruptive occurrences.

Manifestations of the Trickster in Business

Nasim Taleb famously introduced the notion of "black swan" to account for the occurrence of unlikely events.[19] Given his past career as a trader, a considerable part of Taleb's inquiry into such events concerns black swans in the field of finance, such as the 2008 financial crisis.[20] Black swan events are defined as events that lie outside the range of probability but occur anyway. They can be positive (invention of the internet) or negative (the 2008 financial crisis). They can also be trivial (learning that not all swans are white) or life-altering (losing everything in a stock market crash). Their key feature is that, while they are impossible/difficult to predict, they can be relatively easily explained in hindsight.[21]

Taleb's thesis is that we are surprised by such events not because they are random or accidental but because our outlook is too narrow. He points out our tendency to be overconfident in what we know or think we know and ignorant of what we do not know. This ignorance, he claims, is a result of our cognitive biases, currently a popular topic within the field of cognitive psychology, e.g., works of Gigerenzer, Kahneman, Pinker.[22] These basic logical biases include narrative fallacy (our need for linear explanations), confirmation biases (selection of those facts that confirm our existing beliefs) and ludic fallacy (the equation of risk to a game, in which rules and probabilities can be determined).

However, given that Taleb's aim is to explore the black swan phenomenon from the rational perspective (which he does in a brilliant tricksterish fashion), two important questions are left unaddressed. First, while his book focuses on the logical pitfalls that cause us to overlook the bigger picture and thus fall victim to surprises, it touches only momentarily on the nature of what we perceive as these random events. To be specific, Taleb simply states that these events happen. Second, while he describes cognitive biases, he does not explain how and why they come into play on the collective level at a particular time. The answers to these questions lie at the threshold of collective conscious and unconscious dynamics. Thus, I argue that if we wish to understand the nature of these occurrences, *The Red Book* can be of valuable assistance, and the trickster may serve as our guide (despite the likelihood that the trickster will abandon or betray us at the very instant we attempt to turn it into a framework).

As stated earlier, the trickster's prime concern is to link and balance conscious and unconscious dynamics. The "progressive" trickster, rather than acting out this archetypal function, is an astute reader of both conscious and unconscious patterns. After spotting imbalances and weak links, it pulls a surprise from its sleeve. Lewis Hyde calls it "the god of chance events."[23] The trickster puts two or more events together to create an unexpected occurrence. Its surprises are impossible to predict precisely because they are random and may belong to different realities. Black swan events, those unlikely occurrences at the tail of the normal distribution curve, comprise these trickster surprises that disrupt our accustomed patterns of thinking and often force us to reconsider our worldview, even if temporarily. Like the trickster, these black swan events are about uncertainty, shocks, chance occurrences, as well as creativity, which are predominant in the business domain.

The trickster thrives in the capitalist business environment, which provides great freedom and opportunities to pursue one's impulses and interests; thus, there is plenty of shadow material for the trickster to play with. It is particularly important to stress the trickster's function as a pattern-breaker who fractures our identifications with certain psychologically outdated ideas or fantasies. As seen from its disruptive and creative endeavors (e.g., the myths of Hermes or Loki), it is amoral: It does not care about the general good or about the suffering that its surprises might impose on individuals, but only about balancing the diverse components of the personal and collective psyche. In this respect, it is particularly important to emphasize that the trickster works with what is already in existence: Its actions reveal what is unwanted, left behind, repressed, denied or hidden. The hypothesis that the trickster, as a psychological phenomenon and concept, is behind black swan events has vast implications for our consideration of business.

Implications of the Connection between Trickster and Black Swan Events

As is always the case with the trickster, there is more to black swan events than meets the eye. These events are unpredictable precisely because they happen largely as a result of unconscious factors. In the aftermath, however, these factors are given a rational causal narrative that anyone can understand, only to wonder how the elephant in the room could have gone unnoticed. Black swan events are thus never purely accidental. While the trickster certainly plays on our cognitive biases, the definitive nature of its craft is that what emerges from it is far from random: The trickster overthrows the conscious dynamic to reveal the presence of unconscious factors.

The 2008 financial crisis is an example of a black swan event and, as my argument suggests, a negative manifestation of the trickster in the business world. The crisis remains the most recent economic calamity, and today, a decade later, it serves as a particularly useful example of the lessons learned and not learned. The learned lessons include the rational dominants that caused the crisis (the derivatives, the ruling dogmas of the financial market, the lack of regulation, the greediness of bankers). It is on the lessons that were not learned that I wish to concentrate, as many crises of similar nature are or will be in the making, e.g., the current building up of the Bitcoin bubble.

The 2008 financial crisis originated in the collective fantasy of effortless wealth (a *puer* fantasy), which, when turned on, automatically resulted in systemic risks and the ultimate downfall of the entire financial system.[24] In particular, this fantasy pattern can be seen in the collective preoccupation with debt and leverage, as well as a belief that governments can and should protect against economic crisis. This was evident in expectations of a bailout and in the complacency of the "too-big-to-fail" attitude.

In his interview with the Financial Crisis Inquiry Commission, Warren Buffett explained how this patterned way of thinking is related to the booms and busts of the business cycle.[25] He stated that bubbles are always formed on a "very sound premise."[26] When this premise is turned into a pattern, it overtakes our perception of reality, i.e., we identify with the pattern. The premise of the "dot-com bubble" was that the invention of the Internet was a life-changing phenomenon. When this premise became a pattern, its limitations were forgotten, resulting in the overvaluation of almost any company with related content. A similar dynamic lay behind the 2008 financial crisis (and the current Bitcoin bubble), and it is this psychological pattern based dynamic that builds a corresponding physical reality around itself. In this narrative, the derivatives were the mere tools rather than the cause of the crisis.

The trickster's thrill in the modern business environment comes from causing the abundance of unconscious grandiose fantasy bubbles/patterns to burst. Not only "greedy bankers," but also society at large participates in this fantasy in one way or another, as we will see below. The heightened state of ego-inflation results in "collective blindness," which acts as a defense mechanism that protects the unconscious fantasy (by making use of the inherent cognitive biases mentioned above). Yet, as we know from *The Red Book*, which accounts in colorful details for Jung's many struggles with his pride and hero-induced inflation, the unconscious knows better what the difference between fantasy and reality is. When there is an imbalance between a fantasy and reality, the trickster appears. It constructs the bubble, and then it busts it. Arguably, the way of trickster's interference depends on the way of interaction between a fantasy and reality. In *The Red Book*, apart from the major trickster figure of Philemon, who provides some twisted congruence to Jung's journey, we see a wide range of trickster figures (Salome/the soul, the devil, the young maiden, the Red One, the tramp, the *cabiri*, Satan), each representing a certain type of relationship that Jung has with a relating fantasy (we might say, each representing a certain complex), and different ways in which they (the trickster figures) impact Jung.

Trickster Dynamics in the 2008 Financial Crisis: "The Attack of Accidents"

The trickster reads conscious and unconscious patterns, identifies the core issues and imbalances, orchestrates two or more random events to come together, and, in the twist of events, pulls the weakest link. This dynamic is apparent in the 2008 crisis, the official postmortem of which reveals multiple causal factors that can be classified into six general categories: economic policies, bank strategies, derivative usage, deregulation, oversight, and changes in accounting.[27] The first

category, economic policies, includes, *inter alia*, the Federal Reserve's
reduction of the interest rate to promote home ownership, as well as
the Clinton and Bush administrations' support for credit extension
to marginal borrowers. Regarding the second category, following
deregulation and increased competition in the financial services
sector, banks found themselves having to compete almost exclusively
on price given the overall homogeneity of the products.[28] As a result,
they were receptive to any new product capable of generating profits
and in particular to those that helped meet the market demand for
mortgage loans (option adjustable-rate mortgages, subprime loans,
and the related securitization).[29]

There was also ambiguous derivative usage: The appearance and
subsequent popularity of credit default swaps enhanced the credibility
of otherwise questionable mortgages. This was coupled with the
growing demand for highly rated securities by institutional investors
(as diverse as pension funds, insurance companies, and hedge funds),
foreign companies, and governments. Lack of oversight further contributed to the growing inadequacy, and credit rating agencies not
only underestimated the risks involved in collateralized debt
obligations, but also gave high rankings to the riskiest loans. Auditors
and regulators also failed to foresee the risks involved due to their
"inexperience with complex financial instruments, a 'form-over-
substance' perspective prevalent within the accounting industry, and
an unwillingness to potentially disrupt the financial markets by
issuing 'negative' reports."[30]

All these factors collaborated to result in a mortgage frenzy,
which grew into an uncontrollable bubble fueled by strong emotions
and partisan interests. The unconscious fantasy spread like a virus,
further fueling the internal psychological conflict. It is important to
note that most, if not all, of the factors above, albeit happening at the
critical time, were unrelated, yet all collaborated to create the bubble.
This is a signature trickster characteristic and a common pattern of
an unfolding black swan event. From the rational perspective, the
confluence of these events comprises the unlikely occurrence, the tail
event of the normal distribution curve. However, for the trickster
such occurrences are far from random or accidental, as they reflect

the unconscious factors that have been dismissed. In this way, the trickster links the conscious and unconscious, as well as the inner/psychological and outer/physical realities, emphasizing the lack of wholeness in our perspective. Everyone (aspiring homeowners, the financial industry, government, regulators, accountants, pension funds) appeared to add their own brick to the construction of this grandiose castle in the air, as is evident from the diversity of factors above, but the main investments were people's emotional realities.

The only thing remaining for the trickster to do was to burst the bubble. In 2006, there was a sudden increase in interest rates, causing subprime borrowers to default on mortgages. Further, in 2007 the Financial Accounting Standards Board issued a rather "subjective and complex new requirement,"[31] the fair-value reporting rule, which resulted in many U.S. publicly traded companies disclosing their mortgage assets.

Trickster vs. Shadow: It's not Dracula, It's Trickster

When attributing the factors that led to the bubble and its subsequent bursting to trickster dynamics, it is crucial to distinguish these dynamics from the shadow operations in business, as the two have different implications. When a crisis occurs, it is often mistakenly attributed to shadow/evil dynamics. The trickster nature, however, is disruptive rather than destructive: Its primary purpose is to link and balance conscious and unconscious patterns rather than to cause outright damage.

In *The Red Book*, we come across this important distinction when Jung meets Salome. Salome appears with Elijah, her father, and is presented as a blind young woman. When Jung is introduced to her, his initial reaction is to accuse her of murderous sins and to call her a "bloodthirsty horror."[32] Jung treats her as the personification of evil (the shadow) and is appalled by Elijah's intimate alliance with her. Elijah (who later is transformed into Philemon) explains to Jung that he is misunderstanding something important about who this figure is and what she stands for. Salome also undergoes some important transformations in the course of the book, but one thing that remains unchanged is her tricksterish cunning nature, which Jung comes to appreciate for what it is.

In many commentaries on *The Red Book*, Philemon is presented as the wise old man (*senex*) and Salome as Jung's soul/*anima*, who appears as neglected and immature at first but who, through Jung's acceptance and genuine desire to love her, regains her sight and becomes more whole. Some commentators such as Schwartz-Salant show skepticism about the final outcome of this relationship: In spite of the progress that Jung makes with his *anima*, he is unable to fully love or trust her.[33] The integration is incomplete, and Jung's *anima* remains somewhat underdeveloped. An alternative reading, in which Philemon is a trickster figure (and only secondarily a wise old man figure) and Salome is his trickster companion (also Jung's *anima*), allows for a different conclusion. This portrayal of Philemon and Salome contrasts sharply with the original mythological pair of Philemon and Baucis: The latter are a simple, devoted, loving, and trustworthy couple (true worshippers of the gods), while *The Red Book*'s Philemon and Salome are a pair of tricksters who seem to be everything that the first couple is not. In this reading, *The Red Book* would indicate that Jung achieved possibly the best relationship one can have with the soul when one's soul is a trickster. It is the solidity of this relationship that allows Jung in a moment of emotional disturbance to ask the question: "Now what are you up to? What do you see? I should like to know." Jung positively affirms: "After some resistance she regularly produced an image."[34]

While the trickster and shadow represent importantly different psychological energies, Jung nonetheless warns that the trickster can turn into the shadow when it is denied existence and forced to the bottom of the unconscious, from where it returns in a powerful and destructive way.[35] The more the trickster is pushed to the dark corners of the unconscious, the more it accumulates shadow characteristics and the more dramatic will be the consequences of these dynamics in the material world. In *The Red Book*, the presence of the serpent signifies this dynamic.[36] Thus, when an unconscious fantasy has too strong a hold on the conscious mind and the internal conflict/tension is unacknowledged, the trickster's surprises become correspondently darker.

While the trickster is behind black swan events, the shadow contributes what could be called "perfect storm"[37] events, of which the 2008 collapse of Lehman Brothers, the 2010 BP oil rig explosion, and the 2015 Volkswagen scandal are examples. To sum up the importance of the distinction: Negative black swan events involve a collective fantasy, and the bursting of the inflated ego causes the crisis, while perfect storm catastrophes are built around a much heavier and darker dynamic, implicating actual wrongdoing and its concealment (usually on the part of some partisan group).

Practical Difficulties in Distinguishing Between Trickster and Shadow Dynamics

The premise of both negative black swan and perfect storm events is that none of the individual factors, which contribute to the eventual catastrophe, is sufficiently powerful on its own to bring them about, while their confluence produces the observed devastation. Both types of event, given their unconscious nature, involve cognitive biases resulting in collective blindness. Given these premises, it is difficult to distinguish between negative black swan and perfect storm events. For example, according to Ali Velshi, CNN's chief business correspondent, the 2008 crisis was a perfect storm event: "It was a lack of regulation, it was greed and creativity in the financial industry, and it was an American dream that got off track."[38] Perfect storm events require that most, if not all, contributing factors are negative. A negative black swan event, on the other hand, may be the result of negative, neutral, or even positive factors. In the 2008 crisis, it is difficult to make a case that all of the factors involved were negative. Was the reduction of interest rates, which allowed the less wealthy to get their foot on the property ladder during a period of favorable economic conditions, a negative factor when taken by itself? Was the deregulation of the financial industry necessarily a bad idea? Even the securitization of loan purchases cannot on its own be considered negative. Rather, it was the chance nature of the way these factors interacted in service of the collective fantasy that caused the crisis.

In shadow scenarios, negative factors accumulate, and under some "favorable" circumstance, their confluence results in toxic content that further fuels the outcome. This favorable or enabling event, however, appears to be absent from the 2008 crisis. It was the interaction of the above-mentioned factors that created a financial calamity, and, importantly, this interaction was a chance occurrence. It is necessary to distinguish between trickster and shadow dynamics as the two have different implications for meaning as well as for economic policies. I will first consider the implications in terms of meaning before switching to the issue of practical policies.

Implications for Meaning

As stated earlier, in the case of the 2008 crisis, the trickster burst the bubble and brought down a collective fantasy. In this act of rebalancing, it served as an agent of change and progress. However, it needs to be repeated that the trickster only works with what is already in existence and builds external scenarios in the physical world based on the relevant unconscious dynamics. The 2008 crisis could thus be seen as a symbolic representation of the unconscious content in the collective. The trickster, by revealing the underlying dynamics, brings about the potential for understanding the meaning of the entire collective situation. However, the meaning is not transparent, not least because it is unclear who creates this meaning. Modern societies escape the complexity of meaning-making with the help of causal explanations. Consequently, post crisis analyses have not found anything extraordinary in the market crash. As the financial commentator Iain Martin writes: "At root, the causes of the financial crisis were boringly old-fashioned and predictable. An excess of cheap money, pumped out for too long, inflated a bubble and encouraged wild behavior on the part of governments, financiers and many consumers."[39] Martin adds that the only "novelty came with the complex instruments designed inside banks, which too few of those using them properly understood." Most officials have referred to the crisis as a rather ordinary consequence of a "housing-and-credit bubble."[40] The hypothesis that economic booms and busts include collective psychological factors and thus are, to some important degree, psychological in nature remains unexplored. The gift (of meaning) that the trickster brings thus remains unopened.

It is indeed difficult to substantiate the claim that the trickster brings chance events together in a meaningful way, since the unconscious dynamics are hidden. Collective unconscious dynamics are particularly difficult to detect. To see this connection more clearly, we might, as an exercise in mental gymnastics, consider a particular type of chance event that the trickster pulls from its sleeve, namely synchronistic events.[41] The relevance of *The Red Book* for such an exercise will be discussed later. I suggest imagining the 2008 financial crisis as a synchronistic occurrence because it disrupts the accustomed pattern of causal thinking and thus brings us closer to the consideration of meaning.

Synchronicity, or the so-called "acausal connecting principle," refers to events that coincide in time and space and have a meaningful psychological connection but no knowable causal connection.[42] Roderick Main highlights the core concepts in Jung's definition of synchronicity as time, acausality, meaning, improbability, and inexplicability.[43] In his words, synchronicity "suggests that there are uncaused events, that matter has a psychic aspect, that the psyche can relativise time and space, and that there may be a dimension of objective meaning accessible to but not created by humans."[44] For Jung, synchronicity is important in underpinning individuation as it contributes to increasing levels of consciousness.

As Main observes, synchronicity is "central to Jung's criticism of scientific rationalism, the one-sidedness of which it aims to compensate."[45] It "challenges existing models of science by suggesting that matter may have a psychic aspect that needs to be taken into consideration in the investigation of physical reality."[46] He also states that synchronicity applies to both the individual and social realms and thus provides an additional and complementary way of reading the social and political worlds.[47] Murray Stein further points that one of Jung's key preoccupations was with possibilities of incorporating elements of synchronistic thinking into our rational worldview since such events are "of great significance in our experience of life."[48]

The defining feature of synchronistic events is that they "force" meaning upon us. While we may dismiss a dream or escape some other more or less explicit content from the unconscious, synchronistic events catch us off guard and present an opportunity (a gift) for us to reconsider our worldview. It is important to point out that while trickster dynamics suggest that hidden unconscious factors cause certain corresponding outcomes in the physical world (e.g., some unconscious fantasies result in economic bubbles), synchronistic events imply an "acausal" connection. However, the key and most striking feature of synchronistic events is the "as if" condition under which they occur: It is as if a certain mental event somehow causes a physical one while we know at the same time that it does not. Thus, as noted above, imagining the crisis as a synchronistic phenomenon makes it possible to disrupt the cycle of causal thinking regarding the nature of black swan events.

In this imaginary synchronistic scenario, the collective inner state is in the grip of the *puer* fantasy of effortless wealth, which (somehow) coincides with the different factors coming together to create a bubble in the physical world. The presence of this unconscious fantasy produces a conflict between fantasy and reality, which creates psychic tension. As Main writes of the dynamics of synchronistic events: "Eventually, this build-up of energy in the unconscious became so great that it burst into consciousness."[49] Similarly, when the tension reaches some tipping point, the financial crisis erupts. (The latter, as the corresponding tipping point in the physical world, might be either the actual disaster in 2008 or the interest rate increase of 2006, which propelled the downfall. The choice between these two events depends on the chosen interpretation of the tipping point.) In this example, the issue of the meaning of the crisis is evident. Belief in our rationality plays a trick on us. All our so-called inventions that come out of the imbalance between consciousness and the unconscious are atavistic at their core.

Because causal thinking, as the preferred method of engagement with events in the physical world, escapes consideration of meaning, our society collectively dismisses the trickster and even the importance of chance events in fueling creativity and progress. Causal reasoning may successfully deduce that the crisis happened because of A, B, and C, but the curse of such explanations is that the next crisis may not necessarily involve A, B, or C. The rhetoric of "this time is different," which is characteristic of commentaries after many bubbles, shows that the lesson has not been learned.

Cases of synchronicity on the collective level are bound to represent weaker connections between inner and outer events (it would be difficult, for example, to imagine a real-life occurrence of many people having and reporting a dramatic dream of a fall prior to some catastrophe). In Jungian psychology, synchronicity is customarily treated within the personal context. As Stein points out, the meaning of synchronistic events is usually taken as personal: "One must ask: what does this mean to me?"[50] However, *The Red Book* suggests a way of thinking about synchronicity on the collective level. Although outer events are not mentioned directly, one of Jung's key questions is not only how the personal connects with the collective and how they can be differentiated, but also how what is happening on the collective unconscious level relates to and influences the events in the physical world. The next section clarifies this point.

The Red Book and its Red Thread across the Spirit of Our Time

Sonu Shamdasani points out Jung's concerns that he was having psychotic experiences with apocalyptic visions of destruction by flood, blood, and killing cold prior to the World War I and his astonishment at the outbreak of the war, which was accompanied by similar images, only that now they were real.[51] What instigated Jung's risky *Red Book* journey are these prior experiences of his psyche catching up or being caught up in the presence of the autonomous collective unconscious factors in the world around. Jung willingly sailed on his night sea journey to learn more about these factors and experience them more consciously.[52] The figures he meets there were later to be generalized and conceptualized as the archetypes. Thus, Jung's desire to understand World War I in terms of these unconscious factors was a motivation behind *The Red Book*.[53]

This is evident in multiple debates throughout *The Red Book* about rationality and irrationality, as well as discussions about science "killing our souls." In this reading, *The Red Book* is an exploration of the hypothesis that when there is an acute disbalance between the rational and irrational, the conscious and unconscious, "the spirit of our time" and "the spirit of the depths," something dramatic is bound to happen to release this tension. The "death of the gods" and the prevalence of rational ways of being in the world were thus linked with the outburst of irrationality in the two World Wars that followed.

In *The Red Book*, Jung expressed his concern and even fear of the dismissal of the irrational.[54] Since it is customary in Western societies to treat rational truth as facts or plausibility and irrational truth as fantasy, the unconscious is perceived as an enemy, and indeed becomes an enemy. Repression of the irrational is dangerous because it leads to outbreaks of the irrational, which are violent and destructive. It is a "historical necessity to acknowledge the irrational as a psychological factor,"[55] and it is this necessity that Jung addresses directly in *The Red Book* and which constitutes the red thread through all his further work.

To counteract the habitual comfort of rational explanations, Jung had to kill Siegfried ("I killed my intellect"), save Izdubar (the god is reborn rather than "the god is dead"), and undergo many unsettling experiences (such as cutting and eating the liver of a dead child), the significance of which is complex and symbolic. This in its own time— and with the help of Philemon—allows him to arrive at the union of rational and irrational truth, which could be found in the symbol. Symbols are about reconciliation of opposites.[56] They, according to Jung, stem from the unconscious, and "the creation of symbols [is] the most important function of the unconscious. While the compensatory function of the unconscious [is] always present, the symbol-creating function [is] present only when we [are] willing to recognise it."[57]

Policy Implications

What might the union of the rational and irrational look like in the relation to the 2008 crisis? In terms of the trickster's black swan events, policy should be structured around preventing bubbles and facilitate an environment where certain core fantasies can freely manifest on a much smaller scale and fail more quickly. The trickster serves as a reminder that we cannot change just because we rationally decide to do so; we can only change to the extent that the unconscious (both personal and collective) allows. The real change, the one that has lasting consequences, occurs in the unconscious. Our primitive responses must be taken into account and included as a necessary part of any journey.[58] On both personal and collective levels, facilitating a flexible environment is a way of mediating unconscious and conscious dynamics, and thus integrating the trickster.

Taleb's concept of antifragility provides some further points of reference for the policy implications of black swan events.[59] Unlike fragile items, which break under stress, antifragile items benefit from volatility and shock. In Taleb's narrative, black swan events serve the evolutionary process in making it antifragile. Arguably, in a similar way, the trickster is at the service of the self. The physical evolutionary process can be related to the psychological self. (This relationship is usually explored in Jungian literature from the perspective of individual psychology. For example, Anthony Stevens writes about "the two-million-year old self"[60]) Thus, it is the trickster, as a natural life occurrence and an organizing principle, who by its surprises/shocks in the physical world, contributes to the evolutionary process.

It is important to note that even in this scenario, the trickster, as an agent of change, can never serve the system. Whether the trickster brings negative or positive black swan events, it challenges the existing system with its establishment and rules of thumb. Equally, any system, being concerned with its own preservation, tries to tame the trickster. The nature of the relationship is thus always antagonistic. However, by not serving any system, the trickster serves the overall evolutionary process by ensuring its constant movement. Thus, there need not be a contradiction between the two statements: "the trickster

serves no one" and "the trickster serves the self/evolution." The
meaning of "serving" in the second statement can be inferred from
the nature of the relationship between Zeus and Hermes. Zeus
intended Hermes to be the pattern-breaker and disturber of gods (i.e.,
organizing principles and systems) and people. This suggests that he
serves no one. Simultaneously, however, by virtue of his very
existence, he is at the service of Zeus. The fact that, given his nature,
Hermes can always twist and do his own thing while at Zeus' service
is perfectly expected and accepted by Zeus. Through his disruptive
surprises, Hermes fulfils his predestined mission, which makes the
overall order stronger (aka antifragile).

It is crucial to stress here that the trickster cannot be conflated
with evolution, progress or even change. The trickster is not *the* agent
of change, but rather *an* agent. Change can be carried by many archetypes. The trickster, however, is one of the key guardians of change:
It is the trickster who appears when change is resisted. Its task is to
ensure that change takes place by introducing a disruptive element.
The energy released in this way is an essential life force, which the
trickster puts in motion.

Taleb argues that antifragility is the feature of all complex
biological systems.[61] Given its complexity, the business environment
also approximates natural systems and thus is antifragile. For the
business domain to grow, it needs some of its individual parts to fail.
For example, the failure of a technological start-up makes the
industry stronger as others learn from its mistakes. When the
economy/business is deprived of its volatility, it is argued, it also loses
its antifragility. Making antifragile systems tranquil results in bigger
eventual collapses.[62] The key policy implication of the trickster is thus
that when governments attempt to manage the economy, using
regulations and subsidies to smooth out the business cycle, they
remove the vital stressors that contain useful information. With the
loss of this information, the resources are misallocated, and the
economy suffers calamities of a much higher magnitude. This narrative also accords with that of the trickster, who makes existing
problems apparent. If the trickster is tamed by the system, the
problems will lie dormant, growing ever more severe until they reach

massive proportions and turn into a powerful shadow. Taleb's anti-fragility thesis resembles many trickster narratives, e.g., the Nordic myths of the trickster Loki.

Conclusion

In this paper, I have argued, with the help of *The Red Book*, for the hypothesis that the boom and bust cycle has underlying unconscious dynamics that the trickster reveals through black swan events. In this narrative, the derivatives were the mere tools for, rather than the cause of, the 2008 financial crisis. I have emphasized the importance of differentiating between trickster and shadow operations to counteract the tendency to view business cataclysms as evidence of pathology or wrongdoing by partisan groups. Jung's relationship with Salome served as a basis for this distinction. Following *The Red Book*'s proposition that a certain degree of immersion in chaos and disorder is crucial for the soul-finding process, this paper concludes that progress needs the trickster and the meaningful randomness it brings.

Endnotes

I wish to thank Murray Stein for his kind encouragement with this paper and Roisin Tangney for her editorial assistance.

[1] Sonu Shamdasani, "*Liber Novus*: The 'Red Book' of C.G. Jung," in C.G. Jung, *The Red Book: Liber Novus. A Reader's Edition*, ed. Sonu Shamdasani, trans. John Peck, Mark Kyburz, and Sonu Shamdasani (New York, NY: W.W. Norton, 2012), 55.

[2] C.G. Jung, "The Psychology of the Unconscious Processes," in *Collected Papers in Analytical Psychology*, ed. Constance Long (London: Bailliere, Tindall & Cox, 1917, 2nd edition), 435.

[3] Murray Stein, *Soul: Treatment and Recovery: The Selected Works of Murray Stein* (London and New York, NY: Routledge, 2016), 14.

[4] Ibid., 13.

[5] William J. Hynes and William G. Doty, *Mythical Trickster Figures: Contours, Contexts, and Criticisms* (Tuscaloosa, AL: University Alabama Press, 1993), 9.

[6] Andrew Samuels, *The Political Psyche* (London and New York, NY: Routledge, 1993), 84.

[7] Joseph Campbell, *An Open Life: Joseph Campbell in Conversation with Michael Toms* (New York, NY: Perennial Library, 1990), 39.

[8] C.G. Jung, "On the Psychology of the Trickster-Figure," in *CW*, vol. 9/I (Princeton, NJ: Princeton University Press, 1968), par. 465.

[9] Ibid., par. 458.

[10] Ibid., par. 480.

[11] Ibid., par. 477.

[12] C.G. Jung, *Memories, Dreams, Reflections*, ed. Aniela Jaffé (New York, NY: Vintage Books, 1963), 1963, 215.

[13] Ibid., 217.

[14] C.G. Jung, *The Red Book: Liber Novus. A Reader's Edition*, ed. Sonu Shamdasani, trans. John Peck, Mark Kyburz, and Sonu Shamdasani (New York, NY: W.W. Norton, 2012), 555.

[15] C.G. Jung, "Concerning Mandala Symbolism," in *CW*, vol. 9/I (Princeton, NJ: Princeton University Press, 1968), par. 689.

[16] Andrew Samuels, *Jung and the Post-Jungians* (London and New York, NY: Routledge, 1985/2006), 270.

[17] Anna Milashevich, *Re-visioning Business: Archetypal Patterns in the Business Domain and Their Relation to the Concept of Business Creativity* (Essex University, Ph.D. thesis, 2017), 85-98.

[18] Homer, "The Homeric Hymn to Hermes," in Lewis Hyde, *Trickster Makes This World: How Disruptive Imagination Creates Culture* (Edinburgh and London: Canongate, 1998/2008), 317-331.

[19] Nassim Taleb, *The Black Swan: The Impact of the Highly Improbable* (London and New York, NY: Penguin Books, 2008).

[20] The popularity of this book (one of the most influential of the 20th century, according to *The Sunday Times* (Bryan Appleyard, 2009, https://www.thetimes.co.uk/article/books-that-helped-to-change-the-world-qbhxgvg2kwh) at least in part owes to the fact that its author was one of few people who predicted and actively warned about the crisis. One of Taleb's key observations is that it is impossible to calculate tail risks using the current methods of risk analysis, as they cannot keep up with the complexity of the modern financial world. All the metrics have the effect of underestimating the impact of the possibility of very large deviations. Meanwhile, an exponential increase in risks means that if the market drops by 10 percent, one may lose 10 million, but if the market drops by 15 percent, the loss might be 500 million, and an extra 5 percent fall might result in 15 billion (Tim Morrison, 2008, http://content.time.com/time/business/article/0,8599,1853531,00.html). In Taleb's words, the current metrics might at best be able to estimate "how uncomfortable the plane ride is going to be, but tells you nothing about the crash." (Ibid.).

[21] Taleb, *The Black Swan*, xxii-xxxii.

[22] See, for example, Gerd Gigerenzer, *Reckoning with Risk: Learning to Live With Uncertainty* (London: Penguin, 2002); also Gerd Gigerenzer, *Gut Feelings: The Intelligence of the Unconscious* (London: Penguin, 2007); Gerd Gigerenzer, *Risk savvy: How to Make Good Decisions* (London: Penguin, 2014); Daniel Kahneman and Amos Tversky, eds., *Choices, Values and Frames* (New York, NY: Cambridge University Press, 2000); Daniel Kahneman, *Thinking, Fast and Slow* (New York, NY: Farrar, Straus and Giroux, 2011); Steven Pinker, *The Blank Slate: The Modern Denial of Human Nature* (London: Allen Lane, 2002) and Steven Pinker, *The Better Angels of Our Nature: Why Violence Has Declined* (London: Allen Lane, 2011).

[23] Hyde, *Trickster Makes This World: How Disruptive Imagination Creates Culture*, 138.

[24] Milashevich, *Re-visioning Business: Archetypal Patterns in the Business Domain and Their Relation to the Concept of Business Creativity*, 166-189.

[25] Warren Buffett, in an interview with the Financial Crisis Inquiry Commission in 2010, as cited by Elena Holodny, "Warren Buffett Brilliantly Explains How Bubbles Are Formed" (2016), http://uk.business-insider.com/warren-buffett-explains-how-bubbles-are-formed-2016-3?r= #US&IR=T.

[26] Ibid.

[27] Anthony Catanach and Julie Anne Ragatz, "2008 Market Crisis: Black Swan, Perfect Storm or Tipping Point?", in *Bank Accounting and Finance*, 23.3 (2010), 20–26.

[28] Ibid.

[29] Ibid.

[30] Ibid.

[31] Ibid.

[32] Jung, *The Red Book*, 176.

[33] Nathan Schwartz-Salant, "The Mark of One Who Has Seen Chaos: A Review of C.G. Jung's Red Book," in *Quadrant* 40.2 (Summer 2010), 26.

[34] Jung, *Memories, Dreams, Reflections*, 212.

[35] Jung, "On the Psychology of the Trickster-Figure," *CW* 9/I, pars. 477-487.

[36] Jung, *The Red Book*, 564.

[37] The term "perfect storm" was originally coined by writer Sebastian Junger (1997) to refer to the 1991 battle between a fishing boat crew and a nor'easter. The storm in question resulted from a combination of multiple unpredictable factors: warm air from the Great Lakes, storm winds from an Atlantic island and tropical moisture due to Hurricane Grace. As financial scholars Anthony Catanach and Julie Ragatz comment in relation to such events in business: "The perfect storm premise is that none of these factors was individually powerful enough to create the resulting storm; when they came together, however, their confluence created an effect that was exponentially more devastating than anyone could have imagined" (Catanach and Ragatz, "2008 Market Crisis: Black Swan, Perfect Storm or Tipping Point?", 21).

[38] Ali Velshi, CNN, as cited in Manav Tanneeru, "How a 'Perfect Storm' Led to the Economic Crisis" (2009), see http://edition.cnn.com/2009/US/01/29/economic.crisis.explainer/index.html.

[39] Iain Martin, "Farewell to a Decade of Debt and Disaster" (2009), https://www.wsj.com/articles/SB10001424052748704398304574598350918417532.

[40] Jon Hilsenrath, "Fed Debates New Role: Bubble Fighter" (2009), http://online.wsj.com/article/SB125970281466871707.html.

[41] On the connection between the trickster and synchronicity, see Milashevich, *Re-visioning Business: Archetypal Patterns in the Business Domain and Their Relation to the Concept of Business Creativity*, 236-243.

[42] C.G. Jung, "Synchronicity: An Acausal Connecting Principle," in *CW*, vol. 8 (Princeton, NJ: Princeton University Press, 1968), par. 850.

[43] Roderick Main, *The Rupture of Time: Synchronicity and Jung's Critique of Modern Western Culture* (London and New York, NY: Routledge, 2004), 51-62.

[44] Ibid., 2.

[45] Ibid., 177.

[46] Ibid.

[47] Ibid.

[48] Stein, *Soul: Treatment and Recovery: The Selected Works of Murray Stein*, 9.

[49] Main, *The Rupture of Time: Synchronicity and Jung's Critique of Modern Western Culture*, 26.

[50] Stein, *Soul: Treatment and Recovery: The Selected Works of Murray Stein*, 187.

[51] Shamdasani, "*Liber Novus*: The 'Red Book' of C.G. Jung," 54-55.

[52] Ibid.

[53] Ibid.

[54] Jung, *The Red Book*, 117-211; 277-320.

[55] Shamdasani, "*Liber Novus*: The 'Red Book' of C.G. Jung," 56.

[56] C.G. Jung, "The Role of the Unconscious," in *CW*, vol. 10 (Princeton, NJ: Princeton University Press, 1964), par. 24.

[57] Shamdasani, "*Liber Novus*: The 'Red Book' of C.G. Jung," 57.

[58] Jung, "On the Psychology of the Trickster-Figure," in *CW* 9/I, pars. 477-487.

[59] Nassim Taleb, *Antifragile: Things That Gain from Disorder* (London and New York, NY: Penguin Books, 2013).

[60] Anthony Stevens, *The Two-million-year-old Self* (College Station, TX: Texas A&M University Press, 1993).

[61] Taleb, *Antifragile: Things That Gain from Disorder*, 56-60.

[62] Ibid., 54-76.

The Schreber Case and the Origins of the *Red Book*

George B. Hogenson

The publication in 2009 of C.G. Jung's *Liber Novus,* or *The Red Book,* marked a critical turning point in the interpretation of Jung's "project" by making available the text that he claimed formed the primary material for his later theorizing. I want to suggest that *The Red Book's* significance extends beyond the Jungian community and in fact sheds light on the entire history of psychoanalysis. Jung composed the book as we now have it over a period of nearly 20 years, but its form rested largely on experiences he had during roughly six months immediately after the final break with Freud in September of 1913. This period has been somewhat mystified, not least by Jung himself in *Memories, Dreams, Reflections,* where he describes the events leading to his *Red Book* as his "encounter with the unconscious." More importantly, this period in Jung's life is often characterized as an episode of "transient psychosis," to use Zvi Lothane's expression. The consensus among Jung scholars, however, is that there is no evidence that Jung was actually having a psychotic episode. Rather the contrary. As Sonu Shamdasani, the editor of *The Red Book,* describes Jung's work at the time, he was engaged in a process of deep meditative visualization, similar to research by other individuals with whom Jung was familiar. "From December 1913 onward," Shamdasani writes,

> … he [Jung] carried on in the same procedure: deliberately evoking a fantasy in a waking state, and then entering into it as into a drama. These fantasies may be understood as a type of dramatized thinking in pictorial form. In reading his fantasies, the impact of Jung's mythological studies is clear. Some of the figures and conceptions derive directly from his readings, and the form and style bear witness to his fascination with the world of myth and epic. In the *Black Books,* Jung wrote down his fantasies in dated entries,

together with reflections on his state of mind and his difficulties in comprehending the fantasies. The *Black Books* are not diaries of events, and very few dreams are noted in them. Rather, they are the records of an experiment. In December 1913, he referred to the first of the black books as the 'book of my most difficult experiment.'[1]

In 1916, Jung wrote a brief paper, "The Transcendent Function," outlining the process he had used for his experiment. There, he described in some detail the practices by means of which he sought to withdraw all attention from the outside world and, as he remarked in a discussion of the process in 1925, allow himself to "drop down" into the unconscious. What I want to suggest in this paper is that this process—which would become his method of active imagination— was at least in part an attempt to replicate under controlled conditions the experiences of a psychotic episode without in fact succumbing to a psychotic break. The occasion for this experiment was the culmination of his debate with Freud regarding libido theory and the characteristics of the deep structure of the unconscious occasioned by their respective interpretations of *dementia praecox* (schizophrenia), paranoia, and the case of Daniel Paul Schreber.

Daniel Paul Schreber is often referred to as the most discussed psychiatric patient in the history of medicine. His circumstances are well-known. The son of a distinguished physician, he rose to prominence in the law, becoming, while still quite young, the *Senatspräsident,* or presiding judge, of the *Oberlandesgericht* in Dresden—the highest court in Saxony. Prior to this elevation, Schreber had run a failed campaign for a seat in the *Reichstag* following which he suffered a breakdown—perhaps from exhaustion —resulting in a brief hospitalization. His election as president of the Dresden court, however, was followed shortly by a far more severe breakdown, resulting in his hospitalization in 1884. In 1903, as part of an effort to free himself from the Sonnenstein asylum, he composed an extensive account of his delusional—or visionary— system, which he managed to have published under the title *Denkwürdigkeiten eines Nervenkranken,* which was translated into

English as *Memoir of My Nervous Illness*. Accompanied by a carefully constructed legal argument, the *Memoir*, despite its exotic mystical and religious system, led to Schreber's successful plea for release. Another hospitalization, however, was necessary following his wife's death, and Schreber himself died in 1911.

Schreber's delusional system begins with a thought upon waking that "it really must be rather pleasant to be a woman succumbing to intercourse."[2] With this thought Schreber begins a psychic journey into a world where he experiences his body being transformed into that of a woman, while God, through contact with his "nerves," seeks variously to impregnate him or to torture him. As his visionary experiences progressed, he came to the conclusion that it was his destiny to survive the destruction of the world and, by way of his intercourse with God, to be the originator of a new human race. At various points in his account, he experiences those around him in the asylum in increasingly abstract ways, as "fleetingly improvised men." His principal physician in the first stages of his hospitalization, Paul Flechsig, became an agent of torment whom Schreber accused of "soul murder." In his brief to the court seeking release from the asylum, Schreber maintained that while his experiences were beyond normal psychological patterns, and, while also accepting that he was ill, he nevertheless maintained that his religious insights remained as valid as any other religious system. The court accepted this argument and ordered his release from the asylum.

There is an extensive literature on the Schreber case, although the bulk of it is actually directed at Freud's commentary on Schreber in his "Psycho-Analytical Notes on an Autobiographical Account of a Case of Paranoia (*dementia paranoides*)," published in 1911. Freud's central argument was that Schreber suffered from paranoid dementia due to the repression of homosexual desires that began with his childhood love and admiration for his father, which in turn became projected onto Flechsig. The basic dialectic of paranoia followed a pattern that Freud had laid out much earlier, in which paranoia was the result of the failure of an initial repression of a desire to defend against the implications of the desire, which was therefore transformed into a negative projection and perceived as an attack or threat from the outside. Paranoia as an expression of repressed homosexuality, the argument that Freud deployed in his analysis of Schreber, was, however, a more recent development of Freud's model, originating in his collaboration with Sandor Ferenczi. On the other hand, it was Jung who first introduced Schreber's *Denkwürdigkeiten* to Freud following the Second International Psychoanalytic Congress in Nuremburg in March 1910. Jung had already studied Schreber's book at least as early as 1906, referring to it, albeit in passing, at several points in his study of *dementia praecox*, published in 1907. *The Psychology of Dementia Praecox* was also the occasion for the first theoretical exchange between Freud and Jung in their correspondence, and it gave rise to what would become the debate over the nature and the application of the concept of libido. This debate, as both Zvi Lothane and Patrick Vandermeersch point out, would come to a head around the Schreber case several years later, but it is important to understand how it originated, as there has developed a rather extensive and altogether misleading narrative about Jung's objection to Freud's sexual etiology of the neuroses—that he objected to the sexual theory out of some fastidious Victorian moral sensitivity—which in turn flows into his discussion of *dementia praecox* and paranoia.

Any discussion of the debate between Freud and Jung must take into account several critical differences in their experiences prior to their first exchange of letters. Jung was already familiar with Freud's work, having read *The Interpretation of Dreams* upon its publication as part of his training at the Burghölzli hospital, and it is clear from his dissertation that he was at least familiar with some of Freud's other early works. More importantly, however, Jung was involved almost exclusively in the treatment of psychotic patients under the direction of Eugen Bleuler, arguably the leading psychiatric theoretician in Europe at that time. Freud, on the other hand, was primarily engaged with neurotic patients in his private practice in Vienna. Additionally, Jung's work at the Burghölzli involved extensive experimentation with the Word Association Experiment over a wide array of individuals, both in the hospital and from the general population. Jung would continue to rely on evidence from these experiments to validate many of his theoretical proposals well into the 1930s. Taken together, these aspects of the relationship complicated matters from the beginning, as Jung, while deeply admiring of Freud's work on neurosis, brought to the relationship not only a distinctly different clinical experience, but also an experimental base for many of his early objections regarding Freud's theories. These differences would become manifest almost immediately.

In Jung's second letter to Freud, he comments that he cannot entirely accept the idea that sexuality is the only "basic drive," suggesting that hunger, for example, is equally fundamental and informs the infant's eating and sucking. He goes on to suggest that one complex—perhaps sexual in origin—can contaminate another complex that is not sexual in origin and vice versa, writing: "Two complexes existing at the same time are always bound to coalesce psychologically, so that one of them invariably contains constellated aspects of the other."[3] Jung's argument was that Freud relied too heavily on the observation of behavior that appears similar to sexual satisfaction, for example in the nursing infant. Lothane, drawing on Vandermeersh, summarizes the dispute, writing:

> Freud's libido theory envisaged a process of coalescing of sexually-toned infantile component drives into adult forms of sexual aim and love object choice and was the basis of a theory of pathogenesis of neuroses and psychoses according to which symptoms represented a return to fixation points created in the course of libidinal development. By contrast, Jung argued for a genetic, or evolutionary, conception of a holistic, vital drive, or primordial libido, concerned with self-preservation only, which only at a later stage became differentiated into sexuality. Jung's theory of pathogenesis stressed the role of a real, actual conflict in the patient's adult life as a result of which 'libido became introverted and regressively formed the fantasies which Freud has mistakenly considered to be the origin of neurosis.' Jung proposed this theory for psychoses in general and for Schreber in particular. For Freud, the two theories were on an irreconcilable collision course.[4]

By the time of the Schreber debate, however, the issue of libido had become far more acute. Jung was, by this time, arguing that Freud's account of libidinal withdrawal, as spelled out in the *Three Essays on a Theory of Sexuality*, was insufficient for a description of *dementia praecox*. In the Schreber case itself, Freud had acknowledged that his position on withdrawal from a specific object, as was the case in the formation of a neurosis, was problematic when faced with the global withdrawal of the *dementia praecox* patient. Writing to Freud in December 1911, Jung pressed this point home:

> The loss of the reality principle in dementia praecox cannot be reduced to repression of libido (defined as sexual hunger). Not by me, at any rate … The essential point is that I try to replace the descriptive concept of libido with a *genetic* one. Such a concept covers not only the recent sexual libido but all those forms of it which have long since split off into organized activities.[5]

Also in 1911, Jung, using material provided by Theodore Flournoy, published his major study of mythology, *Wandlungen und Symbole der Libido* (*Transformations and Symbols of the Libido*). *Wandlungen* is generally viewed as the final nail in the coffin of the relationship between Freud and Jung. On the one hand, it appeared to be a continuation of the debate over the nature of libido with Jung's position being one of a more general concern for self-preservation that differentiated itself into more specific forms of libidinal investment. But there was another aspect to that book, and to the dispute between Jung and Freud over the nature of *dementia praecox* that is usually overlooked in the commentaries—the role of the symbol, and more particularly the status of psychic imagery, in Jung's theorizing.

In my work on the relationship between Jung and Freud, I identified several axes upon which their disputes rotated that went beyond the dispute over libido, which appeared to me to be more of a proxy for deeper issues. Among these deeper issues was the problem of temporality in the unconscious, which Jung would take up after the break. Another critical distinction concerned the fundamental form of the contents of the unconscious—specifically whether the deep unconscious was populated by previously conscious propositions that came to be lodged in the unconscious by way of repression, or rather by structuring factors that were present as natural constituents of the unconscious—that is, unconscious contents that gave form to images or image schemas that were not the result of repression. Jacques Lacan, who met with Jung in 1954 and may have actually seen the *Red Book* and discussed Jung's technique of active imagination with him, also identified this distinction, taking special notice of Jung's notion that the libido transforms through the agency of the symbol. In the materials for his 1955-56 seminar, "On Questions Prior to Any Possible Treatment of Psychosis," Lacan comments:

> It is of the utmost importance to observe—in the experience of the unconscious Other where Freud is our guide—that the question does not find its outlines in protomorphic proliferations of the image. ... This is the whole difference between Freud's orientation and that of Jung's school, which latches onto such forms: *Wandlungen der Libido.* These forms may be brought to the fore in a mantic, for they can be produced using the proper techniques (promoting imaginary creations such as reveries, drawings, etc.). ... Similarly, it is precisely to the extent that this style of articulation has been maintained, by virtue of the Freudian Word [verba] ... that such a profound difference persists between the two schools.[6]

Not surprisingly, Lacan is dismissive of Jung's emphasis on the image in his understanding of the unconscious. And I would agree that this distinction is a point of fundamental divergence between the systems.

In July 1914, Jung presented a paper at the Psycho-Medical Society in London, where for the first time he commented on the Schreber case at some length and on Freud's analysis of the case. While admiring the sophistication of Freud's analysis, Jung is critical of what he refers to as Freud's "retrospective understanding" of the case, which considers Schreber's fantasies to be entirely bound by earlier repressed desires or experiences. This is the temporal issue that I mentioned, and it has its origins as early as Jung's 1902 dissertation "On the Psychology and Pathology of So-Called Occult Phenomena," which posited a forward-looking or developmental purpose to a fantasy system resulting from mediumistic experiences. For Jung, Schreber is also attempting to find a way forward, not falling prey to the reemergence of threatening repressed homosexual impulses. Jung writes: "But if we look at the delusional system without prejudice and ask ourselves what it is aiming at, we see, first, that it is in fact aiming at something, and second, that the patient devotes all his will-power to the completion of his system ... Schreber belongs in this class."[7] The world system, or *Weltanschauung*, that the patient creates, Jung goes on, is intended to "enable them to assimilate unknown psychic phenomena and so adapt themselves to their own world."[8] To further explain this system building impulse in the psychotic, Jung introduces a discussion of the first elements of his study of personality typology, which came to fruition in 1921 with the publication of *Psychological Types*. Jung had already introduced the orienting attitudes, introversion and extraversion, at the 1912 congress in Munich, where he attempted to account for the divisions occurring within psychoanalysis—specifically between Freud and Adler—by virtue of their differing typologies. Jung's paper upset Freud, as it implied that his theories did not provide the singular perspective on the psyche that he envisioned but rather legitimized competing theories as simply alternative points of view on the same phenomena.

In the 1914 paper, Jung extended the significance of the introversion/extraversion distinction to an understanding of the psychotic experiences of Schreber, arguing that the introvert, precisely by virtue of the orientation toward the interior, of necessity constructs a system that allows for adaptation to the world. "An extravert," he writes, "can barely conceive the necessity that forces the introvert to adapt to the world by means of a system."[9] Jung extends this proposition to the world of the psychotic, arguing that the delusional system is itself an attempt to adapt to the world. The difficulty is that, due to the radical nature of the inward turn in a psychosis, the affectively charged or numinous contents of the unconscious capture the patient who then "remains stuck in this stage and substitutes his subjective formulations for the real world—which is precisely why he remains ill."[10] This understanding of the inward turn and its relationship to psychosis points as well to a significant aspect of Jung's experiment with the induction of near-psychotic states insofar as he was able to contain them by way of active imagination and retain his attachment to reality. Commenting on this process in *Memories, Dreams, Reflections*, Jung writes:

> To the extent that I managed to translate the emotions into images—that is to say, to find the images which were concealed in the emotions—I was inwardly calmed and reassured. Had I left those images hidden in the emotions, I might have been torn to pieces by them. There is a chance that I might have succeeded in splitting them off; but in that case I would inexorably have fallen into a neurosis and so been ultimately destroyed by them anyhow. As a result of my experiment I learned how helpful it can be, from the therapeutic point of view, to find the particular images which lie behind emotions.[11]

The quest for the images that underlie the emotions returns us to Lacan's comments on the "mantic," or method of deep, meditative interiority. In both the *Red Book* and in his later writings, his work is replete with mandala images, some of which are Jung's own creations and some of which, as pointed out by Joseph Cambray, bear a striking resemblance to the luminous paintings of sea creatures by the naturalist Ernst Haeckle. *The Red Book* in its entirety is set in reference to the medieval illuminated manuscript, and as Jeffrey Hamburger has pointed out, the tradition of illuminated manuscripts viewed even the text as an image. It is in Jung's concerted turn to the image, and particularly to the mandala, that he provides a particular counterpoint to Lacan's critical comments on his method.

In a collection of essays devoted to a critique of the philosopher Hans Blumenberg, Erin Labbie and Michael Uebel point to two critical aspects of Schreber's circumstances and delusional system.[12] First, the circumstances: The physician treating Schreber, whom he accused of soul murder, was the distinguished psychologist, and neuroscientist, Paul Flechsig. In 1884, Flechsig assumed the chair in psychiatry at Leipzig University previously held by the humanistic, or "soul psychiatrist," Johann Christian August Heinroth, and he declared in his inaugural address titled, "On the physical basis of mental diseases," that a "chasm ... gaped" between him and Heinroth, "no less deep and wide than the chasm between medieval medicine and modern science."[13] Psychiatric research and treatment, for Flechsig, would thereafter be a matter of attending to the nerves, or nervous system, of his patients, and he established one of the foremost laboratories for the study of brain tissue from deceased patients. I want to add to the analysis of Labbie and Uebel the development in physics around the same time of a far more refined understanding of light, primarily through the Michelson/Moreley experiment, which undermined the ether theory of light transmission and opened the discussion of electromagnetic radiation. What does this have to do with Schreber and the *Red Book*?

The factor I want to focus on, which is outlined by Labbie and Uebel, albeit without reference to Jung's insistence on the need for a system to organize the introverted movement of the psychotic's withdrawal of libido from the entirety of reality, is that Schreber's system involves God's control of his life through rays that engage his nerves. As Labbie and Uebel point out, the irony here is that Schreber's system for organizing his psychotic states involves precisely an engagement with modernity, in response to what they, correctly I believe, view as a medieval problem of spiritual alienation. The argument of Labbie and Uebel is far more complex than this element alone and deeply indebted to a Lacanian reading of Schreber, but this particular aspect of their argument is telling in terms of the problematic that Schreber sets up for himself. I would now join the argument by suggesting that Schreber's paranoia derives from the system he falls into in an effort to organize his experience of the unconscious. The modernity of his system does not allow him to engage constructively with the problematics of his sense of soul murder. He is, if we now turn to the *Red Book*, in the grip of the spirit of the age, rather than the spirit of the depths.

As we have already seen, Freud's analysis of Schreber included his reflections on the extreme form of introversion in a psychosis that amounted to an experience of the destruction of the world. An element in Schreber's delusional system was God's intention to destroy the world and then repopulate it through intercourse with Schreber in his transformed feminine form. Jung's initial fantasies of the immanent destruction of Europe, if not the world, are remarkably similar to the fantasies both Jung and Freud associate with the psychotic's withdrawal of libido from all objects. It is not a wonder that Jung feared he was slipping into a psychosis himself. A reasonable consensus now exists that Jung was not having a psychotic break, but I want to suggest that his attention to the Schreber case, and the growing dispute with Freud over the nature of libido, among other issues that developed out of their divergent perspectives on psychosis, which had been central to their disagreements from the beginning, presented Jung with a problem that required a form of self-experimentation: Jung's own descent to the level of the unconscious experienced by the psychotic. The *Red Book* is, in this context, a response to Freud's interpretation and the paradoxical problems Freud had to admit existed in the analysis of psychosis regarding the withdrawal of libido and an attempt to solve the problem that Schreber failed to solve in his own system.

Following the argument of Labbie and Uebel that Schreber was confronting a medieval problem by way of a modern system, it is possible that Jung's turn to the Middle Ages, as he explicitly remarks in the *Red Book*—"I must catch up with a piece of the Middle Ages—within myself"[14]—reflects his own intuition regarding the nature of Schreber's claim that his soul was being murdered by his physician, the neuroscientist Flechsig.

Where does this leave us today? One aspect of the historiography of psychoanalysis and Analytical Psychology that is rarely commented on is the degree to which Freud and Jung remained engaged with one another even after the break. I have noted Jung's comments from 1914, and one can find similar comments in Freud's papers on metapsychology, particularly "On the History of the Psychoanalytic Movement" and "On Narcissism." In these instances, Freud is critical of Jung, but by 1920, in "Beyond the Pleasure Principle," Freud begins to take on Jung's prospective point of view in the dynamics of the psyche, as pointed out by John Kerr.[15] In 1939, on the occasion of Freud's death, Jung offered a testimony to his continued admirations for Freud, his only critical comment being that Freud had failed to realize that, not unlike the introvert or the psychotic, he had become trapped in the numinosity of his theory and could not see beyond it. In interviews near the end of his life, Jung continued to characterize Freud as the most extraordinary man he had ever known.

I conclude, therefore, by encouraging a deeper examination of *The Red Book* within the context of the conflicts between Freud and Jung, not only by the Jungian community but also by psychoanalysts more generally. When *The Red Book* was published, a feature article in the *New York Times Magazine* referred to the book as "The Holy Grail of the Unconscious."[16] This is perhaps a bit hyperbolic, but failure to delve into the intricacies of Jung's experiment foreshortens our understanding of the psyche more generally and does a disservice not only to Jung but also our understanding of the strange world first uncovered by Freud and those who followed him.

Endnotes

[1] Sonu Shamdasani, "*Liber Novus*: The 'Red Book' of C.G. Jung," in C.G. Jung, *The Red Book: Liber Novus*, ed. Sonu Shamdasani, tr. John Peck, Mark Kyburz, and Sonu Shamdasani (New York, NY: W.W. Norton, 2009), 200.

[2] D.P. Schreber, *Memoir of My Nervous Illness* (New York, NY: The New York Review of Books, 2000), 46.

[3] Sigmund Freud, C.G. Jung, *The Freud/Jung Letters: The Correspondence between Sigmund Freud and C.G. Jung*, (ed.) William McGuire and trans. by Ralph Manheim and R.F.C. Hull (Princeton, NJ: Princeton University Press, 1974), 7.

[4] Zvi Lothane, "The schism between Freud and Jung over Schreber: Its implications for method and doctrine," in *International Forum of Psychoanalysis*, 6(2), 1997, 110.

[5] Sigmund Freud, C.G. Jung, *The Freud/Jung Letters: The Correspondence between Sigmund Freud and C.G. Jung*, 471.

[6] J. Lacan, *Ecrits: The First Complete Edition in English* (New York, NY: W.W. Norton, 2007), 460.

[7] C.G. Jung, "On Psychological Understanding," in *CW*, vol. 3 (Princeton, NJ: Princeton University Press, 1960), par. 410.

[8] Ibid., 416.

[9] Ibid., 420.

[10] Ibid., 416.

[11] C.G. Jung, *Memories, Dreams, Reflections*, ed. Aniela Jaffé (New York, NY: Vintage, 1963), 307-308.

[12] Erin Labbie, Michael Uebel, "We have never been Schreber: Paranoia, Medieval and Modern," in *The Legitimacy of the Middle Ages: On the Unwritten History of Theory*, (eds.) Andrew Cole and D. Vance Smith (Durham, NC: Duke University Press, 2010), 127-158.

[13] Paul Flechsig, *Die körperlichen Grundlagen der Geistesstörungen. Vortrag gehalten beim Antritt des Lehramtes an der Universität Leipzig am 4. März 1882* (Leipzig: Veit, 1882).

[14] Jung, *The Red Book*, 330.

[15] John Kerr, "Beyond the pleasure principle and back again: Freud, Jung and Sabina Spielrein," in *Freud: Appraisals and Reappraisals*, vol. 3, (ed.) P. Stepansky (Hillsdale, NJ: The Analytic Press, 1988), 3-79.

[16] Sara Corbett, "The Holy Grail of the Unconscious," in *The New York Times Magazine*, September 16, 2009.

C.G. Jung's Subversive Christology in *The Red Book* and its Meaning for Our Times

Christine Maillard

I read the gospels and seek their meaning which is yet to come. We know their meaning as it lies before us, but not their hidden meaning which points to the future.[1]

C.G. Jung

Introduction: Jung's *Liber Novus*, a Reflection on the Figure of Christ

The Red Book, titled *Liber Novus* by Jung, was composed from 1914 onward and published posthumously in 2009. It is an extraordinary document, rich in content as well as beautifully crafted, making it unique among Jung's works with respect to the latter. It came into being under special circumstances, which Sonu Shamdasani, editor of *The Red Book*, attempted to reconstruct in his extensive introduction to the book and to present in part a visionary experience.[2]

In previous articles, I have studied the role played by *Liber Novus* in expanding our awareness of Jung's *oeuvre*, from both the psychological perspective and from the viewpoint of religious thought.[3]

Although of a different kind, *Liber Novus* is close, chronologically, to other texts in which Jung attempted to define his idea of *individuation*, that is, his view on psychological and spiritual development, his ideas on adaptation to collective norms and on freedom, and his concerns about gender and its consequences for the process of individuation.[4] Those issues are today more topical than ever in our globalized world.

A century separates us from the production of the *Liber Novus* text, which was elaborated in times of major collective crises. Like the works of many authors of that time, such as those of Hermann Hesse (1877-1962), Alfred Döblin (1878-1957) and Hermann Broch (1886-1951), Jung's text remains a source of inspiration at the beginning of the 21ᵗʰ century. Examining the meaning of such a work as *Liber Novus* for our times is therefore a real issue.

The history of religions plays a huge part in the *Red Book*'s analyses. Many characters fall within a religious world, whether Christian or from other backgrounds. "Every subsequent form of religion is the meaning of the antecedent," as formulated in the dialogue between the narrator and the hermit Ammonius.[5] The topic of religion, in its confessional and personal aspects, is a dominant theme in Jung's entire work. *Liber Novus* conjures up "the gift of religion" as one of the main issues developed in this work.[6]

In this context, the discourse on the figure of Christ, which permeates the entire *Red Book* like a guiding motif, is not only a key element for understanding this work but also relevant for our times. The figure of Christ appears as an element of the narrator's discourse in the first two parts, *Liber Primus* and *Liber Secundus,* and briefly at the end of the third part ("Scrutinies") as a character talking with Philemon, who is one of the main characters of *The Red Book* and in charge of exposing a specific form of knowledge, which could be called "the gnosis" of *Liber Novus.*

The texts compiled in *Liber Novus* are the thoughts of an intellectual who was deeply influenced by German mystical movements, particularly the works of Meister Eckhart (1260-1328), Jacob Boehme (1575-1624) and Angelus Silesius (1624-1677), but also by the religions of India and the Far East. Moreover, Jung's intense preoccupation with Christ was part of a broader discussion of Christology developed in the 19ᵗʰ and 20ᵗʰ centuries by several philosophers whose project was to criticize Christianity, such as Ludwig Feuerbach (1804-1872), Søren Kierkegaard (1813-1855) and Friedrich Nietzsche (1844-1900). Among them was another less-known but very important philosopher, Max Stirner (1806-1856), whose view on Christ in his major work, *Der Einzige und sein*

Eigentum (literally, *The Unique and His Property*; translated as *The Ego and His Own*), resembles the one Jung expresses in *Liber Novus*, which is related to the idea of radical individuation that breaks with the norms and values transmitted by a society or even a whole civilization. David Friedrich Strauss (1808-1874) had already published in 1835 and 1836 the two volumes of his major work, *Das Leben Jesu, kritisch bearbeitet* (*The Life of Jesus, Critically Examined*), in which he explored the Christ myth.

Jung was the son of a Zwinglian pastor and deeply influenced by a very specific Christian background during his childhood. In his adulthood and following upon more than 150 years of deconstruction of religion, especially of Christianity in Europe, he suggested a new reflection on religion and the Christian episode in the history of religions in a group of works written in the 1930s and 1940s and extending into the early 1950's: *Psychology and Religion*, an essay on the psychological approach to the dogma of the Trinity, another essay on the symbol of transubstantiation in the Catholic Mass, a collection of texts on Gnosticism under the title *Aion*, and *Answer to Job.*[7] Most of the major topics of these works appear in germination and in literary form in the three parts of *Liber Novus*.[8] The third part contains the *Seven Sermons to the Dead*. Composed in 1916, it is the only text that was available before *The Red Book* was published.[9]

The figure of Christ appears in each of the three parts of *The Red Book* and is connected to a complex set of symbolic characters. The main characters in relation to the Christ pattern are Salome, representing Eros, the Snake, representing Evil, and Philemon, exposing a Gnostic-like knowledge. The "I" figure, who is related to Jung's own experience and the subject in *The Red Book*'s narrative, appears as a character whose mission is to expose Jung's ideas.

The Red Book displays a critique and deconstruction of the value systems ruling present and past societies. For instance, heroism, male role models, and virtue (*Tugend*) are criticized. Collective values, including the ones inherited from Western Christian culture, are also reassessed. Moreover, together with criticism comes the idea of a necessary "subversion of all values" (*Umwertung der Werte*), as expressed and developed by Nietzsche in *Thus Spoke Zarathustra*, a huge source of inspiration for Jung.[10] The question remains as to whether it is possible to identify in *The Red Book* the expression of new values that would create an ethic for the future. This is a crucial issue, since *The Red Book* evokes first and foremost the "way of what is to come" (*der Weg des Kommenden*) and belongs in that respect to the visionary, almost prophetic genre.[11]

Among the new values espoused in *Liber Novus*, one finds that of the individual subject who is expected to become what the text calls "the unique being" (*Einzelsein*), which prefigures Jung's conceptions of individuation and the self. The other value is collective, with the notion of "hospitality" (*Gastfreundlichkeit*), referring to a particular way of dealing with otherness.[12] These values will be further discussed in the last part of this essay. The enunciation of new values calls upon the figure of Christ and the issue of his status as a role model. This will be dealt with further below. *Liber Novus* outlines the vision of *the coming God*, following the Nietzschean "death of God," as a new value coming after the loss of the highest value in the process of growing secularization of culture and societies.[13]

I will divide the reflection on Christ in *The Red Book* into three major steps: (1) the injunction "not to imitate Christ," but to (2) "become a Christ," which will finally lead to (3) "overcoming Christianity." Each of these steps seems to shape a message emphasizing the deeply subversive nature Jung assigned to the Christian moment of civilization, which we believe remains topical to this day.

(Do not) Imitate Christ

A major part of the discussion of Christ in *Liber Novus* is dedicated to the issue of "imitating Christ" (*imitatio Christi*), as a commandment of the Church to its believers. Christ as an ethical ideal, embodying such capital virtues as modesty, love for the other, and charity, is indeed a fundamental message of the Gospels. However, its dissemination was mostly through a devotional book from the late Middle Ages: *The Imitation of Christ*, reputedly written by Thomas a Kempis (1380-1471). This short work dating from the end of the 14th century was written for clergymen in order to encourage them to withdraw from worldly vanities and dedicate themselves to Christ alone. It was, in fact, very successful and commanded a much larger audience than the regular clergy, and it became most likely the second most printed book after the Bible.[14] Two whole chapters of *Liber Secundus* are dedicated to a debate of this text: The "I" figure mentions it while talking to two secondary characters, the librarian and the cook.[15] In the chapter titled "Divine Folly" (in *Liber Secundus*), the narrator asks a librarian if he can borrow *The Imitation of Christ* in order to read it. A brief dialogue ensues in which the librarian expresses his astonishment at this request. The narrator ("I") explains to him how he appreciated the short book, not so much as a source of knowledge but rather as a way to conjure up the values of the soul,[16] what the *Liber Novus* calls "the spirit of the depths" *(der Geist der Tiefe)*, as opposed to "the spirit of this time" (*der Geist dieser Zeit*). This opposition, as expressed in Jung's theoretical work, distinguishes the collective unconscious and collective consciousness.[17]

The values of the intellect, which lie at the foundation of science and everything deriving from it in modern life, are here opposed to another value: "mercy" (*Gnade*). It brings the individual's life to another dimension, different from the one that is determined by collective consciousness and the dominant values of the time, allowing one to see things from a different perspective:

> The 'imitation of Christ' led me to the master himself and to his astonishing kingdom. I do not know what I want there; I can only follow the master who governs this other realm in me. In this realm other laws are valid than the guidelines of my wisdom. Here, the 'mercy of God,' which I never had relied on, for good practical reasons, is the highest law of action.[18]

The reader then rapidly realizes that the praise for "imitating" Christ in those chapters takes a special turn. Christ is given the value of an individual who rose against the established order and against the values of society and the religious world he was born into. He "violated the laws"[19] of his society. The most important action he accomplished was to "overthrow values" in order to make way for other values that were not imposed by "the spirit of this time" but that he created *against* the spirit of his time. *Liber Novus* recommends to each individual to create their own values and not to live the life of another, not even of Christ's, life but *their own* life. Everyone has to follow their own way, which shall not be someone else's way. Jung's thoughts are very close to the idea of radical individualism exposed in the middle of the 19th century by Max Stirner (1806-1856). In his unique and masterful book, *The Unique and Its Property* (*Der Einzige und sein Eigentum*, 1845), Stirner recommended that any imitation of alienating values, whether social or religious, should be abolished and that each individual should create his/her own values.[20]

According to Jung, the fight against alienation includes the order to "break the Christ" in oneself in order to find oneself, a "unique individual" as Stirner put it. The radical individualism he defended set only one rule to any individual: Be "unique."

> For only one was Christ and only one could violate the laws as he did. ... Break the Christ in yourself so that you may arrive at yourself.[21]

Not to imitate Christ does not mean going away from Christian values in their most advanced outcomes for humanity or opposing it entirely, but rather giving up any imitative posture that enslaves individuals by casting him in a collective mould. Do not imitate anybody, do not fit in any mold, that is the "true" *imitatio Christi*!

> If I imitate Christ, he is always ahead of me and I can never reach the goal, unless I reach it in him. ... But if I am truly to understand Christ, I must realize how Christ actually lived only his own life, and imitated no one. He did not emulate any model.[22]

And the reflection goes on: "If I thus truly imitate Christ, I do not imitate anyone, I emulate no one, but go my own way, and I will also no longer call myself a Christian."[23]

The idea is not to conform to a predefined message transmitted by an institutional religion and its confessional aspects but rather to live what is most radical in the Christian message, namely a subversion of values, just as Christ practiced and taught. The idea is to create and follow a personal way, not a collective one.

"Becoming a Christ": Individuation and "Christification"

The chapter "Divine Folly" also includes a critique of Nietzsche's critique of Christianity. Through his radical critique, the German philosopher had wholly rejected Christianity. As far as Jung is concerned, he lets his narrator say that we are far from being done with Christianity and that there is much more to be found in it than what has been seen.

Once the principle of a servile imitation of a model is set aside, as prestigious as the model might be, the question becomes how the figure of Christ can contribute to the creation of new values at the beginning of the 20th century when the *Liber Novus* was composed, as well as at the beginning of the 21th century, another question that has to be dealt with here. The answer provided in the *Liber Novus* is radical: Do not "imitate" Christ, rather "become" a Christ; do not become *christiani*, that is to say Christians devoted to a collectively dictated doctrine and submissive to it; rather become *christi*, individuals who will live their own life just as Christ did and create new values for their community: "… you should be he himself, not Christians but Christ, otherwise you will be of no use to the coming God."[24] The image of Christ created by Jung thus refuted the "spirit of this time" (*Geist dieser Zeit*), which drove individuals to conformity. On the contrary, it embodied the inspiration of the "spirit of the depths" (*Geist der Tiefe*), enabling people to access individuation through the incorporation of unconscious contents.

One could say that things get more complex from there. The issue of the relation to Evil, another key theme of *Liber Novus*, appears here for the first time in Jung's work and would be at the center of the debate with Christianity until the end of his life, in texts such as the late work, *Answer to Job*. Jung believed that during the whole

Christian era, the highest value was embodied in the figure of Christ, who was identified with the Sovereign Good (*summum bonum*). According to Jung, Christ represented a unilateral ideal built on the ignorance of the reality of Evil. The theme of a somehow "unilateral Christ" is presented in several ways in *Liber Novus*, first through reflections on a God who was identified with love: "Christ taught: God is love. But you should know that love is also terrible."[25] Second, it emerges in the motif of temptation, which is also very present in the *Imitation of Christ* by Thomas a Kempis, who recommended to the pious individual to stay away as much as possible from the temptations offered by the world. In *Liber Novus*, the theme of temptation is subverted and applied to both Good and Evil:

> Christ totally overcomes the temptation of the devil, but not the temptation of God to good and reason. Christ thus succumbs to cursing.
> You still have to learn this, to succumb to no temptation, but to do everything of your own will; then you will be free and beyond Christianity.[26]

The Last Supper, one of the main episodes of the Christian myth, is here interpreted as a "bloody sacrifice": "Did not Christ himself restore bloody human sacrifice, which better customs had expelled from sacred practice since days of old? Did he not himself reinstate the sacred practice of the eating of human sacrifice?"[27]

The relativity of Good and Evil, a major theme in Jung's last works, is already a topic in *Liber Novus*, and the conjunction of opposites, which structures the entire *Red Book*, is here applied to the figure of Christ and his journey to Hell:

> Therefore after his death Christ had to journey to Hell, otherwise the ascent to Heaven would have become impossible for him. Christ first had to become his Antichrist, his underworldly brother.[28]

Christ—as explained by Jung in diverse essays on Christianity, more specifically in *Answer to Job*—was only one step in the process one could call "the individuation of mankind" because of his identification with the Good. Another view on the individual's position, including the Evil and hence transcending it, would represent a new step, for which *The Red Book* offers a prophetic statement:

> I hold together what Christ has kept apart in himself and through his example in others, since the more the one half of my being strives toward the good, the more the other half journeys to Hell.[29]

The "individuated" person is expected to give up certainties that are collectively transmitted regarding Good and the Evil in order to reach a personal ethical code, which implies facing Evil personally and directly.

The "christification" of the individual subject reached its climax in *Liber Novus* with the topic of the identification of the "I" with the crucified: "Becoming a Christ" implies the individual experience of Passion and Crucifixion. Jung was here in line with a medieval tradition. The symbolism of these elements of the Christian myth is here applied to the human experience. The vocabulary of *Liber Novus* presents striking images expressing the phantasmagorical experience of the Crucifixion as experienced by the subject narrator. And it goes one step further with the experience of the Snake on the Crucified subject, as narrated in the dialogue between the "I" and Salome:

> S: 'You are Christ.'
> I stand with outstretched arms like someone crucified, my body taut and horribly entwined by the serpent ...[30]

Liber Novus postulates the "christification" of each individual, symbolizing through this metaphor the evolution of the human personality Jung referred to as "individuation," which would finally lead the individual to go beyond the compliance to any system of values, including the Christian values, considered as a dogmatic and denominational system.

Beyond Christianity: A "Religion of the Future"?

The considerations mentioned before show Jung's paradoxical position in *Liber Novus*. On the one hand, he accepted and advocated Christianity as a heritage. On the other, he called for a post-Christianity that would allow individuals, freed from any forms of collective pressure, to live a personal religion as Goethe had already pleaded for:

> He who possesses art and science, has religion. He who does not possess them, needs religion.[31]

Surpassing Christianity also implies dealing with the other main religions and their messages. One element in *The Red Book* is especially revealing as to the significance Asian religions had on Jung in the 1910s: The references concerning the figure of Buddha are scarce, but particularly meaningful within the thematic framework of a new religion that would overtake Christianity. This theme was powerfully developed in the *Seven Sermons to the Dead*, a key component of the third part of *The Red Book*, "Scrutinies," which Philemon recites in the presence of the narrator. In the Commentaries to *Liber Novus*, Jung briefly compares Christ to Buddha:

> Christ overcame the world by burdening himself with its suffering. But Buddha overcame both the pleasure and suffering of the world by disposing of both. And thus he entered into nonbeing, a condition from which there is no return. Buddha is an even higher spiritual power, that derives no pleasure from controlling the flesh, since he has altogether moved beyond pleasure and suffering. Passion, whose conquest still requires so much effort in the case of

Christ and does so incessantly and in ever greater measure, has left Buddha and surrounds him as a blazing fire. He is unaffected and untouchable.[32]

Among the religions that originated in Asia, Buddhism seems to have most strongly caught Jung's attention. He saw in Buddha the one who paves the spiritual way for the entire world[33] and the representative of the religion of what is to come or of the future. At the time when he wrote the *Red Book*, this way of looking at things already existed. Did Jung actually mean that the Western world should become Buddhist? Certainly not. During his entire life, he distrusted any process of transculturation and identification with a form of cultural otherness, especially a collective one. Buddha, who frequently appeared in German-speaking literature between 1900 and 1930, did not represent a confession according to Jung, but rather a symbol, a figure of radical emancipation and transcendence from any illusory identification.

The last part of *Liber Novus* ("Scrutinies") stages a final dialogue between Philemon and Christ, who appears only briefly in the text. Philemon talks to a "blue shade" that entered his garden. This character is related to Christ in *Black Book* 6.[34] Upon Christ's inquiries about the Kingdom of Heaven and of the Spirit, that is his Kingdom, Philemon informs him about the opening of a new religious era:

> You are, Oh master, here in the world of men. Men have changed. They are no longer the slaves and no longer the swindlers of the Gods and no longer mourn in your name, but they grant hospitality to the Gods.[35]

"Men have changed." What does this mean? They could henceforth adopt a different attitude toward religion. They would not merely reject it in the name of reason or science, they would not submit to the dogmatic or moral orders of the confessions but would rather be able to experience a plurality of divine figures—hence the theme of polytheism developed by Jung in *Septem Sermones ad Mortuos,* that is, a "polytheism of the soul" and a "polytheism of values."[36]

Jung remained Christian, but he favored Esoteric Christianity, or even Christian gnosis.[37] According to him, gnosis was "a special form of knowledge" making possible the formulation of dogma. It was an esoteric knowledge that recognized in dogma a symbolic expression, which was accessible in terms of the exoteric. Jung expressed the idea that the function of religious confessions was to "replace" the immediate experience of religion by providing the individual with a large collection of symbolic elements codified in ritual and dogma. The dogma "owes its continued existence and its form on the one hand to so-called 'revealed' or immediate experiences of the 'Gnosis'—for instance, the God-man, the Cross, the Virgin Birth, the Immaculate Conception, the Trinity, and so on, and on the other hand to the ceaseless collaboration of many minds over many centuries."[38] The dogma was, however, "purged from any weird, insufficiently elaborate or disturbing elements of the individual experience."[39]

According to Jung, the Gnostics had many direct religious experiences, which were directly reflected in theirs myths, and the contemporary person is likely to experience the same through the encounter with the archetypes of collective unconsciousness, a modern source of "gnostic" knowledge.

"The way of what is to come" (der Weg des Kommenden) mentioned in the Liber Novus is also inspired by the eschatological utopia expressed by Gioacchino da Fiore who describes a Trinity whose "persons" would be the three phases of the psychological development of mankind. This mythologem was abundantly used in the history of German thought from Jacob Boehme to Eduard von Hartmann's "religion of the future."[40]

> Just as the disciples of Christ recognized that God had become flesh and lived among them as a man, we now recognize that the anointed of this time is a God who does not appear in the flesh; he is no man and yet is a son of man, but in spirit and not in flesh; hence he can be born only through the spirit of men as the conceiving womb of the God.[41]

Conclusion: Christianity and "Symbolic Life"

According to Jung, the Christian message was not outdated by the successive deconstructions of Christianism carried out by the Enlightenment, by the philosophy of religion of 19th-century post-Hegelians or by Nietzsche, although he took his inspiration from those authors and their critics. Jung felt that the Christian message was still alive and long-lasting. The myth is particularly strong and as such cannot die. Analyzing this myth, Jung's consideration of Christianity, as presented in *The Red Book* and in his later work as a psychologist of religion, has a deep meaning for our time, both for the individual and for collective life and regarding the issues our societies are facing. It is part of our "symbolic life."[42]

Liber Novus is about individuation, individual liberation, as well as hospitality, a value of openness toward the community. It offers a special interpretation of the Christ symbol, conveying the value of individual freedom as opposed to dogmatism. The theme of "hospitality" toward the gods, the acknowledgment of diversity and its reception are very current issues for our times. Indeed, if the figure of Christ is not a main character of *The Red Book*, as opposed to other characters such as Philemon, Salome, the Soul, and the "I," his discreet presence as a figure in the last chapters of the book reminds us of the importance of the Christian myth for our times.

Endnotes

[1] C.G. Jung, *The Red Book: Liber Novus. A Reader's Edition*, ed. Sonu Shamdasani, trans. John Peck, Mark Kyburz, and Sonu Shamdasani (New York, NY: W.W. Norton, 2012), 258.

[2] Sonu Shamdasani, "*Liber Novus*: The 'Red Book' of C.G. Jung," in C.G. Jung, *The Red Book*, 1-110.

[3] See Christine Maillard, ed., *Arts, sciences et psychologie. Autour du Livre Rouge de Carl Gustav Jung (1914-1930)/Kunst, Wissenschaft und Psychologie. Über das Rote Buch von C.G. Jung (1914-1930). Recherches Germaniques*, hors série No. 8, 2011. In this volume, see especially: Karl Baier, "Das *Rote Buch* im Kontext europäischer Spiritualitätsgeschichte," 13-40.

[4] On this aspect, see Christine Maillard: *Au coeur du Livre Rouge: Les Sept Sermons aux Morts. Aux sources de la pensée de C.G. Jung* (Paris: Imago/La Compagnie du Livre Rouge, 2017).

[5] Jung, *The Red Book*, 258.

[6] Jung, *The Red Book*, 376.

[7] C.G. Jung, "Psychology and Religion," in *CW*, vol. 11 (Princeton, NJ: Princeton University Press, 1969); C.G. Jung, *Answer to Job*, in *CW*, vol. 11 (Princeton, NJ: Princeton University Press, 1969); C.G. Jung, "A Psychological Approach to the Dogma of the Trinity," in *CW*, vol. 11 (Princeton, NJ: Princeton University Press, 1969); C.G. Jung, "Transformation Symbolism in the Mass," in *CW*, vol. 11 (Princeton, NJ: Princeton University Press, 1969).

[8] Shamdasani, "*Liber Novus*: The 'Red Book' of C.G. Jung," in C.G. Jung, *The Red Book*, 45.

[9] On *Septem Sermones ad Mortuos*, see Maillard: *Au cœur du Livre Rouge*.

[10] On this aspect, see Paul Bishop, *The Dionysian Self. C.G. Jung's Reception of Friedrich Nietzsche* (Berlin/New York, NY: De Gruyter, 1993); Martin Liebscher, *Libido und Wille zur Macht. C.G. Jungs Auseinandersetzung mit Nietzsche* (Basel: Schwabe, 2012).

[11] On prophetic aspects, see Christine Maillard, "La voie de l'à-venir. Du discours prophétique dans le *Livre Rouge* de Carl Gustav Jung," in *Cahiers jungiens de psychoanalyse* 54, 2011, 119-132.

[12] Jung, *The Red Book*, 553.

[13] Jung, *The Red Book*, 164ff.

[14] On the context of *devotio moderna*, see Karl Baier: "Das *Rote Buch* im Kontext europäischer Spiritualitätsgeschichte," 13-40.

[15] Jung, *The Red Book*, chap. XV, XVI, XVII.

[16] Jung, *The Red Book*, 337.

[17] See Maillard, *Au cœur du Livre Rouge*.

[18] Jung, *The Red Book*, 339.

[19] Ibid., 343.

[20] Max Stirner, *Der Einzige und sein Eigentum* (Stuttgart: Reclam, 2011).

[21] Jung, *The Red Book*, 343.

[22] Ibid., 331-332.

[23] Ibid., 332.

[24] Ibid., 137.

[25] Ibid., 139.

[26] Ibid.

[27] Ibid., 345.

[28] Ibid., 167.

[29] Ibid., 405.

[30] Ibid., 197.

[31] J.W. Goethe, *Zahme Xenien IX*, in *Goethes Werke*, ed. by Erich Trunz, Hamburger Ausgabe, vol. 1: *Die weltanschaulichen Gedichte* (München: Dt. Taschenbuch Verlag, 1998), 367 (translated from German by Christine Maillard).

[32] Ibid., 570.

[33] C.G. Jung, *Memories, Dreams, Reflections*, ed. Aniela Jaffé (New York, NY: Vintage Books, 1963), 279ff.

[34] Jung, *The Red Book*, 541 n137. On the *Black Books*, see Shamdasani, "*Liber Novus*: The 'Red Book' of C.G. Jung."

[35] Ibid., 552.

[36] See Maillard, *Au cœur du Livre Rouge*, 163f.

[37] See Christine Maillard, "La pensée de Carl Gustav Jung et les courants néo-gnostiques de la première moitié du XXème siècle," in Christine Maillard, ed., *Art, sciences et psychologie*, 99-116.

[38] Jung, *Psychology and Religion*, in *CW* 11, par. 81.

[39] Ibid.

[40] See Henri de Lubac, *La postérité spirituelle de Joachim de Flore*, 2 vol. (Paris/Namur: Lethellieux, Culture et Vérité, 1979/1980).

[41] Jung, *The Red Book*, 353.

[42] C.G. Jung, "The Symbolic Life," in *CW*, vol. 18 (Princeton, NJ: Princeton University Press, 1980).

Transformation of the God-Image in Jung's *Red Book*: Foundations for a New Psychology of Religion

Ingrid Riedel

Jung's "Religious Mission"

The god-image and its transformation, along with the topic of religion in general, together combine one of the major themes in *The Red Book*. This runs like a red thread through the entire book. Sonu Shamdasani, in his Introduction, notes a passage where Jung reports receiving instructions regarding his vocation in a conversation with Soul on January 5, 1922:

> I: "But what is my calling?"
> Soul: "The new religion and its proclamation."
> I: "Oh God, how should I do this?"
> Soul: "Do not be of such little faith. No one knows it as you do. There is no one who could say it as well as you could."[1]

Reading these sentences, one is involuntarily taken aback—and so was Jung when he heard what Soul was demanding. "But you are not thinking that I should publish what I have written? That would be a misfortune. And who would understand it?"[2]

Despite Jung's confusion, this is exactly what his Soul pointedly demands, namely, to bring his inner experiences to a public audience and to explain his encounters with his psyche. And though he meticulously worked on his self-experiment from 1913 onward—while also wrestling with a new god-image—and created his *Red Book* with its beautiful images, he decided not to publish this work during his lifetime, since "… who would understand it?" Only 50 years after Jung's death was it finally decided to publish this impressive book that laid the foundations for his entire life work.

The Red Book is not at all a scientific *opus*. On the contrary, this book compiles Jung's psychic experiences during his times of personal upheaval and crisis. The inner turmoil after the break with Freud and the outer events of World War I brought with them a constant stream of inner images and thoughts and forced Jung to search for new solutions to overcome "the contemporary malaise of spiritual alienation."[3] It is especially Jung's wrestling with the traditional Christian god-image and his attempt to transform this outdated image that we today can relate to when we in our own lives encounter crises in which the god-image our culture has handed down to us does not suffice and leaves us in a spiritual void. "... to no longer be a Christian is easy," Soul says to Jung, "But what next?"[4]— Jung personally endured his psychic ordeal as his traditional god-image started to crumble.

After his break with Freud, for whom religion was an illusion, Jung, the son of a protestant clergyman, started to reassess the importance of a religious attitude. His publication in 1912 of *Wandlungen und Symbole der Libido* (*Symbols of Transformation*) postulated a much broader concept of psychic libido than Freud's— a concept that would also embrace mythology and religious phenomena. The relationship between the psyche and religion, i.e., the psychology of religion, would increasingly become Jung's main interest in the course of his work on *The Red Book*. But, as Shamdasani cautiously notes:

> He (Jung) attempted to develop a psychology of the religion-making process. Rather than proclaiming a new prophetic revelation, his interest lay in the psychology of religious experiences. The task was to depict the translation and transposition of the numinous experience of individuals into symbols, and eventually into the dogmas and creeds of organized religions, and, finally, to study the psychological functions of such symbols. For such a psychology of the religion-making process to succeed, it was essential that analytical psychology, while providing

an affirmation of the religious attitude, did not succumb
to becoming a creed.[5]

A selection of certain of Jung's statements regarding religion from
The Red Book can even today lead to misunderstandings if they are
not seen in the context of the whole process of his inner experiences
and his findings.

At the time of working on his *Red Book*, Jung was deeply
influenced by Nietzsche's *Zarathustra* and the announcement of "the
death of God." The pathetic language of *Zarathustra* as well as the
ceremonious and ancient tone of the Bible both determine Jung's style
of language in the *Red Book*: They lead to a prophetic ductus in his
writings.

What is new in comparison to Nietzsche is Jung's emphasis on
the psyche as the dwelling place of the numinous—the soul becomes
the realm for a new birth of God, just as Meister Eckhart had envisioned as well as the Gnostics, for whom God is born in the soul, a
God that can embrace the *complexio oppositorum*. Jung calls this God
Abraxas.

First and foremost, Jung wanted to fundamentally change the
Judeo-Christian god-image so that it could account for aspects that
in the course of history had been excluded, namely matter, the
feminine, and evil. This new god-image was necessary due to
experiences humans clearly encounter in their dealings with the
numinous, experiences that cannot be compared to experiences with
the outer objects of the world since they are highly subjective.

The Gods—a Phantasy

How Western man has lost his gods because of a worldview based
entirely upon rational-scientific thinking, and is also unable to find
them in the religions of the East, is shown in Jung's encounter with
Izdubar, the Sumerian bull-god (Image 36 in *The Red Book*). I quote
the text of Jung's active imagination from January 8, 1914, in which
he meets Izdubar:

But on the third night, a desolate mountain range blocks my way, though a narrow valley gorge allows me to enter. The way leads inevitably between two high rock faces. My feet are bare and injure themselves on the jagged rocks. Here the path becomes slippery. One-half of the way is white, the other black. I step onto the black side and recoil horrified: it is hot iron. I step onto the white half: it is ice. But so it must be. I dart across and onward, and finally the valley widens into a mighty rocky basin. A narrow path winds up along vertical rocks to the mountain ridge at the top.

As I approach the top, a mighty booming resounds from the other side of the mountain like ore being pounded. The sound gradually swells, and echoes thunderously in the mountain. As I reach the pass, I see an enormous man approach from the other side.

Two bull horns rise from his great head, and a rattling suit of armour covers his chest. His black beard is ruffled and decked with exquisite stones. The giant is carrying a sparkling double axe in his hands, like those to strike bulls. Before I can recover from my amazed fright, the giant is standing before me. I look at his face: it is faint and pale and deeply wrinkled. His almond-shaped eyes look at me astonished.[6]

Image 36 in *The Red Book* shows the huge giant Izdubar standing in front of a blue background filled with winged snakes. At the bottom if this image kneels a tiny human figure surrounded by crocodiles to the left and right side. This is Jung's "I" who now addresses the giant:

I: "Oh, Izdubar, most powerful, spare my life and forgive me for lying like a worm in your path."

Iz: "I do not want your life. Where do you come from?"

I: "I come from the West."

Iz: "You come from the West? Do you know of the Western lands? Is this the right way to the Western lands?"

I: "I come from a Western land, whose coasts washes against the great Western sea."

Iz: "Does the sun sink in that sea? Or does it touch the solid land in its decline?"

I: "The sun sinks far beyond the sea."

Iz: "Beyond the sea? What lies there?"

I: "There is nothing but empty space there. As you know, the earth is round and moreover it turns around the sun."

Iz: "Damned one, where do you get such knowledge? So there is no immortal land where the sun goes down to be reborn? Are you speaking the truth?"

His eyes flicker with fury and fear. He steps a thundering pace closer. I tremble.[7]

When Jung's "I" continues to talk about the sun as a "celestial body that lies unspeakably far out in unending space," Izdubar is seized by suffocating fear. To become immortal and to reach his sun is his deep desire, which now is shown to be impossible. In despair Izdubar smashes his ax on a rock with a powerful, clanging blow.

Here, a massive conflict between the scientific and the mythological worldview appears. Who of us has not experienced this conflict himself when the scientific mode of thought has collided with the faith given to us in our childhood, the belief in a God who would take care of us and guide us?

Izdubar, the giant, now collapses and sobs like a child. He lays stretched out on the ground, paralyzed by the poison of science:

Iz: "You call poison truth? Is poison truth? Or is truth poison? Do not our astrologers and priests also speak the truth? And yet theirs does not act like poison."

....

Iz: "Are there then two sorts of truths?"

I: "It seems to me to be so. Our truth is that what comes to us from the knowledge of outer things. The truth of your priests is that which comes to you from the inner things."

Iz (half sitting up): "That was a salutary word."

After Jung's "I" collects some wood and lights a fire, he and Izdubar continue their conversation while sitting in front of the flickering flames:

> Iz: "… Have you no Gods anymore?"
> I: "No, words are all we have."
> Iz: "But are these words powerful?"
> I: "So they claim, but one notices nothing of this."
> Iz: "We do not see the Gods either and yet we believe that they exist. We recognize their workings in natural events."
> I: "Science has taken from us the capacity of belief."
> Iz: "What, you have lost that, too? How then do you live?"[8]

Jung's "I" now stays with Izdubar during the long cold night, since he senses that Izdubar needs him. "And yet again I feel it quite clearly that my life would have broken in half had I failed to heal my God."[9] This sentence leads to the fundamental questions that force Jung into a crisis: How can we live without the Gods, without symbols for the divine realm that transcends us, encompasses and saves us? Jung's life is at risk to break apart if he should lose his God forever. So, during the long night at the fire at which Jung's "I" and Izdubar warm each other without finding a way out of their dilemma, Jung's "I" finally says: "My heart bleeds at the thought of leaving you here without having done the upmost to help you."[10]

What is the "upmost" that Jung's "I" can envision to save his fallen God? It is the attempt to resurrect the God, a resurrection that is accomplished via an imaginative approach. What a brilliant and creative thought! However, some critical thoughts step in:

> What can be done? … I am basically convinced that Izdubar is hardly real in the ordinary sense, but is a fantasy. … He will of course not accept that he is a fantasy, but instead claim that he is completely real and that he only can be helped in a real way: nevertheless, it would be worth trying this means once. I will appeal to him.[11]

And this is exactly what Jung's "I" does:

> I: "My prince, Powerful One, listen: a thought came to me that might save us. I think that you are not at all real, but only a fantasy."
>
> Iz: "I am terrified by this thought. It is murderous. Do you even mean to declare me unreal—now that you have lamed me so pitifully?"
>
> I: "Perhaps I have not made myself clear enough, and have spoken too much in the language of the Western lands. I do not mean to say that you are not real at all, of course, but only as real as a fantasy. If you could accept this, much would be gained."
>
> Iz: "What would be gained by this? You are a tormenting devil."
>
> I: "Pitiful one. I will not torment you. The hand of the doctor does not seek to torment even if it causes grief. Can you relay not accept that you are a fantasy?"
>
> Iz: Woe betide me! In what magic do you want to entangle me? Should it help me if I take myself for a fantasy?"
>
> I: "... You also know that one often gives the sick new names to heal them, for with a new name, they come by a new essence. Your name is your essence."
>
> Iz: "You are right, our priests also say this."
>
> I: "So you are prepared to admit that you are a fantasy?"
>
> Iz: "If it helps—yes."[12]

What is Jung doing here? It is not really convincing that he compares the essence of this god with a fantasy. Only later does this become more convincing when he calls the god a "symbol" and then goes to great lengths to show what a symbol is and what its effectiveness is. Insofar as he relates the *imago dei* to a symbol, he relativizes its ontological objectivity but not its effectiveness. A god-image has the strongest influence not only within the human soul but also in the collective consciousness of a culture. Even where it would be consciously suppressed, it continues to be most effective in the collective unconscious of a culture.

However, Izdubar himself now seems to believe in his resurrection while being a fantasy. Though the situation remains very complex, he acknowledges Jung's attempt:

> Iz: "That was a masterstroke. Where are you carrying me?"
> I: "I am going to carry you down into the Western land."[13]

Jung comments on this while carrying Izdubar to a quiet dark garden and a secluded house:

> This tangible and apparent world is one reality, but fantasy is the other reality. So long as we leave the God outside us apparent and tangible, he is unbearable and hopeless. But if we turn the God to a fantasy, he is in us and easy to bear.[14]

How deeply the myth of Gilgamesh (i.e., Izdubar) is still rooted in contemporary individuals I have witnessed in good friends of mine, who made that myth the symbolic background of their relationship. Another friend of mine, an artist, set up—after the death of a beloved artist friend—a collection of images showing the lamentation of Gilgamesh after the death of Enkidu.

Contemporary individuals, who are acquainted with the myth of Gilgamesh, are slightly baffled when they read *The Red Book* and find out that in his imagination Jung squeezes Izdubar into an egg to get him into the door of the house. This seems not consistent, since a fantasy should be able to get through a door of any size. This inconsistency was also felt by Jung himself, when he later mentioned to Aniela Jaffé that some of his fantasies "were driven by fear, such as the chapter on the devil and the chapter on Gilgamesh-Izdubar. From one perspective it was stupid that he [Jung] had to find a way to help the giant, but he felt that if he didn't do so, he would have failed. He paid for the ridiculous solution through realizing that he had captured a God. Many of these fantasies were a hellish combination of the sublime and the ridiculous."[15]

What needs to be taken very seriously though—since it belongs to the treasure house of humanity—is the image of the transformation of a God into an egg. This is a widespread mythological motive that describes the beginning of a divine development, the new birth of a God.

Incantations: Songs for a New God

Is it not rather grandiose to transform a God into an egg and hide him away in one's own pocket? As if now some kind of *enantiodromia* sets in moving from grandiosity to a devoted hatching, Jung starts his incantations:

> Thus do not speak and do not show the God, but sit in a
> solitary place and sing incantations in the ancient manner:
> Set the egg before you, the God in his beginning.
> And behold it.
> And incubate it with the magical warmth of your gaze.[16]

In the following incantations, Jung combines the Christian image of the birth of the divine child during Christmas with the Eastern Vedic hymns of an egg from which a God is born. Thus, he knits Eastern and Western traditions into his process of creating a new god-image. In doing so, he created a series of images (Images 50 to 64) in which festive colors such as red and gold dominate to celebrate Izdubar's incubation and resurrection—an impressive example of a renewal of God. Jung starts his incantations as follows (Image 50):

> Christmas has come. The God is in the egg.
> I have prepared a rug for my God, an expensive rug
> from the land of morning.
> He shall be surrounded by the shimmer of
> magnificence of his Eastern land.
> I am the mother, the simple maiden, who gave birth
> and did not know how.
> I am the careful father, who protects the maiden.
> I am the shepherd, who received the message as he
> guarded his herd at night on the dark fields.[17]

Indeed, Image 50 in *The Red Book* is similar to a deep red eastern prayer rug with sacred motives worked into it. The "God on the egg," representing a symbolic pregnancy, is shown as a golden egg positioned on a brown field in the lower part of the image, the field itself having a triangular shape as a symbol of the fertile feminine.

Image 51, too, is similar with a beautiful prayer rug colored in red with a green ribbon ornamentally worked in. In the upper section of the image, the "wise man of the Eastern land" resides, the lower section again shows the egg, the right and the left side show eagle and snake that are both combined with the sun symbol. In the incantations of Image 51, Jung identifies himself with the animals in the Christmas narrative:

> I am the holy animal that stood astonished and cannot
> grasp the becoming of the God.
> I am the wise man who came from the East, suspecting
> the miracle from afar.[18]

After Jung emulates all the figures of the Christmas saga by creating an "inner Christmas crib," he then says: "And I am the egg that surrounds and nurtures the seed of the God in me."[19] Here we find Meister Eckhart's approach of a "mystic Christianity" pointing toward the birth of God within the soul, an approach that is also well-known in Hinduism and Gnosticism.

With the incantation of Image 52, Jung starts to consider himself as someone who brings the God to life, like Maria, and, therefore, takes a feminine identity:

> The solemn hours lengthen.
> And my humanity is wretched and suffers torment.
> Since I am a giver of birth.
> Whence do you delight me, Oh God?[20]

Jung is becoming delighted, seized by the joy of ecstasy. He then describes the coming godhead as a *complexio oppositorum*, which he later, in the third part of *The Red Book*, will give the name Abraxas. This leads to a god-image that is beyond any rational comprehension:

> He is the eternal emptiness and the eternal fullness.
> Nothing resembles him and he resembles everything.
> Eternal darkness and eternal brightness.
> Eternal below and eternal above.
> Double nature in one.
> Simple in the manifold.
> Meaning in absurdity.
> Freedom in bondage.
> Subjugated when victorious.
> Old in youth.
> Yes in no.[21]

These incantations are positioned in the center of Image 52, encircled by various types of motifs and ornaments. Important to emphasize are the four circles in blue as well as half of a mandala-like structure at the bottom of the image obviously symbolizing an awareness of growing wholeness. After the elevated spirit of this incantation, Jung's mood shockingly swings into a state of hubris when his "I" states: "Nothing remains of the Gods other than an egg. And I possess this egg."[22] After another *enantiodromia* in his emotions, he finally opens the egg with great awe. It seems as if in these incantations one strong emotion produces a strong antithetical emotion—the opposites are hardly integrated in this phase of Jung's imaginations. Now, however, he can get on his knees:

On the evening of the third day, I kneel down on the rug and carefully open the egg. Something resembling smoke rises up from it and suddenly Izdubar is standing before me, enormous, transformed, and complete. ... It's as if he had awoken from a deep sleep. He says: '... Where was I? I was completely sun.'[23]

His desire for the sun and immortality has finally been fulfilled. In Sumerian mythology, Izdubar is associated with the sun god. The incubation and rebirth of Izdubar follows the classic pattern of solar myths.[24] This is related to the setting and rising of the sun in the sea—we experience the rising and setting of the sun as a "golden egg" in the sea.

Jung had a thorough and extensive knowledge of humanity's mythologies and knew that the figures appearing in his imaginations were rooted in this knowledge, that something was at work in what we today refer to as the "cultural memory." His imagination here ends with the following scene: "... when I thought that I had caught the mighty one and held him in my cupped hands, he was the sun himself."[25] Obviously envying the rising God, Jung continues in the following imagination:

I wandered toward the East where the sun rises. I probably wanted to rise, too, as if I were the sun and rise with it to daybreak. ... While he rises, however, I go down. When I conquered the God, his force streamed into me. But when the God rested in the egg and awaited his beginning, my force went into him. And when he rose up radiantly, I lay on my face. ... I lay there like a child-bearer cruelly mauled and bleeding her life into the child. ... My God has torn me apart terribly, he had drunk the juice of my life, he had drunk my highest power into him and became marvelous and strong like the sun, an unblemished God who bore no stigma or flaw. He had taken my wings from me. ... He left me powerless and groaning.[26]

What kind of a strange "either-or" does Jung here reflect on? It seems to be either my God or me—what can this mean for Jung? It has always been an important issue in the history of religious thought how the relationship between God and man can be comprehended, whether this relationship is indeed an opposition or whether man is contained in God in the sense of an all-efficacy of God, including the aspect of unfreedom of man's will. As understood in Hinduism, the Mithraic cult, and Christian mysticism, this means an essential unity of man with the divine. That man contains the divine and that man is the creator and inventor of God would become commonly accepted only in modernity, finally leading to Nietzsche's proclamation of the death of God. However, Jung—who was strongly influenced by Nietzsche's *Zarathustra*—decided in his deep longing and need for a new God to resurrect God, first as a fantasy and imagination, later as a symbol. But then Jung encounters the problem that man always must devote himself to a living God. And were not the old symbols of the divine handed down since ancient times not images and personifications of real forces that transcend man, be it the forces of nature, of the universe, or the life force itself? When Jung wants to revive the old god-images "with the *magical warmth* of your gaze," he must take their power seriously, and he finally succeeds by putting man in front of God and God in front of man without intermixing them.

Nonetheless, after opening the egg, Jung feels too much the creator of his God who then pulls all the power out of him and will leave him feeling empty. This leads to a conflict that Jung cannot really resolve in this passage of his *Red Book,* with the result that he will descend into hell in the next chapter.

The Inner Christ

In the chapter "Divine Folly," Jung revisits Christianity. Do his experiences and insights regarding the rather remote and foreign image of Sumerian Izdubar also hold in the face of the Christian god-image and the faith still alive in so many of his contemporaries? In this active imagination, Jung's "I" visits a large library with an atmosphere filled with wounded scholarly vanity and asks for a copy of the book *The Imitation of Christ* by Thomas a Kempis. The librarian seems to be surprised, and Jung's "I" mentions that he is seeking this book not out of scholarly interest but because it is written from the soul: "We haven't come to an end with Christianity by simply putting it aside. It seems to me that there's more to it than we see."[27] And:

> The divine wants to live with me. My resistance is in vain. I asked my thinking, and it said: 'Take as your model one that shows how to live the divine.' Our natural model is Christ. … We fought against Christ, we disposed him, and we seemed to be conquerors. But he remained in us and mastered us. … You can certainly leave Christianity but it does not leave you.[28]

We should not misunderstand Jung's intention: He is looking for a completely new understanding of Christ: "But if I am truly to understand Christ, I must realize how Christ actually lived only his own life, and imitated no one. … If I thus truly imitate Christ, I do not imitate anyone, I emulate no one, but go my own way, and I will also no longer call myself a Christian."[29]

In the chapter "Nox secunda," Jung's "I" sits in a kitchen besides a library and shows the cook the book he just borrowed, *The Imitation of Christ* by Thomas a Kempis, which the cook also knows like so many devotional Catholics and which is used for prayer. She is astonished to see a man like Jung wanting to read it, and Jung spots the following sentences in the book: "The righteous base their intentions more on the mercy of God, which in whatever they undertake they trust more than their wisdom."[30] Jung then meditates on the "intuitive method" of Thomas a Kempis, when suddenly a roaring sound fills the room, many shadowlike human forms appear, and he hears a manifold babble of voices uttering: "Let us pray in the temple. … We are wandering to Jerusalem to pray at the utmost holy sepulcher."[31] These shadow-like human forms that suddenly appear to Jung and create a strange desire in him are Anabaptists: "Take me with you,"[32] he cries. But they cannot because they are the Dead who still have no peace and have not come to a proper end with life. "And what was it that had not been lived?" asks one of the Dead, greedily and uncannily reaching out for Jung, who then answers: "Let go, daimon, you did not live your animal."[33] Jung is convinced that Christianity has suppressed the instinctual realm that wants to be acknowledged in life too—this suppression indeed keeps the Dead restless and without peace. The cook gets horrified after Jung's statement and together with the librarian calls for the police, who take him to the madhouse. There, a friendly superintendent, two doctors, and a small fat professor welcome Jung:

> Professor: "What's that book you've got there?"
> "It's Thomas a Kempis, *The Imitation of Christ.*"
> Professor: "So, a form of religious madness, perfectly clear, religious paranoia—You see, my dear, nowadays, the imitation of Christ leads to the madhouse."
> "That is hardly to be doubted, professor."
> Professor: "The man has wit—he is obviously somewhat maniacally aroused. Do you hear voices?
> You bet! Today it was a huge throng of Anabaptists that swarmed through the kitchen."
> Professor: "Now, there we have it. Are the voices following you?"
> "Oh no, Heaven forbid, I summoned them."
> Professor: "Ah, this is yet another case that clearly indicates that hallucinations directly call up voices. This belongs in the case history. Would you immediately make a note of that, doctor?"
> "With all due respect, Professor, may I say that it is absolutely not abnormal, but much rather the intuitive method."
> Professor: "Excellent. The fellow also uses neologisms. Well—I suppose we have an adequately clear diagnosis. Anyway, I wish you good recovery, and make sure you stay quiet."

"But professor, I'm not at all sick, I feel perfectly well."
Professor: "Look, my dear. You don't have any insights
into your illness yet. The prognosis is naturally pretty
bad, with at best limited recovery."[34]

After these self-critical and ironic statements, Jung remarks: "The
problem of madness is profound. Divine madness—a higher form of
the irrationality of the life streaming through us—at any rate a madness that cannot be integrated into present-day society—but how?
What if the form of society were integrated into madness? At this point
things grow dark, and there is no end in sight."[35] Jung closes this
section with the following remarks: "I leave the spirit of this world
which has thought Christ through to the end, and step over into that
other funny-frightful realm in which I can find Christ again."[36]

In dealing with *The Imitation of Christ,* Jung finds himself on the
way to the madhouse. Yet, as described in *Liber Primus,* closer to a
psychotic episode seems to be his identification with the crucifixion
of Christ, in which Salome, his *anima*, tells him: "You are Christ."[37] It
seems to Jung that he experiences his own crucifixion in the service
of God, or in the service of the rediscovery of God: "I stand with
outstretched arms like someone crucified, my body taut and horribly
entwined by the serpent: You, Salome, say that I am Christ?"[38]

What does it mean that Salome whispers this to him? Jung
should remark later in his famous 1925 seminar: "I felt her in-
sinuations as a most evil spell. One is assailed by the fear that perhaps
this is madness."[39] Continuing his active imaginations, he writes:

It is as if I stood alone on a high mountain with stiff
outstretched arms. The serpent squeezes my body in its
terrible coils and blood streams from my body, spilling
down the mountainside. Salome bends down to my feet
and wraps her black hair round them. She lies thus for a
long time.[40]

This scene reminds us of Christ's crucifixion with Mary Magdalene at his feet. In Jung's active imagination, the blind Salome suddenly cries: "I see light!" Jung then states: "Truly, she sees, her eyes are open. The serpent falls from my body and lies languidly on the ground. I stride over it and kneel at the feet of the prophet, whose form shines like a flame."[41] Elijah then says to Jung: "Your work is fulfilled here. Other things will come. Seek untiringly, and above all write exactly what you see."[42] In the biblical tradition, Elijah is an important *psychopompos* since he himself found his own path after a terrifying encounter with God. Here he appears and speaks to Jung's "I".

Driven by his interaction with Salome, his *anima*, the frightening possibility for Jung is a potential inflation caused by how much he leans in this active imagination toward an identification with the figure of Christ. However, what distinguishes this imagination from psychosis is that it is the blind Salome, herself a symbol, who has suggested to him such a state of hubris. What also distinguishes this active imagination from a real identification with Christ, which often is experienced by psychotics, is its embeddedness in the context of the history of religion, namely the narrative of Jesus' passion or the *imitatio Christi*. Moreover, there is the identification with the godhead in the mysteries of Mithras, which were well-known to Jung and fascinated him. On the same page of *Liber Primus* where he imagines the narrative of Jesus' passion, he also experiences himself as an initiate of Mithras: "The serpent has wound itself around my whole body, and my countenance is that of a lion."[43] In the cult of Mithras, this corresponds to the deification of the *myste*. In his seminar of 1925 Jung would critically assess his experiences:

When the images come to you and are not understood, you are in the society of the gods or, if you will, the lunatic society; you are no longer in human society, for you cannot express yourself. Only when you can say, 'This image is so and so,' only then do you remain in human society.[44]

Therefore, it is highly important to understand and structure these inner psychic processes. Jung would later integrate his experiences with reference to the Mythraic cult and interpret them within the history of religion. As a result, he avoids identification with the inner figures. Yet, these deep experiences remain important for him: "In this deification mystery you make yourself into a vessel, and are a vessel of creation in which the opposites reconcile."[45] At the time when Jung experienced these active imaginations and put them down in his *Red Book*, he was undergoing a fundamental process of transformation that made him a vessel, which profoundly changed him as well his god-image. In his later works, Jung would relate the god-image to the psychological concept of the self, a concept that was not yet available to him during the time of his *Red Book* experiences.

A New Psychology of Religion

With regard to the "wholeness of God," Jung ultimately considered all the god-images in the history of religion and—through "the magical warmth of your gaze"—revived them. These ranged from the Sumerian Gilgamesh-Izdubar narrative to the Egyptian sun cult to the Mediterranean Greek gods and from there to the late mystery cults such as the Mithraic cult. In addition, ideas and images from Hinduism were a significant influence on Jung, especially the concept of *atman* and *brahman* in which the deep and essential participation of man in the divine as well as the idea of wholeness are fundamentally emphasized. Jung dedicated numerous paintings and carvings to the revitalization of "old" gods such as, for example, "Atmanvictu" in his *Red Book*: "This is Atmanvictu, the old one, after he has withdrawn from creation. He has returned to endless history, where he took his beginning."[46]

The image on page 122 in *The Red Book* exhibits the "other side" of the *lapis philosophorum*, which is in alchemy the goal of man's lifelong quest. The "stone" is shown in Image 121 as a mandala with an incorruptible diamond in its center: "This stone, set so beautifully,

is certainly the Lapis Philosophorum. It is harder than
diamond. But it expands into
space through four distinct
qualities, namely breadth, height,
depth, and time. It is hence
invisible and you can pass through
it without noticing it."[47] In his
later work the mandala would
become the symbol for psychic
wholeness.

There are so many images
of the divinities that Jung created
—despite the biblical prohibition
against making icons and images
of God. I think, however, that
one cannot observe this prohibition by a nonpictorial attitude,

Atmanvictu—"The Breath of Life"
— in Jung's garden in Küsnacht

but rather by populating the heavens with a plethora of images of the
countless aspects of the divine. This would approach the totality of
the divine realm, which transcends each single image.

Jung, the psychologist, always speaks of "god-images" and the
symbols of the divine as the only statement we can make with
respect to God. However, if he encounters God within his active
imaginations, he addresses the God directly, and he then mentions
the word "God." This accounts for some inconsistencies with respect
to the issues of the god-image in his *Red Book* as well as in his later
works, for example in *Answer to Job*.

Philemon, Jung's wise *psychopompos* in *The Red Book*, explained
to him the mystery of hospitably receiving the Gods who once
wandered the earth: "But what mystery are you intimating to me with
your name, Oh ΦΙΛΗΜΩΝ? Truly you are the lover who once took
in the Gods as they wandered the earth when everyone refused them
lodging."[48] We remember the classical story of Philemon and Baucis
from Ovid's *Metamorphoses*, which was also taken up by Goethe in
his *Faust*. There, Philemon is the "host of the Gods" who granted

hospitality after they were refused by the rest of the population. As Jung says to Philemon: "You are the one who unsuspectingly gave hospitality to the Gods; they thanked you by transforming your house into a golden temple, while the flood swallowed everyone else. ... The animal fled to the Gods who then revealed themselves to their poor hosts, who had given their last, Thus I saw that the lover survives, and that he is the one who unwittingly grants hospitality to the Gods."[49]

If I may venture an image: Jung himself was perhaps the "host of the Gods." He considered the human soul as the "house of the Gods," which they would enter and leave. He welcomed them—*vocatus atque non vocatus deus aderit* ("Summoned or not, the god is present") is written above the door of his house in Küsnacht. Though he conceives the Gods as symbols, he understands that these symbols have a reality of their own and that they are "vessels" of a reality they transmit. They act as "images of the senses" for a reality that lies beyond them, which they convey.

In the history of religions, there is in Buddhism a development parallel to Jung's encounter with images and symbols in his active imaginations. Although Buddhism itself does not deal with a specific god-image, its Tibetan version is a generous host of the old Gods handed down from the Bon religion of the Himalayan people. The old Tibetan Gods are seen as symbols of emotional forces and, being either wrathful or kind, are visualized by the initiate and, therefore, experienced. For example, there is the compassionate and wisdom-filled energy of the Green or White Tara. The process of imagination as well as of modeling the symbols of divinity in sand or a thangka is of utmost importance in Tibetan Buddhism. Jung has given us something similar with the method of active imagination and his artistic creation of divine symbols. This can open the way to the cultural memory of mankind by putting the individual into the context of a bigger and more encompassing realm of meaning and thereby healing a spiritual malaise.

Without proclaiming a new religion, *The Red Book* in a certain sense is a prophetic book insofar as it brings forth a new view on religious phenomena. Jung considers religious matters by and large in the context of a psychology of religion, a depth psychology of religion, which draws its symbols constantly from the collective unconscious but at the same time stays in touch with the cultural unconscious of mankind. Jung's view could be highly important for the present-day dialogue of religions. It could revive that dialogue if a "symbolic view" on religious phenomena would be appreciated, since the "mother tongue" of religion exists on the symbolic level. Whereas spiritual knowledge is alive and draws on experienced images and narratives, rational terminology and dogmatic fixations lose touch with vivid experiences.

Lived experiences of the unconscious form the basis of Jung's *Red Book* by which he developed the method of active imagination. Since then, this method has become an integral part of therapeutic work with clients in order to find new paths to spirituality. Together with dreams and work on inner images, this can provide experienced "meaning," which since ancient times always has been the goal of religion.

Endnotes

[1] Sonu Shamdasani, "*Liber Novus*: The 'Red Book' of C.G. Jung," in C.G. Jung, *The Red Book: Liber Novus*, ed. Sonu Shamdasani, tr. John Peck, Mark Kyburz, and Sonu Shamdasani (New York, NY: W.W. Norton, 2009), 211.

[2] Ibid.

[3] Ibid., 207.

[4] Ibid., 211.

[5] Ibid., 212.

[6] Jung, *The Red Book*, 277.

[7] Ibid., 278.

[8] Ibid., 279.

[9] Ibid., 281.

[10] Ibid., 282.

[11] Ibid.

[12] Ibid.

[13] Ibid.

[14] Ibid., 283.

[15] Ibid., n114.

[16] Ibid., 284.

[17] Ibid.

[18] Ibid.

[19] Ibid.

[20] Ibid.

[21] Ibid.

[22] Ibid., 285.

[23] Ibid., 286.

[24] Ibid., n136.

[25] Ibid., 286.

[26] Ibid., 287.

[27] Ibid., 292.

[28] Ibid., 293.

[29] Ibid.

[30] Ibid., 294.

[31] Ibid.

[32] Ibid.

[33] Ibid.

[34] Ibid., 295.

[35] Ibid.

[36] Ibid.

[37] Ibid., 252.

[38] Ibid.

[39] C.G. Jung, *Analytical Psychology. Notes of the Seminar given in 1925*, ed. W. McGuire (Princeton, NJ: Princeton University Press, 1991), 97.

[40] Jung, *The Red Book*, 252.

[41] Ibid.

[42] Ibid.

[43] Ibid.

[44] Jung, *Analytical Psychology. Notes of the Seminar given in 1925*, 99.

[45] Ibid.

[46] Jung, *The Red Book*, 122 and 305 n231.

[47] Ibid., 305 n229.

[48] Ibid., 315.

[49] Ibid.

The Quest for One's Own *Red Book* in the Digital Age

Stephen A. Aizenstat

> If your creative force now turns to the place of soul, you
> will see how your soul becomes green and how its field
> bears wonderful fruit.[1]
>
> C.G. Jung

Introduction

There are real threats to our existence and well-being in this world—
and in the worlds behind and beyond this world. Toxins and
pollutants are wreaking havoc with our environment and our health.
Earthquakes, forest fires, floods, hurricanes, and other natural
disasters ravage one portion of the globe or another with blinding
frequency. Through it all, we are swept up in a perfect storm of
scientific and technological advancements that has produced cars
without drivers; computers with soaring IQs; watches that administer
EKGs and email them to your doctor; and space centers with the
potential to launch humans into galactic orbit. Meanwhile, back on
Earth, millions of people feel more alone and spiritually impoverished
than ever.

Embracing *The Red Book* as a personal meditative journey can
help us better envision our places in a multidimensional universe and
reconnect us to the abundance of our unique genius, that seminal
soul spark sourced in the animated psyche. *The Red Book* offers
neither answers nor solutions, but rather portends an arrival: a
surfacing of creative imagination and the emergence of the possible.

This discussion of the relevance of Jung's *Red Book* in helping us to nurture "the spirit of the depths" in tumultuous times unfolds in three parts. The first is an account of my life's work in the praxes of Dream Tending and the ritual of digs, which are Jungian-inspired journeys into the inner reaches of the psyche.

In the second section, I offer perspectives on how the genius and vision of Jung's *Red Book* can illuminate the inherent paradoxes of advanced technology and help us deal with the ever-growing omnipotence of our cyberworld.

Lastly, I share reflections on *The Red Book* as a tool for personal exploration into the depths of one's own relationship to psyche and offer suggestions as to how one might embark upon that enlivening journey.

Let me begin with how most things begin: in imagination and dream.

I. Dream Tending: A Portal to Journeying

> Dreams are the guiding words of the soul. Why should I henceforth not love my dreams and not make their riddling images into objects of my daily consideration? ... The spirit of the depths even taught me to consider my action and my decision as dependent on dreams. Dreams pave the way for life, and they determine you without you understanding their language.[2]

My early experiences with the transcendent have shaped my life's work, my approach to dreams, and the praxis of tending illuminated images. These same experiences have offered me a living relationship with the visions and ideologies of *The Red Book*.

Tending to dreams began for me at the tide pools on Zuma Beach, outside Los Angeles, when I was 12. A rock jetty on the beach extended into the sea and separated the north beach from the south beach. The north side was a public beach, which was popular with families. A sentry of lifeguards stood equidistantly across the beach next to a massive paved parking lot and a dozen food huts.

Looming out into the sea, the rocky reef served as a great divide between north and south. The north beach was supervised and civilized. The south beach was a mystery. The accepted "rules of order" stipulated that no curious kid should ever venture over to the other side. I was troubled. "Were there people on that beach?" I wondered, and, if so, "Why are we not allowed there?"

When the tide was at its lowest, one could simply walk over the exposed jetty to the south, and on a family outing one hot July day, my curiosity got the best of me. After the towels had been laid out, swim gear donned, and sunscreen applied, I quietly slipped away and wove through the crowds to the reef. The tide was out, and I walked over the point and jumped down onto the sand. I looked all around me, taking it all in. Glistening tide pools appeared in every direction; the receding waves had exposed long lines of brightly colored iridescent coral, and hundreds of sea anemone and starfish still trembling with life dotted the beach. There were only a few people lying on the sand farther down the coastline, and they were all naked! That made quite an impression on this preadolescent kid, too—but paled next to the kaleidoscope of dazzling marine life surrounding me.

Sitting down on a rounded piece of sea-worn coral, I watched and listened to the teeming activity in this majestic corner of nature's universe. Mesmerized, I was suspended in time but was startled to attention by a voice behind me.

"Did you know that rocks can talk?" The words were haunting and prophetic. I was speechless. Who was speaking, and how did he know? I did not think that anybody other than I could hear such things!

I turned around to see that the prophesy emanated from a surfer in his late teens, a "god" of the highest order to a 12-year-old. He smiled at me and walked on down the beach. As I returned to the living energy of the tide pools, his transcendent utterance permeated the atmosphere. Having had their soulful eloquence affirmed by the other, the animated voices around me became more expressive, and my hearing was sharper. Eventually, I was jolted from this psychic communion by an earthly reality: The tide was coming in! In a minute, the reef would be underwater. I leaped up and sloshed through the rising tide pools, scrambling over the flooding jetty. As I hopped off the reef and landed safely on the civilized side, I breathed a sigh of relief.

My parents awaited.

"Steve, where have you been?" my mother asked. For me, this was an all too familiar question! What could I say? I have been to a place where gods exist, where rocks can talk, and where the landscape has stories to tell? No. This explanation would fall on deaf and suspicious ears. Here on the civilized side, where food stands, parking lots, and lifeguards secure the beachscape, rocks do not speak, and the ocean and her creatures remain mute.

Dream Tending is rooted in the realization that at multiple levels of psyche, everything is dreaming: the creatures, the landscapes, and all things in and of the world. The inner subjectivities of living things, their particular soul-sparks, their voices, and their pleas, appear as images in our dream life. When we take the time to listen closely, as I did that afternoon long ago on Zuma Beach, the inscapes come to life in new and wondrous ways. I have come to see and hear these living dream images of the animated world in the actuality of their being, not just my own.

I have discovered that when tending dreams or reading *The Red Book*, what matters most is not what I see, but how I see. When we engage different modes of perception, we ask new questions. Our inquires originate from the other side of the rational mind, from the other side of the reef. The explanatory yields to the experiential. "Who is visiting now?" and "What is happening here?" evoke an imploring imagination, and they are much more interesting questions than the prosaic, familiar, rational queries, "What does this mean?" and "Why did this happen?"

I remember as a child, high-play invited the world to display itself in magic, mystery, and beauty. When I met these wonders with an innocent, poetic eye, the world responded poetically. It was only when I went into my head, encouraged by school, and fueled by the new "miracle sciences" of the times, that I seemed to go deaf and blind. Adults were working so hard trying to "make sense out of it all," that they failed to see the inner luminescence of all being, the human-made and the nature-made. In *The Red Book*, Jung notes:

> And when you sleep, you rest, like everything that was, and your dreams echo softly again from distant temple chants. You sleep down through the thousand solar years, and you wake up through the thousand solar years, and your dreams full of ancient lore adorn the walls of your bed-chamber.[3]

Animated images come to life when given attention and regard; they tell their deeper stories and offer lustrous light from the inside out. During this quintessential process, two essential questions arise: "What is the dream's desire?" and "Who journeys now?" These queries move dreamwork and discovery in a distinctly vertical descent: down, further still, into deep imagination and into explorations that I have come to know as the digs.

The Digs, Journeying, and Deep Imagination

Underground. Down-under. In the worlds below the world. I have come to observe that the numinous, for the most part, has been banished from above-ground viewing: not destroyed, but forgotten; not lost, but abandoned. Only as an adult have I come to fully remember and see with new eyes the psychic radiance that sparks all creation. Over recent years, and particularly after my reading of *The Red Book*, I have made my way back to the homeplace of the illuminated imagination.

The downward expeditions of the digs may be incubated during struggle and strife, or apprehension and fears. However, my inaugural descent did not germinate in a state of personal or professional crisis. Although the plunge was down, vertical, and deep, the initiation itself was spawned by insatiable curiosity. Similar to my youthful passions on Zuma Beach, I was driven by a desire to rediscover the unknown in the known.

My inaugural dive into the depths began not in a sacred ceremony deep in the Amazon rainforest, but rather in one of the small ubiquitous coffee houses in the Pacific Northwest, in the town of Everett, Washington. I sat in the cafe with my journal to do what I most often do with my dreams: I write them down. The dream the night before had been a simple showing of a scene, rather than a major announcement or revelation. The tableau was of a bubbling creek behind a shopping mall in the California neighborhood that I grew up in.

Between coffees and homemade pastry, I sketched the locale in my journal. As I drew, visual images opened up. The creek came to life, animated by a remembrance of the actual creek bed that I had visited secretly when growing up. I drew a circle, over and again; it became denser and more spiraling, inviting a journey, down—down below the brook, into the wet sludge at the bottom. The earth, pebbles, and soil beneath the creek were unfamiliar, very different from the underwater sand and seas in which I had spent a lifetime free-diving and exploring in oceanic dream time.

A portal was opening into foreign geologic places, and I was reluctant to go there. I hesitated. "This is dirt, not ocean. How mundane," I thought, "there is not much life in this inanimate landscape." I packed up my journal and left the coffee shop. That afternoon, a friend and mentor encouraged me to return:

"A portal has presented, now go explore."

So, in the "white-night" of the Pacific Northwest, when the evening light softens but never quite gives way to darkness, I sat at the same table in the same coffee shop and began the geologic dig. Down I drifted, weightlessly, into the vast expanse below. A rock formation at the familiar childhood creek had become a portal into an awe-inspiring underworld.

Once landed, I was face-to-face with others: fellow journeyers, or emergents, as I have come to call them, were streaming in from far and wide. Many who arrived were elders and mentors; others emerged from the lands of the dead in the forms of ancestors and ancients, immortals of the deep soul. There were long-familiar figures, too: the personage of a forgotten lover, dream animals that had lingered in my imagination, and soul-companions of dreams who had afforded wise counsel over many years.

My companions on the creek dig were friendly. Greetings all around! It seemed like a reunion, and I felt privileged to be included. After everyone was introduced, the procession continued to descend, and we were directed into caves where a guide told us that to go deeper, to see the worlds behind the world more clearly, we needed to be grounded in "skeletal resonance."

"Before you go further, you must feel it in your bones," he said. We began an embodied singing and chanting the songs of the dead. I felt my body soften and my breathing deepen; I looked around and was relieved to see that my companions were also transforming in ways that made safe passage possible. I remembered Orpheus had been put to death for being unprepared for his underworld journey, and I did not relish the same fate.

What I witnessed next will shape my work with others, particularly the next generations of students and family members, for the rest of my life.

From the caves we were led into the catacombs, a dazzling place of light, where a galaxy of shimmering gems and crystals served as lenses through which we could see into the deep imagination without upper-world light. These worlds beyond the world revealed a stunning display of what was, what is, and what will be possible. In *The Red Book*, Jung says, "Because I have fallen into the source of chaos, into the primordial beginning, I myself become smelted anew in the connection with the primordial beginning, which at the same time is what has been and what is becoming."[4]

My digs continue to this day, each one delving deeper, around, and through the unknown, the unseen, and the uninhabited dimensions of deep imagination. The landscapes in my initial explorations were mostly familiar to me, places that had been cultivated over years in the practice of active imagination. As they continued, the digs descended to new and unfamiliar expanses beyond the known and oceanic.

During these voyages into the depths, I am not alone, nor am I leading a team. The success of any dig is inseparable from the guidance and grace-filled presences of the others, the co-journeyers. In each pilgrimage, I am joined by new and unexpected figures. Look there, in the distance, other entities approach! Indigenous to the world of pain, emergent are among the most vital companions on these underworld treks. Some of the formidable presences I've met include "Vulture," who knows the fear of death; "Left-out," rejection's sultry twin; and "Kali," the enraged.

The synergism of the digs gives voice to darkness as well as light, anger as well as joy, alienation as well as communion. Pilgrimages into the abyss conjoin the horrific and the beatific, as well as other polar opposites that thrive in the world above. In *The Red Book*, Jung addresses the inseparability of goodness and evil in "the spirit of the depths":

> I understood that the new God would be in the relative. If the God is absolute beauty and goodness, how should he encompass the fullness of life, which is beautiful and hateful, good and evil, laughable and serious, human and inhuman? How can man live in the womb of the God if the Godhead himself attends only to one-half of him?[5]

Every time I descend further into a dig, I am opening myself to the imagination matrix, the dominion where soulful discoveries are nurtured and thrive. Like the universe itself, the imagination matrix reveals the psychic dynamism of all being and all nonbeing. I do not know who or what will show up on a dig, just as I do not know what birds will fly above me in the light of the daytime sky. The personalities, animals, and landscapes of the underworld have their own lives, and they move in and out of my sight in their own time. Unlike the constructed algorithms of the programmer's code or the avatars in a computer game, the figures and manifestations that flourish in deep imagination have an unpredictable spontaneity; and when they do come forward and announce themselves, I am surprised. The theater of the depths presents dramatic and restorative shows that entertain as they enlighten.

I have been privileged over these past years to be able to take a quantum leap, or more aptly, a leap of faith, into learning the ways of illuminating dream images. By peering through the translucent screens affixed to the imaginal bodies of dream images, modes of perception have opened that allow me to see a metaverse of interacting soul-sparks and to hear a symphony of song-lines reverberating in dreamtime. Engaged in the praxes of dream tending and digs, we must meet the embodied dream image with our imaginal or arche-typal ego-bodies, not our rational minds. We use our senses. We touch the ocean. Is it warm, cold, or freezing? We taste and smell the seawater. Is it tropical or arctic? "Ocean" enters the room with us, not as a category of thought, but as a living, autonomous embodied image of the dreaming psyche.

Through the transcendent we can discover our transparence. Through dream tending and the explorations of the digs, we become permeable. We find our places in the translucent fields of the deep imagination, where we are connected to more than what exists out there, and we experience a recovery—an awakening—of uniquely intimate places in here. Just as the psyche knows no bounds other than those that have been placed on her, the matrix of imagination is a free-flowing channel to the infinite. The "sky is the limit," and the earth opens into the vast depths of inner space.

II. New World Technology and *The Red Book*: Perils, Possibilities, and Mixed Realities

> He whose desire turns away from outer things, reaches the place of the soul. If he does not find the soul, the horror of emptiness will overcome him, and fear will drive him with a whip lashing time and again in a desperate endeavor and a blind desire for the hollow things of the world.[6]

Caught up in a technological monsoon, we are experiencing constant torrents of advancement in global communications. Daily, we interact with an international cyber community that contains billions of websites, processes trillions of gigabytes, and transmits millions of emails per second. Our lives, work, and relationships rely on an ever-expanding collective of internet information and entertainment. Given the amount of time we occupy in cyberspace, our time in the dream-space becomes ever more diminished.

Humanity has crossed a threshold in which, on average, we spend over 51 percent of our time living in cyberspace (for those in their teens and 20s, that number is above 75 percent). Given this technological maelstrom, many of us fear that cybertechnology and artificial intelligence is threatening to supplant psychic life and imagination altogether—that programmed "counterfeit images" (products of artificial intelligence) are threatening the psychic home ground of the "living images" that are expressions of an autonomous psyche.

Will our reliance upon technology altogether usurp our spontaneous imaginal lives? Will authentic imagination eventually succumb to computerization of all sorts, including the algorithmic manipulation of a marketplace whose single-minded intention is profit-making? Jung noted that to become a "knower of the human soul," one must hang up "exact science and put away the scholar's gown ... and wander with human heart through the world ... to experience love, hate and passion in every form in one's body."[7] In today's high-tech frenzy, for example, online time is supplanting the song-lines of dreamtime. Psyche finds herself an endangered species, a forgotten muse. Her poetry, her wisdom, her otherness are diminishing presences. When she does come forth, speaking through dreams or cultural arts most often, her voice is commandeered and channeled in service to the next YouTube stars or cultural trends, which, in the end, do not become truly "big, real, or legit" until they have sent a slew of "bottom lines" into orbit.

Today, the Jungian-influenced practice of Dream Tending holds that not all dream images are created equally because not all dream images are harvested from the same loam. Dream images that emerge from "the spirit of the depths" have been gestated and birthed in the deepest chambers of the imagination, and they make manifest the Neoplatonism of the *mundus imaginalis*. In contrast, the avatars and computerized images of cyber reality are designed and created from the Aristotelian logic of programmers' codes.

While writing this essay, I had a dream in which I saw myself carrying a gun and climbing up two circular flights of stairs in a modern building located in the sleek, high-rise, commercial sector of New Tech, Los Angeles. My strides were purposeful, mechanical, and virtually programmed. I got to the top floor, opened an office door, saw four robotic figures—two males and two females—and pulled the trigger, shooting them "dead." I had no emotions. The act felt clean, efficient, and final.

The next day I was troubled. What deep fear and rage had created these automated beings? More disturbing, what dread had turned me into their cold, calculated assassin? Was my soul engaged in a life-or-death battle with cyber technology? As much as I gladly join the technological tidal wave every day, relying on it for personal and professional communication and information, I still often feel that I am frolicking in the devil's sea. Is my imaginative self—like the tenor of my voice—being replaced by mechanistic, robotic avatars who are simply carrying out the digital instructions of a programmer's code?

That afternoon I went to a video studio for a nine-hour taping, introducing my praxis of Dream Tending. Greeting me was a film crew of 10. There were no shortages of cameras, lights, or screens. Highly talented young people were running the studio, and they were astutely aware of the need to meet an exacting set of technological requisites in the making of the film, including search engine optimization, keywords, and digital repurposing.

During the first hours of the taping, my "robot assassin" role in the dream was still haunting me, and I could feel that distress compromising my effectiveness in front of the camera. Then, a surprise. In a break between director's "cuts," my heart softened, and something other nestled in—a remembering of what brought me to this high-tech studio, fully staffed by millennials who think, breathe, and speak in megabytes. I truly love this generation of young people. I appreciate their intelligence, wit, and agility (particularly tech-nologic); and I am touched deeply when they share with me their yearnings (often of vocation and belonging). I enjoy tending their dreams; guiding them in this way reminds me how the spontaneous psyche, offering image and sensation, opens the humility of our humanity. Even as we are surrounded by screens, handheld and otherwise, we are tending dreams; although we are not really offline, we have opened ourselves to sharing the expansive breadth of psyche's beauty. In the midst of the spirit(s) of the times, we are tending the spirit(s) of the depths.

Soon after the day of the taping, I had a welcome visit from the Woman with Many Screens, a regular emergent from my dreamtime; her cyberwisdom and benevolent techno presence cast further light on the darkness of the robot-killer dream. Woman with Many Screens first appeared three years ago. In the dream, I was sitting by a bucolic lake, and she beckoned for me to join her. Together we traveled through vast imaginal space and landed in her community. Once there, I relaxed and looked around. I had never before seen so many computer screens in one place. The pervasive mood was one of revelation, peace, and creative energy. Every screen was a looking-glass through which one could view all aspects of their inner and outer lives. From compassion to competition, from love to hate, all was revealed in their techno translucent screens.

In Woman with Many Screens' neighborhood, the projections emitted empathy and understanding. Misunderstandings, territorial conflicts, anger, and shame gave way to collective harmony and mutual regard. I was fascinated by the thousands of live computer screens. The atmosphere was humming. Individuals communicated to one another verbally and through their translucent computer screens. These cyborgs were living in a blended harmonious community with capacities for love and compassion far beyond our own. They were more humane than humans, and upon waking I felt an overwhelming sense of awe and deep regard.

Sound utopian? You bet. And, what a place to visit! I have come to feel affection for the kind and expressive faces of Woman with

Many Screens and her hybrid computerized neighbors; this thriving cyber-human community has helped me recognize that rapidly advancing technologies need not be dire. If we are vigilant about integrating advancing technology with the inner realities of dreams, imagination, and personhood, there is no threat to the depths of the spirit. Upon waking from this most recent visit to Woman with Many Screens' vibrant community, my first thought was: Maybe our contemporary dilemma is not a matter of technological threat, but, instead, could be a matter of technological evolution, in which cyber-space offers another complementary dimension of a new, extending dream-space.

Woman with Many Screens has been a frequent companion in my daily digs, and her affable cyber presence in my dreams is a stark and enlightening contrast to my recurrent fears in the waking world that our imaginal lives are on the brink of a high-tech takeover. Her presence is particularly reassuring to me, because, in today's world, in one way or another, we are all cyborgs.

A luminous guide, Woman with Many Screens traces a lineage reaching back to the ancients, yet her wisdom imbues light into the present and the future. Her visions make it difficult to divide today's technological universe into incompatible opposites: good and evil, dark and light. Advanced technology and deep imagination can coexist and enhance each other; as dream images become increasingly "hybrid," some being both technological and imaginative, we must embrace the human, mechanical, and psychical as one. I am reminded of Joseph Campbell's observation that simultaneous levels of existence function in concert: the corporeal of waking consciousness; the spiritual of dream; and the ineffable of the absolute unknowable.

* * *

Each autumn for over 30 years, I have traveled to the "Big Sky" state of Montana, where I offer a weeklong Dream Tending workshop and retreat at the B-Bar Ranch. The retreat unfolds in the deep imagination of the open mountain landscapes. The natural beauty that surrounds us greatly enhances our art projects, storytelling, music, dance movement, yoga, as well as the tending of our dreams. This last fall an early snow fell over the valley, making the bright yellows, radiant oranges, and fiery reds of the changing leaves even more dramatic. The panoply of color added its drama to our dream-sharing experiences.

In one session, as I worked with a dreamer, the others listened while writing and drawing in their journals. There were a number of young people in their late 20s and early 30s, and most of them were chronicling their thoughts and experiences on tablets and iPads, for some, today's journals of choice. After the formal dreamwork, others were invited to come forward and share their art and reflections.

One young woman showed us her interpretation of the living, moving, "imaginal" figures in the dream that she had drawn on her iPad, using an illustrator app and program. The animated images were alive, vital, and three-dimensional. And, the figures were accompanied by an audio of the song that the dreamer had mentioned hearing in the dream! In a word, the whole visual interpretation was breathtaking. The dreamer was deeply touched.

"Thank you so much!" she said.

"No problem!" the artist replied. "By the way, what is your email? I'm sending it to you, right now!"

* * *

The Red Book has its own unique, technological "coming out" story. In 2010, shortly before the original *Red Book* manuscript made its West Coast debut at UCLA's Hammer Museum, Pacifica Graduate Institute hosted a weekend immersion symposium in which experts gave presentations describing some of the many advanced print technologies that had been used to preserve the integrity of the original *Red Book* manuscript for W.W. Norton's publication. Highly advanced computer technologies had been utilized to faithfully restore and replicate the print, images, and artwork in Jung's original journals. Without the implementation of this extraordinary, high-tech computer technology, the genius of *The Red Book*, which Jung described as the "prima materia for a lifetime's work," might never have been preserved and made available to us.

Cutting-edge software and highly advanced print technology have played leading roles in delivering Jung's enlightening reflections from *The Red Book* to the world. Countless visitants in dreams possess a hybrid quality that originates from the confluence of cyber and innate sources. Virtual realities are becoming increasingly more sophisticated, creating computer avatars that are sentient and sympathetic. Virtual images and psychically generated images are less distinguishable and more interactive with each other. The question is posed: Can avatars that exist in virtual and augmented realities be experienced as living images of dreams and imagination? Can "the spirits of the depths" in *The Red Book* be illuminated technologically as avatars to reveal the blood soul of Jung's original phantasmagorical world in an interactive multidimensional experience for today's readers?

No. I suspect not. But, only, "Not yet."

III. Closing Reflections: Embarking Upon One's Own *Red Book* Journey

> The way is within us, but not in Gods, nor in teachings, nor in laws. Within us is the way, the truth, and the life.[8]

In what ways can Jung's excursions into "the spirit of the depths," as named in *The Red Book*, be applied to today's increasingly technological world? How are the symbols and mythical figures that emerge from his underworld excursions germane to our modern, high-speed, outward-facing cyber reality?

What would today's *Red Book* look like? How would it evolve? How could the unfathomable depths of the imagination in *The Red Book* come to life in a Silicon Valley-centered universe?

I believe that if Jung—at least the Jung who lives in my imagination—had a wish, it would be that each of us would create our own *Red Book*. That we would receive inspiration and guidance from Jung's expeditions into "the spirit of the depths" and then take the deep dive ourselves, writing, drawing, and describing the images, figures, symbols, landscapes, and events that emerge from the *opus* of our own encounters with psyche, as they orchestrate our underworld explorations.

All too often, we reduce the wondrous to causal explanations, and the "magic" disappears and goes underground. Perhaps better to read and experience Jung's *Red Book* as a dream, rather than a textbook. In his journal, Jung lets the images take the lead; he meets them in their world and allows them to display themselves and tell their stories. Images first, explanations second. "The ancients devised magic to compel fate. They needed it to determine outer fate. We need it to determine inner fate and to find the way that we are unable to conceive."[9]

The study and clinical application of depth psychology has been the mainstay of my adult life; it provides a template, a psychological, emotional, and cultural map from which I can begin to discern and understand Jung's "spirit of the depths" in "the spirit of the times." Depth Psychology is the inspiration for and foundation of Pacifica Graduate Institute in Santa Barbara, California, a school that I established in the mid-1970s with the assistance of other Jungian-inspired visionaries.

Opus Archives and Library at Pacifica Graduate Institute holds in perpetuity the works of Joseph Campbell, James Hillman, and Marion Woodman, all of whom were ongoing presences at Pacifica for decades, teaching in the classroom, meeting with faculty and staff, and generously offering me advice and consultation in developing and tending an Institute of Depth Psychology. At Pacifica, the pedagogical legacy of these luminous mentors lives on forever.

Tenacious, disciplined, and determined, one of our mentors, James Hillman, was driven to follow the Eros of ideas—"pressing" the known, while embracing the unknown and the unknowable. His classroom presentations, essays, and books stand as testaments to his daring in describing the indescribable and attempting to articulate the psychologically real, but inherently ineffable, dimensions of underworld consciousness.

When the story of *The Red Book's* discovery, restoration, and publication was told during a weekend symposium at Pacifica, James

Hillman and Sonu Shamdasani held a seminar in which they read passages and dialogue from *The Red Book* and addressed the meaning and role of those particular passages in the *oeuvre* of Jung's thought. Then they invited each of us to reflect upon the passage's relevance in our own explorations of the deep psyche.

"To meet the dead," Hillman said, required not a day-world point of view but instead a sojourn through underworld consciousness. And to embark upon that journey, we must "die into the realm of the eternals," a sentiment that echoed Jung's reflections in *The Red Book*. "Peace and blue night spread over you while you dream in the grave of the millennia."[10]

Before entering the "places of the visitants" of Jung's psychic world—his *mysterium coniunctionis*—we would do well to companion with an immortal who is active in the alchemy of our own imaginal depths, and then introduce ourselves through the entities of our souls' longings.

When embarking upon a meditative reading of *The Red Book*, something other is needed. Before opening the cover of the *Liber Novus*, take heed of the wise counsel that Hillman and other Jungian mentors have offered: Open yourself to "night mysteries," and suspend yourself in a state of "not-knowing." Turn to a council of soul figures and ancient ones.

Place the closed *Red Book* in front of you. Listen closely to what awakens in your psychic reality, then receive the images, ideas, and hints that come forward. Let the images and figures find each other and exchange their regard. Then settle in and listen for an invitation.

At first, we might be intimidated and ask, "What if no one invites me in when I make the request?" Here, again, we must turn to Jung's light. Above the doors of his family home in Küsnacht is this Latin inscription: *vocatus atque non vocatus deus aderit*: "Called or Not Called, God Will Be There."

Once summoned, open *The Red Book* and read slowly. Allow the words and figures to emerge from the pages and greet you. Follow the phenomenology of experience and the poetics of imagination, not simply your rational mind. As you immerse yourself in a slow, reflective reading of the text, watch, listen, and absorb the interplay and interactions between images. Pause at the open spaces in the text and allow images to come forward and announce themselves: "Here we are." Meet the emergents with an aesthetic eye, noticing what animates from the interior as well as the surface.

Our personal *Red Books* would make visible our own unique Journeys of Becoming. In the process of tending our dreams and imaginal realities, we would receive hints from the images and figures evolving from the autonomous psyche—hints of what is, but also, intimations of what is intended for us and can be realized. "Through comprehending the dark, the nocturnal, the abyssal in you, you become utterly simple … and you sleep down into the womb of the millennia, and your walls resound with ancient temple chants. Since the simple is what always was."[11]

A dream, or a dream-inspired *opus*, such as Jung's *Red Book*, desires to be approached poetically, rather than advanced on rationally. Animated images, when given time and regard, illuminate. They tell their deeper stories and offer their radiant endowment. How glorious would it be to vivify Jung's journeys in *The Red Book* and to thrive, ourselves, in that magical place where "the spirit of the depths" and "the spirit of the times" are one?

Can you imagine?

Endnotes

[1] C.G. Jung, *The Red Book: Liber Novus. A Reader's Edition*, ed. Sonu Shamdasani, trans. John Peck, Mark Kyburz, and Sonu Shamdasani (New York, NY: W.W. Norton, 2012), 142.

[2] Ibid., 131-132.

[3] Ibid., 248-249.

[4] Ibid., 178.

[5] Ibid., 166.

[6] Ibid., 128.

[7] C.G. Jung, "New Paths of Psychology," in *CW*, vol. 7 (Princeton, NJ: Princeton University Press, 1966), par. 409.

[8] Jung, *The Red Book*, 125.

[9] Ibid., 396.

[10] Ibid., 251.

[11] Ibid.

Bibliography

A

Adler, Gerhard. *C.G. Jung Letters.* Trans. by R.F.C. Hull. Vol. 1, 1906-1950. Princeton, NJ: Princeton University Press, 1973.

Adler, Gerhard. *C.G. Jung Letters.* Trans. by R.F.C. Hull. Vol. 2, 1951-1961. Princeton, NJ: Princeton University Press, 1975.

Arnheim, Rudolf. *Visual Thinking.* Berkeley/Los Angeles, CA and London: University of California Press, 1969.

Arzt, Thomas, ed. *Das Rote Buch: C.G. Jungs Reise zum "anderen Pol der Welt." Studienreihe zur Analytischen Psychologie,* Bd. 5. Würzburg: Königshausen & Neumann, 2015.

Arzt, Thomas. "The Way of What Is to Come: Searching for Soul under Postmodern Conditions." In Stein, Murray, and Thomas Arzt, eds., *Jung's Red Book for Our Time: Searching for Soul under Postmodern Conditions.* Volume 1. Asheville, NC: Chiron Publications, 2017.

B

Bair, Deirdre. *Jung: A Biography.* Boston, MA: Little, Brown and Company, 2003.

Bishop, Paul. *The Dionysian Self. C.G. Jung's Reception of Friedrich Nietzsche.* Berlin/New York, NY: De Gruyter, 1993.

Bollas, Christopher. *The Shadow of the Object: Psychoanalysis of the Unthought Known.* New York, NY: Columbia University Press, 1987.

Brooke, Roger. *Jung and Phenomenology.* London: Routledge, 1991.

Brown, Norman O. *Apocalypse and/or Metamorphosis.* Berkeley and Los Angeles, CA: University of California Press, 1992.

Burckhardt, Titus. *Mirror of the Intellect: Essays on Traditional Science & Sacred Art.* New York, NY: State University of New York Press, 1987.

C

Cambray, Joseph. "*The Red Book*: Entrances and Exits." In *The Red Book: Reflections on C.G. Jung's Liber Novus,* ed. T. Kirsch and G. Hogenson. New York, NY & London: Routledge, 2014.

Cambray, Joseph. *Synchronicity: Nature & Psyche in an Interconnected Universe* (Fay Lecture Series). College Station, TX: Texas A&M University Press, 2009.

Cambray, Joseph. "Cosmos and Culture in the Play of Synchronicity." In Stacy Wirth, Isabelle Meier, and John Hill, eds. *The Playful Psyche: Entering Chaos, Coincidence, Creation*. New Orleans, LA: Spring Journal Books, 2012.

Campbell, Joseph. *The Masks of God: Occidental Mythology*. Harmondsworth, England, Penguin Books, 1991.

Campbell, Joseph. *An Open Life: Joseph Campbell in Conversation with Michael Toms*. New York, NY: Perennial Library, 1990.

Casey, Edward. *Spirit and Soul: Essays in Philosophical Psychology*. Dallas, TX: Spring, 1991.

Catanach, Anthony and Julie Anne Ragatz. "2008 Market Crisis: Black Swan, Perfect Storm or Tipping Point?" In *Bank Accounting and Finance*, 23.3, 2010.

Chodorow, Joan, ed. *Jung on Active Imagination*. Princeton, NJ: Princeton University Press, 1997.

Clark, Margaret. *Understanding Religion and Spirituality in Clinical Practice*. London: Karnac Books, 2012.

Connolly, Angela. "Cognitive aesthetics of Alchemical Imagery." In *Journal of Analytical Psychology*, 58 (1), 2013.

Corbett, Sara. "The Holy Grail of the Unconscious." In *The New York Times Magazine*, September 16, 2009.

Corbin, Henry. "Mundus Imaginalis or the Imaginary and the Imaginal." In Spring 1972, Zürich.

Corbin, Henry. *Alone with the Alone: Creative Imagination in the Sufism of Ibn Arabi*, trans. by Ralph Manheim. Princeton, NJ: Princeton University Press, 1998.

Corbin, Henry. *Man of Light in Iranian Sufism*. New Lebanon, NY: Omega Publications, 1994.

Corbin, Henry. *Temple and Contemplation*, trans. by Philip Sherrard and Liadain Sherrard. London: KPI & Islamic Publications, 1986.

Corbin, Henry. *Swedenborg and Esoteric Islam*, trans. by Leonard Fox. West Chester, PA: Swedenborg Foundation, 1999.

Corbin, Henry. *Spiritual Body and Celestial Earth: From Mazdean Iran to Shi'ite Iran*, trans. by Nancy Pearson. Princeton, NJ: Princeton University Press, 1977.

Coomaraswamy, A.K. "On the Indian and Traditional Psychology, or rather, Pneumatology." In *Coomaraswamy Vol 2. Selected Papers: Metaphysics*, Roger Lipsey, ed. Princeton, NJ: Princeton University Press, 1977.

Covington, Coline, and Barbara Wharton, eds. *Sabina Spielrein: Forgotten Pioneer of Psychoanalysis, Second Edition*. London: Routledge, 2015.

D

de Lubac, Henri. *La postérité spirituelle de Joachim de Flore*, 2 vol. Paris/Namur: Lethellieux, Culture et Vérité, 1979/1980.

E

Edinger, Edward F. *The New God-Image. A Study of Jung's Key Letters Concerning the Evolution of the Western God-Image*. Wilmette, IL: Chiron Publications, 1996.

Edinger, Edward F. *The Creation of Consciousness: Jung's Myth for Modern Man*. Toronto: Inner City Books, 1984.

El Shakry, Omni. *The Arabic Freud: Psychoanalysis and Islam in Modern Egypt*. Princeton, NJ: Princeton University Press, 2017.

F

Flechsig, Paul. *Die körperlichen Grundlagen der Geistesstörungen. Vortrag gehalten beim Antritt des Lehramtes an der Universität Leipzig am 4. März 1882*. Leipzig: Veit, 1882.

Freud, Sigmund and C.G. Jung. *The Freud/Jung Letters*. Ed. William McGuire and trans. by Ralph Manheim and R.F.C. Hull. Princeton, NJ: Princeton University Press, 1974.

Fukushima, Akiho. *A study of Japanese myth and legend in Kojiki* (Nihon-shoki: Rokko Shuppan, 1988) (福島秋穗著. -記紀神話伝説の研究- 六興出版, 1988).

G

Gergen, Kenneth J. *Social Construction in Context*. London: Sage, 2001.

Gergen, Kenneth J. *Relational Being. Beyond Self and Community*. Oxford: Oxford University Press, 2009.

Giegerich, Wolfgang. "*Liber Novus*, That is, The New Bible: A First Analysis of C.G. Jung's *Red Book*." In *Spring: A Journal of Archetype and Culture* 83 (*Spring* 2010).

Giegerich, Wolfgang. "Psychology—The Study of the Soul's Logical Life." In A. Casement, ed., *Who Owns Jung?* London: Karnac Books, 2007.

Gigerenzer, Gerd. *Reckoning With Risk: Learning to Live With Uncertainty*. London: Penguin, 2002.

Gigerenzer, Gerd. *Gut Feelings: The Intelligence of the Unconscious*. London: Penguin, 2007.

Gigerenzer, Gerd. *Risk Savvy: How to Make Good Decisions*. London: Penguin, 2014.

Gravino, P., B. Monechi, V.D.P. Servedio, F. Tria, and V. Loreto. "Crossing the Horizon: Exploring the Adjacent Possible in a Cultural System." In *Proceedings of the Seventh International Conference on Computational Creativity (ICCC 2016)*. François Pachet, Amilcar Cardoso, Vincent Corruble, Fiammetta Ghedini (Editors). Paris, France, June 27 – July 1, 2016. Publisher: Sony CSL Paris, France. ISBN 9782746691551.

Greene, Liz. *The Astrological World of Jung's Liber Novus: Daimons, Gods, and the Planetary Journey*. London/New York, NY: Routledge, 2018.

Greene, Liz. *Jung's Studies in Astrology: Prophecy, Magic and the Qualities of Time*. London/New York, NY: Routledge, 2018.

Greene, Liz. "The Way of What is to Come: Jung's Vision of the Aquarian Age." In Stein, Murray, and Thomas Arzt, eds., *Jung's Red Book for Our Time: Searching for Soul under Postmodern Conditions*. Volume 1. Asheville, NC: Chiron Publications, 2017.

Guénon, René. *The Reign of Quantity and The Signs of The Times*, trans. Lord Northbourne. Hillsdale, NY: Sophia Perennis, 2001.

Guénon, René. *The Symbolism of the Cross*. London: Luzac and Company, 1958.

Guilfoyle, Michael. *The Person in Narrative Therapy. A Post-structural, Foucauldian Account.* Houndmills, Basingstoke: Palgrave Macmillan, 2014.

H

Harré, Rom. *The Singular Self.* London: Sage, 1998.

Harré, Rom. *Social Being.* Oxford & Cambridge: Blackwell, 1993.

Heidegger, Martin. "'Only a God can save us': The *Spiegel* Interview." In Thomas Sheehan, ed., *Heidegger: The Man and the Thinker.* Chicago, IL: Precedent, 1981.

Heisig, James W. *Imago Dei: A Study of C.G. Jung's Psychology of Religion.* London: Lewisburg Bucknell University Press, 1979.

Hermans, Hubert J. M., and Giancarlo Dimaggio, eds. *The Dialogical Self in Psychotherapy.* Hove and New York, NY: Brunner-Routledge, 2004.

Hermans, Hubert J. M., and Agnieszka Hermans-Konopka. *Dialogical Self Theory.* Cambridge: Cambridge University Press, 2010.

Hesse, Hermann. *Demian.* London: Penguin Modern Classics, 1919/2017.

Hillman, James and Sonu Shamdasani. *Lament of the Dead: Psychology After Jung's Red Book.* New York, NY: W.W. Norton, 2013.

Homer. "The Homeric Hymn to Hermes," trans. Lewis Hyde. In Lewis Hyde, *Trickster Makes This World: How Disruptive Imagination Creates Culture.* Edinburgh and London: Canongate, 1998/2008.

Hynes, William J., and William G. Doty. *Mythical Trickster Figures.* Tuscaloosa, AL: University Alabama Press. 1993.

I

Ibsen, Henrik. *Peer Gynt.* Mineola, NY: Dover Publications, 2003.

Izutsu, Toshihiko. *Toward a Philosophy of Zen Buddhism.* Boulder, CO: Prajna Press, 1982.

J

Jacobs, Hans. *Western Psychotherapy and Hindu Sadhana.* London: Allen and Unwin, 1961.

Johnson, Steven. *Where Good Ideas Come From: The Natural History of Innovation.* New York, NY: Riverhead Books, 2010.

Jung, C.G. *Aion. Researches into the Phenomenology of the Self.* In *CW*, vol. 9/II. Princeton, NJ: Princeton University Press, 1959.

Jung, C.G. *Analytical Psychology. Notes of the Seminar Given in 1925,* ed. W. McGuire. Princeton, NJ: Princeton University Press, 1991.

Jung, C.G. "A Psychological Approach to the Dogma of the Trinity." In *CW*, vol. 11. Princeton, NJ: Princeton University Press, 1969.

Jung, C.G. "Basic Postulates of Analytical Psychology." In *CW*, vol. 8. Princeton, NJ: Princeton University Press, 1969.

Jung, C.G. "Concerning Rebirth." In *CW*, vol. 9/I. Princeton, NJ: Princeton University Press, 1968.

Jung, C.G. "Concerning Mandala Symbolism." In *CW*, vol. 9/I. Princeton, NJ: Princeton University Press, 1968.

Jung, C.G. "Flying Saucers. A Modern Myth of Things Seen in the Skies." In *CW*, vol. 10. Princeton, NJ: Princeton University Press, 1964.

Jung, C.G. "General Problems of Psychotherapy." In *CW*, vol. 16. Princeton, NJ: Princeton University Press, 1966.

Jung, C.G. *History of Modern Psychology: Lectures Delivered at ETH Zurich. Volume 1, 1933-1934,* ed. Ernst Falzeder, trans. Mark Kyburz, John Peck, and Ernst Falzeder. Princeton, NJ: Princeton University Press, 2018.

Jung, C.G. *Introduction to Jungian Psychology. Notes on the Seminar on Analytical Psychology Given in 1925.* Princeton, NJ and Oxford: Princeton University Press, 2012.

Jung, C.G. *Memories, Dreams, Reflections,* ed. Aniela Jaffé. New York, NY: Vintage Books, 1963.

Jung, C.G. *Mysterium Coniunctionis.* In *CW*, vol. 14. Princeton, NJ: Princeton University Press, 1963.

Jung, C.G. "New Paths of Psychology." In *CW*, vol. 7. Princeton, NJ: Princeton University Press, 1966.

Jung, C.G. "On the Psychology of the Trickster-Figure." In *CW*, vol. 9/I. Princeton, NJ: Princeton University Press, 1968.

Jung, C.G. "On the Nature of the Psyche." In *CW*, vol. 8. Princeton, NJ: Princeton University Press, 1969.

Jung, C.G. "On Psychological Understanding." In *CW*, vol. 3. Princeton, NJ: Princeton University Press, 1960.

Jung, C.G. "Paracelsus as Spiritual Phenomenon." In *CW*, vol. 13. Princeton, NJ: Princeton University Press, 1967.

Jung, C.G. *Psychology and Alchemy*. In *CW*, vol. 12. Princeton, NJ: Princeton University Press, 1968.

Jung, C.G. "Psychology and Religion." In *CW*, vol. 11. Princeton, NJ: Princeton University Press, 1969.

Jung, C.G. "Psychological Factors Determining Human Behaviour." In *CW*, vol. 8. Princeton, NJ: Princeton University Press, 1969.

Jung, C.G. "Psychological Commentary on 'The Secret of the Golden Flower." In *CW*, vol. 13. Princeton, NJ: Princeton University Press, 1967.

Jung, C.G. *Psychological Types*. In *CW*, vol. 6. Princeton, NJ: Princeton University Press, 1971.

Jung, C.G. "Psychological Commentary on 'The Tibetan Book of the Great Liberation." In *CW*, vol. 11. Princeton, NJ: Princeton University Press, 1969.

Jung, C.G. "Spirit and Life." In *CW*, vol. 8. Princeton, NJ: Princeton University Press, 1969.

Jung, C.G. *Symbols of Transformation*. In *CW*, vol. 5. Princeton, NJ: Princeton University Press, 1956.

Jung, C.G. "Synchronicity: An Acausal Connecting Principle." In *CW*, vol. 8. Princeton, NJ: Princeton University Press, 1969.

Jung, C.G. "The Psychology of the Unconscious Processes." In *Collected Papers in Analytical Psychology*, ed. Constance Long. London: Bailliere, Tindall & Cox, 1917.

Jung, C.G. *The Red Book: Liber Novus. A Reader's Edition*, ed. Sonu Shamdasani, trans. John Peck, Mark Kyburz, and Sonu Shamdasani. New York, NY: W.W. Norton, 2012.

Jung, C.G. *The Red Book: Liber Novus*, ed. Sonu Shamdasani, trans. John Peck, Mark Kyburz, and Sonu Shamdasani. New York, NY: W.W. Norton, 2009.

Jung, C.G. "The Philosophical Tree." In *CW*, vol. 13. Princeton, NJ: Princeton University Press, 1967.

Jung, C.G. "The Psychology of the Child Archetype." In *CW*, vol. 9/I. Princeton, NJ: Princeton University Press, 1968.

Jung, C.G. *The Psychology of Kundalini Yoga: Notes of the Seminar Given in 1932 by C.G. Jung.* Princeton, NJ: Princeton University Press, 1996.

Jung, C.G. "The Psychology of the Transference." In *CW*, vol. 16. Princeton, NJ: Princeton University Press, 1966.

Jung, C.G. *The Psychogenesis of Mental Disease.* In CW, vol. 3. New York, NY: Pantheon Books, 1960.

Jung, C.G. "The Relations between the Ego and the Unconscious." In *CW*, vol. 7. Princeton, NJ: Princeton University Press, 1966.

Jung, C.G. "The Role of the Unconscious." In *CW*, vol. 10. Princeton, NJ: Princeton University Press, 1964.

Jung, C.G. "The Spirit Mercurius." In *CW*, vol. 13. Princeton, NJ: Princeton University Press, 1967.

Jung, C.G. "The Structure of the Psyche." In *CW*, vol. 8. Princeton, NJ: Princeton University Press, 1969.

Jung, C.G. "The Symbolic Life." In *CW*, vol. 18. Princeton, NJ: Princeton University Press, 1980.

Jung, C.G. "The Tavistock Lectures." In *CW*, vol. 18. Princeton, NJ: Princeton University Press, 1976.

Jung, C.G. "The Transcendent Function." In *CW*, vol. 18. Princeton, NJ: Princeton University Press, 1969.

Jung, C.G. *The Zofingia Lectures.* Princeton, NJ: Princeton University Press, 1983.

Jung, C.G. "Transformation Symbolism in the Mass." In *CW*, vol. 11. Princeton, NJ: Princeton University Press, 1969.

Junger, Sebastian. *The Perfect Storm: A True Story of Men Against the Sea.* New York, NY: W.W. Norton & Company, 1997.

K

Kahneman, Daniel and Amos Tversky, eds. *Choices, Values and Frames.* New York, NY: Cambridge University Press, 2000.

Kahneman, Daniel. *Thinking, Fast and Slow.* New York, NY: Farrar, Straus and Giroux, 2011.

Kauffman, Stuart. *Humanity in a Creative Universe.* New York, NY: Oxford University Press. 2016.

Kawai, Toshio. "The experience of the numinous today: from the novels of Haruki Murakami." In A. Casement and D. Tacey, eds. *The Idea of the Numinous: Contemporary Jungian and Psychoanalytic Perspectives.* London & New York: Routledge, 2006.

Kawai, Hayao. *Mukashibanashi to Nihonjin no Kokoro.* Tokyo: Iwanami Shoten, 1982.

Kawai, Hayao. *Dreams, Myths and Fairy Tales in Japan.* Einsiedeln: Daimon, 1995.

Kearney, Richard. *Poetics of Imagination: Modern and Post-Modern.* Edinburgh: Edinburgh University Press, 1998.

Kerr, John. "Beyond the pleasure principle and back again: Freud, Jung, and Sabina Spielrein." In P. Stepansky, ed., *Freud: Appraisals and Reappraisals* (Vol. 3). Hillsdale, NJ: The Analytic Press, 1988.

L

Labbie, Erin, and Michael Uebel. "We have never been Schreber: Paranoia, Medieval and Modern." In *The Legitimacy of the Middle Ages: On the Unwritten History of Theory*, (eds.) Andrew Cole and D. Vance Smith. Durham, NC: Duke University Press, 2010.

Lacan, J. *Ecrits: The First Complete Edition in English.* New York, NY: W.W. Norton, 2007.

Lagerlöf, S. *Trollmusik. En julberättelse.* In *Skilda Tider.* Stockholm: Albert Bonniers Förlag, 1949.

Lammers, Ann Conrad and Adrian Cunningham, eds. *The Jung-White Letters.* London: Routledge, 2007.

Lieblich, Amia, Dan P. McAdams, and Ruthellen Josselson. *Healing Plots. The Narrative Basis of Psychotherapy.* Washington, D.C.: American Psychological Association, 2004.

Liebscher, Martin. *Libido und Wille zur Macht. C.G. Jungs Auseinandersetzung mit Nietzsche.* Basel: Schwabe, 2012.

Lothane, Zvi. "The schism between Freud and Jung over Schreber: Its implications for method and doctrine." In *International Forum of Psychoanalysis*, 6(2), 1997.

Lovejoy, Arthur O. *The Great Chain of Being: A Study of the History of an Idea.* Cambridge, MA: Harvard University Press, 1964.

M

Maillard, Christine, ed. *Arts, sciences et psychologie. Autour du Livre Rouge de Carl Gustav Jung (1914-1930)/Kunst, Wissenschaft und Psychologie. Über das Rote Buch von C.G. Jung (1914-1930).* In *Recherches germaniques*, hors série N°8, 2011.

Maillard, Christine. *Au cœur du Livre Rouge: Les Sept Sermons aux Morts. Aux sources de la pensée de C.G. Jung.* Paris: Imago/La Compagnie du Livre Rouge, 2017.

Maillard, Christine. "La voie de l'àvenir. Du discours prophétique dans le Livre Rouge de Carl Gustav Jung." In *Cahiers jungiens de psychanalyse* 54, 2011.

Mahmoud, Samir. "Henry Corbin and Jung's Visionary Recital: A Personal Journey with Jung." In Thomas Arzt, ed., *Das Rote Buch: C.G. Jungs Reise zum "anderen Pol der Welt." Studienreihe zur Analytischen Psychologie*, Bd. 5. Würzburg: Königshausen & Neumann, 2015.

Main, Roderick. *The Rupture of Time: Synchronicity and Jung's Critique of Modern Western Culture.* London and New York, NY: Routledge, 2004.

Mather, Mathew. *The Alchemical Mercurius: Esoteric Symbol of Jung's Life and Works.* London and New York, NY: Routledge, 2014.

McAdams, Dan P., Ruthellen Josselson, and Amia Lieblich. *Identity and Story. Creating Self in Narrative.* Washington, D.C.: American Psychological Association, 2006.

McLeod, John. "Counselling as a social process." In *Counselling*, 10, 1999.

Midbøe, Gunilla. *The Elliptical Dialogue.* Asheville, NC: Chiron Publications, 2017.

Milashevich, Anna. *Re-visioning Business: Archetypal Patterns in the Business Domain and Their Relation to the Concept of Business Creativity.* Essex University, Ph.D. thesis, 2017.

Murakami, Haruki. *Kafka On The Shore*, trans. P. Gabriel. London: Vintage, 2005.

N

Needleman, Jacob, and Antoine Faivre. *Modern Esoteric Spirituality.* New York, NY: Crossroad, 1992.

Nietzsche, Friedrich. *Thus Spoke Zarathustra*, trans. by Richard J. Hollingdale. New York, NY: Penguin, 1968.

Nisbet, H.B. *German Aesthetic and Literary Criticism: Winckelman, Lessing, Hamann, Herder, Schiller, and Goethe*. Cambridge: Cambridge University Press, 1985.

Noll, Richard. *The Jung Cult: Origins of a Charismatic Movement*. Princeton, NJ: Princeton University Press, 1994.

Novak, Philip. "C.G. Jung in the Light of Asian Psychology." In *Religious Traditions: A Journal in the Study of Religions*, vol. 14, 1991.

O

Okuno, Shuj. *Tamashii, demo iikara soba ni ite*: 3 11go no reitaiken o kiku. Tokyo: Shin-yo-sha Publishing Ltd, 2017.

Orel, Vladimir. *A Handbook of Germanic Etymology*. Leiden, Boston: Brill, 2003.

P

Pilard, Nathalie. *Jung and Intuition: On the Centrality and Variety of Forms of Intuition in Jung and Post-Jungians*. London: Karnac, 2015.

Pinker, Steven. *The Blank Slate: The Modern Denial of Human Nature*. London: Allen Lane, 2002.

Pinker, Steven. *The Better Angels of Our Nature: Why Violence Has Declined*. London: Allen Lane, 2011.

R

Raine, Kathleen. *Golgonooza City of Imagination: Last Studies in William Blake*. Ipswich: Golgonooza Press, 1991.

Ricoeur, Paul. *Freud and Philosophy: An Essay on Interpretation*, trans. Denis Savage. New Haven, CT: Yale University Press, 1970.

Rieff, Philip. *The Triumph of the Therapeutic: Uses of Faith after Freud*. New York, NY: Harper & Row, 1966.

Rose, Nikolas. *Inventing Our Selves. Psychology, Power, and Personhood*. Cambridge: Cambridge University Press, 1996.

Rose, Nikolas. *Governing the Soul. The Shaping of the Private Self.* London/New York, NY: Free Association Books, 1989.

S

Samuels, Andrew. *Jung and the Post-Jungians.* London: Routledge & Kegan Paul, 1985.

Samuels, Andrew. *The Political Psyche.* London and New York: Routledge, 1993.

Sarbin, Theodore, ed. *Narrative Psychology: The Storied Nature of Human Conduct.* Westport, CT: Praeger, 1986.

Satinover, Jeffrey. *The Empty Self: C.G. Jung and the Gnostic Foundations of Modern Identity.* Westport, CT: Hamewith Books, 1996.

Schrag, Calvin. *The Self after Postmodernity.* New Haven and London: Yale University Press, 1997.

Schreber, D. P. *Memories of My Nervous Illness* (I. Macalpine & R. A. Hunter, trans.). New York, NY: The New York Review of Books, 2000.

Schuon, Frithjof. "No Activity Without Truth." In Jacob Needleman, ed., *The Sword of Gnosis: Metaphysics, Cosmology, Tradition, Symbolism.* Baltimore, MD: Penguin Books, 1988.

Schuon, Frithjof. *Esoterism as Principle and as Way.* Bedfont: Perennial Books, 1981.

Schuon, Frithjof. *Logic and Transcendence.* London: Perennial Books, 1984.

Schwartz-Salant, Nathan. "The Mark of One Who Has Seen Chaos: A Review of C.G. Jung's Red Book." In *Quadrant* 40.2 (Summer 2010).

Shamdasani, Sonu. *Cult Fictions: C.G. Jung and the Founding of Analytical Psychology.* London and New York, NY: Routledge, 1998.

Shamdasani, Sonu. *Jung Stripped Bare: By His Biographers, Even.* London: Routledge, 2018.

Simic, Charles. *The Voice at 3:00 A.M.: Selected Late and New Poems.* Orlando, FL: Mariner Books, 2003.

Sinha, Jadunath. *Indian Psychology: Perception.* London: Kegan Paul, Trench, Trubner & Co., 1934.

Singer, Thomas and Joerg Rasche, eds. *Europe's Many Souls: Exploring Cultural Complexes and Identities.* New Orleans, LA: Spring Journal Books, 2016.

Spiegelman, J. Marvin. *Sufism, Islam, and Jungian Psychology*. Scottsdale, AZ: New Falcon Publications, 1991.

Stein, Murray. *Jung's Map of the Soul: An Introduction*. Peru, IL: Open Court Publishing, 1998.

Stein, Murray. *Jung on Christianity*. Princeton, NJ: Princeton University Press, 1999.

Stein, Murray, and Thomas Arzt, eds. *Jung's Red Book for Our Time: Searching for Soul under Postmodern Conditions*. Volume 1. Asheville, NC: Chiron Publications, 2017.

Stein, Murray. *In Midlife: A Jungian Perspective*, Dallas, TX: Spring, 1983.

Stein, Murray. *Soul: Treatment and Recovery: The Selected Works of Murray Stein*. London and New York, NY: Routledge, 2016.

Stevens, Anthony. *The Two-million-year-old Self*. College Station, Texas: Texas A&M University Press, 1993.

Stirner, Max. *Der Einzige und sein Eigentum*. Stuttgart: Reclam, 2011.

T

Takeda,Y., ed. *Kojiki*. Tokyo: Kadokawa-shoten, 1995.

Taleb, Nassim. *The Black Swan: The Impact of the Highly Improbable*. London and New York, NY: Penguin Books, 2007/2008.

Taleb, Nassim. *Antifragile: Things That Gain from Disorder*. London and New York, NY: Penguin Books, 2013.

Turkle, Sherry. *Alone Together: Why We Expect More from Technology and Less from Each Other*. New York, NY: Basic Books, 2011.

Turkle, Sherry. *Reclaiming Conversation: The Power of Talk in a Digital Age*. New York, NY: Penguin Random House. 2015.

U

Upton, Charles. "Can Jung Be Saved?" In *The Greater Jihad: Essays in Principial Psychology*. San Rafael, CA: Sophia Perennis, 2011.

V

von Franz, Marie-Louise. "What Happens When We Interpret Dreams?" In Mahdi, L. C., ed., *Betwixt and Between. Patterns of Masculine and Feminine Initiation*. La Salle and London: Open Court, 1987.

W

Wahba, Liliana Liviano. "Imagination and Evil." In Stein, Murray, and Thomas Arzt, eds., *Jung's Red Book for Our Time: Searching for Soul under Postmodern Conditions*. Volume 1. Asheville, NC: Chiron Publications, 2017.

Wasserstrom, Stephen M. *Religion After Religion: Gershom Scholem, Mircea Eliade, and Henry Corbin at Eranos*. Princeton, NJ: Princeton University Press, 1999.

Wittgenstein, Ludwig. *Tractatus Logico-Philosophicus,* London: Routledge and Kegan Paul, 1976.

Wittgenstein, Ludwig. *Philosophical Investigations*. Oxford: Basil Blackwell 1953.

Y

Yama, Megumi. "Ego consciousness in the Japanese psyche: culture, myth and disaster." In *Journal of Analytical Psychology*, vol. 58, 2013.

Yamaori, Tetsuo. *Kami to Hotoke: Nihonjin no shukyoukan (Kami and Buddha: Japanese view on religion)*. Tokyo: Kodansha, 35th edition, 2014.

Yamaori, Tetsuo. *Kindai Nihonjin no shuukyou ishiki (Modern Religious Consciousness of Japanese)*. Tokyo: Iwanami-shoten, 2007.

Yasumaro, Ono. *The Kojiki: An Account of Ancient Matters*, trans. Gustav Heldt. New York, NY: Columbia University Press, 1983.

About the Contributors

Stephen Aizenstat, Ph.D., is chancellor, founding president of Pacifica Graduate Institute, and ex-officio Board of Trustees member. He is a professor of depth psychology with a Ph.D. in clinical psychology, a licensed marriage and family therapist, and a credentialed public school teacher and counselor. He has served as an organizational consultant to companies and agencies worldwide and teaches extensively. Dr. Aizenstat has explored the potential of dreams through depth psychology and his own research for more than 35 years. His Dream Tending Methodologies extend traditional dreamwork to the vision of an animated world, where the living images in dreams are experienced as embodied and originating in both the psyche of nature and the psyche of persons. His book, *Dream Tending*, describes multiple applications of dreamwork in relation to health and healing, nightmares, the world's dream, relationships, and the creative process. Web page: www.dreamtending.com; contact email: saizenstat@gmail.com.

Thomas Arzt, Ph.D., was educated in physics and mathematics at Giessen University (Germany). Research assistant at Princeton University (USA) with the special focus on atomic, nuclear, and plasma physics. 1988 training and certification in Initiatic Therapy at the "Schule für Initiatische Therapie" of Karlfried Graf Dürckheim and Maria Hippius-Gräfin Dürckheim in Todtmoos-Rütte (Black Forest, Germany). 2016 Training Programm Continuing Education in Analytical Psychology at ISAP Zurich. Since 1999, president and managing director of Strategic Advisors for Transformation GmbH, an international consulting company for simulation technology, complexity management, and "Strategic Foresight under Deep Uncertainty" in Freiburg, Germany. He resides in Lenzkirch (Black Forest), Germany. Major publications: Various publications on Naturphilosophie in the context of Wolfgang Pauli und C.G. Jung: *Unus Mundus: Kosmos und Sympathie* (ed., 1992), *Philosophia Naturalis* (ed., 1996), *Wolfgang Pauli und der Geist der Materie* (ed., 2002). Editor of the German series

Studienreihe zur Analytischen Psychologie. Web page: www.thomasarzt.de; contact email: thomasdrarzt@ gmail.com.

Paul Brutsche, D.Phil., studied philosophy and theology in Fribourg, Paris, and Innsbruck (1963-1971) and Anthropological Psychology at the University of Zurich (1971-1975). He earned the diploma in Analytical Psychology at the C.G. Jung-Institute Zurich in 1975. He practices as Jungian analyst in Zurich and functions as a training and supervising analyst at ISAP Zurich. Dr. Brutsche is a former president of SGAP, CGJI, and ISAP Zurich. Publication: *Creativity: Patterns of Creative Imagination as Seen Through Art* (Spring Journal Books, 2018). Contact email: paul.brutsche@gmx.net.

Joe Cambray, Ph.D. is currently president of Pacifica Graduate Institute and past president of the International Association for Analytical Psychology. He has served as the U.S. editor for the *Journal of Analytical Psychology* and is on various editorial boards. He was a faculty member at Harvard Medical School in the Department of Psychiatry at Massachusetts General Hospital, Center for Psycho-analytic Studies. His numerous publications include the book based on his Fay Lectures: *Synchronicity: Nature and Psyche in an Inter-connected Universe* and a volume edited with Linda Carter, *Analytical Psychology: Contemporary Perspectives in Jungian Psychology*. He has published numerous papers in various international journals. Contact email: cambrayj@earthlink.net.

Linda Carter, MSN, CS, is a Jungian analyst who was in private practice in Boston and in Providence, Rhode Island, for more than 30 years. Currently, she practices in Carpinteria, California, and teaches at Pacifica Graduate Institute. She is a graduate of George-town University and Yale University. She has been the book review editor and the U.S. Editor of the *Journal of Analytical Psychology*. She is a co-editor of *Analytical Psychology, Contemporary Perspectives in Jungian Analysis* (2004) and co-author of a chapter in that book titled "Analytic Methods." She is currently the chair of the Art and Psyche Working Group whose mission is to bring together members of the art world with therapists and anyone interested in depth psychology. Contact email: lcarter20@cox.net.

George B. Hogenson, Ph.D., LCSW, is a Jungian analyst with a private practice in Chicago, Illinois. He received his Ph.D. in philosophy from Yale University (1979) and his M.A. in clinical social work from the University of Chicago (1991) before receiving the Diploma in Analytical Psychology from the C.G. Jung Institute of Chicago (1998). He has published widely on the history and theory of Analytical Psychology and is the author of *Jung's Struggle with Freud*. He is currently vice president of the International Association for Analytical Psychology and a member of the editorial board of the *Journal of Analytical Psychology*. Contact email: hogenson@mac.com.

Toshio Kawai, Ph.D., is professor at the Kokoro Research Center, Kyoto University for Clinical Psychology. He is president-elect of the IAAP. He was educated in clinical psychology at Kyoto University and in philosophical psychology at Zurich University, where he received a Ph.D. in 1987. He obtained his diploma from the C.G. Jung Institute Zurich in 1990. He has published articles and books and book chapters in English, German, and Japanese. He has been involved with psychological relief work after the earthquake in 2011. Publications include "The 2011 Earthquake in Japan: Psychotherapeutic Interventions and Change of Worldview," "Big stories and small stories in the psychological relief work after the earthquake disaster," "Psychological Relief Work after the 11 March 2011 Earthquake in Japan: Jungian Perspectives and the Shadow of Activism," "Jung in the Japanese Academy," and "Jungian Psychology in Japan: Between mythological world and contemporary consciousness." Contact email: kawai.toshio.6c@kyoto-u.ac.jp.

Samir Mahmoud, Ph.D., is a graduate of the University of Cambridge (2012) in philosophical aesthetics. He is currently assistant professor of architectural history and theory at the Lebanese American University (LAU). Between 2013 and 2016, he was visiting assistant professor of architecture at the American University of Beirut (AUB). He was postdoctoral fellow at the University of Oxford (2012-2013) and Agha Khan postdoctoral fellow at MIT (2012). Samir's interests vary widely. He is the author of several publications, including the book chapters: "Henry Corbin and Jung's Visionary Recital: A

Personal Journey with Jung," in Thomas Arzt, ed., *Das Rote Buch: C.G. Jungs Reise zum "anderen Pol der Welt,"* in *Studienreihe zur Analytischen Psychologie,* Bd. 5 (Würzburg: Königshausen & Neumann, 2015), "The Taste (*Dhawq*) of Things: Taking the Appearances (*Mazahir*) Seriously," in *The Beacon of Mind: Reason and Intuition in the Ancient and Modern World,* edited by Andrea Blackie and Dr. John H. Spencer (Param Media Publishing, 2015), "Suhrawardi and Plotinus on Self-Knowledge as Illumination," in *Selections of Papers from Prometheus Trust Conferences 2006-2010,* Prometheus Trust Publishers, June, 2011, and "From Heidegger to Suhrawardi: An Introduction to the Thought of Henry Corbin" (published on official website of Henry Corbin edited by Pierre Lory, 2006). Contact email: samir.mahmoud.cantab@gmail.com.

Christine Maillard, Docteur ès Lettres, is professor of German Studies and History of Ideas at Strasbourg University and the director of the interdisciplinary institution "*Maison interuniversitaire des Sciences de l'Homme–Alsace*" (CNRS/Strasbourg University). Her main research fields include C.G. Jung's work and history of psychological theories and the reception of Oriental cultures and religions (India, Persia, Japan) in German literature and culture from the 18th to the 20th century. She translated Jung's *Red Book* into French (2011) and published or co-published several books and numerous papers on Jung in French, German and English. Her works include *Arts, sciences et psychologie: Autour du Livre Rouge de Carl Gustav Jung*, (with Véronique Liard) *Pour une réévaluation de l'œuvre de Carl Gustav Jung, Au coeur du Livre Rouge: Les Sept Sermons aux Morts. Aux sources de la pensée de C.G. Jung.* Christine Maillard supervises several Ph.D. theses on Jung's work at Strasbourg University. She is an honorary member of The International Association for Analytical Psychology. Contact email: christine.maillard@ unistra.fr.

Mathew Mather, BSc, MSc, Ph.D., is a graduate of the University of Essex, where he specialized in Jung and Alchemy. He is a lecturer at Limerick School of Art and Design and course director of the Certificate in Jungian Psychology with Art Therapy. He regularly presents at international conferences, has been a guest lecturer at ISAP Zurich, and is especially interested in synchronicity, alchemy, astrology, the environment, visual culture as well as personal and cultural mythologies. He is author of *The Alchemical Mercurius: Esoteric Symbol of Jung's Life and Works* (Routledge, 2014) and lectures in Narrative, Media Psychology and Film Studies. Contact email: mathew.mather@lit.ie.

Patricia Michan, M.A., is a Jungian psychoanalyst certified in 1995. She has a private practice in Mexico City. She is the founder and director of the Centro Mexicano C.G. Jung, a member of the IAAP's Communication and Resources Working Group, assistant editor for the JAP's Editorial Board, and a founding member of the Mexican C.G. Jung Society (SOMEJ). She has published widely about the relationship between Analytical Psychology and the myths of the ancient cultures of Mexico, including: "Reiterative Disintegration: Historical and Cultural Patterns and the Contemporary Mexican Psyche" in *Confronting Collective Trauma: Jungian Approaches to Treatment and Healing*, edited by Gražina Gudaitė and Murray Stein, "Analysis and Individuation in the Mexican Psyche: Culture and Context" in *The Journal of Jungian Theory and Practice*, "Analysis and Individuation in Latin Cultures and Contexts: The Mexican Psyche" in *Proceedings of the Fifteenth International Congress for Analytical Psychology*, and "Dismemberment and Reintegration: Aztec Themes" in *Journal of Analytical Psychology*. Contact email: pgmichan@gmail.com.

Gunilla Midbøe, MSW, is a certified psychotherapist, supervisor and Jungian psychoanalyst. She studied at Socialhögskolan i Östersund (1972-1976), Lund University (1988-1991) and Uppsala University (1998-2000). She has worked over 30 years in public health care and is currently in private practice in Sweden. She is a training analyst and supervisor at C.G. Jung Institute in Copenhagen and a member of DSAP training committee, a board member of the Swedish C.G. Jung Foundation and an editor of the net journal *Coniunctio*. She has presented clinical papers at IAAP conferences and the Congress in Kyoto, Japan. Her book, *The Elliptical Dialogue*, was published in 2017. Contact email: gunilla@ midboe.se.

Anna Milashevich, Ph.D., read philosophy, politics and economics as an undergraduate at the University of Oxford. This was followed by work in management consultancy. Her interest in Jungian psychology and psychoanalysis led her to take a Master's Degree in Jungian and post-Jungian Studies and later a Ph.D. in Psychoanalytic Studies at the University of Essex. Being intrigued by the phenomenon of start-up culture and the practical applications of depth psychology to the business world, her thesis explored the concept of business creativity and in particular how archetypal energies structured the business domain's creative dynamics. Currently, Anna works in London as a business consultant for start-ups. Contact email: am.wildeast@hotmail.com.

Velimir B. Popović, Ph.D., is a Jungian psychoanalyst, also trained in clinical psychology and Freudian psychoanalysis, and maintains a private practice in Belgrade, Serbia. He is an assistant professor at the Department of Psychology of the University of Belgrade, Serbia, where he teaches clinical psychology, personality assessment, Rorschach Inkblot Technique, and Analytical and Archetypal Psychology. He has lectured internationally and is a faculty member and lecturer at the Gestalt Psychotherapy Training Institute on Malta. His current and long-standing interests include Archetypal Psychology, phenomenology, narrative psychology, hermeneutics, and Orthodox mystical theology. He has published a number of articles on archetypal and analytical psychology, including two books: *The Psychology of Feminine* (1995) and *On Soul and Gods: Theory and Practice of Archetypal Psychology* (2001). Contact e-mail: velimirb. popovic@yahoo.com.

Ingrid Riedel, Dr. theol., Dr. phil., studied theology, literature and psychology. After a parish vicarage from 1970-1984 she became the director of studies at the Evangelische Akademie Hofgeismar. She then obtained her diploma from the C.G. Jung Institute Zurich and works as a Jungian analyst with a private practice in Konstanz, Germany. She lectures at C.G. Jung Institute Zurich, Kassel University, and Frankfurt University. Major publications: Various publications on the psychology of religion as well as on art, creativity and psychology, for example, *Das Buch der Bilder: Schätze aus dem Archiv des C.G. Jung-Instituts Zürich*. Contact email: Dr.Ingrid-Riedel@t-online.de.

Murray Stein, Ph.D., studied at Yale University (B.A. in English) and attended graduate student at Yale Divinity School (M.Div.) and the University of Chicago (Ph.D. in Religion and Psychological Studies). He trained as a Jungian psychoanalyst at the C.G. Jung Institute of Zurich. From 1976 to 2003, he was a training analyst at the C.G. Jung Institute of Chicago, of which he was a founding member and president from 1980-85. In 1989, he joined the executive committee of IAAP as honorary secretary for Dr. Thomas Kirsch (1989-1995) and served as president of the IAAP from 2001-2004. He was president of ISAP Zurich 2008-2012 and is currently a training and supervising analyst there. He resides in Goldiwil (Thun), Switzerland. His special interests are psychotherapy and spirituality, methods of Jungian psychoanalytic treatment, and the individuation process. Major publications: *In Midlife, Jung's Map of the Soul, Minding the Self, Soul: Retrieval and Treatment, Transformation: Emergence of the Self*, and *Outside, Inside and All Around*. Web page: www.murraystein.com; contact email: murraywstein@gmail.com.

Žanet Prinčevac de Villablanca, B.A., M.A., studied at the Faculty of Special Education and Rehabilitation, University of Belgrade, Yugoslavia (1985-1989, 1999-2002). She is a Jungian analyst, IM, IAAP (2007) and has served as president of the Belgrade Analytical Circle, the IAAP Developing Group in Serbia, and is a past director of Center for Education in Jungian Psychotherapy (2004-2007). She has given lectures widely on Analytical Psychology: "Precognitive Dreams and Synchronicity" (ISAP Zurich, 2007), several lectures given at the University of Macedonia, Skopje (Psychology Department for postgraduate students, 2009) and many lectures open for professional and the general public at the Belgrade Analytical Circle. She translated *Jung's Map of the Soul* by Murray Stein and *The Border Zones of Exact Science* (November 1986) from *Zofingia Lectures: Supplementary Volume A* (*CW* of C.G. Jung) into Serbian. She contributed to the article "The Developmental Theories of

Analytical Psychology" (with Velimir. B. Popović) in *The Handbook of Developmental Psychiatry* (2012). She works in private practice in Belgrade. Contact e-mail: z.villablanca@gmail.com.

Megumi Yama, Ph.D., studied at Kyoto University (undergraduate, graduate school, Ph.D.). She is a professor in the Faculty of Humanities at Kyoto University of Advanced Science, where she teaches clinical psychology and depth psychology. She also engages in psychotherapy, supervision, and training based mainly on Jungian thought. She was a visiting scholar at Harvard University in 2015 and a visiting fellow at University of Essex from 2008-2009. She has published many articles and books, including translations both in English and Japanese. Her major publications in English are: "Ego consciousness in the Japanese psyche: Culture, myth and disaster," in *Journal of Analytical Psychology* 58, 2013, "Haruki Murakami: Modern myth-maker beyond culture," in *Jung Journal Culture & Psyche* 10(1), 2016, "Non-fixed multiple perspectives in the Japanese Psyche: Traditional Japanese art, dream and myth," in Blocian, I. and Kuzmicki, A. (eds.) *Contemporary Influence of C.G. Jung's Thought*, in *Contemporary Psychoanalytic Studies 24*, Brill, 2018. Contact email: memeyam2008@gmail.com.

Mari Yoshikawa, Ph.D., is originally from Osaka, Japan, and educated at Kyoto University (Ph.D.). She is professor of Gakushuin University in Tokyo, being engaged in training certified clinical psychologists in Japan. In 2008, she studied at ISAP in Zurich, and got a diploma of AJAJ (Association of Jungian Analysts, Japan) in 2016. She manages Yamanashi Hakoniwa Institute (https://www.yamanashi-hakoniwa.com/) for practices with imagery. She collaborated on many Japanese books on psychological assessment, personality psychology and psychotherapy. Her publication in English is: "The Shadow of Modernization in Japan as Seen in Natsume Soseki's Ten Night's Dreams," in *Confronting Cultural Trauma-Jungian Approaches to Understanding and Healing*, edited by Gražina Gudaitė and Murray Stein (*Spring Journal*, 2014). Contact email: mari.yoshikawa@gakushuin.ac.jp.